To Cindy

Best cooking!

JACQUES PEPIN'S
THE ART OF COOKING
Volume 2

ALFRED A. KNOPF · NEW YORK 1992

JACQUES PEPIN'S
THE ART OF COOKING
Volume 2

THIS IS A BORZOI BOOK PUBLISHED BY
ALFRED A. KNOPF, INC.

Copyright © 1988 by Jacques Pepin, Inc.

Photographs copyright © 1988 by Tom Hopkins

All rights reserved under international and Pan-
American Copyright Conventions. Published in
the United States by Alfred A. Knopf, Inc.,
New York, and simultaneously in Canada by
Random House of Canada Limited, Toronto.
Distributed by Random House, Inc.,
New York.

Portions of this book were originally published in
Gourmet magazine.

Library of Congress Cataloging-in-Publication Data

Pépin, Jacques.
  Jacques Pepin's the art of cooking.

  Includes index.
  1. Cookery. I. Title. II. Title: Art of cooking.
TX651.P388   1987   641.5   87-4253
ISBN 0-679-74270-0 (v. 1)
ISBN 0-679-74271-9 (v. 2)

Manufactured in the United States of America
Published July 1988
First paperback edition, September 1992

CONTENTS

INTRODUCTION

A large part of this second volume of The Art of Cooking deals with baking, the area of cooking that is the most structured, lending itself to rigid formulas rather than improvisation. If an ingredient is inadvertently omitted from a cake formula, there is no way to rescue the cake while it is baking.

A great cake that you may have baked again and again at home is often uncooperative in an unfamiliar kitchen. Differences in even the same brand of equipment — from cookie sheets to ovens — to say nothing of altitude, the degree of humidity, and the temperature, can account for variables in the end result. If you were making a stew, you would simply adjust as necessary as the stew cooks, but with breads, pies, meringues, and cakes you can't tell if they are right until after they have been baked, so you are unable to make adjustments until the next time around.

Unless otherwise specified, you should use the middle rack of the oven for baking. If you find that your cake, for instance, has gotten too brown on the bottom, then next time you may want to bake it on the next rung up. Or if it has baked unevenly, you may need to turn it next time. Every cook has to work out his or her own method of compensation when faced with a temperamental oven.

Ingredients vary, too — the size of eggs, the moisture content of the flour, the quality of the water, all of which will affect whatever you are baking. Nothing can take the place of a knowledgeable cook's watchful eyes, so try to be observant and take note of these variables and their effects. Try, also, to understand the goal of a recipe or the idea behind it so that you can establish a standard and acquire a taste memory

of the dish as it should be. Then you will be able to recognize signs of trouble and adjust accordingly.

The first section of this second volume deals with charcuterie, which in French has several meanings and usages. Traditionally, a plate of charcuterie is a plate of cold cuts. It is also the name of an establishment, a type of delicatessen, that sells more than cold cuts. The master charcutier is a pâté and sausage maker and an expert at curing hams and other meats. In addition, modern charcuteries are catering establishments that sell take-out food, including all kinds of salads, as well as aspic dishes, pasta, hams, sausages, cold roasts, hot and cold pâtés, fish quenelles, and gratins, to name a few of their specialties. I have also included in the charcuterie chapter luxury products such as caviar, truffles, and goose liver pâté along with instructions for preserving cherries in alcohol or vinegar, and making small sour gherkins (cornichons), homemade mustard, and other condiments.

The bread section that follows offers a good selection of my family's favorite breads, including sweet as well as savory recipes.

In the pastry section I offer several methods for making puff pastry and pie along with sweet doughs, giving extensive examples of using these doughs in savory as well as sweet dishes, from oyster and asparagus to raspberry filling. I have also included several tarts and galettes.

The section that follows features my favorite great summer fruit desserts from a Stew of Red Summer Fruits to Cabernet Sauvignon Plums with Wine Plum Sherbet and Cinnamon Lemon Cake. Several ice creams and sherbets, flavored with ingredients such as espresso and grapefruit, are served in different ways. Then custards follow, along with several chocolate cakes and a series of soufflés, including caramel and lime and apricot and pistachio. You will also find cream puffs, meringue cakes, mousses, and my favorite cookies.

Although the scope of The Art of Cooking doesn't — and wasn't intended to — cover all

of French and modern American cooking, the selection is large and the many techniques included in the making of these dishes will teach the cook just about all the basics of good cooking.

A series of very personal illustrated menus offers a glimpse of the possible arrangement of the dishes in simple and elaborate combinations. If cooking is, as Lévi-Strauss says, ". . . a process which transforms nature into culture . . ." or establishes the difference between the savage and the civilized, my hope is that some of my food will contribute a small amount to the enjoyment and advancement of the art of cooking.

Finally, and most important, always be aware that food is to be enjoyed and shared with friends. As Brillat-Savarin suggests, "To invite someone for dinner is to take care of his/her happiness the entire time he/she is under your roof."

The recipes in this book have been designed to demonstrate important cooking techniques. The techniques are noted with their step numbers at the top of the page where they appear so that you can locate them easily and refer to them again when needed.

JACQUES PEPIN'S
THE ART OF COOKING
Volume 2

- FISH AND SHELLFISH ASPIC
- SALMON TARTARE
- SALMON GRAVLAX EVELYN
- BLACK BASS GRAVLAX
- SMOKED SALMON ETHEL
- SMOKED TROUT SALAD CLAUDINE
- MINUTE-SMOKED SEAFOOD
- SMOKED EEL PATE WITH EGGPLANT
  MARMALADE
- SARDINES IN PARSLEY SALAD
- CLAM AND FISH CEVICHE ZIM ZIM
- EGGS IN ASPIC GLORIA
- COLD MOUSSE OF CHICKEN AND PISTACHIOS
- SUPREME OF CHICKEN SANDRINE
- CHICKEN GALANTINE WITH PRUNES
- RABBIT BALLOTINE JEANNE
- PATE OF PHEASANT AND SWEETBREAD
- COUNTRY PATE WITH WALNUTS AND HOT
  HONEY MUSTARD
- COLD STUFFED BREAST OF VEAL
  IN NATURAL ASPIC
- BRAISED DAUBE OF BEEF IN RED WINE ASPIC
- PARSLEYED HAM
- CIVIER VICTOR
- PRESSED HEAD CHEESE
- RILLETTES OF RABBIT
- DUCK LIVERS IN PORT ASPIC
- FRESH FOIE GRAS WITH COGNAC ASPIC
- HARD COUNTRY SALAMI
- SAUSAGE AND POTATO SALAD RICHARD
- CURED AND DRIED COUNTRY-STYLE HAM
- CARPACCIO OF BEEF MARIE-FRANCOISE
- CHICKEN SALAD DANNY
- RED OAK DUCK SALAD
- SALAD TULIPE
- BRESSANE SALAD
- WILD DANDELION SALADE LYONNAISE
- SALAD OF FRESH FOIE GRAS NICOLE
- CARPACCIO OF WHITE TRUFFLES
- RISOTTO WITH WHITE TRUFFLES
- BLACK TRUFFLE SALAD
- WHITE TRUFFLE BRIOCHE TOAST
- BLACK TRUFFLES IN BRIOCHE WITH
  TRUFFLE SAUCE
- CAVIAR PUFF
- CAVIAR CANAPES
- RED OR GOLDEN CAVIAR POTATOES
- CAVIAR WITH BLINIS AND FROZEN VODKA
- FROMAGE BLANC JEAN-VICTOR WITH
  ROASTED GARLIC
- PLUMS AND CHERRIES IN MOUNTAIN BREW,
  CHERRIES IN VINEGAR, AND CORNICHONS

COLD CHARCUTERIE, SALADS & CONDIMENTS

FISH AND SHELLFISH ASPIC

Although my recipe is made with fish and shellfish that has been specially cooked for this dish, any leftover cooked fish or shellfish can be used. The fish aspic can be made up to 48 hours ahead and is both delectable and attractive for a summer lunch or light dinner.

When the aspic is made from the stock of scallops, as it is here, it never clarifies as well as when it is done with a fish stock, although the flavor is excellent.

Yield: 8–10 servings (8-c. mold)

FOR COOKING THE FISH AND SHELLFISH

¾ lb. fish fillets (sole, scrod, cod, bass, etc.)
¾ lb. large sea scallops
¾ lb. shrimp, medium to small, with shells removed (reserve shells for aspic)
1 c. dry white wine
2 c. water
1 tsp. salt
¼ tsp. freshly ground black pepper

ASPIC

1 c. each celery, leeks, parsley stems, and carrots, chopped coarse
2 egg whites and shells, crushed
3½ envelopes gelatin (2½–3 Tb.)
½ tsp. salt
¼ tsp. pepper
5 c. cooking liquid from shrimp and fish
1 tsp. soy sauce

DECORATION

2 hard-cooked eggs, peeled
1 large carrot

GARNISHES

1½ c. peeled cucumbers, cut into ¼-in. dice
½ tsp. salt
1½ c. carrots, cut into ¼-in. dice
1 Tb. oil
1 tsp. mild vinegar (rice vinegar)
Dash freshly ground black pepper

BEET SALAD

1½ lb. small beets, peeled (leaving about ½ in. of stem), sliced in half, and each half cut into 5 or 6 wedges.
1 Tb. distilled white vinegar
¼ tsp. freshly ground black pepper
⅓ tsp. salt
1 Tb. white wine vinegar
1 Tb. good olive oil
1 Tb. chopped fresh dill

1 To prepare the garnishes: In a bowl, mix the 1½ c. diced cucumbers with the ½ tsp. salt and macerate for 20 minutes. Drain on paper towels to remove some of the moisture and set aside. Place the 1½ c. diced carrots in water to cover, bring to a boil, and cook for 2 minutes. Drain and set aside. Mix the carrots with the 1 Tb. oil, 1 tsp. vinegar, and dash of pepper.

To prepare beet salad: Cover the beets with cold water, add the 1 Tb. distilled vinegar, bring to a boil, and cook 10 minutes, just until tender but still firm. Cool under cold water to stop the cooking and set the color. Add the ¼ tsp. pepper, ⅓ tsp. salt, 1 Tb. wine vinegar, 1 Tb. olive oil, and 1 Tb. chopped dill, and mix well. Arrange on a serving platter to serve with the Fish and Shellfish Aspic.

2 To cook the fish and shellfish: Place the ¾ lb. each fish fillets, scallops, and shrimp in one layer in a large stainless steel saucepan. Add the 1 c. white wine, 2 c. water, 1 tsp. salt, and ¼ tsp. pepper. Bring to a simmer, covered, and remove from heat. Keep covered and let stand for 5 minutes. Using a slotted spoon, transfer all the solids to a plate and cover to prevent drying. Place in the refrigerator to cool.

Add water to the stock to bring it up to 5 c.

For the clarification: Put the 1 c. each celery, leeks, parsley stems, and carrots, 2 egg whites and shells, 3½ envelopes gelatin, ½ tsp. salt, and ¼ tsp. pepper in a large saucepan, and mix thoroughly. →

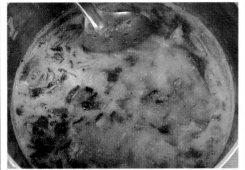

3 Add the 5 c. of cooking liquid from the shrimp and fish and the 1 tsp. soy sauce, and bring to a boil, stirring. You will notice that as the liquid approaches the boil, it will get very cloudy and, as it boils, it will form a crust with the egg whites on top. Let it come to a rolling boil and set aside to rest for 5 minutes.

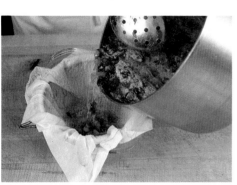

4 Strain the liquid through a strainer lined with a dampened paper towel. You should have approximately 3½ to 4 c. of clear liquid. Set aside.

5 Pour about ¼-in. thickness of the clear liquid aspic into the bottom of a dish (I am using an 8-c. Pyrex dish about 2 in. deep). Place in the refrigerator to set while you are preparing the decoration.

6 Draw a decoration on a piece of paper about the same diameter as the bowl. Using an egg slicer or a knife, cut the egg whites into shapes to fit your drawing. Note: I am making a design with two birds.

7 Use cutouts of blanched carrot for your decoration: Peel off a few thin slices of carrot with a vegetable peeler and blanch in boiling water for approximately 1 minute. Cool under cold water and make cutouts for the eyes and the branch between the two birds.

8 When the aspic is well-set in the bottom of the dish, lift up the paper with your decoration on it with one hand and with the other invert the aspic on top of it. Return the aspic and paper to the bowl, set the bowl upright, and press the paper to make the design adhere to the surface of the aspic. Remove and discard the paper.

9 **To make little butterflies:** Start with a fairly large piece of the carrot, approximately 3 to 4 in. long. On one cut end, using the tip of the knife, "draw" the outline of a butterfly. Then, carve out the carrot flesh following the outline of your butterfly so that when you cut across the carrot the slice will have a butterfly shape.

10 The shape of a butterfly has been carved into the carrot now. Cover the carrot with cold water, bring to a boil, and cook 1½ to 2 minutes to soften it slightly. Cool under cold water.

11 Slice the carrot. Each slice now has a little butterfly shape. This decoration can be used, of course, in many other dishes – in a salad, for example, or even as a garnish for hot meat or fish.

12 Arrange the little butterflies around your decoration on the aspic.

Place about ½ c. of aspic on ice and stir until it gets syrupy and almost ready to set. Pour it on top of the decoration to hold it in place.

13 Remove the little sinews still attached to each of the scallops (very often these tend to be tough).

14 Slice the scallops about ¼ in. thick and cover the design to create a whole flat layer of scallops.

15 Mix together the rest of the fish and shellfish and ½ c. each of the prepared garnishes of diced carrots and cucumber, then place on top of the scallop layer. Cool the remainder of the aspic on ice and, when it begins to get syrupy, spoon it on top of the seafood and vegetables. Cover with plastic wrap and refrigerate at least 4 hours.

16 At serving time, unmold the aspic by loosening the mold slightly around the edge and pulling it away with your fingers or running a knife around the edge so a little air gets underneath. It should unmold easily. Arrange the remaining diced cucumber and carrot salad around the aspic and serve with the beet salad.

SALMON

Salmon is one of the best and most versatile fish, especially when very fresh. Although frozen salmon is adequate for certain dishes, especially if defrosted very slowly under refrigeration, the texture of the meat changes and it does not compare to fresh salmon. Of the Pacific salmon, the king and the silver are the best and close to the quality of the Norwegian and Atlantic species.

The salmon lends itself to many preparations and, most of the time, it is boned first. Particularly good for broiling and smoking because of its fat content, it is often served with acidic sauces such as tomato or sorrel to offset the richness of the meat.

As with most fatty fish, the salmon bones make a fairly weak stock and the fatty skin should not be used in the stock. The head, if used, should be split into halves and the gills as well as any other bloody parts removed or the stock will be bitter.

The beautiful, refreshing salmon tartare can be served in smaller portions. The chopped salmon mixture can be served on open snow peas or on buttered black bread as well as on slices of cucumber or in the presentation shown here.

Scandinavian gravlax is traditionally made with more sugar and less salt, and is flavored with dill. My version produces a firmer, easier-to-slice salmon that is quite flavorful and can be kept for at least one week in the refrigerator.

I have used one whole salmon to make the Salmon Tartare and the gravlax.

TWO RECIPES USING RAW SALMON

BONING OUT THE SALMON

1 seven-pound salmon, gutted, with the head on (approximately 2½ to 3 lb. completely clean flesh)

SALMON TARTARE

Yield: 8 servings
INSTANT-CURED SALMON SLICES

8 thin slices salmon, ½ oz. each (4 oz. total)
¼ tsp. salt
1 Tb. peanut oil

TARTARE MIXTURE

1 lb. pieces or scrapings of salmon, chopped coarse
½ c. finely chopped onion, washed in a sieve under cold water and pressed dry in a towel
1 tsp. salt
½ tsp. freshly ground black pepper
¼ c. good olive oil
8 to 10 drops Tabasco sauce
1 tsp. grated lemon rind
4 Tb. chopped fresh herbs (a mixture of chives, chervil, and basil)
CUCUMBER SALAD GARNISH

1 medium cucumber, peeled
½ tsp. salt
¼ tsp. freshly ground black pepper
1 Tb. vegetable oil
1 tsp. red wine vinegar
A few pieces of skin from the cucumber

About 2 Tb. red salmon caviar
About 1 Tb. drained capers

Pumpernickel or rye bread

SALMON GRAVLAX EVELYN

Yield: about 10–12 servings for a buffet party
¼ c. kosher-type salt
2 Tb. sugar
1½ lb. salmon fillet, completely cleaned
1 Tb. cognac
1 Tb. grated lime rind
½ tsp. freshly ground black pepper
½ c. chopped fresh herbs (a mixture of parsley, tarragon, chives, and chervil – tarragon, being stronger, should be only in the proportion of 1 chopped Tb. of the herbs)

ONION AND CUCUMBER GARNISH

1 English or seedless cucumber
1 c. coarsely chopped onion
1 tsp. sugar
½ tsp. salt
2 Tb. rice vinegar
¼ c. corn oil

Olive oil
Danish-style rye bread

1 **Bone out the salmon,** using a long, strong, very sharp knife. Start by sliding your knife under the front gill toward the head.

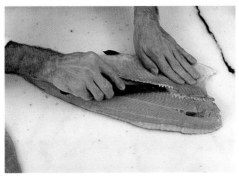

4 Using a thin knife, slide the blade beneath the rib cage to remove the ribs on each of the fillets.

6 With a large knife, remove the skin of the salmon. Using your knife at a 45-degree angle, push the knife forward, cutting gently back and forth in a jigsaw motion with the right hand, while pulling the skin with the left hand.

2 Twist the knife so the blade faces the other way and cut down in one swoop, through the rib cage bones right on top of the main central bone, to remove the whole fillet in one piece. Turn the salmon upside down and remove the other fillet in the same manner.

5 There is a central line of bones that extends straight down into the fillet that must be removed. Using a strawberry huller or a small pair of pliers, pull each of the small bones, one by one, to remove. There are more than 30 of these small bones and they extend from the neck three-quarters down the fillet.

7 Using your knife horizontally, gently cut off all the dark flesh on top of the fillet, just under the skin. That dark flesh is mostly fat and should be discarded. In a poached salmon, it is the part under the skin that turns black and slides off after cooking.

3 Do not worry if you leave some of the salmon flesh on the bones. Using a spoon, scrape the bones of the salmon and inside the gill and the corner toward the head to remove as much of the flesh as possible. That purée of flesh will be used for salmon tartare.

8 Although the whole half side of salmon can be used for gravlax, if you intend to make salmon tartare or to poach pieces of salmon for aspic, cut away the thin section of the belly and the end of the tail and save them for these dishes, using only the thickest part for the gravlax. →

9 **For the Salmon Tartare:** Start by making the instant-cured salmon slices. Cut 8 small slices of salmon very thin, approximately ½ oz. each. Arrange on a plate. Sprinkle with ¼ tsp. salt and 1 Tb. peanut oil. Let macerate for 1 hour while you prepare the remainder of the ingredients. For the tartare mixture, mix all the chopped salmon with the ½ c. onion, 1 tsp. salt, ½ tsp. pepper, ¼ c. olive oil, 8 to 10 drops Tabasco, 1 tsp. lemon rind, and 4 Tb. herbs, and refrigerate.

11 At serving time, arrange equal portions of the shaved cucumbers on eight plates. Place about 2 oz. of the chopped salmon in the center and cover each mound of salmon with a slice of the instant-cured salmon.

14 After the curing, open the salmon. The salt-sugar mixture will have melted and most of the liquid will have been absorbed by the salmon. There shouldn't be any more salt or liquid visible. If the salt is still apparent on the salmon, just rinse it briefly under cold water and pat it dry with paper towels. Rub the 1 Tb. cognac on top and around the salmon and sprinkle with the rind of lime and the black pepper.

10 **For the cucumber salad garnish:** Use a vegetable peeler to cut the cucumber into thin shavings about 3 in. long, cutting all around until you get to the seeds in the center. You should have approximately 2 c. of shaved cucumber. Mix with the ½ tsp. salt, ¼ tsp. pepper, 1 Tb. vegetable oil, and 1 tsp. vinegar. Cut little oval shapes from the skin of the cucumber to resemble little leaves. Set aside for the decoration.

12 Arrange about 3 of the green ovals of cucumber skin on top of each salmon tartare and place about ½ tsp. salmon eggs in the center and some capers around. Serve with buttered pumpernickel or rye bread.

15 Finally, cover with the fresh herbs, patting them gently on top to cover the whole surface of the salmon. Rewrap the salmon in the plastic wrap and aluminum foil and place in the refrigerator on a tray with another tray, weighted with the equivalent of at least 5 lb., to press the salmon and tighten the meat. Refrigerate, weighted, at least 2 hours or overnight (to develop more taste).

13 **For the Salmon Gravlax Evelyn:** Mix the ¼ c. kosher salt and 2 Tb. sugar together. Arrange the fillet of salmon on a piece of plastic wrap placed on top of a piece of aluminum foil. Rub the salt-sugar mixture all over the salmon, on top and underneath. Enclose the fillet tightly in the plastic wrap and then in the aluminum foil and place in the refrigerator for at least 6 hours or overnight.

16 To make the onion and cucumber garnish: Peel the seedless cucumber, cut it in half, remove any seeds, and cut into 3 slices ¼ in. thick. Pile the slices together to cut them into ¼-in. strips and finally into ¼-in. dice. Set aside. Bring 2 c. of water to a boil, add the 1 c. chopped onions, and stir well for about 10 seconds. Pour in a sieve. Wash under cold water, place in a towel, and press to extract most of the water. Blanching the onions prevents discoloration and makes them milder in flavor. Mix the onion, cucumber, 1 tsp. sugar, ½ tsp. salt, 2 Tb. rice vinegar, and ¼ c. oil.

Spread out the cucumber-onion mixture on two or three large platters. Using a long, thin serrated knife, cut the salmon into thin slices, about 1 to 1¼ oz. each. Arrange on top of the cucumber-onion mixture. Be sure that the green border on one side of the salmon lines up, one next to another, to form a design around the edge of the plate. You should have approximately 20 slices of salmon. If you like, sprinkle with a little good olive oil.

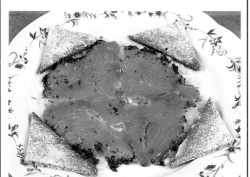

17 Serve with thin, buttered slices of hard Danish-style rye bread, cut into wedges and arranged around the salmon.

BLACK BASS GRAVLAX

Although gravlax made with salmon, a fatty fish, will be very moist and rich, it can also be made with waxy, very firm, thinner, white fleshed fish. Red snapper, black fish, and black bass all work particularly well for this type of gravlax. The bones of black bass are very good for stock or soup, so be sure to clean them and set them aside or freeze for later use. It is imperative that the freshest possible fish be used for gravlax.

Yield: 12 servings as a first course

CURING

2 black bass (each weighing about 1½ lb.), cleaned (each fillet weighing about 5 to 6 oz.)
1½ Tb. sugar
2½ Tb. kosher-type salt

FLAVORING

1 Tb. gin
½ tsp. freshly ground black pepper
2 tsp. grated lime rind
2 tsp. chopped fresh mint
1 Tb. chopped fresh dill
3 Tb. chopped fresh parsley

CUCUMBER AND EGG GARNISH

2 cucumbers, peeled, seeded, and cut into ¼-in. dice
4 hard-cooked eggs, chopped coarse
8 oz. sour cream
¼ tsp. salt
¼ tsp. freshly ground black pepper
12 large slices rye (or other type) bread, crusts removed, cut into an oval shape

GARNISH

Sprigs of parsley, mint, or dill

1 To bone the fish, insert a long, sturdy, sharp knife under the gill toward the head. Twist the knife so the blade faces out and, in one swoop, cut down through the rib cage and along the top of the central bone to remove the whole fillet in one piece. →

2 Turn the fish on the other side and repeat this procedure to remove the other fillet. You will notice that the line of rib bones is still attached to each of the fillets.

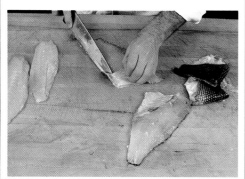

3 Slide the point of your knife under the rib bones on each of the fillets and remove the bones.

4 To remove the skin, make a cut at the tail end down through the fillet to the skin. Hold the end of the skin with one hand and pull while pushing your knife in the other direction, moving your knife forward in a jigsaw motion with the blade at about a 45-degree angle. The fish fillet will slide off the skin.

5 Notice that in the center of the fillet, on the side of the head, there is a line of bones about one-third of the way down. Cut a strip down the center to remove those bones. The fillets should be completely free of skin, bones, and sinew.

6 Mix the 1½ Tb. sugar and 2½ Tb. salt together. Place the fillets on a piece of plastic wrap on top of a piece of aluminum foil. Sprinkle the salt and sugar mixture over them, patting it all around the fillets. Wrap in the plastic wrap and aluminum foil, and refrigerate on a tray for 5 to 6 hours to cure. When cured, you will notice that the fillets have absorbed most of the sugar-salt mixture and are firm. Rub the fillets with the gin. Mix the ½ tsp. pepper, 2 tsp. each lime and mint, 1 Tb. dill, and 3 Tb. parsley together, and pat this over the fillets. Wrap again and refrigerate with a 3- or 4-pound weight on top to press the fish down and make the flesh more compact. Refrigerate for a few hours or overnight.

7 Remove the wrappings and place the fillets flat on the table. Using a long, thin knife, cut on the bias into thin slices about 2 to 3 in. long and the width of the fillet. Each of the slices should be bordered with a thin layer of the green.

8 Mix together the 2 diced cucumbers, 4 chopped hard-cooked eggs, 8 oz. sour cream, and ¼ tsp. each salt and pepper (you should have about 4 c.).

Toast the 12 bread ovals until nicely browned. Cover each slice with approximately ⅓ c. of the sour cream–cucumber-egg mixture and cover with 3 or 4 slices cured fish.

9 Arrange on a platter. Notice that the fish should be arranged on the bread so the border on the fish remains on the outside, forming a design. Decorate by placing a piece of parsley, mint, or dill in the center of each and serve as soon as possible, one large slice toast per person.

SMOKING FISH

Smoking fish at home is fun, rewarding, and the product is usually better than what you can buy commercially. The commercial variety is usually cured too much so it can be kept longer and, as a result, often tastes too salty and smoky. However, fish smoked at home, because it has less salt, cannot be kept for more than about 1½ weeks.

I have limited myself here to smoking only salmon and trout, but other fish, such as sturgeon, eel, porgie, and even large shrimp, can be cured and smoked in the same manner. As you can see in photograph 4, an old metal locker or refrigerator can be transformed into a smoker.

I have used hickory here but other kinds of wood can be used. Most fruit tree wood is good and, in some parts of the country, resiniferous wood (such as pine and spruce) are used for a stronger, darker, and more potent smoke flavor. Fresh thyme, sprigs of dried oregano and coriander, as well as bay leaves, can be added to the wood for flavor.

Before the fish is smoked, it must first be cured with salt. Two different methods are used here – a dry-cure for the salmon and a liquid-cure for the trout. They can be applied interchangeably. The salt will leach the moisture out of the fish, ridding it of bacteria (which would make it spoil) and preserving it. Kosher-type salt tends to give a better result than iodized salt, although either could be used.

There are two different types of smoking: high temperature – up to 250 degrees – known as the hot smoke method, for harder fish (such as eel and sturgeon, and the trout here smoked at about 200 degrees); and the cold smoke method. At about 120 degrees, the protein in salmon will coagulate and leach out (it looks like an egg white custard) and the flesh will flake (meaning that the salmon is cooked). Consequently, the salmon is always cold smoked.

To achieve the cold smoke, as demonstrated in the following recipe, the source of smoke is kept on the outside of the smoker (in this case, my old refrigerator) so the temperature never goes much higher than 90 degrees inside the smoking cabinet. But for the hot smoke method – the method I used for the trout – the source of heat is inside the cabinet and the temperature will reach at least 200 to 250 degrees.

SMOKED SALMON ETHEL

This smoked salmon should be done at least a day ahead since it is easier to slice if it has had time to cure and set. Although it can be served plain, in my recipe it is stuffed with a cucumber salad and garnished with asparagus – a delicious combination and delightful presentation.

Yield: 12–14 servings for each half salmon

1 salmon, head off and gutted, about 6¾ lb. (yielding 5½ lb. for both salmon fillets; 2 to 2¼ lb. for each fillet after boning)

DRY BRINE

⅔ c. kosher-type salt
¼ c. sugar

1 Tb. corn or safflower oil
CUCUMBER SALAD

2 large cucumbers, peeled, seeded, and cut into ¼-in. dice (about 3 c.)
2 tsp. salt
1 Tb. coarsely chopped dill, tarragon, or parsley
½ tsp. freshly ground black pepper
Salt, if needed
⅓ c. sour cream
2 tsp. lemon juice

GARNISHES

3 hard-cooked eggs
12 long chives, dropped in boiling water for a few seconds to wilt, and then refreshed under cold water, for use as a "string"
About 24 asparagus spears (peeled, cooked, and split, see steps 4–6, page 154)
1 Tb. lemon juice (8 to 10 drops per portion)
½ c. good virgin olive oil

1 Follow the technique for boning out salmon (Salmon Gravlax Evelyn, page 9, steps 1–5), and leave the skin on.

Place each half of salmon on a piece of plastic wrap. Mix the ⅔ c. salt and ¼ c. sugar together and divide it between the fillets. Wrap the fillets in the plastic wrap and then in aluminum foil and set aside, refrigerated, to cure for at least 6 hours, but preferably overnight, turning the packages occasionally so the salt (which will transform into liquid) runs through the salmon.

2 When the salmon is cured, you will notice that there is practically no liquid remaining because the salt has been transformed into liquid and been absorbed into the salmon and the salmon has firmed up considerably. At this point, the salmon can be rinsed briefly under cold water and dried with paper towels. It is ready to smoke.

3 Use a large flowerpot and an electric barbecue starter. Push the starter into the pot and fill the pot with wood chips.

4 To transform an old refrigerator into a cold smoker, make a hole with a hacksaw through one of the sides toward the bottom of the refrigerator (low enough so that the flowerpot can be positioned directly under it on the floor). The hole should be large enough to hold an elbow downspout (available at a hardware store). Fit the downspout into the hole and push aluminum foil around it so it fits tightly.

Plug in the barbecue starter and position the flowerpot under the downspout. Place a piece of aluminum foil around the top of the pot.

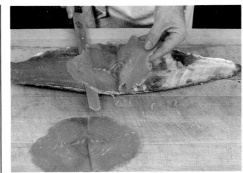

5 The foil should wrap around the pot and downspout so most of the smoke from the smoldering chips in the pot will go into the refrigerator. (If left open in a draft, the wood would eventually ignite and burn when, in fact, it should smolder.)

6 Place each salmon fillet on a wire rack in the refrigerator and close the door tightly. Plug in the smoker for 5 minutes and then unplug it. During the 5 minutes the smoker is plugged in, smoke will fill the refrigerator. The smoke will stay in the refrigerator, seeping out slowly. After an hour, plug in the smoker again for another 5 minutes. Then unplug it and, again, leave it for 1 hour. Do this a third time. The salmon should get approximately 15 minutes of smoking, 5 minutes every hour, and remain in the refrigerator for 4 hours. For a more penetrating smoke flavor, fill up the flowerpot with wood chips again and repeat the procedure a few more times.

7 Remove the salmon from the smoker, rub it on top with the 1 Tb. oil, wrap it in plastic wrap, and keep in a cool place in the refrigerator for at least 1 day before slicing.

To cut the salmon into the large slices needed for my recipe, use a long, thin-bladed knife and cut thinly on the bias, slicing almost to the bottom of the flesh but still keeping the slice attached at the base. Then cut another slice next to the first but cut it through so that both thin slices are attached at the base and when opened create one large, thin butterflied slice of salmon. Repeat until you have 12 to 14 butterflied pieces.

8 Place each butterflied piece of salmon in a little Pyrex bowl to make it easier to stuff.

Mix the 3 c. diced cucumber with the 2 tsp. of salt. Let the cucumber macerate for 10 to 15 minutes, then rinse it lightly in a strainer under cold water and pat dry. Add the 1 Tb. chopped dill (or tarragon or parsley), ½ tsp. pepper, and a dash of salt to taste, if needed. Mix in the ⅓ c. sour cream and 2 tsp. lemon juice.

Separate the 3 hard-cooked egg whites from the yolks, press the yolks through a sieve, and set aside. Cut the whites into a little dice and add them to the salad. Place approximately 2 to 3 Tb. of the salad mixture inside the salmon-lined bowl.

9 Fold the edges of the slices over the stuffing, turn upside down, and tie into a "package," crisscrossing the strips of blanched chives and tying them like string, making a knot on top. Repeat with the remaining pieces of salmon.

10 Arrange the salmon "packages" on serving plates and sprinkle sieved egg yolk on top. Arrange 2 split asparagus spears attractively on each plate and sprinkle with 8 to 10 drops of lemon juice and 2 tsp. of very good olive oil. Serve right away.

1 For best results, the trout should be freshly killed (live trout are available). Bash its head with the side of your hand or a piece of wood to kill it. Then plunge a knife into the trout and open it up 2 to 3 in. along the belly. Remove the gills and guts and wash the fish carefully under cold, running water, being sure to remove the strip of blood in the bottom of the cavity. In a stainless steel bowl, combine the 4 c. cool water, 2 c. kosher-type salt, and ¼ c. sugar. Place the trout in the brine and soak for approximately 2 hours. Notice that an egg placed in the brine rises to the surface with approximately one-fourth of the egg showing above the brine. This demonstrates that the gravity of the brine is very high in salt, what is called a saturated brine. It contains the maximum amount of salt possible; if any more salt is added to the mixture, it would not dissolve. Place a plate on top of the trout so they stay immersed in the water.

SMOKED TROUT SALAD CLAUDINE

This smoked trout, as explained in the introduction to the recipe, is hot smoked at a temperature between 180 and 200 degrees. The trout is excellent served with scrambled eggs and can also be made into pâtés, such as the eel pâté, page 20, or served whole (with just the skin removed, as shown in photograph 3), with some sour cream or butter and croutons.

The trout will keep for approximately 10 days in the refrigerator. Don't remove the skin ahead of serving. When they are cold, the trout should be wrapped individually in plastic wrap and refrigerated. Otherwise, the smoky odor will permeate the refrigerator.

Yield: about 12 servings

6 trout, about 10 oz. ungutted (about 8 oz. gutted with heads on)
BRINE
4 c. cool water
2 c. kosher-type salt
¼ c. sugar

EGG AND PEPPER SALAD
4 Tb. cream
2 tsp. freshly grated horseradish
4 tsp. red wine vinegar
1 tsp. salt
½ tsp. freshly ground black pepper
2 c. peeled red pepper, cut into ¼-in. dice
½ c. loose coriander leaves
6 hard-cooked eggs
Sliced bread, toasted in a toaster, then buttered lightly and cut into sticks

2 After curing the trout for 2 hours, rinse under cold water and pat dry, inside and out, with paper towels. Follow the directions in Smoked Salmon Ethel, pages 14–15, steps 2–5, for making a smoker. Place the trout on the wire rack in the smoker and fill the flowerpot with wood chips. Completely immerse the barbecue starter in the chips and place the pot inside the smoker (in this case, the old refrigerator, although a standard smoker will work as well). Cover it with a large piece of aluminum foil wrapped fairly tightly around it. Make a couple of small holes in the foil so the smoke can escape. Place the pot under the trout, running the cord from the barbecue starter through the hinge of the door. Leave the barbecue starter on for 2 hours. After a while, most of the wood will be smoldering. The pot should be quite full of wood – as much as it will hold – and if it is kept tightly wrapped and closed in the refrigerator, the wood won't ignite because there is no air; only the smoke and heat will come through to smoke and cook the trout.

3 The trout should be left in the smoker for another hour to cool slowly after the barbecue starter has been unplugged. Then wrap them individually in plastic wrap and refrigerate at least overnight. The following day, peel the skin off the trout. It will come off easily.

4 Remove the heads from the trout and cut down the line in the center of the fillet. With the side of the knife, ease the fillet off the central bone.

5 Repeat and ease the belly part of the fillet off the bone, also. Then turn the trout over and repeat to remove the fillet on the other side in 2 pieces. Each trout should be divided into 4 pieces.

6 To make the salad: Combine the 4 Tb. cream, 2 tsp. horseradish, 4 tsp. vinegar, 1 tsp. salt, and ½ tsp. pepper in a bowl, and stir with a whisk for 15 to 20 seconds. The mixture will thicken slightly. Add the 2 c. diced red pepper and ½ c. coriander leaves. Dice the 6 hard-cooked eggs by placing them in an egg slicer and cutting them one way, then turning them and cutting them the other way, and add them to the salad.

Arrange the fillets on a serving platter. On the platter here, we have one trout, i.e., 4 pieces of fish, arranged around the edge in an overlapping oval with the salad in the center. The salad can also be arranged on individual plates with the smoked trout around it.

7 Arrange the bread sticks attractively at either end of the serving platter and serve immediately.

MINUTE-SMOKED SEAFOOD

Fish as well as shellfish cooks quickly and absorbs seasonings well, making them both ideal for smoking. The fast cooking and smoking of the fish described here yields a juicy, flavorful, and delicate meat.

Although I use a commercial smoker (see Smoked Eel Pâté with Eggplant Marmalade, page 21, step 5), which is a rectangular container with a lid and wire rack inside, any old pot could be used, provided it is deep enough to accommodate a layer of sawdust in the bottom with a rack positioned about 1 ½ to 2 in. above the sawdust with enough room for a lid. The fish is partially cured ahead with a dash of salt, pepper, and lemon juice, and smoking and cooking are done in a few minutes. Different herbs can be added to the cure or to the sawdust, although the smoky flavor tends to dominate and destroy the flavor of herbs.

Fish that are more porous and have a softer texture, such as salmon, will cook and smoke faster than a firmer fish like monkfish. Firmer fleshed seafood (in this case, the prawns) will take longer to cook and is, therefore, cut in half so that the thinner pieces cook in the same amount of time as the salmon and swordfish, which

are left in larger pieces. The fish should be barely cooked; the inside moist with a center that looks a little transparent. Serve the seafood lukewarm or at room temperature coated with the dressing.

The tomato-orange dressing is acidic as well as sweet, and the tomato-onion vinaigrette is milder and less assertive. Choose according to your own taste. Because the seafood is only lightly smoked and cured, it cannot be kept as long as commercially smoked fish. It should be consumed within a day.

Yield: 8 servings

SEAFOOD MIXTURE

8 oz. cleaned swordfish
8 oz. salmon, bones removed
4 large prawns (about ½ lb.)
6 oz. scallops (about 16 large bay scallops or small sea scallops)
1 tsp. salt
¼ tsp. freshly ground black pepper
2 tsp. lemon juice

About ⅔ c. hardwood sawdust to make smoke

TOMATO-ORANGE DRESSING

2 tomatoes (about 12 oz.)
¼ c. red wine vinegar
½ c. chopped onion
¾ c. orange juice with pulp
½ tsp. salt
¼ tsp. freshly ground black pepper

TOMATO-ONION DRESSING

⅓ c. chopped onion, washed and pressed in a towel to remove excess water
½ c. tomato flesh, cut into ½-in. pieces
⅔ c. olive oil
3 Tb. red wine vinegar
¾ tsp. salt
¾ tsp. freshly ground black pepper

GARNISH

Basil leaves

1 Cut the swordfish and salmon (8 oz. each) into strips about 1 in. wide (about 1 oz. each). You should have 1 piece per person. Split the ½ lb. of prawns lengthwise down the center. Put the fish and shellfish in a bowl and sprinkle with the 1 tsp. salt, ¼ tsp. pepper, and 2 tsp. lemon juice. Cover, and refrigerate for at least 1 hour.

2 Sometimes the wires are too far apart on the smoker rack and the fish tend to fall through the openings between. To prevent this, place a piece of metal screen over the rack and arrange the fish and shellfish on it. Be sure that the fish that are softer and will cook faster are packed a little closer to each other and the firmer fish arranged more loosely.

4 At serving time, cut the pieces of fish on the diagonal into 1-in. pieces so the inside flesh contrasts with the smoky and more golden outside. Cut the fish, scallops, and shrimp on the diagonal into slices.

3 Sprinkle the sawdust in the bottom of the smoker and place it over fairly high heat for about 1 minute, or until it starts smoking. Place the rack containing the fish on top of the sawdust. Cover tightly with the lid and cook over high heat until the fish has smoked for approximately 3 minutes. Remove from the heat and set aside with the lid still in place for a few more minutes so the fish continue cooking gently in their own heat. The fish and shellfish should be golden but still juicy. Make the dressing of your choice.

5 Arrange the seafood on a platter or individual plates with some of your favorite sauce on top. (The sauce here is the tomato-onion vinaigrette.) Decorate with basil leaves and serve.

For the tomato-orange dressing: Skin and seed the 2 tomatoes. Cut the flesh into ¼-in. dice. Bring the ¼ c. vinegar and ½ c. chopped onion to a boil and cook approximately 1 minute. Remove from the heat and add the ¾ c. orange juice, ½ tsp. salt, and ¼ tsp. pepper, stirring to combine.

For the tomato-onion dressing: Combine the ⅓ c. chopped onion, ½ c. tomato flesh, ⅔ c. olive oil, 3 Tb. vinegar, and ¾ tsp. each of salt and pepper.

SMOKED EEL PATE WITH EGGPLANT MARMALADE

The recipe here is made with home-smoked eel, but it could also be done with commercially smoked eel as well as smoked trout or smoked sturgeon. The smoked fish should account for half of the mixture in the pâté, and the mousse is used as a binder to hold pieces of the smoked fish together.

The skin of eggplant, used as a wrapper, simulates the skin of eel and makes a flavorful envelope for the pâté. Although I have poached the pâté, it can also be steamed or baked dry in a low-temperature oven.

The spicy eggplant marmalade complements cold cuts as well as fish pâtés, and the sweet, acidic sauce, made with raspberry purée and Balsamico vinegar, should be used sparingly so it does not overpower the flavor of the pâté. Buttered toast always goes well with smoked fish.

The dried tomatoes lend a pungent taste and a beautiful color to the dish. The ones used here have been reconstituted in water because they were completely dried. This is not necessary if dried tomatoes packed in oil are used.

The pâté should be served cool but not ice cold. It will keep properly wrapped and refrigerated for a week after cooking and is actually better 24 hours later, when it has set and developed flavor.

Yield: 10–12 servings

4 to 5 small eels, about 2¼ to 2½ lb. total, about 1½ lb. skinned and gutted

CURING MIXTURE

2 Tb. salt
1 Tb. brown sugar
1 tsp. dried oregano leaves
½ tsp. freshly ground black pepper

About ¾ c. hardwood sawdust

GARNISH OF EGGPLANT SKIN AND DRIED TOMATOES

2 large eggplants (about 1¼ lb. each)
1 Tb. peanut oil
½ c. water
1 doz. sun-dried tomato halves, reconstituted in ½ c. boiling water for ½ hour and drained. (Reserve the tomato water for soups and stocks.)

SOLE MOUSSE

1 lb. fillet of gray or lemon sole
1 egg white
1 c. cream
⅛ tsp. freshly ground black pepper
½ tsp. salt

EGGPLANT MARMALADE

Eggplant flesh (about 4 c.)
3 large cloves garlic
1 piece peeled ginger (size of 2 cloves garlic)
1 tsp. sesame oil
2 tsp. sugar
¼ tsp. Chinese hot oil
2 Tb. rice wine vinegar
2 Tb. dark soy sauce
¼ tsp. salt
1 Tb. peanut oil
1 tsp. fennel seed
2 tsp. coarsely chopped coriander

RASPBERRY-VINEGAR SAUCE

½ c. purée of unsweetened raspberries
3 Tb. Balsamico vinegar
¼ tsp. salt
¼ tsp. freshly ground black pepper

GARNISH

Parsley and arugula leaves

1 Cut all around the head of the eel just under the side fin to loosen the skin.

2 Hold the slippery head with a towel. Using pliers, pull the skin, which should come off easily. Cut off the head.

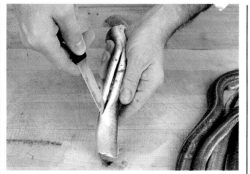

3 Using a sharp knife, open the belly of the eel from the anus to the head and clean the inside, removing all the guts and blood. Clean and dress the rest of the eels in the same way.

4 Wash the eels and cut them into 2- to 2½-in. pieces. Mix the 2 Tb. salt, 1 Tb. brown sugar, 1 tsp. oregano, and ½ tsp. black pepper together. Put the pieces of eel with the curing mixture in a plastic bag. Seal the bag and let the eel cure, refrigerated, for at least 2 hours, turning the bag occasionally to redistribute the curing mixture.

5 To smoke the eels, an old pot could be used, provided it is at least 3 to 4 in. deep so there is room for the sawdust, a wire rack approximately 1½ in. above the sawdust, and a lid on top. In this recipe, I have used a commercial smoker. Sprinkle the sawdust in the bottom of the pan and place the rack on top.

6 Arrange the eel in one layer on the wire rack. Cover with the lid and place the smoker on top of the stove over medium to high heat, until the sawdust starts smoking. Keep over medium to low heat so the sawdust (made from hardwood) smokes and the eel continues cooking for approximately 10 minutes. Then, set the smoker, still covered, off the heat and let it cool to lukewarm.

7 The eel becomes golden in color as it smokes. It should be firm and barely cooked in the center at the bone.

8 Scrape some of the black, fatty underskin from the eel, bone the pieces, and set the meat aside. (You should have about ¾ lb. of cooked, boned eel.) Discard the trimmings and bones.

9 **To prepare the eggplants:** Trim the stems from the 2 large eggplants and place in a saucepan large enough to accommodate them. Add the 1 Tb. peanut oil and ½ c. water. Place over high heat for about 1 minute, then reduce the heat to medium-low and cover. (If the eggplants are too high and the lid doesn't fit, press down on them with the lid; as they soften during cooking, the lid will eventually fit.) Turn the eggplants every 5 to 6 minutes to make sure that they cook throughout, and continue cooking over low heat for a total of about 30 to 40 minutes. Cool.

10 Place the eggplants on a platter and peel off the skin in pieces as large as possible.

11 Arrange the skin of the eggplant on a piece of plastic wrap, making sure that the shiny side is touching the plastic. Overlap the pieces, if necessary, to form a tight seal and create a rectangle about 9 × 14 in.

To make the mousse: Cut the 1 lb. of sole fillets into 1-in. pieces and put them in the bowl of the food processor with the egg white. Process for several seconds and then scrape down the sides of the bowl with a rubber spatula and process again until the mixture is smooth and slightly spongy. Add the 1 c. cream in a steady pour while the machine is running. (It should take about 10 to 15 seconds.) Add the ⅛ tsp. pepper and ½ tsp. salt, and process for a few more seconds, until the mixture is fluffy and smooth. Place the mixture in a bowl and refrigerate it until ready to use.

12 Spread half of the mousse over about one-half to two-thirds of the eggplant skin and arrange half the pieces of smoked eel on top, pressing them down so they become embedded in the mousse. Cover with more mousse.

13 Press the 12 pieces of reconstituted sun-dried tomatoes into the mousse. Cover with the rest of the mousse and eel meat.

14 Lifting the plastic wrap, roll up the mixture to create a "sausage."

15 Tighten the plastic wrap around and at each end so the "sausage" is tight and completely wrapped in the eggplant skin. The dimensions of the "sausage" should be approximately 2 to 3 in. thick by about 12 in. long.

16 Wrap the plastic-wrapped "sausage" in aluminum foil and tightly seal the foil at the ends. Place on a rack in a fish poacher and cover with water. Place a lid or weight on the sausage to hold it under the water. Bring the temperature of the water to approximately 180 degrees, and cook the "sausage" about 20 minutes. (The internal temperature should reach about 120 to 125 degrees.) Remove from the hot water, let cool at room temperature, and then refrigerate.

17 **To make the eggplant marmalade:** Coarsely chop the reserved eggplant flesh (about 4 c.). Crush and chop finely together the 3 large cloves of garlic and 2 garlic clove–size pieces of peeled ginger. Put in a bowl with the 1 tsp. sesame oil, 2 tsp. sugar, ¼ tsp. Chinese hot oil, 2 Tb. rice wine vinegar, 2 Tb. soy sauce, ¼ tsp. salt, 1 Tb. peanut oil, and 1 tsp. fennel seed, and mix well. Add the eggplant flesh and mix to incorporate. Stir in some of the 2 tsp. chopped coriander and arrange on a serving dish with the remainder of the coriander sprinkled on top.

To make the raspberry-vinegar sauce: Combine the ½ c. purée of unsweetened raspberries with the 3 Tb. Balsamico vinegar, and ¼ tsp. each salt and pepper.

Cut the eel pâté into slices about ¾ in. thick. Arrange on a platter with the parsley and arugula leaves around it and serve with the eggplant marmalade and raspberry-vinegar sauce.

2 Mix the ¼ c. kosher-type salt with the 2 Tb. brown sugar and sprinkle on top of the sardines. Cover with plastic wrap and cure for 3 or more hours – they could be left overnight.

3 Remove the sardines from the salt, rinse briefly under cold water, and pat dry. Then, open the sardines by running your thumb along the central bone on each side. The flesh will be quite soft and will separate from the bone easily.

SARDINES IN PARSLEY SALAD

The sardine, from the small smelt to the large sardine often called "pilchard" in France, comes from the herring family. Sardines of varying sizes are often served raw cured with salt, as in this recipe, or, in Mediterranean countries like Spain and Portugal, grilled over charcoal and sold on the streets. The sardine lends itself well to grilling since it is a fatty fish with soft bones. The smoke imparts a nice flavor and, although messy to eat, grilled or broiled sardines are most delicious.

In this recipe, the sardines are cured in salt, boned, and covered with olive oil. They can remain in olive oil for several days to develop flavor. I have added roasted and skinned yellow and red pepper and a very garlicky parsley salad.

Yield: about 12 servings

3 lb. sardines, about 24 fairly large sardines (1½ oz. each)
¼ c. kosher-type salt
2 Tb. brown sugar
2 to 3 Tb. fresh thyme leaves
About ½ c. olive oil

6 peppers: 3 red, 3 yellow
SALAD
6 c. flat parsley leaves, separated
2 c. grated carrots
2 Tb. chopped onion

2 Tb. chopped garlic (6 to 8 cloves)
½ tsp. freshly ground black pepper
½ tsp. salt
1 Tb. red wine vinegar
¼ c. good olive oil

1 Scale the sardines gently with the back of a knife, or by rubbing them under cold water (the scales will slide off). Then, cut off the heads and a strip of the belly so the insides can be cleaned out. Wash under water and pat dry.

4 Pull off the central bone. It will come off without much meat with it. Cut off the tail and remove any black skin or visible bones. →

5 Pat the butterflied sardines dry with a towel and arrange them in a dish. Strew 2 to 3 Tb. fresh thyme leaves on top and sprinkle with about ½ c. olive oil. Cover with plastic wrap and refrigerate for several days, if desired.

6 To prepare the peppers: Arrange the 3 yellow and 3 red peppers on a broiling rack and place under the hot broiler about 1 in. from the heat. Broil, turning occasionally, for about 12 to 15 minutes, until fairly brown all around. Place the hot peppers in a plastic bag for 10 minutes to steam them and soften the skin, making it easy to remove.

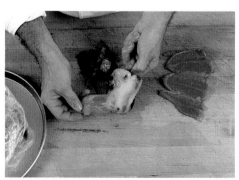

7 The skin will now slide off. Pull to remove it all around and remove the core. Open the peppers and remove the seeds from the insides – this can also be done under running water.

8 If rinsed under running water, pat the pieces of pepper dry. Flatten them and cut into large pieces for our recipe. (For another recipe, the peppers can be sliced into strips and placed in a jar with olive oil, a dash of salt, a lot of ground pepper and chopped garlic, and kept as marinated peppers. This way they will keep for a couple of weeks in the refrigerator and can be used in sandwiches or for seasoning pasta or other things.)

9 Prepare the parsley salad: Wash the 6 c. flat parsley carefully and dry. Remove the tough stems and combine the leaves with the 2 c. grated carrots, 2 Tb. each chopped onion and garlic, ½ tsp. each pepper and salt, 1 Tb. vinegar, and ¼ c. olive oil, mixing well.

10 Arrange the parsley salad on a serving platter with the pieces of red and yellow pepper, and place the sardines on top.

11 Sprinkle lightly with the oil from the sardines, adding a bit more cracked pepper, if desired. Serve.

Note: These are ideal eaten on thick, crusty bread, or buttered black bread, and served with a dry white wine.

1 Wash 1½ doz. clams, rubbing them against one another carefully under cold water. To open a clam, hold it with a towel or pot holder or, if you feel sure enough of yourself, grasp it in your unprotected hand. Place the cutting blade of the paring knife on the line between the two shells and, with the fingers of one hand, press on the blade, sliding it between the two shells, and cut the sinew that holds the clam closed.

CLAM AND FISH CEVICHE ZIM ZIM

The mixture of raw fish and citrus juice called ceviche can be flavored with many different seasonings. In the recipe here, clams and their salty juices are added to a mixture of raw fish to help cure and flavor it. If you feel the flavor is too assertive, omit the clams and their juices and, instead, increase the amount of salt and vinegar slightly.

The variety of vegetables added to the fish — from cucumbers to avocados, tomatoes, peppers, onions, scallions, etc. — gives wonderful flavor, varied texture, and beautiful color to the dish.

The ceviche should macerate at least 2 hours before being served, but it will keep, refrigerated, for as long as 3 or 4 days. (Don't add the avocado too far ahead, however, as it tends to disintegrate and will muddy the dish.) The fish is cured by the acidity of the vinegar and lemon as well as by the salt. The inside flesh of the tomatoes is mixed into the ceviche, while the shells make elegant receptacles, which can be filled with other salads as well.

This ideal summer dish makes a great buffet centerpiece and the selection of fish and shellfish should be varied to take advantage of the freshest available ingredients.

Yield: 10–12 servings

1½ doz. cherrystone clams (about 1 to 1¼ lb.)
8 oz. large bay scallops or small sea scallops (about 24 pieces)
¾ lb. cleaned sea bass
¾ lb. cleaned fish fillets with a different texture from the sea bass, such as cod, haddock, or bluefish
About 10 strips of lemon peel, removed with a vegetable peeler
4 finely chopped cloves garlic (1 Tb.)
1 large cucumber, peeled, seeded, and cut into ¼-in. dice (about 2 c.)
1 c. coriander leaves, chopped coarse
1 small jalapeño pepper, cut in half, seeded, and chopped (1 tsp.)
1 large red onion, chopped coarse (1¼ c.)
4 scallions, cut into ½-in. pieces (½ c.)
10 to 12 tomatoes
1 medium ripe avocado
⅓ c. oil (half peanut and half good olive oil)
2 tsp. salt
½ tsp. freshly ground black pepper
3 Tb. red wine vinegar
2 Tb. lemon juice
¼ tsp. Tabasco sauce

GARNISH

Basil or mint leaves

2 Holding the clam over a bowl to catch the juice, cut with the knife until the clam shells are completely split in half.

3 After all the clams have been cut open, pry both shells apart with your fingers and, using a spoon, scrape the meat out. →

4 When all the meat has been extracted, shake each clam in the clam juice to wash off any sand that may be clinging to it. Cut the large clams in pieces and put them in a large bowl. Reserve the juice, letting it rest until the sediment falls to the bottom. Mix the 8 oz. of scallops in with the clams.

5 After making sure that all sinews and bones are removed, cut the 1½ lb. of fish into ½-in. pieces. Add them to the clams and scallops.

6 Cut the lemon peel into julienne slices (about 1 Tb.) and add them to the seafood along with the 1 Tb. finely chopped garlic, 2 c. diced cucumbers, 1 c. chopped coriander leaves, 1 tsp. chopped jalapeño pepper, 1¼ c. chopped red onion, and ½ c. scallions. Pour the clam juice into the ceviche slowly so as not to disturb the sediment settled on the bottom. (Discard the sand and sediment.)

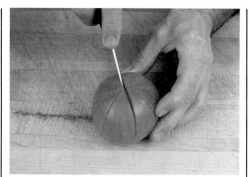

7 **To make the tomato receptacles:** Cut a tomato in eighths, going approximately two-thirds to three-fourths of the way through from the top to the bottom.

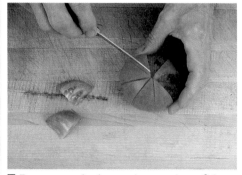

8 Remove each alternating section of the tomato. Then, using a spoon, remove the inside pulp of the tomato and press the juice out to create a receptacle. The inside pulp can now be sorted out, setting aside the juice, seeds, and skin for use later in a stock, and keeping the flesh to chop up and add to the ceviche.

9 To give a more elegant effect to the receptacle, one by one lay each of the cut points flat on the table and, using a knife held flat, separate the skin from the flesh.

10 The tomato is a hollow shell, ready to be filled, and each of the four points has been split into skin and flesh. Prepare the rest of the tomato receptacles, adding all the flesh to the ceviche mixture.

11 **For the avocado:** Cut a ripe avocado in half from top to bottom with a knife until you reach the pit. Twist the halves in opposite directions until they separate. Remove and discard the pit.

12 With the point of a knife, gently cut each half first in strips going one way and then the other at ½-in. intervals through the flesh (being careful not to penetrate the skin).

13 With a spoon, scoop out the diced flesh of the avocado and add it to the ceviche.

14 Add the ⅓ c. oil, 2 tsp. salt, ½ tsp. pepper, 3 Tb. vinegar, 2 Tb. lemon juice, and ¼ tsp. Tabasco to the ceviche and mix well. Taste to make sure that the dish is highly seasoned. Cover tightly with plastic wrap and let macerate in the refrigerator for at least 2 hours before serving.

15 At serving time, fill each tomato with ceviche and arrange it in the center of an individual serving plate. Surround with additional ceviche. Decorate with a little sprig of basil or mint, and serve immediately.

EGGS IN ASPIC GLORIA

My wife, Gloria, loves eggs in aspic. In addition, she often prepares Hanoi soup, flavoring the stock she makes for it with blackened shallots, pieces of ginger, and star anise – a Vietnamese combination that enriches the flavor and gives the soup an incomparable aroma. In this recipe, I have used her stock for the aspic surrounding the poached eggs and created a garnish of fresh and dried mushrooms, red pepper, and cooked ham. The poached egg garnish can be varied ad infinitum with pieces of chicken, fresh herbs, vegetables, fish, or shellfish.

This is an appealing summer party dish of eggs glistening in a beautiful, dark, rich aspic. Get large eggs that are as fresh as possible – they will hold their shape better as they poach than older eggs will. A little white vinegar added to the water tends to tighten the albumen and give the egg whites a rounder shape. After the eggs have been poached, they are plunged into ice water, which stops the cooking and washes off the taste of the vinegar.

The eggs in this recipe are used cold in aspic but can be served hot with a hollandaise or other sauce. In that case, reheat them, when needed, for a minute or so in simmering water.

The Salad Olga, a mixture of celeriac and carrots with a mustard-mayonnaise sauce, is a nutty salad, one that is always welcome for a summer buffet. The dressing is also good with poached fish or combined with beef salad made from leftover boiled beef.

Yield: 8 servings

POACHED EGGS

8 large eggs, as fresh as possible
3 qt. water
2 Tb. distilled white vinegar

RICH BROWN STOCK

3 large shallots, peeled (about 2 oz.)
1 piece ginger, about 1½ to 2 in., cut in half
4 lb. chicken bones, cut into 3-in. pieces
5 qt. water
3 pieces star anise
Approximately 1½ c. mushroom soaking liquid (from dried mushrooms for garnish)

ASPIC GLORIA

1 c. coarsely chopped green of leeks
1 c. coarsely chopped parsley
1 c. coarsely chopped celery
4 envelopes gelatin (about 3 Tb.)
3 egg whites
½ tsp. freshly ground black pepper
2 tsp. salt

GARNISHES

½ oz. dried mushrooms (shiitake, cèpe, or black Polish mushrooms)
½ red pepper, peeled and cut into a thin julienne about 3 in. long
3 large fresh mushrooms (about 3 oz.)
1 c. cooked ham strips

SALAD OLGA

Yield: 6 servings
1 celeriac, about 1 lb.
2 carrots, peeled (about 6 oz.)

MUSTARD DRESSING

3 egg yolks
4 Tb. French mustard, Dijon-style
½ tsp. freshly ground black pepper
½ tsp. salt
1 c. oil (mixture of half olive, half peanut)

GARNISH

Parsley sprigs

1 For the poached eggs: The eggs can be poached up to a day ahead and kept, refrigerated, in water, until ready to use. To poach the eggs, combine the water and vinegar in a shallow saucepan about 10 in. wide. The depth of the water should be about 1½ to 2 in. Bring the water to a boil. (In theory, the eggs should not be cooked in boiling water since this will toughen the albumen. I begin with boiling water, however, since as soon as the first egg is added, the water temperature will go down and the boiling will cease.)

Break the egg on a flat surface to crack it. (Breaking eggs on the edge of a pan or table can push the shell inside and break the yolk.) Insert your thumb in the little opening created and break the shell directly above the water, close enough so the water doesn't splash as the egg drops into it. Repeat with the other eggs, working as fast as you can. You can poach 8 to 10 eggs at one time in one saucepan, dropping them into the water quickly – all within about ½ minute.

2 The heat is still on high under the eggs and you will see threads of the egg whites rise to the surface and float a little. Drag the back of a skimmer or slotted spoon across the surface of the water to catch those threads and to move the eggs enough that they don't stick to the bottom of the pan. After the eggs have been moved once, they won't stick anymore.

3 Let the water return almost to the boil (about 200 degrees). When it begins to simmer, lower the heat and continue poaching the eggs approximately 3 to 4 minutes, depending on how well done you like your eggs. At this point, lift one of the eggs out of the water with a slotted spoon and press on it gently with your finger to determine the degree of "doneness." The yolk should be soft to the touch, indicating it is soft and runny inside. Transfer the cooked eggs to ice-cold water.

4 After 10 to 15 minutes, the eggs will be cold. Lift them out of the water and trim off any hanging pieces of white to create a nice oval shape.

5 Notice that the yolk is more apparent on one side while the other side of the egg is more evenly rounded and no yolk is visible. Serve the eggs smoother side up (i.e., the one on the right). The trimmed eggs can be kept in water in the refrigerator for up to 24 hours.

6 To make the stock: Impale the 3 shallots and piece of ginger on a skewer and char them over a gas flame. After about 3 to 4 minutes, they should be nicely browned and slightly blackened all around. Set aside.

Meanwhile, spread out the 4 lb. chicken bone pieces in a roasting pan and then roast them in a preheated 400-degree oven for 75 minutes, turning them once or twice during the cooking so they are nicely browned on all sides.

7 Notice that the bones are brown, dry, and all of the fat from the skin on the chicken back has melted. With a slotted spoon, transfer the bones to a large saucepan containing 5 qt. of water and add 2 of the pieces of star anise. Discard the fat that has accumulated in the roasting pan and add 2 c. of water from the saucepan. Bring to a boil, scraping the bottom of the pan with a flat wooden spatula to dislodge the solidified fat in the roasting pan. Add this mixture to the kettle, lower the heat, and boil gently, uncovered, over medium to high heat for 2 hours. Then, add the remaining piece of star anise and the blackened shallots and ginger, and boil for 1 hour more.

8 As the stock boils gently, skim off the fat that accumulates on the surface.

Strain the stock through a strainer with a very fine screen and let it cool. When cold, spoon off any additional fat that has risen to the surface. There should be 4½ to 5½ c. of stock.

Soak the ½ oz. dried mushrooms (for the garnish) in 2 c. water for about 1 hour. Remove the mushrooms from the water and add the soaking liquid (approximately 1½ c.) to the stock. Boil the stock and soaking liquid together. (You will now have approximately 6 c.)

9 To make the aspic: In a large stockpot (preferably stainless steel), combine the 1 c. each green of leeks, parsley, and celery and 4 envelopes gelatin. (Although there are 4 envelopes added, the strength of the gelatin will lessen as the stock boils.)

Add to the pot the 3 egg whites, ½ tsp. freshly ground pepper, and 2 tsp. salt. Mix well. Add the boiling stock and return the pot to the stove. Cook over high heat, stirring constantly, until the mixture comes to a strong boil. Lower the heat and continue to simmer very gently for 3 to 4 minutes, then set aside and allow to rest for ½ hour before straining. Strain through a strainer lined with wet paper towels. You should have about 5 c. of strong stock.

10 For the garnishes: With a vegetable peeler, remove as much skin from ½ red pepper as possible; then cut the pepper into sections at the pleats and peel off any remaining skin, which will now be accessible. Remove the ribs and seeds from the pepper and cut the flesh into julienne strips, about ¼ in. thick. Put the strips into a saucepan, add ½ c. of water, bring to a boil, and cook for about 10 seconds. Drain. Reserve the remaining ½ pepper for use in a soup or salad.

11 Cut the caps of the 3 large mushrooms into ⅛- to ¼-in. slices. Stack the slices up together and cut them into sticks. You should have about ¾ c.

Remove any sand or tough areas from the stems of the dried presoaked mushrooms, and cut them into little strips about ¼ in. thick. The yield should be about ¾ c.

Place the cut fresh and dried mushrooms in a saucepan, and add ½ c. of the aspic to cover. Bring to a boil and cook for about 1 minute. Remove the pan from the heat and stir in the pepper strips. →

12 For the eggs that are to be un-molded: Pour some of the aspic into a small stainless steel bowl over ice and stir until it starts to get syrupy. Spoon about 2 Tb. of the cold aspic into the bottom of each ramekin – about ⅜ in. deep. Refrigerate until the aspic is set.

13 When the aspic is set, arrange 3 or 4 ham strips on top, then a few strips of red pepper and mushrooms.

14 Place the poached eggs on top of the pre-set aspic and garnishes (see step 13), then top and surround with more garnishes. Cool additional aspic over ice and, when it becomes syrupy, pour it over the eggs and garnishes, filling up the molds. The aspic is cooled over ice before using because the finished dish will be shinier and more beautiful than if the aspic were poured directly on top of the eggs while lukewarm or just cool.

15 To unmold the eggs, run the blade of a small knife gently all around the inside edge of the molds, holding the knife tightly against the mold so you don't cut into the eggs. Invert over a plate and shake to unmold.

16 As an alternative, serve the eggs molded either in a serving dish or in individual molds. Drain 3 of the poached eggs on a paper towel and dry them thoroughly. Sprinkle some of the garnishes over the bottom of a gratin dish and arrange the eggs on top. Sprinkle more of the garnishes over the eggs. To serve the eggs individually, sprinkle a few of the garnishes in small ramekins and place an egg on top. Sprinkle with more of the garnishes.

17 Place about 1½ to 2 c. of the aspic in a bowl over ice and stir until it gets syrupy. With a large spoon, nap the eggs with the aspic until they are completely covered and the aspic is almost set. Refrigerate until set hard.

18 To make the celeriac Salad Olga: Peel the celeriac to remove all the skin and cut it in half. Sometimes the center of the celeriac gets slightly soft; if that is the case, remove any soft areas. The peeled celeriac should weigh 13 to 14 oz.

19 Cut each half of the celeriac into thin slices (no more than ⅛ in. thick) and stack the slices up.

20 Cut the slices into a fine julienne. (You should have about 4 c.)

23 The finished dressing will be quite thick.

21 Peel the carrots and cut lengthwise into thin slices (about 1/16 to 1/8 inch thick). Stack a pile of the slices up and cut into a very fine julienne, yielding about 1 1/4 c.

24 Combine the julienne of celeriac and carrot with the dressing and toss to mix well. Arrange in an attractive serving bowl and garnish with parsley. Serve with the Eggs in Aspic Gloria, unmolded, in the gratin dish, or in the small ramekins. Notice that the yolk of the cut egg on the serving plate in the foreground is still runny, as it should be. Eggs in Aspic will keep, covered with plastic wrap (so they don't dry out), in the refrigerator for a couple of days.

22 Place the 3 egg yolks, 4 Tb. mustard, and 1/2 tsp. each pepper and salt in a bowl, and whisk until well-blended. Add the oil (at room temperature* or it won't mix properly), pouring it slowly in a stream while whisking continuously.

*Expensive oil is sometimes stored in the refrigerator, especially in warm areas of the country.

1 Place the 8 oz. of pieces of chicken fat in a large skillet over medium to high heat and cook until most of the fat is rendered and the pieces of chicken fat are like cracklings, dry and brown. Meanwhile, in a small spice or coffee grinder, place the 4 to 5 sprigs thyme, 2 bay leaves, 1 tsp. peppercorns, ½ tsp. each allspice and coriander, and ¼ tsp. fennel seeds. Process for a few seconds to grind into powder.

Add ½ c. sliced shallots to the hot fat, cook for 8 to 10 seconds, and add the pieces of chicken, 1 tsp. salt, and the 1 tsp. chopped garlic. Cook over medium heat, stirring, for 2 to 3 minutes. Then, add the 10 oz. livers. Continue cooking over medium to high heat for another 3 to 4 minutes.

COLD MOUSSE OF CHICKEN AND PISTACHIOS

This combination of chicken meat, chicken fat, liver, cognac, and seasonings could be called a terrine because it is served in a dish that is called a terrine. It could also be called a pâté, as a cold loaf commonly is, or a mousse. Mousse, regardless of whether it is a scallop, a chocolate, or a chicken mousse, means foam in French; it is a mixture that is usually whipped or emulsified to make it foamy, or mixed with whipped cream or beaten egg white.

Always welcome for a party, it can be made ahead and is attractive and showy as a centerpiece when it is decorated. It can also be done without the decoration, poured into small containers, and served with toast on different tables. Unlike regular pâté, where the meat is ground, seasoned, then cooked slowly in the oven, the ingredients in this dish are precooked and emulsified in the food processor and molded afterward. It is prepared quickly, but requires a few hours to set properly. The mousse can be made the day before and the decoration and glazing done the day of serving.

Yield: 14–16 servings

8 oz. chicken fat, cut into ½-in. pieces
4 to 5 sprigs fresh thyme, or 1 tsp. dried
2 large bay leaves, crushed
1 tsp. black peppercorns
½ tsp. whole allspice
½ tsp. coriander seeds
¼ tsp. fennel seeds
½ c. sliced shallots (about 3 to 4 medium shallots)
18 oz. chicken meat, cleaned of skin, sinews, and fat, and cut into 1-in. pieces
1 tsp. salt
1 to 2 cloves garlic, chopped (about 1 tsp.)
10 oz. chicken livers, cleaned of sinews
3 sticks butter, softened (12 oz.)
1 Tb. cognac
⅔ c. shelled pistachios

ASPIC

1 egg white
1 envelope gelatin (about ¾ Tb.)
½ c. green of leeks, celery, and parsley
¼ tsp. freshly ground black pepper
Salt, if needed, depending on the saltiness of the stock
1 c. chicken stock

GARNISH

A few thin strips of red pepper, chives, green of leeks and scallions, carrot, radishes, and tomatoes

2 The liver should be barely cooked through, still pink in the center. Set aside on the stove and let everything rest 10 minutes.

Put the entire mixture into the bowl of a food processor and emulsify for ½ minute, until smooth. Add the 3 sticks butter and process only until the ingredients are well-blended and smooth. Add the 1 Tb. cognac.

3 Push the mixture through a food mill fitted with a small screen or through a sieve. Then, fold in the ⅔ c. pistachios. Place the mixture in a bowl and let cool in the refrigerator until it begins to set hard. Mix well to assure that it doesn't look broken.

4 When it is smooth, pack into a pâté mold or terrine, cover tightly with plastic wrap, and refrigerate overnight.

5 The following day, decorate, using very thinly cut red pepper pieces (which can be used for flowers as well as for the vase in my decoration), chives, and green of leeks and scallions. All the greens should be dropped in boiling water, blanched for approximately 10 to 15 seconds until wilted, and cooled under cold water. Pieces of sliced carrot, blanched in water for 1 minute, can be used, as well as pieces of radish, tomato, and red pepper, which do not need to be blanched. Be sure not to use any vegetable or fruit that will impart a taste to the pâté, such as lemon skin, or beets, which would discolor it.

Decorate according to your own taste, making a frame with the long pieces of scallion. Tamp down the decoration with the point of your knife or the tip of your finger to set it into the pâté.

6 Make stems and leaves of flowers with the green of leeks and chives. Make calyxes with green and flowers with red of tomato.

7 Create a vase and flowers with cutouts from tomato skin. Use your imagination.

For the aspic: In a saucepan, mix together the egg white, 1 envelope gelatin, the ½ c. green of leeks, celery, and parsley, ¼ tsp. pepper, optional salt, and the 1 c. chicken stock. Bring to a boil over high heat and set aside for 5 minutes. Strain through a sieve lined with wet paper towels. Place on ice and stir gently until the mixture gets very syrupy and ready to set. This is the time to use it, when it is at its shiniest and most translucent. Using a spoon, coat the top of the pâté, working quickly, with some of the aspic, until the entire surface is covered. Place again in the refrigerator until well-set. The extra aspic can be coarsely chopped when set and served with the pâté later on.

8 The decorated pâté makes a stunning presentation as a buffet centerpiece. Be sure to keep it as cold as possible until serving time. At serving time, use a cold spoon to dish it out. Serve with small pieces of Melba toast or black bread.

SUPREME OF CHICKEN SANDRINE

In a classic chaud-froid, chicken is spread with goose liver pâté, but in the recipe here it is coated with a savory mousse made with the fat and liver of the chicken flavored with cognac and heavy cream. This chicken mousse could also be served by itself on toast for a party.

The chickens are simmered for a short time and are allowed to continue cooking off the heat in the poaching liquid. This produces a moist, flavorful meat. After the chickens are removed, the liquid is cooked further with the chicken feet (to increase the gelatin content), carrots, leeks, celery, onion, and seasonings to make a stronger stock. Some of the stock is reduced further and made into a rich, concentrated chicken suprême sauce that is used to coat the chicken pieces, and the remainder of the stock is turned into an aspic.

The decoration is fanciful and striking for a summer buffet and should be done only with vegetables or edible flower petals. The green from scallions, leeks, and chives as well as the carrot strips and any other vegetables that have a hard texture are first blanched in boiling water to make them limp and pliable. Do not use any decorative elements that would impart a bitter or other unpleasant taste to the chicken pieces.

This beautiful dish can be done in steps. The chicken can be poached, the mousse prepared, and the chicken pieces coated with the suprême sauce the day before serving. The decoration and aspic glazing, however, should be done only a few hours ahead or the aspic will tend to dry, crack, and get rubbery. The dish should be served cool to cold but not ice cold.

The suprême sauce, the aspic, and the mousse should be highly seasoned as the taste of spices and salt tends to diminish in a dish that is eaten cold.

Yield: 8 servings

POACHING THE CHICKENS

About ½ lb. chicken feet, if obtainable
2 chickens, about 3 lb. each, eviscerated, heads and necks included
1 large leek, cleaned
2 medium carrots, peeled
1 large rib celery
1 medium onion studded with 6 cloves
1 tsp. salt
2 to 3 bay leaves
1 tsp. dried thyme
3 qt. water

CHICKEN MOUSSE

2 lumps fat from inside the chicken near the tail. (They should be about the weight of the chicken livers, below.)
1 large shallot, peeled and sliced (2 tsp.)
1 small clove garlic, crushed and peeled
¼ tsp. thyme leaves
2 chicken livers
1 Tb. butter
1 Tb. cognac
1¼ tsp. salt
½ tsp. freshly ground black pepper
12 drops Tabasco sauce
½ c. heavy cream

CHICKEN ASPIC

4 c. stock
2 envelopes gelatin (about 1½ Tb.—use only 1 envelope if stock is already gelatinous due to the addition of chicken feet)
1 c. coarsely chopped green of leeks
½ c. coarsely chopped carrots
1 c. coarsely chopped parsley
1 large sprig fresh tarragon, or ½ tsp. dried
2 egg whites
1½ tsp. salt
½ tsp. freshly ground black pepper

SUPREME SAUCE

2 c. reduced stock
1 envelope gelatin (about ¾ Tb.)
¼ tsp. salt
⅛ tsp. freshly ground white pepper
1½ tsp. potato starch dissolved in 1 Tb. water
1⅓ c. heavy cream

GARNISHES

Leaves of chives, leeks, and scallions
2 to 3 pieces red pepper skin peeling
2 to 3 pieces carrot peeling
Petals of edible flowers (violets, roses, or nasturtiums)
Sieved yolk of 1 hard-cooked egg

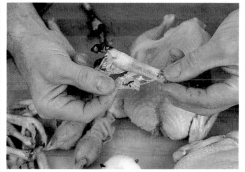

1 If you can obtain them, chicken feet will give taste and a lot of gelatinous elements to the stock. Wash the feet first thoroughly under water and dry them. Char them over an open flame until the skin becomes darkened in spots and starts to blister. Pull the skin off the feet. It will slip off easily. Once the scaly surface of the skin has been removed, clean the feet underneath.

2 Place the chickens, breast-side down, in a deep saucepan, preferably stainless steel, with the optional feet, 1 large leek, 2 medium carrots, 1 large rib celery, 1 medium onion studded with 6 cloves, and 1 tsp. salt. Add the 2 to 3 bay leaves, 1 tsp. thyme, and 3 qt. water.

3 Bring to a boil (it should take 12 to 15 minutes), cover, and simmer at a gentle boil for about 10 minutes. Remove the pot from the heat and set aside, still covered, to allow the chickens to poach simply in their own accumulated heat for 45 minutes. Remove the chickens from the lukewarm poaching liquid.

4 After the chickens have cooled slightly and can be handled, bone them out. Using your hands, remove the wishbone and the two legs. Split the breast in half.

5 The breast meat should be moist in the center and pull off the bone easily.

6 Separate the thigh from the drumstick and bone the pieces. Separate the wing from the breast. Discard the chicken skin. Each breast will weigh about 4 to 5 oz. With each thigh and some meat from each drumstick, make 2 additional pieces also weighing about 4 to 5 oz. each. (Note: If the leg meat pieces are still smaller than the breasts, the fillet pieces from the breasts can be placed with the legs so the pieces (leg and breast) are about equal in size. The trimmings (without fat or sinew) from one chicken should weigh about 6 oz. Set this aside for the mousse. Repeat with the second chicken.

Return the bones (without the skin) back to the stock with the vegetables and boil gently until the stock is reduced to 6 c. Strain the stock and refrigerate it.

7 To make the mousse: Cut the fat into little pieces and place in a skillet over medium heat, until it starts melting and most of the fat is released. Cook for a few minutes and add the 2 tsp. chopped shallot, 1 crushed garlic clove, ¼ tsp. thyme, and the 2 chicken livers, quartered. Sauté briefly over medium to high heat for 1½ minutes. The liver should still be pink inside. →

8 Place the contents of the skillet in the bowl of a food processor and process until smooth. While the machine is running, add the 1 Tb. butter, 1 Tb. cognac, 1¼ tsp. salt, ½ tsp. pepper, and 12 drops Tabasco, and continue processing for a few seconds, until very smooth. Push the mixture through a food mill fitted with the fine screen to remove any pieces of sinew that were not puréed in the food processor.

9 Allow the mixture to cool to room temperature. Whip the ½ c. of cream until it forms a soft peak and mix into the mousse mixture. Taste again and correct the seasoning, if needed. Refrigerate.

10 Spread the underside of the chicken breasts and the pieces of combined thigh and drumstick with the mousse.

11 When the stock is cold, remove any remaining fat. The 6 c. of concentrated stock left should be gelatinous.

12 To make the aspic: In a saucepan, preferably stainless steel, combine the 4 c. of stock with 1–2 envelopes of gelatin, 1 c. chopped green of leeks, ½ c. chopped carrots, 1 c. chopped parsley, 1 sprig tarragon, 2 egg whites, 1½ tsp. salt, and ½ tsp. pepper. Mix well and bring the mixture to a strong boil, stirring often to prevent it from scorching. As soon as it comes to a strong boil, set aside and do not disturb for 15 minutes. Strain through a sieve lined with wet paper towels. You should have approximately 2½ c. of very clear aspic.

13 For the suprême sauce: Reduce the remaining 2 c. of stock to 1 c. of concentrated stock. Strain through a fine strainer. Sprinkle the 1 envelope of gelatin on top of the stock and add the ¼ tsp. salt, ⅛ tsp. white pepper, and the 1½ tsp. potato starch dissolved in 1 Tb. water. Bring to a boil, stirring, so the mixture thickens and the gelatin melts. Add the 1⅓ c. cream, stirring gently to incorporate, and strain again through a fine strainer into a bowl. You should have 2 c. of sauce.

14 Place the chicken pieces meat-side up on a wire rack set on a cookie sheet lined with plastic wrap. Transfer half the suprême sauce to a bowl and place it over ice. Stir gently until the mixture starts to set.

15 As soon as the mixture starts to set, using a large tablespoon, coat the chicken pieces with the sauce, working as quickly as you can. Coat them as thoroughly as possible but don't be concerned if some of the sauce runs down the chicken and falls onto the plastic-lined tray beneath.

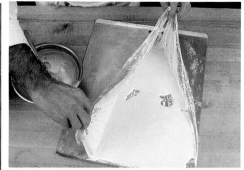

16 Lift up the rack containing the coated chicken, place on a clean tray and refrigerate. Carefully lift the plastic wrap containing the sauce that dripped down during the coating procedure and return it to the bowl. Remelt the sauce, then stir gently again over ice and repeat the process, coating each chicken piece two or three times, until it has a good ⅛-in. thickness of sauce all over. Most of the sauce should be used.

17 To prepare the garnish: Blanch the chive, leek, and scallion leaves for 10 to 15 seconds in boiling water, then lift them out, immediately run cold water over them, and dry them thoroughly with paper towels. Do the same with the 2 to 3 red pepper and carrot peels, blanching them for 30 seconds, and the edible flowers, blanching them for only a few seconds. Blanching the vegetables makes them limp and pliable so they can be arranged more attractively on the chicken pieces.

Cut pieces of green from the chives, leeks, and scallions to make "stems" of flowers. Cut out little triangle shapes and "flowers" from the red pepper skin and carrot peel and arrange them on the chicken pieces. Add a little sieved egg yolk to make the "calyx" for each flower.

18 Although the decoration can be the same for each piece, you can create a different design for each suprême.

19 Cool some of the aspic over ice until syrupy. With the rack containing the chicken pieces positioned over a plastic-lined tray, coat the top of the decorated chicken pieces with the aspic. As when coating the chicken with the sauce, don't worry if some of the aspic falls through onto the tray; it is retrievable. Place the coated chicken in the refrigerator until cold. Retrieve the aspic from the tray, remelt, and cool it over ice until syrupy and coat the chicken again. Repeat the process a third time to be sure the chicken is well-coated. Place the remaining aspic in a bowl and refrigerate until set.

20 At serving time, arrange the chicken pieces attractively on a large platter, preferably porcelain (because the mousse on the bottom should not be on metal for too long).

21 Unmold the aspic that has solidified. Cut it into ¼-in.-thick slices and cut the slices into strips.

22 Cut the strips crosswise into small squares of shiny aspic that resemble jewels. →

23 Arrange the aspic squares attractively around the suprême of chicken and place the platter on the buffet table.

24 Serve on individual plates. Notice that the chicken is moist and tender and the mousse underneath flavorful. Serve cool but not ice cold.

CHICKEN GALANTINE WITH PRUNES

A galantine is usually made from boned poultry that is stuffed with a forcemeat and then poached in a strong stock. It is served cold with its natural jelly. The two chickens in the recipe here make two galantines. Although the recipe can be cut in half, it makes sense, because of the long preparation, to make two instead of one. The chickens are skinned and the skin used as a wrapper for the forcemeat, seasonings, and other ingredients. If possible, keep the wrapped galantines refrigerated for at least one day before cooking to develop flavor.

The galantines are studded with pistachios and prunes to give a sweet taste and cut the richness of the meat. The black mushrooms not only give taste but lend beautiful color to the dish. Most of the chicken and pork meat is kept in large pieces with only enough of it ground to bind all the ingredients together.

The galantines can be roasted in a pâté mold lined with caul fat – the fatty membrane that encases a pig's stomach (see page 51, photograph 2). Leaf lard as well as the skin of the chicken can be placed in a pâté mold as a wrapper. In this recipe, the skin is spread on a piece of cheesecloth, filled, wrapped, tied loosely with string, and poached in a stock made from the bones of the chickens. The galantines are cooled in the stock, which is reduced further and served with the galantines as a natural aspic.

Galantines can be kept, properly wrapped, in the refrigerator for a week after cooking.

The spicy, flavorful cherry-ginger chutney complements the galantine particularly, but it will also accent the taste of most pâtés and cold meats. It can be made ahead and, refrigerated, will keep almost indefinitely.

Yield: 12–14 servings

2 chickens (about 3 lb. each)

FORCEMEAT

2 lb. white chicken meat (from chickens above)
1½ lb. dark chicken meat and trimmings (from chickens above)
12 chicken hearts
4 large chicken livers (about 8 oz.)
2 lb. pork shoulder meat (about one-third fat)

SPICE MIXTURE

(the following ingredients placed in an electric spice grinder or coffee grinder and processed into a powder)
2 tsp. whole black peppercorns
12 juniper berries
¼ tsp. whole cloves
¼ tsp. fennel seeds
½ tsp. dried thyme leaves
¼ tsp. powdered nutmeg
¼ tsp. powdered cinnamon
⅛ tsp. cayenne pepper

2 Tb. Armagnac
½ c. dry white wine
2 Tb. salt
¼ tsp. saltpeter (optional)
1 Tb. cornstarch
½ c. shelled pistachios

MUSHROOM MIXTURE

3 Tb. butter
⅓ c. finely chopped shallots
3 oz. black mushrooms (Horn of Plenty), washed
1 clove garlic, chopped (½ tsp.)

12 to 16 pitted prunes

COOKING STOCK

2 Tb. butter
About 2¼ lb. chicken bones (from above chickens)
1 large onion, diced
1 carrot, cut into cubes
6 qt. water
2 bay leaves
1 rib celery
1 c. white wine
½ tsp. thyme leaves
1 tsp. salt

CHERRY-GINGER CHUTNEY SUSIE

¾ c. light brown sugar
½ c. granulated sugar
½ c. cider vinegar
½ tsp. salt
2 tsp. mustard seed
1½ tsp. red pepper flakes
1 c. sliced red onions
1 large clove garlic, peeled and thinly sliced
1 c. raisins
½ c. julienned fresh ginger
1½ lb. large Bing cherries, pitted

1 Skinning and boning out the chickens: Lift the skin at the neck of the chicken and run a knife on each side of the triangular bone (wishbone). Pry out the wishbone with your finger. (Running your thumb behind it will help release it.)

2 To skin the chicken, cut through the skin all the way down the backbone and start lifting it, pulling and cutting as necessary, to make it come off.

3 Keep pulling on the skin and cutting; you will notice that most of the skin, except for that on the thigh bones, will come off without cutting. Pull the skin down the length of the drumstick and off the bone.

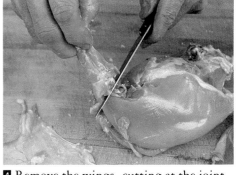

4 Remove the wings, cutting at the joint of the shoulder. The meat from the wings will be ground up.

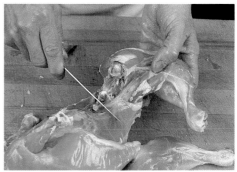

5 To separate the legs from the carcass, cut the little "oyster" off the backbone so it stays attached to the leg and break the leg open at the pelvic bone (the joint of the hip). Cut through the joint and pull the leg off.

6 Cut the breast alongside the breastbone. Grab the breast meat, including the fillet, with one hand and pull it off; it should come off the carcass in one piece. →

7 Continue boning and scraping the remaining meat from the carcass. Cut the white meat of the breast and thigh meat into 1½-in. pieces. Remove the sinew from the breast fillet.

8 Remove most of the sinews from the drumstick by holding one end of each sinew with a towel and scraping off the meat with a sharp knife. Both chickens, which are approximately 3 lb. each, should yield about 2 lb. of large, cubed pieces (1–1½ in.) of chicken (mostly from the white meat, but some from the dark), about 1½ lb. of dark meat and little pieces of meat from around the wing (to be ground), and approximately 2¼ lb. of bones. The rest of the weight is in the skin.

9 **For the forcemeat:** Cut the ends off the 12 chicken hearts, removing the fatty portion, which will go into the ground meat. Reserve the hearts. Cut the 4 large chicken livers into quarters. The liver will separate by itself into 2 pieces and each piece should be cut in half and set aside with the hearts. Remove approximately ¾ lb. of the leanest part of the pork shoulder and cut it into ½-in. pieces.

10 Cut the remaining 1¼ lb. of fattier pork shoulder into pieces, and then in a meat grinder grind them with the trimmings of the chicken hearts, and combine in a bowl with the spice mixture, 2 Tb. Armagnac, ½ c. white wine, 2 Tb. salt, optional ¼ tsp. saltpeter, 1 Tb. cornstarch, and ½ c. shelled pistachios. Add the cubed pieces of white chicken meat, the cubed pork shoulder, the chicken livers, and the chicken hearts, and mix well.

11 Melt the 3 Tb. butter and, when hot, add the ⅓ c. chopped shallots and 3 oz. mushrooms, and cook for about 3 to 4 minutes, until the vegetables are wilted and most of the juices have evaporated. Add the ½ tsp. chopped garlic. Scrape the mushroom mixture into the forcemeat and mix thoroughly.

12 Spread the skin of one chicken, which should be in one piece, out on the table. Notice that the area where the drumstick was is like a tube. Cut this off and open it up. The extra little pieces of skin can be used to patch where needed.

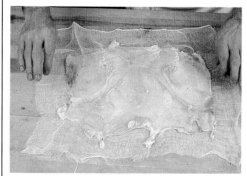

13 Flatten the skin (outside down) on a piece of cheesecloth about 20 × 20 in., extending and patching it with extra pieces of skin from the drumstick, to form a rectangle.

14 Divide the forcemeat into two equal batches. Place approximately half of one batch in the center of the chicken skin and embed 6 to 8 pitted prunes in the center. Place the rest of one batch of the forcemeat on top.

15 Bring the skin of the chicken back up over the forcemeat carefully to enclose it as much as possible.

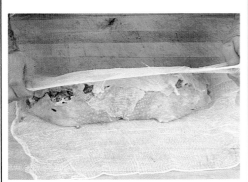

16 Bring the cheesecloth back on top of the skin, and roll it up tightly.

17 Twist each end of the cheesecloth to create a tubelike package and tie at the ends. The galantine will be approximately 12 in. long by 2½ to 3 in. in diameter. Make the second galantine in the same way.

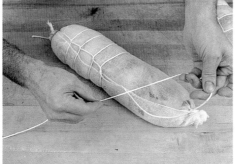

18 Attach a piece of string with a double knot on the end closest to you. Make a loop with the loose end of the string, slide it underneath the galantine about 1½ in. away from the tied end, and pull gently to create one loop. This is called a half-hitch. Make additional loops every 1½ to 2 in., repeating until the galantine is completely tied on one side. If this is too difficult to do, make single ties at 1½-in. intervals the length of the galantine to achieve the same effect.

19 When the galantine is tied on one side, secure the string at the other end and turn the galantine over. Slide the rest of the string around each of the loops, bringing it under and over each cross-string so the galantine looks the same on the top and bottom. Secure it again at the end where you started. Repeat the entire filling, rolling, and tying procedure for the other galantine. This tying technique can be used for tying breast of lamb, breast of veal, etc., for roasting. Now the galantines should be left to macerate overnight in the refrigerator to develop flavor before they are cooked.

20 **To make the stock:** Put the 2 Tb. butter in a large pot and, when hot, add the 2¼ lb. chicken bones, and brown over medium to high heat for at least 15 minutes. (You need a little butter because there is practically no fat left on the bones and the skin has been used for the galantine.) When the bones are browned, add the 1 diced large onion and carrot, and continue browning for 10 minutes. Add the 6 qt. water, 2 bay leaves, celery rib, 1 c. white wine, ½ tsp. thyme, and 1 tsp. salt, bring to a boil, and skim off any foam that forms on the surface. Boil gently for 2½ hours. You should have about 7 c. →

21 To cook, arrange the galantines so they fit snugly side by side in a large pot. Remove most of the fat that has risen to the top of the stock and pour the stock into the galantine pot. Heat to a temperature of approximately 180 to 190 degrees (the stock should not boil) and cook 1½ hours, partially covered, turning the galantines in the liquid every 20 minutes or so, until they reach an internal temperature of 155 to 160 degrees. Let cool overnight, refrigerated, in the stock.

22 Remove the galantines from the cooking liquid, which should be jellied.

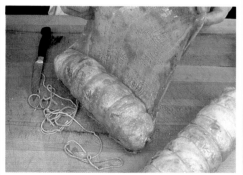

23 Unwrap the cheesecloth from the galantines and dry them with paper towels. At this point, they can be wrapped in plastic wrap and stored in the refrigerator to use as needed. They will keep for at least one week.

24 Bring the galantine liquid to a boil, then strain it through either a sieve lined with paper towels or a kitchen towel to remove any particles. You should have about 6 c. Boil the liquid down to reduce to 2½ c. and cool.

25 At serving time, cut one of the galantines. It should have a nice design, showing the different colors and outlines of the large pieces of meat and garnishes.

26 Dry the galantine thoroughly so the aspic will adhere to it. Cut several ½- to ¾-in. slices from the galantine and put the remaining whole piece on a serving platter. Cool the reduced liquid over ice until it becomes syrupy and is ready to set, coat the galantine and the bottom of the platter with it, and allow to set. Arrange the slices of the galantine around the uncut piece.

27 The spicy cherry-ginger chutney can be made several days ahead since it will keep almost indefinitely in the refrigerator.

To make the chutney: In a saucepan (preferably stainless steel), put the ¾ c. brown sugar, ½ c. each granulated sugar and vinegar, ½ tsp. salt, 2 tsp. mustard seed, 1½ tsp. red pepper flakes, 1 c. sliced red onion, and 1 large clove of thinly sliced garlic, and bring to the boil. Add the 1 c. raisins, ½ c. julienned ginger, and 1½ lb. cherries, return to the boil, and cook 10 minutes without a lid. Cool. The chutney should be thick, with only enough juice remaining to moisten the cherries.

28 Serve the galantine cold with the chutney.

1 After the rabbit has been eviscerated, reserve the liver, kidney, and heart for later use or sauté separately and serve, since they are not used in my recipe. Cut the skin in the center back of the rabbit enough so you can insert two fingers from each hand and pull to separate the skin into 2 pieces. Pull on one half, making the skin slide off the flesh, push the legs through and sever at the foot of the front leg and the neck. Do the same thing with the other half, pulling the skin, severing it at the tail and the foot of the 2 back legs. (For illustrated technique, see Volume I, Rabbit Blanquette, pages 197–8, steps 1–4.) Cut the rabbit into 3 pieces: the 2 back legs, the front legs, and part of the rib area and the back in 1 piece.

RABBIT BALLOTINE JEANNE

This small ballotine or galantine of rabbit has to be made with a young rabbit, not more than 3 to 4 months old, with tender and very white meat. These are referred to as frying rabbits and will range from approximately 1 ¾ to 2 ½ pounds gutted and skinned. If you use a larger, older rabbit (stewing rabbit), the meat will be tougher and will have to be braised much longer.

In this recipe, the ballotine is served cold with the juices reduced, clarified, and cooled. The same dish can be served hot with the reduced stock thickened lightly with potato starch or arrowroot to make a sauce for the hot ballotine. It is more flavorful if assembled two days ahead of cooking, to allow the stuffing to develop more taste by macerating with the seasonings for two days.

Yield: 6–8 servings

1 young, tender rabbit (about 2½ lb.)
8 oz. pork shoulder (half fat and half lean, to grind)
8 oz. chicken bones and gizzard
½ tsp. finely chopped fresh thyme
1½ Tb. chopped shallot (about 1 shallot)
2 tsp. finely chopped fresh tarragon
2 Tb. white wine
1 Tb. cognac

1 Tb. finely chopped parsley
1 tsp. salt
½ tsp. freshly ground black pepper
2 Tb. butter
1 c. red wine
6 c. water

FOR THE ASPIC

½ c. finely diced carrots
½ c. coarsely chopped celery leaves
½ c. coarsely chopped parsley
½ tsp. salt
¼ tsp. freshly ground black pepper
2 envelopes gelatin (about 1½ Tb.)
1 egg white
2 c. rabbit stock

2 Cut the back legs at the joint and keep only the thigh segments, which are the fleshiest and nicest parts; bone them out and set aside the two large pieces of meat from each leg to roast. Bone the sinewy part in the shank area of the back legs and set the meat aside for the stuffing. →

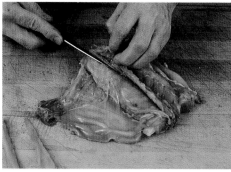

3 Bone out the two front legs and the neck and rib area to remove as much meat as possible. You should have about 8 oz. of meat set aside for the stuffing.

6 When boning the central backbone in one piece, be particularly careful not to make too many holes in the center of the back where the bones are very close to the surface of the skin.

9 You should have approximately ¾ lb. bones altogether, ½ lb. pieces of meat to grind, the whole boned saddle (about 18 to 20 oz.), the 2 solid pieces from the back legs, and ½ lb. of fatty pork shoulder to grind. Cut the bone of the rabbit and the chicken bones and gizzards into 1-in. pieces. Set aside.

4 The boning of the back is the most delicate procedure. The bones should be removed without making too many holes in the back skin so it can be stuffed with the pâté mixture. Remove the two fillets and set aside. Slide your knife behind the rib cage to separate the bones from the flesh.

7 Butterfly the flank of the rabbit to make it larger so that all the stuffing can be held inside securely. Although the flank is already thin, you still need to cut it open where it is not large enough to hold the stuffing in; do so by holding your knife almost flat.

10 Grind the 8 oz. pork and the meat from the rabbit in a meat grinder, which gives a better texture than the food processor. Combine the ground rabbit well with the ground pork, ½ tsp. fresh thyme, 1½ Tb. chopped shallot, 2 tsp. fresh tarragon, 2 Tb. white wine, 1 Tb. cognac, 1 Tb. chopped parsley, 1 tsp. salt, and ½ tsp. pepper. Arrange the ground forcemeat in the center of the saddle and bring the flank on top. It should just enclose the filling.

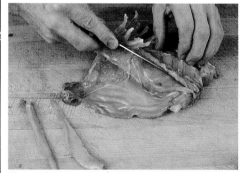

5 Work around the bones gently.

8 Place the 2 small fillets (set aside in step 4) in the center of the back to cover the holes.

11 Place a piece of aluminum foil to cover where the flaps of the flanks join together, especially if they are a bit short. Be sure that the aluminum is long enough to extend to the sides and ends to help hold the stuffing inside. Secure the mixture inside by tying with string. Use the simple loop shown (called a half-hitch knot) every 1 to 2 in.

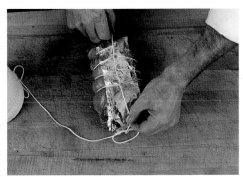

12 Turn the saddle and secure with twine on the other side. Cover, wrap with plastic wrap, and place in the refrigerator for 24 to 48 hours to develop the flavor.

13 When ready to cook, melt 1 Tb. butter in a large, sturdy saucepan, add the chicken and rabbit bones, and brown on medium to high heat for about 15 minutes, stirring occasionally. Push the bones to the side to make a space in the center and place the saddle, stuffed-side down, in the saucepan. Cook gently for 20 minutes on top of the stove over medium to low heat. The object here is to precook the stuffing as much as possible so the two fillets from the back do not end up being overcooked. Sprinkle the saddle lightly with salt, baste with some of the pan juices, and place in a preheated 400-degree oven for 15 to 20 minutes, basting every 5 minutes.

14 Meanwhile, place the remaining 1 Tb. of butter in a small skillet. Sprinkle the two pieces of meat from the back legs with salt and a dash of pepper, and sauté over medium to high heat on top of the stove for 2 to 3 minutes on each side (5 to 6 minutes altogether). At that point, cover the skillet and set aside on top of the stove to let the meat cool slowly.

15 When the saddle is done (it should have an internal temperature of approximately 145 degrees), remove from the saucepan and let sit upside down on a plate (so the fillets of the back are underneath and the juice runs into them) for 30 minutes to cool off slightly. Meanwhile, take the juice rendered from the 2 pieces of back leg meat and add to the saucepan.

When the saddle has cooled enough, remove it to a platter with the 2 pieces of back leg meat, cover everything with plastic wrap, and refrigerate overnight, or for at least a few hours, until thoroughly cold inside.

Add the 1 c. red wine and 6 c. water to the saucepan with the bones, bring to a boil, and cook gently 1 hour on top of the stove, occasionally skimming off the scum and fat from the top.

16 Strain the juice through a fine sieve and reduce to 2 c. Cool overnight in the refrigerator. When cold, remove fat from the top. →

17 **For the aspic:** Combine ½ c. each diced carrots, chopped celery, and parsley, ½ tsp. salt, ¼ tsp. pepper, 1½ Tb. gelatin, and 1 egg white with the 2 c. of rabbit stock, and place on top of the stove, stirring almost constantly over high heat until it comes to a strong boil. Remove from the heat and allow to set 5 to 10 minutes.

Strain the liquid through a sieve lined with a dampened paper towel.

19 Meanwhile, unwrap the saddle, trim it a little if necessary, and slice half of it into ½-in. pieces. Arrange on a serving platter. Cut each of the 2 pieces of the back legs in half and arrange next to the saddle.

When the aspic is very syrupy and ready to set, coat the ballotine and the pieces of meat around it with the aspic. If it sets too quickly, you can remelt the aspic and, again, re-cool on ice and coat the ballotine and meat until all the aspic has been used.

18 Squeeze and press gently at the last to extract as much liquid as possible. You should have approximately 1⅓ c. of liquid remaining. Cool the liquid on ice.

20 Cover and refrigerate until serving time.

FOR EACH PATE

1½ lb. puff paste dough
10 to 12 cabbage leaves, cooked gently 10
   minutes in boiling water, cooled under
   cold water, and drained

Egg wash made with 1 egg with half the
   white removed, beaten

MUSHROOM GARNISH FOR HOT PATE

2 Tb. butter
3 c. mushrooms, cut into 1 × ¼-in.
   sticks
¼ tsp. salt
¼ tsp. freshly ground black pepper
2 Tb. chopped chives

1 Front row, left to right: pork butt, livers, boned pheasant leg meat and boned pheasant breast meat; back row, left to right: sweetbread, a whole baby pheasant, bones of the boned pheasant.

2 Bone out the other pheasant. Separate the skin, the bones, and the meat. Pull out as much sinew and filament as possible from the leg meat, scraping the meat from the bones. Cut the breast meat into ½-in.-long strips. Cut the lean piece from the pork butt into a 1-in. dice (about 1 c.). The rest of the pork will be ground with the meat from the pheasant legs. The nicest pieces of meat from the pork as well as the pheasant are left whole so they will stud the pâté when it is sliced, while the more sinewy, fatty pieces are finely ground and used as the binding agent of the forcemeat.

PATE OF PHEASANT AND SWEETBREAD

This large, free-form pâté could also be made into small, individual pâtés and served hot. There is enough forcemeat mixture to make two pâtés. They can be served hot or cold, with or without the crust. The cabbage leaves could be left out in the hot as well as cold pâté.

To develop the proper taste, the forcemeat should macerate 2 to 3 days before being cooked. However, if you cook it sooner, be sure to refrigerate it for a couple of days before serving so it develops more taste. This will not work as well after the pâté has been encased in the dough.

The pheasants I have used are baby pheasants, available on the market sometimes fresh but most often frozen. If frozen, they should be defrosted slowly under refrigeration. These raised pheasants are tender and milder than wild pheasants, which have a more pronounced gamey taste.

The pork shoulder should not be too lean; it should be approximately one-third fat to two-thirds lean, because there is no other fat added to the forcemeat.

Yield: 2 pâtés

PATE FORCEMEAT

2 baby pheasants or partridges (about ¾
   to 1 lb. each)
1½-lb. piece of pork shoulder or butt
1 large sweetbread (about ¾ lb.)
1 Tb. butter
3 to 4 shallots, chopped fine (⅓ c.)
1 clove garlic, chopped fine (½ tsp.)
1 chicken liver plus the livers, gizzards,
   and hearts of the pheasants
¾ oz. dry cèpe (*Boletus edulis*) mushrooms,
   soaked in 2 c. water, drained (reserving
   liquid), and chopped coarse
2½ tsp. salt
2 Tb. cognac
⅓ c. dry white wine
2 tsp. cornstarch

SPICE MIXTURE

(the following ingredients placed in an
electric spice grinder or coffee grinder and
processed into a powder)
1½ tsp. black peppercorns
4 to 5 cloves
12 dried allspice berries
1 tsp. dried thyme
¼ tsp. coriander seeds
1 large bay leaf

STOCK FOR ASPIC

Bones of pheasants
1½ lb. chicken bones
1 onion, quartered (3 oz.)
1 carrot, cut into chunks (3 oz.)
3 qt. water

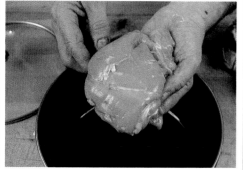

3 The best sweetbread is the large, round type. If it is not very pale, soak for a few hours in cold water to remove any traces of blood. Drain, then cover with cold water in a saucepan and bring to a boil. Lower the heat and continue cooking slowly for 6 to 8 minutes. Then place in cold water to cool.

4 Using a meat grinder, grind the pork trimmings and pheasant leg meat. In a skillet, melt the 1 Tb. butter and, when hot, add the 1/3 c. shallots. Sauté for 10 seconds, then add the chopped garlic clove, livers, gizzards, and hearts. Sauté for 1 minute. While the mixture is still hot, put it through the meat grinder. As it emerges from the grinder, put it back into the grinder and grind again; it should be ground twice so it is very fine and thus acts as a binder in the pâté. To the mixture, add the chopped cèpes, 2 1/2 tsp. salt, 2 Tb. cognac, 1/3 c. white wine, 2 tsp. cornstarch, and spice seasoning. Mix well. Remove the filament from the sweetbread and separate it into lumps of approximately 1 in., pulling out and discarding little pieces of sinew. Mix with the forcemeat – that is, the ground meat mixture – add the breast meat and pork pieces from step 2, cover with plastic wrap, and refrigerate, preferably 3 to 4 days so the flavor develops well. There is enough here for two pâtés.

5 Place the skin and bones of the pheasants (cut into 2- to 3-in. pieces) with the chicken bones in a large saucepan and brown on top of the stove for approximately 20 minutes. There is enough fat released from the skin of the pheasants and chicken bones so the bones properly brown. Add the onion and carrot, and brown 2 to 3 minutes.

Drain off as much of the fat as possible and add 3 qt. of water and the mushroom liquid from the cèpes to the saucepan. Bring the stock to a boil and cook gently for 2 hours. Strain. You should have 7 c. of liquid. Cool overnight and skim off any fat remaining on the surface. Reduce to 5 c. to make the aspic. Make the aspic with the stock, following the recipe on page 36.

6 Roll out half the puff paste (3/4 lb.) to form a rectangle approximately 10 in. wide by 14 in. long. Remove the stems from the 10 to 12 cabbage leaves and place them on top of the dough. Arrange half the pâté mixture on top of the cabbage leaves, using a piece of plastic wrap to press the forcemeat into an oblong shape. The forcemeat should be about 12 in. long by 4 in. wide and 1 1/2 in. deep. The remaining forcemeat can be used for a second pâté, served cold (see steps 13–17).

7 Bring the cabbage leaves and the dough back up around the pâté and brush the dough with the egg wash.

8 Roll out the remaining (3/4 lb.) dough until it is approximately 14 in. long by 10 in. wide and place it on top of the pâté. Press it all around the top and sides so it adheres well, and trim away the extra dough to give the pâté a neat shape.

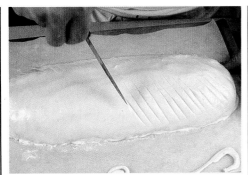

9 Brush the dough with egg wash and score crosses on each side, using the point of a knife dull-side down.

10 With the trimmings of the dough, create a design on top. Brush the design with the egg wash and place the pâté in the refrigerator for at least 1 hour, or in the freezer for 30 minutes to firm up the dough and relax it before cooking.

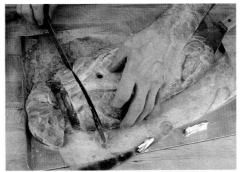

11 At cooking time, make three little holes on top of the pâté. Using a pencil as a mold, make three little cylinders of aluminum foil and place in the holes, like chimneys, so the steam can come out of the pâté and the dough doesn't crack too much during cooking. (Note the foil chimney in photograph 13.) Place in a preheated 400-degree oven for about 10 minutes. Reduce the heat to 375 degrees and continue cooking for about 40 minutes. At that point, the pâté should be well-done, with an internal temperature of around 140 degrees. Remove the chimneys and let the pâté rest about 10 to 15 minutes before cutting.

During that time, prepare the mushroom garnish: Melt 2 Tb. butter in a large skillet, add the 3 c. mushrooms and ¼ tsp. each salt and pepper, and sauté for 1 to 2 minutes, just long enough for the mushrooms to wilt a little and soften. Add 2 to 3 Tb. of the stock made from the bones and bring to a boil. Sprinkle with the 2 Tb. chives and remove from the heat. Cut the pâté into 1- to 1¼-in. slices.

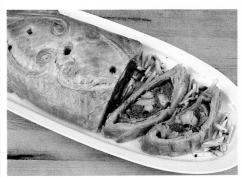

12 Arrange the pâté on a tray with the mushroom garnish around it and serve immediately.

13 **For cold pâté:** Prepare and cook the second pâté according to the previous instructions. You should have about 1 qt. of aspic prepared in step 5. Reserve about one-third of the aspic and let set in the refrigerator until hard. Place the remaining aspic over ice until it starts getting thicker and more syrupy. Use the holes created for the chimneys to pour the aspic inside the pâté. If there are holes in the pastry, the aspic will leak out, so plug the holes with butter or wrap the pâté tightly in plastic wrap and aluminum foil. Pour the aspic through the chimneys until any cavities in the pâté are completely filled. If the aspic doesn't go in, other holes can be made in the pastry so the aspic fills areas around and on each side where the meat has shrunk away from the crust.

14 Cut the reserved aspic into a little dice that looks like jewels: Cut slices of aspic, jiggling your knife back and forth as you cut, to create ridges in the slices. →

15 Pile the slices together and cut again, rocking your knife again back and forth to create ridges on the strips of aspic.

16 Finally, gather the strips together and cut, again in the same back-and-forth manner, to create a dice with ridges.

17 Slice the cold pâté into ½- to ¾-in.-thick slices and arrange on a platter with the aspic around. Serve with a cold white wine.

COUNTRY PATE WITH WALNUTS AND HOT HONEY MUSTARD

This chunky, rough country pâté made with pork and veal is full-flavored, easy to make, and inexpensive.

In the cooking of a pâté, three things are important: The mixture has to be properly seasoned (i.e., slightly overseasoned). It can be tested by sautéing a little of it in a skillet and tasting it. The seasonings tend to diminish as the pâté cools. The right proportion of fat is important, also. A mixture that is too lean will yield a dry, grainy pâté, and a fatty mixture will result in a gooey, over-rich, unpleasant-tasting pâté. Finally, the pâté must be cooked properly. If it cooks too fast, the fat will melt and the pâté will end up being dry and too highly seasoned.

It is not necessary to press a pâté after cooking. The pressing makes the pâté more compact by extracting some of its fat but, if the proportion of fat is right, there is no need for pressing.

The pork liver used here could be replaced with chicken or other poultry liver. It can be puréed in the food processor or ground several times; the purpose of the liver is to bind the ingredients together.

As much of the lean pork and veal as possible is cut into large pieces, which will be visible when the pâté is sliced and give tex-ture as well as taste. The tougher remaining meat is ground (like hamburger meat) and used to hold the pieces together. A dash of saltpeter can be added for aesthetic reasons (the sodium nitrate gives a nice pink color to the meat), but it is optional. The salt also gives the meat a pink color, although not quite as pink as the saltpeter.

The cooked pâté is fuller in taste after 1 or 2 days and can be kept, refrigerated, for 8 to 10 days. It is excellent with an earthy Country French Bread (page 118) and the hot, spicy, and sweet honey mustard.

The butter flowers served with the pâté grace a table attractively and can be served with oysters as well as cheeses or at any time butter is to be served at the table.

Yield: 12–14 servings

FORCEMEAT

½ lb. pork liver
2¼ lb. pork shoulder or butt
1 lb. veal shoulder or lean stew
1 c. walnut halves
1 egg
1 Tb. cornstarch
¼ c. chopped shallots
1 large clove garlic, chopped fine (½ tsp.)

SPICE MIXTURE

(the following ingredients placed in an electric spice grinder or coffee grinder and processed into a powder)
2 large bay leaves
1 tsp. dried thyme
½ tsp. coriander seeds
1 tsp. black peppercorns
¼ tsp. cassia buds or cinnamon pieces

1½ Tb. salt
½ c. white wine
⅛ tsp. saltpeter (optional)
½ to ¾ lb. caul fat (or leaf lard cut from hard fatback)

GARNISHES

2 bay leaves (for top of loaf)
¼ tsp. thyme

HOT HONEY MUSTARD

⅓ c. mustard seed
2 cloves
¼ tsp. anise seed
¼ tsp. black peppercorns
3 Tb. raw honey
¾ tsp. salt
3 Tb. white wine
3 Tb. cider vinegar

BUTTER ROSES

2 sticks unsalted, cool butter
Paprika

1 Clean the ½ lb. pork liver of any sinews and trim the 2¼ lb. of pork shoulder and 1 lb. veal shoulder, cutting the leaner pieces into a ½-in. dice. (Here, from a 2¼-lb. pork shoulder, 1 lb. of the meat is cut into ½-in. pieces and the remainder ground. The 1 lb. of veal shoulder yields ½ lb. of ½-in. pieces and the remainder is ground.) Push the pork liver twice through the grinding machine fitted with the fine screen so it is well-puréed. (This could also be done in a food processor.) Then, grind the remaining 1¼ lb. of pork and the ½ lb. of veal. Mix it with the ground liver along with the diced veal and pork. Add the 1 c. of walnut halves, the egg, 1 Tb. cornstarch, ¼ c. chopped shallots, ½ tsp. garlic, the spice mixture, 1½ Tb. salt, ½ c. wine, and optional ⅛ tsp. saltpeter, combining it well with the sliced and ground meat.

2 Place the ½ to ¾ lb. caul fat in tepid water to make it easier to handle (it tends to tear when very cold). Line a 5- to 6-c. mold with the caul fat, letting the edge of the fat extend over the sides of the mold.

3 Pack the pâté mixture into the mold.

4 Bring up the edges of the caul fat to cover the pâté, trimming away any excess.

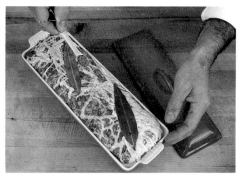

5 Place 2 bay leaves on top of the pâté and sprinkle with ¼ tsp. thyme. Cover with plastic wrap and a lid and let macerate a couple of hours or overnight, if possible.

For the hot honey mustard: Place the ⅓ c. mustard seed, 2 cloves, ¼ tsp. anise seed, and ¼ tsp. peppercorns in the bowl of a spice grinder or mini-chop and grind until almost smooth. Combine with the 3 Tb. honey, ¾ tsp. salt, and 3 Tb. each white wine and cider vinegar. (Note: At this point the mixture will be soft, but it will eventually thicken.) Allow to macerate at least 3 hours before using. →

6 At cooking time, remove the plastic wrap and place the lid back on the pâté. Place the pâté in the center of a deep roasting pan, surround it with lukewarm water, and put it in a preheated 325-degree oven for approximately 45 minutes. Reduce the heat to 300 degrees and cook for 1 hour longer (a total of 1 hour and 45 minutes). The internal temperature of the pâté should be between 150 and 155 degrees. (Remember that our cast-iron mold is fairly narrow and long. If the same amount of meat is cooked in a shallower, thicker loaf pan, the cooking time should be increased until the internal temperature of the pâté reaches 150 to 155 degrees.) Remove the pâté from the hot water and let cool, refrigerated, at least overnight.

8 Notice the coarse texture and nice color of the pâté.

11 Scrape the top of the butter several times from one end to the other to collect a long strip of butter on top of the blade. The repeated scraping will create a thin strip of butter striated on the top side.

9 Cut the pâté into ¾- to 1-in.-thick slices, and serve it with hot honey mustard, crusty French bread (page 118), cornichons or cherries in vinegar (page 111), and the butter roses.

12 Curl the strip of butter around the tip of the blade, making sure that the surface with the jagged look is inside the "flower." Form the strip into one large corolla or cup.

7 Run a knife around the pâté or place the pot in warm water for a few seconds to warm it and unmold the pâté. Trim off excess pieces of caul fat, dry the pâté with paper towels, and wrap it in plastic wrap.

10 **To make the butter roses:** The temperature and quality of the butter are important here. If the butter is too soft, the knife will make it mushy and if it is too cold, it will flake on top and you will not be able to create the roses. Unsalted, high-quality butter tends to have less water, is more pliable, and is the best.

Using the point plus about 1 in. of the blade of a small paring knife held vertically, scrape across the butter from one end of the stick to the other.

13 Place the butter corolla stem-side down on a plate.

14 Pick up another long strip of butter and, this time, curl it more tightly on the point of a knife. (You are making the center of a rose.)

15 Slide the center of the rose off the tip of the knife blade . . .

16 . . . and place it in the center of the corolla.

17 Drop the butter roses into ice cold water and refrigerate. Immersed in water, the flowers don't pick up tastes in the refrigerator. In addition, they will get very hard, making them easier to handle.

18 For another effect, lift one of the ice-cold flowers from the water, impale it with the point of a knife through the base, and, holding it upside down, lower it so the very outer edges of the petals touch the paprika.

19 Two flowers, one with the paprika, one without.

20 The flowers, with and without paprika, are presented on a plate or arranged around individual dinner plates.

COLD STUFFED BREAST OF VEAL IN NATURAL ASPIC

Although the stuffed breast of veal here is served cold as a centerpiece for a buffet, it is also very good served hot. One whole breast of milk-fed or so-called fancy veal, as shown in photograph 1, is about 16 pounds. For this recipe, only one piece of about 6 pounds, preferably the thin end (available at your butcher shop), is used.

Some of the remaining veal can be made into a flavorful stew and some can be braised in large pieces or barbecued with a spicy sauce or an herb butter. The thick part of the breast tends to have large pieces of cartilaginous white, crunchy bones, which are appreciated by the real aficionado.

The ribs are removed after the breast of veal is cooked, which is easier than boning out the meat before cooking. The ribs keep the meat from shrinking during cooking and also add flavor to the dish. The bones are twisted out and easily removed from the cooked breast while it is lukewarm or cold.

The stuffing is a mixture of pork shoulder, spinach, onions, garlic, pine nuts,

sweetbreads, and spices. The vegetables and meat can be changed to suit your personal taste.

The breast of veal yields flavorful juices and, because of the pig's foot added to the braising liquid, there is no need for extra gelatin to jell the stock for the aspic. The meat tightens as it cools and holds together well. Trim some of the cartilage, bones, fat, and sinew from the meat before glazing it with the stock, as shown in photograph 21.

The braised onions with raisins make a flavorful and spicy accompaniment to the stuffed breast of veal. They could also be served with any kind of meat pâté, as well as cold meat, or be part of hors d'oeuvre on a buffet.

Yield: 8–10 servings

1 six-pound breast of veal, cut from a whole veal breast (about 16 lb.)

STUFFING

About 1 lb. veal trimmings (from breast, above)
1 lb. pork shoulder
1 Tb. butter
1 Tb. virgin olive oil
1½ c. chopped leek (about 1 leek)
½ c. chopped onion (about 1 medium onion)
⅓ c. pine nuts
1 Tb. chopped garlic (about 3 to 4 cloves garlic)
1 lb. spinach (big stems removed), washed*
1 lb. sweetbreads
½ tsp. fennel seed
2 tsp. salt
1½ tsp. freshly ground black pepper
1½ tsp. chopped dried sage, crushed
¼ tsp. crushed red pepper flakes

BRAISING

2 Tb. butter
1½ tsp. salt
2 large carrots, washed (about 10 oz.) and coarsely chopped
2 onions (about 12 oz.), chopped coarse
1 head garlic, unpeeled
1 pig's foot (about 12 oz.), cut into 4 pieces
2 c. good fat-free, saltless chicken stock
1 c. dry white wine

TO FINISH STOCK

3 c. defatted braising liquid (from above)
1 tsp. potato starch dissolved in 1 Tb. water
Salt and freshly ground black pepper to taste

BRAISED ONIONS WITH RAISINS

1½ lb. small pearl onions (about 50), each the size of a giant olive
5 Tb. tomato paste
2 Tb. sugar
3 Tb. good virgin olive oil
2 bay leaves
1½ tsp. salt
1 tsp. freshly ground black pepper
¾ c. dark raisins
2 Tb. white vinegar
2½ c. water
1 tsp. coriander seeds

GARNISH

Small bunch of watercress or parsley

---

* Note: Swiss chard can be substituted for the spinach.

1 Although the home cook does not have access to a whole breast of veal at the market, a complete one weighs approximately 16 lb. This cut is from a fancy, or milk-fed, veal, the calf weighing approximately 300 to 320 lb. when slaughtered. The breast is divided into pieces and used for roasts, stews, or braises. Cut the breast in half.

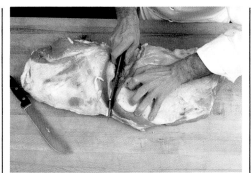

2 Cut off the thick part of one half to leave a thin piece weighing approximately 6 lb. The thick part, which I am not using here, is opposite the ribs and has large bones and cartilage. The meat can be frozen, used for stewing and braising, or boned out for pâté, and the bones and sinews used for stock.

3 From one side of the piece to be stuffed, remove the hanging piece of meat that is part of the skirt steak. It will be used in the stuffing.

4 Remove any skin from the skirt. Trim other pieces of fat and/or meat from the breast to have approximately 1 lb. of trimmings and fat for the stuffing. Grind the 1 lb. pork shoulder with the veal trimmings and set aside.

5 To create a pocket in the veal breast, place it rib-side down on the table. Holding your knife so the blade is parallel to the table, cut directly on top of the bones to create the largest possible pocket.

6 Note that I have not cut through the breast at either end or in the back; only the front is opened up. There should be approximately 1 to 1½ in. left intact on three sides.

7 To make the stuffing: Melt the 1 Tb. each butter and olive oil in a skillet. Add the 1½ c. chopped leek, ½ c. chopped onion, and ⅓ c. pine nuts, and sauté for 1 to 2 minutes, until the mixture starts browning. Add the 1 Tb. chopped garlic and stir it in. Add the 1 lb. of spinach, still wet from washing, place a lid on top, and cook for 1 to 2 minutes over high heat, until the spinach wilts. Then, remove the lid and continue cooking over high heat until most of the moisture is gone, about 4 to 5 minutes, and the spinach is almost dry in the butter again.

8 Cover the 1 lb. of sweetbreads with cold water. Bring to a boil, and simmer for about 5 minutes. Cool under cold water and, when cool enough to handle, peel to remove the tough membrane and break the sweetbreads into chunks; they will separate into little pieces of about 1 to 1½ in. Remove some of the skin, but it is not necessary to remove all the skin between each lump. Add the spinach mixture to the ground veal and pork, then stir in the sweetbreads with the ½ tsp. fennel seed, 2 tsp. salt, 1½ tsp. each pepper and crushed sage, and ¼ tsp. red pepper flakes. Mix thoroughly. →

9 Stuff the mixture into the breast, pushing it inside the opening to make certain it goes into all the corners.

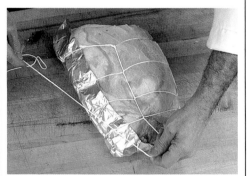

10 Place a strip of aluminum foil around the opening and tie it in place with cotton kitchen twine, following the technique used in the Chicken Galantine with Prunes (page 41), or just tie simply at 1- to 2-in. intervals with separate loops and knots.

11 To braise the meat: Melt the 2 Tb. butter in a large saucepan or roasting pan. Sprinkle the roast with 1½ tsp. salt and, when the butter is hot, place the roast, stuffed-side down, in the skillet, and sauté gently over medium heat for about 10 minutes. It should be nicely browned. Turn the roast over and add the 2 chopped carrots, 2 chopped onions, and head of garlic cloves. Brown for about 10 minutes, bone-side down.

12 Turn the meat again, bone-side up, and add the 4 pieces of pig's foot, 2 c. chicken stock, and 1 c. white wine. Cover the roast with a large piece of aluminum foil or, if the pan is deep enough, with a lid. Bring to a boil, reduce the heat, and continue cooking at a very slow simmer for approximately 2 hours. The internal temperature of the stuffed breast should be 160 to 170 degrees. Let cool to lukewarm before handling.

13 Place the roast on a baking sheet and remove the string and foil. Cut along the bones and twist them out; they should pull out easily. (This can be done while the meat is lukewarm or when it is completely cold.) The roast could be served hot at this point with the braising liquid.

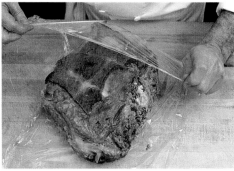

14 To serve it cold, wrap the meat in a piece of plastic wrap to keep it from drying out, and refrigerate until cool. The meat will harden as it cools.

15 Strain the braising liquid into a bowl.

16 Then, strain the liquid again, either through cheesecloth or a very fine strainer. Cool.

17 When the meat is cold, there will be a little jelly around it. Add it to the jellied braising liquid, and scoop all the solidified fat from the top. There should be about 3 c. of jellied liquid left.

18 Place the defatted stock in a saucepan and bring it to a boil. Add the 1 tsp. potato starch dissolved in 1 Tb. water, and salt and pepper to taste. The stock should be highly seasoned.

19 If to be served cold, cut the meat in half.

20 Remove some of the cartilaginous bones from underneath and trim the bottom and all sides of the veal breast as you feel it is necessary.

21 Place half the meat on a large chilled serving platter. Cool the stock over ice until syrupy and almost ready to set. Spoon over the top of the veal and around it on the platter. Slice the remaining half of stuffed breast on top of the aspic.

22 **To make the braised onions and raisins:** Peel the 1½ lb. pearl onions and place in a saucepan with the 5 Tb. tomato paste, 2 Tb. sugar, 3 Tb. olive oil, 2 bay leaves, 1½ tsp. salt, 1 tsp. pepper, ¾ c. raisins, 2 Tb. white vinegar, 2½ c. water, and 1 tsp. coriander seeds. Bring to a boil over medium to high heat. Reduce the heat, cover, and simmer for approximately 20 minutes.

23 Remove the cover and boil for about 5 minutes to reduce the liquid to a thick saucelike consistency. Place in a bowl and cool in the refrigerator until serving time. These onions with raisins will keep for a couple of weeks if refrigerated and can be used as a condiment with any type of cold cut or cold meat.

24 Decorate the veal serving platter with watercress or parsley and serve cold with crunchy bread, cold white wine, and the onion and raisin garnish.

COLD OR HOT BRAISED DAUBE OF BEEF

Traditionally, a daube of beef is cooked in red wine. The meat used is often one large piece, such as brisket or chuck. The underblade of the chuck, which is next to the short ribs, is tender and moist, as is the shank, which is also gelatinous. Either cut is a good choice for daube. The slow braising of the meat produces a juicy, tasty piece of meat, and the pork rind yields the necessary gelatin for the sauce to hold in jelly when the dish is served cold.

A daube can be served hot as well as cold with the same vegetable garnishes. The meat can be braised several days ahead but the garnishes should be done at the last. If the dish is to be served hot, the glazed vegetables should be reheated with the meat mixture just before serving. The cold dish can be prepared and kept for several days; in fact, it must be done at least several hours ahead for the sauce to set and the dish to develop flavor.

This is an ideal country dish for a hot summer meal. It is earthy, rich, and savory and, when served hot, is excellent with mashed potatoes flavored with garlic, or a purée of turnips.

The Salad Anita is quite assertive and excellent as a first course or to complement cold meat. The artichoke cases could also be used as receptacles for poached eggs, vegetable purées, peas, or glazed carrots, as well as for salad.

Yield: 8–10 servings

FOR BRAISING

6 lb. beef underblade of chuck (part of chuck or shoulder)
1½ tsp. salt
2 Tb. butter
5 to 6 cloves garlic, unpeeled
1 c. coarsely chopped onion
1 c. carrot trimmings (see Vegetable Garnishes, below)
1 Tb. flour
1 qt. robust red wine
1 c. water
2 c. brown stock (without salt and fat free)
8 strips of orange peel, removed with a vegetable peeler
¾ lb. pork rind

BOUQUET GARNI

1 stalk celery
¼ tsp. dried thyme
2 bay leaves
4 parsley sprigs

½ tsp. salt
½ tsp. freshly ground black pepper

VEGETABLE GARNISHES

1¼ lb. butternut squash,* cut into pieces 1 in. long by ½ in. wide (about 30 pieces)
5 carrots (about 14 oz.), cut into pieces 1 in. long by ½ in. wide (about 35 to 40 pieces), reserving 1 c. trimmings for braising (see above)
12 oz. boiled pearl onions (25 to 30 pieces)
1½ c. water
1 Tb. sugar
½ tsp. salt
3 Tb. butter
¼ tsp. freshly ground black pepper

TO FINISH THE SAUCE

4 c. solidified cooking juices (from braising)
¾ c. red wine
1 Tb. potato starch dissolved in 2 Tb. water
1 tsp. salt
½ tsp. freshly ground black pepper

SALAD ANITA IN ARTICHOKE CASES

Yield: 6 servings as a main course; 12 servings as a garnish for the beef

ARTICHOKE BOTTOMS

6 artichokes
3 c. water
2 Tb. lemon juice
1 Tb. oil
½ tsp. salt

* Note: White turnips can be substituted for the squash.

VEGETABLE FILLING

3 Tb. virgin olive oil
1 jalapeño pepper, seeded and chopped (about 1 Tb.)
1 lb. red pepper (about 3), seeded and cut into 1-in. strips
1 lb. zucchini, cut into 1½-in. dice
¾ lb. mushrooms, left whole or cut into large pieces
1½ Tb. sliced garlic
1 tsp. salt
½ tsp. freshly ground black pepper
1 c. dried tomatoes
1 tsp. sesame oil

2 Melt the 2 Tb. butter in a very heavy saucepan (copper or aluminum to give the right heat transfer) or two skillets. When hot, add the meat and cook over medium heat, turning the pieces occasionally, for 15 to 20 minutes, until they are brown on all sides. Note that the juices have crusted in the bottom of the pan. Transfer the pieces to a large pot.

3 Meanwhile, prepare the vegetable garnishes: Trim the 1-in.-long and ½-in.-wide pieces of squash and carrot into football-shaped pieces. (This is done mostly for aesthetic reasons.) The carrot trimmings are added to the beef and the butternut squash trimmings can be kept for soup.

4 Discard all but 1 Tb. of the fat in the saucepan. Add the 5 to 6 garlic cloves, 1 c. each chopped onions and carrot trimmings, and cook for 3 to 4 minutes over medium heat to brown and crystallize the vegetables a little. Then, sprinkle the 1 Tb. flour on top, and cook for another 1 to 2 minutes.

1 Although there are some sinews and gelatinous segments in it, the underblade chuck is tender and can also be served as a rare roast.

Separate the beef into pieces approximately ½ lb. each and remove any large pieces of fat. Try to divide the pieces where there is a natural separation, such as between the muscles or sinews. Sprinkle the 1½ tsp. salt over the beef.

5 Add the quart of red wine, 1 c. water, and 2 c. brown stock to the skillet with the vegetables, and cook on top of the stove, stirring with a wooden spatula (preferably straight-edged) to melt all the crystallized juices. Add the 8 strips of orange peel, ¾ lb. pork rind, and bouquet garni to the beef, and pour in the wine mixture. Add the ½ tsp. each salt and pepper.

Place the pot on the stove over medium to high heat, bring to a strong boil, cover, and place in a preheated 275-degree oven for 2½ hours to braise slowly.

6 Gently remove the meat to a dish.

7 When the meat is cool enough to handle, pull off any pieces of fat that cling to the outside, especially if the meat is to be served cold, so you have a nice chunk of meat without too much gristle or fat. Cover and refrigerate. →

8 Pour the juice from the pot through a very fine strainer.

9 Skim as much fat from the top as possible and let the juices in the pot cool, preferably overnight.

10 Remove the solidified fat from the top of the stock. You should have approximately 4 c. of solidified, gelatinous juice.

11 Put the carrots and 25 to 30 pearl onions in a saucepan in one layer. Add the 1½ c. water, 1 Tb. sugar, ½ tsp. salt, 3 Tb. butter, and ¼ tsp. pepper. Place over high heat, bring to a boil, cover, and cook about 4 minutes, until the vegetables start to get tender. Add the squash and cook for another 1 to 2 minutes. Then remove the lid and boil the mixture until all the liquid has evaporated and only the butter and sugar are left to create a glaze. Roll the vegetables in the glaze and keep cooking until they pick up the caramelized color.

12 To assemble the dish, place the cleaned pieces of beef on a serving pan, arranging them fairly snugly together with the vegetables in between and on top.

13 To finish the sauce: Be sure there is no fat left in the solidified juices. Put them (about 4 c.) in a saucepan with the ¾ c. red wine, bring to a boil, and cook about 1 minute, skimming off any impurities that come to the surface. Add the 1 Tb. potato starch dissolved in 2 Tb. water, 1 tsp. salt, and ½ tsp. pepper. If the dish is to be served cold, it should be fairly highly seasoned; if served hot, it should be seasoned a little less.

Pour approximately three-quarters of the sauce over the beef and vegetables. Cover with plastic wrap and allow to set for a few hours in the refrigerator.

14 The remainder of the sauce is added after the beef and vegetables have set. This final addition of sauce makes the top glossier and more attractive. Reheat the remaining stock until liquid, then cool it over ice until syrupy. Pour it over the meat and vegetables to glaze the top of the dish. The *daube* is now ready to be served cold.

To serve hot, reheat the meat for 10 to 15 minutes in the gently simmering sauce, adding the vegetables at the end, just far enough ahead to warm them before serving.

15 **For the Salad Anita in Artichoke Cases:** First, prepare the artichokes. Cut off the stems of the 6 artichokes at the base, trim them all around, and rub with lemon so they don't discolor; they are cooked and used in the salad.

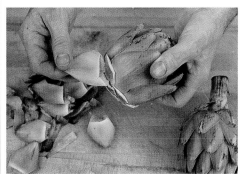

16 **To prepare the artichoke bottoms:** First method: Fold the artichoke leaves down on themselves; they will snap and break at the base, leaving the "meat" of the leaves attached to the bottom. Continue until all the outer leaves have been snapped off in this manner and most of the heart is exposed.

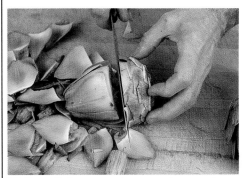

17 Cut off the center leaves to leave only the heart.

18 With a vegetable peeler or a sharp knife, trim the remaining green from around the artichoke bottom. There should be only the tender green flesh remaining.

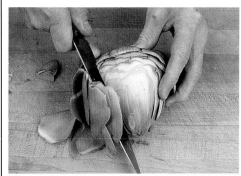

19 Alternate method: For someone proficient with a knife, there is a faster way to trim the artichoke bottoms. Using a very sharp knife, cut slightly on the bias all around to expose the heart and remove the inside leaves. Be careful not to cut into the heart itself.

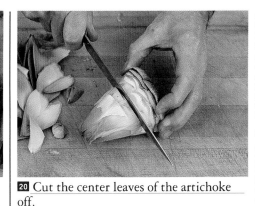

20 Cut the center leaves of the artichoke off.

21 Trim the bottom with a small paring knife. This method requires a little more practice than using a vegetable peeler.

22 The bottoms should be roundish with all the "meat" of the leaves left on. To cook the artichoke bottoms and the trimmed stems, place them in a saucepan with the 3 c. water, 2 Tb. lemon juice, 1 Tb. oil, and ½ tsp. salt. Bring to a boil, cover, reduce the heat, and cook gently for 20 to 25 minutes, until the artichoke hearts are tender when pierced with the point of a knife. Allow to cool in the liquid. →

23 With a spoon or your thumb, remove the choke, which should slide off the heart.

24 To create a thin-shelled receptacle, use a measuring spoon (the edges are sharper than on a regular spoon) and scoop out the insides of the artichoke bottoms to make a thin case. Set aside the artichoke trimmings for the salad.

25 **For the vegetable filling:** Heat the 3 Tb. olive oil in a large saucepan and add the 1 Tb. chopped pepper. Sauté for about 30 seconds, then add the 1 lb. of red pepper strips and sauté for 2 to 3 minutes longer. Add the 1 lb. zucchini dice, ¾ lb. mushrooms, 1½ Tb. sliced garlic, 1 tsp. salt, and ½ tsp. pepper, cover, and cook over medium to high heat for 4 to 5 minutes. Add the 1 c. dried tomatoes, and cook for another 2 minutes. Remove from the heat, and add the 1 tsp. sesame oil and reserved pieces of artichoke heart, stirring them into the salad. Cool.

26 At serving time, spoon the Salad Anita into the artichoke bottoms on a serving plate. Spoon out a piece of the meat with some of the vegetables and solidified juices, and arrange on the plate. Serve immediately.

PARSLEYED HAM

A specialty of Burgundy, parsleyed ham is an ideal way to use leftovers from a whole ham. It you are making it from scratch, buy fully cooked ham, either boiled ham or shoulder butt, the taste of which will be improved greatly by being recooked as it is in my recipe. Attractive on a buffet table, this dish is splendid for an outing (when the weather is not too hot); it should be served with hot French mustard or cornichons (small vinegar gherkins), a rémoulade sauce, crusty French bread, and cool, dry white wine or fruity red wine.

The pigs' feet will give the body and proper texture to the dish. Curing the feet improves the flavor and color of the dish slightly but it is optional, and it works just as well without the curing. However, if you elect not to cure, add 1½ tsp. salt to the cooking liquid of the feet to replace the curing salt.

Yield: 16–20 slices

FOR DRY CURING

1 c. (5 oz.) kosher-type salt
¼ c. sugar
¼ tsp. powdered cloves
¼ tsp. powdered thyme
¼ tsp. powdered allspice
3 large bay leaves, crushed
¼ tsp. saltpeter (optional)
4 pigs' feet split into 8 halves, about 2½–3 lb. (If you have a choice, choose the front feet, which are fleshier.)

PARSLEYED HAM

2 qt. cold water
1½ c. thinly sliced leek, white and tender green parts (about 1 large leek)
¾ c. sliced shallots (about 6 to 8 shallots)
1½ tsp. peeled, crushed, and chopped garlic (about 4 to 5 cloves)
½ tsp. dried thyme
1½ c. dry white wine
2 tsp. freshly ground black pepper
2¾ lb. ham, cleaned and cut into 1¼- to 1½-in. cubes
1½ c. chopped parsley, preferably flat-leaved kind

REMOULADE SAUCE

Yield: about 4 cups
¾ c. finely chopped onions
½ c. capers (preferably small), drained
1 c. coarsely chopped flat-leaved parsley
1 Tb. Dijon-style mustard
1 tsp. freshly ground black pepper
½ tsp. salt
¼ c. red wine vinegar
1 c. peanut oil
½ c. good olive oil

1 For the curing: Combine the 1 c. salt, ¼ c. sugar, ¼ tsp. each cloves, thyme, and allspice, 3 crushed bay leaves, the optional ¼ tsp. saltpeter, and 4 split pigs' feet in a large plastic bag, and refrigerate for 2 to 4 days. The dry ingredients will turn to liquid in a few hours. A few times a day, turn the bag from one side to the other to distribute the brine evenly. Although curing the pigs' feet is not absolutely essential, it improves the flavor and color of the dish (the saltpeter gives a beautiful pink color).

2 When ready, wash the feet under cold water and place in a kettle. Cover with plenty of cold water, bring to a boil, and cook for 5 minutes. Drain the feet into a colander, discard the liquid, and wash the feet under water. →

3 Place back in a clean kettle with 2 qt. cold water. Bring to a boil, cover, and boil gently for 2½ hours. Remove from the stock and pick the meat off the bones as soon as it is cold enough to handle. Cut the meat into ½-in. pieces. You should have 2 c. of leftover broth. If you have more, reduce to 2 c.

4 Place the meat back in the 2 c. of stock with 1½ c. leek, ¾ c. shallots, 1½ tsp. garlic, ½ tsp. thyme, 1½ c. white wine, 2 tsp. pepper, and 2¾ lb. ham cubes. Bring to a boil, cover, and boil gently for 20 minutes. Let cool to lukewarm and add the parsley.

5 Pour into a 3-qt. mold. Cover tightly with plastic wrap and refrigerate overnight.

Meanwhile make the rémoulade sauce: Place the ¾ c. chopped onions in a sieve and rinse under cold water. This washes off the sulfur molecules, which make the eyes water, and also prevents the onions from turning black and getting too strong in taste. Combine with ½ c. capers, 1 c. chopped parsley, 1 Tb. mustard, 1 tsp. pepper, ½ tsp. salt, ¼ c. wine vinegar, 1 c. peanut oil, and ½ c. olive oil, and refrigerate.

6 When ready to unmold, use a spoon to scrape away any fat from the top and discard it.

7 Unmold (it will weigh about 6 lb.) and serve cold in slices with the rémoulade sauce.

8 Slices of parsleyed ham with the cut ham in the background.

9 You should be able to cut about 25 to 30 slices (about 4 oz. each) from the whole parsleyed ham.

1 Place the 2 ham hocks, 3 pigs' feet, and pork rind in a kettle with 1 tsp. of the salt, and cover with the 9 c. cold water. Bring to a boil and skim off any scum that comes to the top. Boil gently, covered, for 2 hours. Drain the solids, reserving the juices, and set aside until cool enough to handle.

CIVIER VICTOR

This kind of rough head cheese was a favorite of my father, Victor, who made it when I was a child. In Bourg-en-Bresse, my birthplace, it is called a civier. *Often made in a soup bowl, it is unmolded as a large, round, jellied type of head cheese, then sliced and served with a mustard-vinegar sauce.*

Similar to head cheese, civier *has more of the liquid of the gelatin in it and the meat is not usually cured. Made in a pressure cooker, the cooking time is reduced from 2 hours to approximately 1 hour for the first stage of the cooking.*

Civier *is an inexpensive, flavorful, and rustic type of pâté that can even be made without the ham hocks, using only the pork rind and pigs' feet.*

Yield: 20–24 servings (makes 2 molded civier *in 6-c. loaf pans)*

2 ham hocks (about 2½ lb.)
3 pigs' feet, cut in half (about 2 lb.) (If you can, buy the front legs, which are fleshier than the back legs.)
1 piece pork rind (about ½ lb.)
1½ tsp. salt

9 c. cold water
5 carrots (½ lb.) peeled and cut into sticks about 1½ in. long, ½ in. thick
2 c. peeled and coarsely chopped onions (½ lb.)
1 c. dry white wine
1 c. coarsely chopped parsley
⅓ c. French mustard
½ c. thinly sliced tiny French sour gherkins (cornichons)
1 tsp. freshly ground black pepper

MUSTARD AND PICKLE SAUCE

Yield: enough for about 8 slices of civier
1 c. finely sliced onions
¼ c. sliced cornichons
¼ tsp. salt
¼ tsp. freshly ground black pepper
2 Tb. Dijon mustard
1½ Tb. red wine vinegar
5 Tb. oil (peanut, corn, or sunflower)

2 Pick the meat from the bones and cut the rind and meat into 1-in. pieces. Meanwhile, prepare the 5 carrots and 2 c. onions.

3 Place the boned out meat, rind, carrots, and onions in a kettle with 5 c. of the reserved cooking liquid and the 1 c. wine. Bring to a boil and cook gently for 35 minutes. Remove from the heat and add the 1 c. parsley, ⅓ c. mustard, the ½ c. sliced gherkins, 1 tsp. pepper, and ½ tsp. salt. Adjust seasoning to taste. →

4 Ladle the mixture into two 6-c. loaf pans. (They should be completely filled.) Refrigerate. When set, after an hour or so, cover with plastic wrap and refrigerate overnight.

5 At serving time, run a knife around the edge of each of the pans and unmold. Cut into good ½-in. slices. Although *civier* can be served without a sauce, it is good with a mustard and pickle sauce.

6 For the mustard and pickle sauce: Rinse the 1 c. sliced onions under cold water and wring out in a cloth towel. Sprinkle the onions and the ¼ c. sliced cornichons on a serving platter.

Combine the ¼ tsp. each salt and pepper, 2 Tb. mustard, and 1½ Tb. vinegar in a bowl, and whisk in the 5 Tb. oil. Pour over the onion and cornichon mixture and arrange the slices of *civier* on top. Serve with country bread.

PRESSED HEAD CHEESE

Pressed head cheese is part of the same family of cold, jellied, cured pork dishes as *civier* and parsleyed ham. Made only from the head and tongue of the pig, the meat is rolled in the rind to make a tight, chewy, and flavorful loaf. The small pieces are rolled inside the larger pieces of rind, pressed and formed into solid loaves. Curing is necessary and greatly improves not only the appearance but the taste of the head cheese. The quantities given here can make one very large head cheese but are hard to roll and poach. It is easier to make two, as I have done, or even three loaves.

Although I used a whole pig's head, which I boned (the bones can be used for stock or soup), it will be easier to find boned pieces of heads in your market, and it will be just as good, provided you buy the largest possible pieces of rind for use as the wrapper to hold the head cheese together. At least half of the meat should be covered with the rind. If it stays in the brine more than a week, it should be kept in a cold place, such as a cold cellar or refrigerator. If kept several weeks in the brine, soak it afterward in water a couple of hours before blanching to remove some of the salt.

This is an ideal dish for a picnic or a country type of dinner, buffet, or lunch and is excellent with anything from a young Beaujolais to a dry white wine, served with crunchy French bread, mustard, and pickles.

Yield: 18–20 servings (for two head cheeses)

BRINE

3 qt. water
2 lb. kosher-type salt
1 c. sugar (about 8 oz.)
1 Tb. saltpeter (optional)
1 tsp. crushed coriander seeds
¼ tsp. powdered cloves
½ tsp. powdered allspice
1 tsp. crushed juniper berries
1 Tb. crushed black peppercorns
4 bay leaves, crushed

HEAD CHEESE

13½-lb. whole pig's head, unboned: 8 lb. meat and tongue and 5½ lb. bones, including brains
1 Tb. butter
¾ c. chopped shallots
1 c. finely sliced scallions or leeks
1 Tb. fresh thyme leaves, or 1 Tb. dried
1 Tb. chopped garlic (about 3 to 4 cloves)
½ tsp. freshly ground black pepper
1 c. dry white wine

1 To make the brine: Put all the brine ingredients together in a large kettle. Bring to a boil, lower the heat, and cook gently for 10 minutes. Let cool before using.

Bone out the head, staying as close to the bone as you can. Keep large pieces that can be used as the wrapper to enclose the meat. Cut the bones into pieces and freeze for later use in stock or soup. The brain can be poached and used separately. You will notice that the boned pieces of meat have a heavy layer of fat, especially by the skull. With a knife, lift up the rind and remove as much of the thick layer of fat as you can. You should remove at least 1½ lb. of fat, which can be used for pâtés and dumplings or it can be rendered or even frozen.

Put the boned-out pieces of head cheese in the brine, placing a plate on top and even a weight, if possible, to make sure the meat is completely immersed in the liquid. Let it macerate for 1 week.

2 The longer it macerates, the pinker and more flavorful the meat will be. Keep in a cold place, refrigerated if possible.

3 When ready to use, rinse the meat under water, put in a large kettle, and cover with cold water. Bring to a boil and cook gently for approximately 1 minute. Drain into the sink, wash, put back in a clean kettle, and cover again with cold water. Place a plate upside down on top of the meat to push it down into the liquid while it cooks. Bring to a boil, cover, and simmer very gently for 1¼ hours.

Remove the meat and place on a large cookie sheet until cool enough to handle. Reserve the liquid.

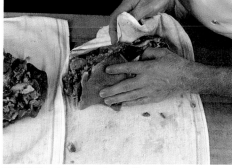

4 While the meat is cooling, heat the 1 Tb. butter in a skillet over medium heat, add the ¾ c. chopped shallots, 1 c. sliced scallions or leeks, 1 Tb. fresh thyme, 1 Tb. chopped garlic, and ½ tsp. pepper, and sauté very gently for 3 to 4 minutes, until soft. When the meat is cold enough to handle, make 2 head cheeses. Spread the two larger pieces of rind on two different wet towels. Cut each of the ears in half lengthwise and place in the center with the tongue (also split in half) and sprinkle with the shallot, scallion, thyme, and garlic mixture. Roll the meat into a sausage shape.

5 Try to enclose as much of the meat as possible in the rind. When the meat is securely inside, tighten the towel around it and tie at one end with a string.

6 Stand the sausage straight up and press it at the open end so as to squeeze, tighten, and press the meat more compactly inside. Secure the other end as well as the center with twine. It should be tightly packed inside. Repeat with the other sausage.

7 Place the 2 head cheeses in a casserole just large enough to accommodate them snugly; add the 1 c. white wine and enough reserved cooking liquid (about 10 to 12 c.) to cover the meat. Place on top of the stove, bring to a simmer, and simmer, covered, very gently for 30 minutes. Remove from the heat and let cool, covered (so it will cool slowly), in the stock overnight, refrigerated. →

8 The following day, remove the sausage rolls from the stock, unwrap, pack in plastic wrap, and keep refrigerated until serving time. The stock should be degreased and can be packed and frozen or used in soup or with other stocks.

9 At serving time, slice and serve the head cheese cold either plain, as above, or with a Rémoulade Sauce (such as the one for the Parsleyed Ham, page 64, step 5), or with mustard, pickles, and crusty French bread.

RILLETTES OF RABBIT

Rillettes are a pork spread that is always made with fatty pork and other meat. They are served very cold with country bread, a dry white wine or a light red wine, and are ideal served in little crock containers for a party.

Sometimes duck, goose, or, as in this instance, rabbit is added to the pork. Game can also be used to flavor the rillettes in a different way. As with the parsleyed ham or head cheese, the quantity I have here is for about 18 to 20 people, since this type of dish is usually done for large parties. It can be cut down easily. Remember, however, that rillettes have to cook a long time and, whether you prepare them for 4 or 20, the time of cooking and the amount of electricity or gas used will remain the same.

After the mixture is packed in small earthenware crocks, it can be covered with rendered pork fat, lard, or even vegetable shortening, and it will keep for weeks refrigerated, as the fat will seal the top and prevent oxidation and spoilage.

Just before serving, scrape off the top layer of fat.

Yield: 18–20 servings (3 containers, 2 c. each)

1½ lb. rabbit, bones in, cut into 3 or 4 pieces
2½ lb. fatty pork shoulder, cut into 3-in. pieces (The proportion of fat to lean meat should be approximately the same.)
1 c. dry, fruity white wine
5 c. water
2 tsp. salt
¼ tsp. powdered thyme
¼ tsp. powdered allspice
1¼ tsp. freshly ground black pepper

GARNISH

A few sprigs parsley

1 Put the 3 or 4 pieces of rabbit, 2½ lb. pork, 1 c. wine, 5 c. water, 2 tsp. salt, ¼ tsp. each powdered thyme and allspice, and 1¼ tsp. pepper in a large kettle (preferably not aluminum), and bring to a boil on top of the stove. Cover, and boil very, very gently for 2 hours. Remove the cover and continue cooking, gently boiling, for another 2½ hours.

2 At the end of the cooking time, all of the liquid should have evaporated and what remains should be mostly fat. At that point, also, the mixture will start sizzling a little and begin to stick to the bottom of the pan. A little browning will impart a nutty taste to the rillettes. Remove from the heat and let cool at room temperature until the meat can be handled.

3 Scoop out the solids and, using your hands, pick all the bones out of the meat, then break the pieces of meat into fibers. Return the meat to the fat and bring the mixture to a boil, stirring.

4 Let cool again and stir with a heavy metal or wooden spoon to mix well and achieve a homogenized texture. If the quantity is too large or too hard to mix, place the mixture in the bowl of a heavy-duty mixer and, using the flat beater, mix on speed 1 for a few seconds, just long enough for the mixture to blend together. Do not overmix or the fat will emulsify and the rillettes will get too white and creamy. Pack into earthenware crocks.

5 Smooth the top. If the rillettes are to be kept more than several days, cover with about a ¼-in. layer of rendered pork fat, lard, or vegetable shortening. When the fat is cold and hard, cover with plastic wrap and keep refrigerated until serving time.

6 At serving time, scrape the fat from the top, make a cross-hatch pattern with your knife, garnish with parsley, and serve with toast, black bread, or crunchy French bread.

DUCK LIVERS IN PORT ASPIC

Although this recipe uses duck livers, other poultry livers, such as chicken or goose, could be substituted. The livers are cured in salt, garlic, and seasonings for at least 48 hours and as long as 3 days, and then they are briefly poached in a strong stock. It is imperative that you do not overcook – the livers should remain pink in the center.

Be sure that the stock and the aspic are highly seasoned when you taste the liquid hot, as the flavor lessens when the aspic cools. This dish makes an elegant first course or an attractive addition to a summer buffet. Although the wrapping of the little timbales with a slice of carrot held by a strip of leek is not necessary, it makes the dish look lovely.

The Bosc pears served with the livers are not peeled but each segment is rubbed with lemon juice to prevent discoloration. Cracked black pepper could also be sprinkled on top of the pears.

Yield: 6 servings

1 lb. duck livers, cleaned (see Grilled
    Duck Livers with Half-Dried Tomatoes,
    Volume I, page 299)

FOR THE MARINADE

1 Tb. cognac
½ tsp. salt
½ tsp. freshly ground black pepper
½ tsp. sugar
2 cloves garlic, chopped (½ tsp.)

STOCK

2½ c. chicken stock
½ tsp. salt
¼ tsp. freshly ground black pepper

ASPIC

½ c. chopped celery, including some of
    the leaves
½ c. chopped green of scallions
½ c. chopped parsley leaves and stems
½ c. chopped green of leeks
¼ c. chopped carrots
¼ tsp. freshly ground black pepper
1 egg white
2 envelopes gelatin (about 1½ Tb.)
¼ c. port wine

GARNISHES

6 large carrot strips
1 strip leek, including white and green
3 ripe Bosc pears (about 1 lb.)
Lemon juice
¼ tsp. cracked black pepper

1 Clean the 1 lb. duck livers. Combine the livers with the 1 Tb. cognac, ½ tsp. each salt, pepper, sugar, and chopped garlic. Cover with plastic wrap and macerate in the refrigerator for 48 hours.

The day before the party, remove the cured livers and put them in a saucepan with 2½ c. of chicken stock, ½ tsp. salt, and ¼ tsp. pepper, and heat it to just under the boil. Turn off the heat and let the livers stand in the hot liquid of the stock for about 5 minutes, then remove the livers with a slotted spoon to a plate. After a while, some liquid will come out of the livers. Discard that liquid and dry the livers with paper towels. Set aside.

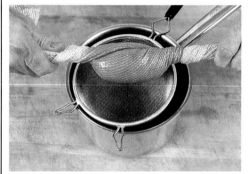

2 To make a clear stock, it is necessary to strain it through a clean dish towel, which will give the final sauce a very fine texture; all the little particles in the stock that would go through an ordinary sieve are removed. Line a sieve with a wet towel and pour the stock in it. Some of the liquid will go through; the remainder will get clogged. Lift up the top of the towel, overlapping and twisting it in opposite directions while pulling it from both ends. Keep pulling and twisting the towel until most of the liquid inside has been pushed through the cloth. (You can use this same method to strain a custard or hollandaise sauce if it has curdled; it will get rid of the grainy appearance.)

3 **To make the clarification:** Place the ½ c. each celery, green of scallions, parsley leaves and stems, and green of leeks, ¼ c. carrots, ¼ tsp. pepper, 1 egg white, and 2 envelopes of gelatin in a saucepan. Mix well together and add the stock from the livers to the pan. Bring to a strong boil on top of the stove while stirring. A foam will form as the stock comes to a boil. As soon as it boils, remove from the heat, set aside 4 to 5 minutes, then strain through a sieve lined with paper towels.

5 For an attractive presentation, cut 6 slices from a long carrot with a vegetable peeler and detach an unblemished leaf from a leek. Cover the carrot slices with water in a saucepan and bring to a boil. Boil for about 1 minute and add the leek leaf. Cook another 30 to 60 seconds, until the vegetables are softened. Remove, cool under cold water, and drain on paper towels. The cooking liquid can be used in a stock.

Run a knife around the edge of the aspic-coated molds and shake each one in your hand to loosen it. Unmold by inverting on a plate.

8 Cut each of the 3 pears into 4 wedges, remove the seeds, and moisten the exposed flesh with lemon juice to prevent discoloration. Sprinkle with the cracked pepper. Place the liver aspic rounds on a platter, arrange the pear sections around them, and place on a buffet table.

4 Place the stock over ice and stir to cool. Add the ¼ c. port wine. Pour some of the stock, about ¼ in. thick, in the bottom of 6 half-cup molds, and place the molds on ice until the liquid sets. When set, arrange some of the liver pieces (2 or 3) in each, on top of the layer of aspic. Cool the remainder of the aspic over ice, stirring it gently until it is syrupy. Pour over the liver to fill the molds. Cover the filled molds with plastic wrap and refrigerate.

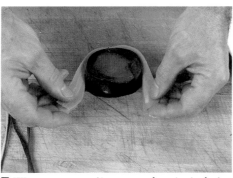

6 Wrap a carrot slice around each timbale.

7 Secure each of the carrot pieces with a thin strip cut from the leek leaf, tying the leek with a double knot and even a bow, if desired.

1½ tsp. salt
4 envelopes gelatin (about 3 Tb.)
2 egg whites
1 c. dry white wine
4 c. good white stock
3 Tb. good cognac
1 small truffle, sliced and cut into julienne
   strips (optional)

1 The large foie gras (1 lb. 10 oz.) comes sealed in plastic.

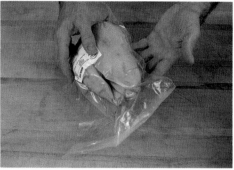

2 Remove the foie gras from the plastic. You will notice that it has 2 lobes. Separate by breaking it apart. Remove as much of the sinews, veins, and gristle running through it as possible and discard. For my recipe, it does not matter if the liver is broken into several pieces since it will join together during cooking. When the foie gras is to be sliced and sautéed (see Salad of Fresh Foie Gras Nicole, page 94, step 1), it is better to slice it before cleaning and remove the pieces of sinews from the slivers afterward.

FRESH FOIE GRAS WITH COGNAC ASPIC

The large liver from a force-fed goose or duck makes one of the greatest delicacies known to epicureans. The areas in France where the best livers are produced are Alsace and the Perigord region. Foie gras is also produced in Israel, Czechoslovakia, Hungary, and, now, in the United States.

The fresh foie gras available in the United States is the fattened liver of duck, and it reaches, at the maximum, 2 lb. There are different grades of liver. The best quality is pale pink in color, is firm, and has a pleasant, mild odor. Inferior foie gras will tend to shrink and melt considerably during cooking and has a bitter taste.

Foie gras is sometimes sautéed fresh in slivers (see Salad of Fresh Foie Gras Nicole, page 94) and other times in large slices, like calves' liver, with different garnishes. My preference, however, is to serve it cold in a strong-flavored aspic, as done in this recipe. Truffles and, if possible, a sweet Sauternes, such as Château d'Yquem, along with a slice of brioche bring the foie gras to its pinnacle. The sweet and complex wine of Yquem tends to complement and balance the richness of the foie gras, making

for an exceptional combination. It is important not to over-cook the foie gras, as it would shrink and become dry.

In my recipe, the foie gras is served within 48 hours after preparation. If it is to be kept longer, it should be wiped with a paper towel to remove any juice or liquid, placed back in a terrine, and covered with clear fat, preferably duck or goose fat and butter, so the liver is completely immersed in the fat and air cannot get to it. Packed this way, it can be kept, refrigerated, for several weeks. At serving time, clean the fat off the liver before slicing. The fat can be used to sauté potatoes or to make stew.

Yield: 8–10 servings

1 duck liver (about 1 lb. 10 oz.)
SEASONING MIXTURE

1½ tsp. salt
1 tsp. sugar
½ tsp. freshly ground white pepper
2 tsp. gelatin (about 1 envelope)
¼ tsp. saltpeter (optional)

3 Tb. good cognac
COGNAC ASPIC

1 c. coarsely chopped green of leeks
1 c. coarsely chopped celery
½ c. coarsely chopped carrots
½ c. loosely packed fresh chervil
2 large sprigs fresh tarragon
¾ tsp. freshly ground black pepper

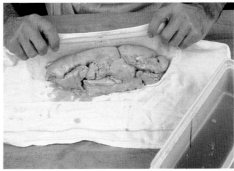

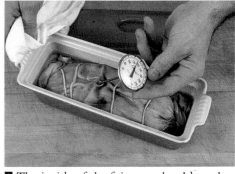

3 Wherever sinews and bloody strips are visible, pull gently to remove, using your fingers and the point of a knife to go deeply into the foie gras.

6 Combine the seasoning ingredients – 1½ tsp. salt, 1 tsp. sugar, ½ tsp. pepper, 2 tsp. gelatin, and ¼ tsp. optional salt-peter – and sprinkle the foie gras with the mixture. Place some of the large pieces of the foie gras on a kitchen towel, arrange the smaller pieces in the center, and cover with the remaining larger pieces. Wrap the towel carefully around the foie gras to compact it into a tight mass.

9 The inside of the foie gras should reach approximately 130 degrees. Cut a piece of wood to fit the terrine, and place it on top of the foie gras with a weight of about 1 to 1½ lb. on top. Let cool, refrigerated, overnight. The weight will press out any remaining blood and juice.

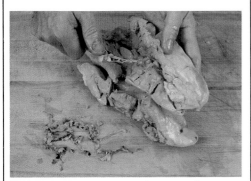

4 To remove even more sinews and nerves, split open the lobes again and probe with your knife where red strips are visible.

7 Tie the ends of the towel tightly with string and place the foie gras in a terrine. Pour 3 Tb. of cognac on top.

10 The following day, scrape off the surface fat and remove the piece of wood. The fat can be used to sauté vegetables or added to sauces for flavor. Run a knife around the towel-encased foie gras to release it. Pull on the towel to unmold. If it doesn't unmold easily, warm up slightly to release.

5 If any part of the foie gras looks slightly greenish, it probably indicates that the gall bladder has broken and run slightly onto the foie gras. This liquid is extremely bitter and any green areas should be sliced off and discarded.

Place the broken pieces of foie gras in ice water and leave for at least 3 hours; the object is to drain more blood out of the foie gras to make it whiter. Drain and dry the foie gras with paper towels.

8 Cover the terrine with a lid and then with aluminum foil, securing it tightly around the edges. Place in a roasting pan with tepid tap water around it that comes at least two-thirds of the way up the outside of the terrine. Cook in a preheated 225-degree oven for 1 hour.

11 Unwrap the foie gras and clean by wiping with a paper towel. The foie gras could be placed back in a clean terrine with fat enough to cover and kept in this manner in the refrigerator for several weeks. Here, it is sliced right away. →

12 **To make the aspic:** In a saucepan, combine the 1 c. each leeks and celery, ½ c. each chopped carrots and chervil, 2 sprigs tarragon, ¾ tsp. pepper, 1½ tsp. salt, and 4 envelopes gelatin. Add the 2 egg whites and stir in with the 1 c. white wine. Bring the 4 c. white stock to a boil in a separate saucepan and add it to the aspic mixture, stirring to combine well. Cook on top of the stove, stirring until it comes to a strong boil. Stop stirring, remove from the heat, and set the mixture aside for about 15 minutes—do not stir further.

13 Strain the aspic through a cloth towel into a saucepan. There should be about 2 good cups. Let cool for 3 minutes and add the 3 Tb. cognac.

14 Pour half the aspic into a large, fairly shallow crystal bowl and set in the refrigerator until hardened. Cut 7 to 8 slices (each about ¾ to 1 in. thick) of foie gras. (The remaining liver can be kept, refrigerated, for a few days.)

15 Place the slices on top of the set aspic in a single layer and sprinkle, if desired, with the julienned truffle. Place the remaining aspic (about ¾ to 1 c.) into a bowl over ice and stir until syrupy and almost ready to set. Spoon on top of the foie gras slices to coat the foie gras and the truffles completely. Refrigerate at least 1 hour before serving.

16 The foie gras can be served with a spoon, dishing out a slice per person with some of the aspic underneath. It is excellent served with a sweet Château d'Yquem and a slice of toasted brioche (see Brioche Mousseline, page 136) or bread.

1 The beef middle (left) and hog casing (right) usually come packed in salt and can be kept in the refrigerator or frozen until ready to use.

Wash thoroughly in cold water.

2 Fit the end of the casing over the water spigot and run lukewarm water through the casing to wash it inside. Drain.

HARD COUNTRY SALAMI

Hard country salami, called <u>saucisson</u> *in French, is usually made of cured ground pork that is stuffed in natural casings and air dried. After three or four days of drying, the fresh sausages are good served cooked with potato salad or cooked in a brioche or puff paste. If allowed to dry longer in a well-ventilated area, the sausage will eventually shrink and get hard, becoming what we know as dried sausage or salami. Even without the use of saltpeter (potassium nitrate), it will turn pink in the process of drying.*

Commercial salami is made with special stuffing machines, which fill the casings very tight, eliminating any air bubbles. When stuffed by hand, as done here, sometimes air bubbles remain and, when the salami is cut, they leave dark areas because the meat there has oxidized. The salami is still edible, but the color will not be quite as appealing.

Sometimes the small sausages are eaten before they have turned hard (after six to seven weeks), when they are what we call half-dried, or <u>demi-sec</u> *in French, but, as a*

general rule, they are allowed to dry longer and are eaten very hard.

The casing called the beef middle, which is from the middle part of the intestine, will give a larger sausage (¾ to 1 lb. each) while the hog casing, which is thinner, will yield a smaller sausage, approximately ½ lb. each and about 8 to 10 in. long.

Yield: 7 large salamis

Beef middle and hog casings
6½ lb. pork shoulder or butt
4 Tb. + 1 tsp. salt
4 tsp. coarsely ground black pepper
2 Tb. sugar
¼ tsp. saltpeter (optional)
1 medium clove garlic, chopped fine

3 The pork butt or shoulder is the best cut for salami because it has the right proportion of fat to lean (about one-quarter fat). Cut approximately 1½ lb. of the leanest part of the meat into ⅜- to ½-in. pieces. Grind the remainder coarse.→

4 To make the sausage: There is a sausage attachment that can be adapted to a KitchenAid mixer (see page 118, step 3). Leave the vise inside and remove the knife and the screen. Attach the deep funnel under the vise at the end and screw it onto the machine. If a special attachment is not available, use a hand stuffer or even a pastry bag with the largest plain tip opening you have. Combine the 5 lb. ground meat, 1½ lb. cut meat, 4⅓ Tb. salt, 4 tsp. pepper, 2 Tb. sugar, ¼ tsp. optional saltpeter (we used it in our recipe), and 1 chopped garlic clove together thoroughly.

5 Fit the casing over the funnel, bunching it up so that most of it is around the funnel. With the machine at high speed, push the meat down through the feeder while holding the casing with your other hand so that as the meat comes out you can regulate its flow and see that the casing fills evenly. Keep filling, trying to pack the casing as tightly as possible without breaking it.

6 When the casing is filled, slip it off the funnel and cut it about 1½ in. above the stuffing. To tie the end of the casing, make a standard knot with kitchen twine about 1 to 1½ in. from the end of the casing.

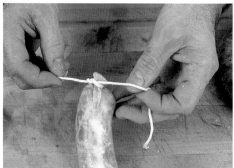

7 Fold the end of the casing over the knot and tie another double knot on top, leaving a little loop of casing at the end. This way, the knots can't slip, so the casing will not open at the ends.

8 Press the casing, squeezing to compact the meat, and prick with a fork wherever you see air bubbles. If the casing (especially a thinner hog casing) bursts, cut it at the break, remove the meat, and repeat the stuffing procedure.

9 Tie each sausage as indicated in steps 6–8 and cut them into 10-in. lengths. Make a loop at one end with the kitchen twine so the salami can be hung. The five smaller salami (lighter in color because the meat is more clearly visible through the thinner hog casing) on the left are about 6 to 8 oz. each and the seven larger salami on the right about 10 to 12 oz. each. Hang in a cool (40 to 60 degrees), well-ventilated place for at least eight weeks before slicing and eating.

10 After a few weeks, the salami should be firm and dry. If white dry spots develop on the surface, it indicates that the salami is drying well.

11 After eight weeks, the salami is ready to eat. Rub the dry salami with paper towels to clean any dirt from the surface and wrap each one in plastic wrap to store in the refrigerator. It will keep, refrigerated, for 4 to 6 weeks. Serve sliced with bread and butter.

SAUSAGE AND POTATO SALAD RICHARD

This rough potato salad goes particularly well with the hot sausage. A country dish, it is served ideally with a green salad, fresh bread, and a robust red wine.

Yield: 6–8 servings

SAUSAGE MIXTURE

2 lb. coarsely ground pork, about one-quarter fat and three-quarters lean (The shoulder or Boston butt is ideal.)
1 Tb. salt
1 tsp. coarsely ground black pepper
1 tsp. sugar
1/4 tsp. saltpeter (potassium nitrate) for color (optional)
2 Tb. red wine
1 small clove garlic, crushed and chopped (1/4 tsp.)
1/4 cup shelled pistachio nuts, with most of the dry skin removed

POTATO SALAD

2 1/2 lb. (about 6) large red-skinned potatoes, cleaned
2 Tb. olive oil, to sauté the leek
1 leek, tough leaves removed, finely sliced (1 1/2 c.)
1/2 c. coarsely chopped parsley
1/2 c. chopped onions, rinsed under cold water and drained
1/4 c. coarsely chopped chervil
3 cloves garlic, chopped fine (1 1/2 tsp.)
3 Tb. French mustard, Dijon-type

3 Tb. white wine
2 Tb. red wine vinegar
3/4 tsp. salt
1/2 tsp. freshly ground black pepper
1/3 c. oil (olive or vegetable, or a mixture of both)

1 Combine the 2 lb. coarsely ground pork (being sure you have at least one-quarter fat and three-quarters lean) with the 1 Tb. salt, 1 tsp. each pepper and sugar, 1/4 tsp. optional saltpeter, 2 Tb. red wine, 1/4 tsp. chopped garlic, and 1/4 cup pistachios and mix well. Cover the mixture with plastic wrap and store in the refrigerator for at least 4 days to cure. (It can be kept for as long as 1 week.) Form 2 sausage rolls of approximately 1 lb. each: Using a piece of wax paper, press the sausage into a thickness of 1 1/2 in. and a length of about 10 in. Be sure to press

firmly so there are no air bubbles inside. Place each on a piece of aluminum foil lined with parchment paper and roll, twisting the ends to enclose the meat.

Place in a large saucepan, cover with cold water, and bring the water to approximately 180 degrees (no higher). Poach the sausage at that temperature for about 30 minutes. Keep in the hot water until ready to serve.

2 For the potato salad: Cook the 2 1/2 lb. of large, washed, red-skinned, waxy potatoes approximately 30 minutes, until they are just tender when pierced with the point of a knife. (This type of potato will tend to absorb the dressing better than baking potatoes.) Drain off the hot liquid and keep the potatoes at room temperature. The moisture in the potatoes, still being very hot, will evaporate. When cool enough to handle (still lukewarm), cut into 1/8-in. slices.

Heat the 2 Tb. oil in a skillet and, when hot, slice the leek and add it to the skillet. Sauté over high heat for about 1 1/2 minutes. Place in a bowl with the 1/2 c. each chopped parsley and onion, 1/4 c. chopped chervil, 1 1/2 tsp. chopped garlic, 3 Tb. each mustard and white wine, 2 Tb. vinegar, 3/4 tsp. salt, 1/2 tsp. pepper, and 1/3 c. olive oil. Mix the ingredients well, add the potatoes, and toss gently, making sure that the potato slices are well-coated with the mixture. →

3 At serving time, arrange the warm potato salad in a serving dish. Cut the sausage into 1-in.-thick slices and place on top of the salad.

4 The potato salad should be served at room temperature. Be sure to keep the foil-wrapped sausage submerged in hot water until serving time.

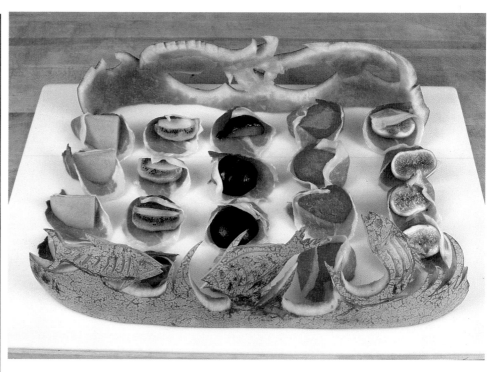

CURED AND DRIED COUNTRY-STYLE HAM

The curing of meat — whether beef for pastrami or corned beef or pork for ham, shoulders, or salami — can be done in dry salt or in a brine made of water, salt, sugar, and seasonings (see Pressed Head Cheese, page 66). The salt drains the moisture from the meat and, at the same time, deprives bacteria of a necessary living condition, hence preserving the meat.

Country hams, such as Westphalia or Black Forest hams, are often smoked or cooked after curing as is done for the great hams of Smithfield, Virginia, or Tennessee as well as Kentucky hams. The smoking adds to the preserving and gives a distinctive flavor to the meat.

The great cured and dried hams of France, such as Bayonne, or of Italy, such as Parma, are not smoked, and this recipe produces a ham similar to those. One day of curing per pound of meat is approximately

what is needed for the recipe, regardless of whether the curing is dry or liquid. The addition of herbs and brandy flavors the meat, and the cheesecloth encloses the seasonings and prevents flies and other insects from touching the meat.

The drying of the meat is crucial since too much heat or humidity and lack of ventilation will cause it to spoil before it has a chance to dry. Therefore, it is preferable to prepare the ham in the winter and hang it in a well-ventilated area so it has a chance to dry before the temperatures rise. Even if it freezes slightly during the drying process — and it would have to be a very low temperature because of the salt — that would not hurt the ham. It will also dry well in a frost-free refrigerator, which will draw out the moisture, provided it is placed on a wire rack so the air can circulate around the ham.

Because country ham is to be consumed raw, we recommend freezing the ham for at least 4 or 5 days in at least 10 degrees Fahrenheit before the curing to kill any possible trichinosis. Be sure to defrost the ham slowly under refrigeration (it will take 2 to 3 days) to prevent loss of moisture. Our cured dried ham weighs approximately

12 lb. after 8 months of drying, a one-third weight loss from an 18-lb. fresh ham. The ham can be dried for 2 years or more, as the Virginia, Tennessee, and European hams are.

The ham, when ready, can be sliced thinly and eaten with buttered bread as well as chopped for use in certain types of stuffings. Sliced, it is excellent with fried eggs and ratatouille together in the style of Bayonne. It is often served with fruit, traditionally with figs. In addition to the figs, I am serving it with watermelon, cantaloupe, kiwi fruit (the acidity of which goes well with the ham), and large plums. Any fruit to your liking will work.

After the ham has been cut into, it is best kept hung in a cool, dry place or in the refrigerator. When a few slices have been removed, cover the remainder with a piece of plastic wrap secured with a rubber band and store in a cold place until ready to slice more.

Yield: 50–60 servings

CURED HAM

1 eighteen-pound whole frozen ham, with the shank bone in, defrosted slowly under refrigeration for at least 3 days
3 lb. kosher-type salt
1½ c. sugar
2 Tb. Armagnac or other alcohol (whiskey, gin, rum, or grain alcohol)
⅓ c. coarsely ground black pepper
⅓ c. dry herbs of Provence
1 bunch fresh thyme

AT SERVING TIME

1 small round watermelon (usually called sugar melon) for decoration, or 1 large watermelon
3 figs
3 kiwi fruit
1 cantaloupe
3 large plums
Freshly ground black pepper

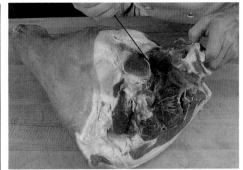

1 Remove the pelvic bone from the ham.

2 Place the ham in a plastic bag. Mix the 3 lb. salt and 1½ c. sugar together and rub over the ham, especially on the areas where there is no rind. Leave in the open plastic bag in a cool place (about 50 degrees or lower), checking on it every couple of days and, with a spoon, pressing any fallen salt mixture back into place on the ham. Let it cure for approximately 16 to 18 days, which is almost 1 day per pound.

3 After 16 to 18 days, some of the salt should have melted around the ham and the meat should be wet and red from the mixture of still dry salt and brine. Rinse the ham carefully under water and dry it with paper towels. Rub with the Armagnac, then the mixture of black pepper and herbs of Provence, rubbing them over the ham so it is well-covered all over. Pack the fresh thyme all around the ham. Be sure that you push the herb mixture with

your fingers around the bone, where there may be little holes, so that you saturate the ham with the seasonings.

4 Place in a piece of canvas or cheesecloth, or even an old pillow case, so it is protected from flies and other insects. Secure with twine and hang it to dry for a minimum of 8 months. It should be in a place that is cool (it can range from freezing to 50°), especially for the first 3 to 4 months, and well-ventilated, such as a garage, or a place where you have good air circulation to prevent the ham from spoiling. If you have space in your refrigerator, the ham will dry well there, provided it is a frost-free refrigerator that has good air circulation and the ham is placed on a wire rack so it dries from underneath as well as on top.

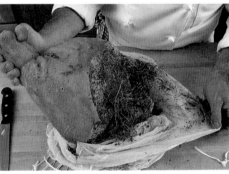

5 **Eight months later:** The ham has dried. Remove the wrapping. The ham can be brushed and washed under water. If you feel that it is too salty, let it soak in cold water for one day and then let it dry again for a few days. →

6 The rind as well as the fat is very good and can be kept for cooking with beans, potatoes, and the like. Trim some of the rind and fat from the top.

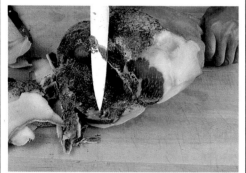

7 Trim off the hard surface of the ham to expose the meat underneath. Trim only a few inches down and around the ham and start slicing.

8 Keep slicing until you reach the level at which the ham is untrimmed around. Then, trim some more around and continue slicing.

To facilitate the carving of the ham, place it in a large container. I have used a pâté mold to hold it securely, making it steadier and easier to slice.

Cut into the thinnest possible slices with a long, thin knife (this requires a little practice) or, if you have access to a slicing machine, slice the ham on it.

9 For a special party, the small, dark green melon (sugar melon) makes a decorative centerpiece. Around the stem, carve a series of leaves to look like the petals of a flower.

10 Continue making a design to your liking with a sharp knife, cutting and removing little strips to create a pattern.

11 The design is becoming more complicated and sophisticated.

12 When you are satisfied with the look, cut away the lower half of the melon and remove the inside flesh. Keep chunks of this flesh to serve with the ham.

13 Another alternative is to use a larger melon and create a fresco-type design (in this instance, of fish), which can be used to make a border for a large tray. Make your design with the point of a knife, carving a strip representing a series of fish and waves all around.

14 When you have completed the basic carving, cut the melon in half lengthwise and remove the melon flesh. Cut away the two carved strips and complete the details of your designs.

15 Cut the 3 figs in halves, the kiwis in wedges, and the melons and plums into pieces, sprinkle the freshly ground pepper on the melon pieces, and wrap slices of the ham around the fruit.

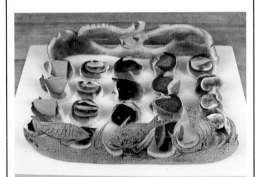

16 On a large white tray, arrange the melon and fruit with the melon-carved fish and waves as a border.

17 As an alternative, serve the ham-wrapped fruit with the carved sugar melon as a decorative centerpiece for a beautiful buffet presentation.

CARPACCIO OF BEEF MARIE-FRANCOISE

Carpaccio of beef is named after the famous Venetian painter of the fifteenth century, red and white being his favorite colors. Thin slices of beef are arranged on a plate and a white, well-flavored mayonnaise is placed on top. In this recipe, I flavor the carpaccio with garlic, oil, onion, and herbs rather than the traditional mayonnaise.

Carpaccio is often prepared in restaurants with the fillet of beef or shell steak, which is more flavorful, in my opinion, than the fillet, and the meat is partially frozen before it is sliced extremely thin, like prosciutto, on a slicing machine. However, the meat releases water as it defrosts on the plate and the finished product is often watery and bland. In the recipe here, the trimmed meat is sliced into small pieces and pounded very thin before being arranged on the plate.

The little tartlets of red, green, and yellow peppers are flavorful and attractive, ideal for a buffet with pâté and other cold meat. Highly flavored with garlic and olive oil, the filling will keep weeks in the refrig-erator and can be used, as well, to enhance sandwiches and salads.

Carpaccio can be made several hours ahead and arranged on individual plates with a piece of plastic wrap touching the meat to prevent discoloration. It can also be seasoned ahead with the salt and seasonings, but vinegar or lemon juice should be added at the last moment, as the acid will coagulate the protein, turning the meat whitish.

Yield: 6–8 servings (3 pieces of meat per person)

SHELL TARTLET DOUGH

Yield: about 30 small tartlets
1½ c. flour (8 oz.)
¾ stick soft butter (3 oz.)
2 Tb. vegetable shortening
4 Tb. milk
⅛ tsp. salt
¼ tsp. sugar

PEPPER MIXTURE MARIE-FRANCOISE

2 large red peppers (1 lb.), 1¼ c. peeled and diced
2 large green peppers (1 lb.), 1¼ c. peeled and diced
2 large yellow peppers (1 lb.), 1¼ c. peeled and diced
5 to 6 cloves garlic, chopped (1½ Tb.)
¾ tsp. freshly ground black pepper
¾ tsp. salt
6 Tb. olive oil

CARPACCIO

2½ lb. untrimmed shell steak (1¼ lb. trimmed)

½ c. chopped onion, washed under cold water and dried

2 cloves garlic, puréed

½ c. oil (half peanut and half olive)

2 to 3 Tb. capers

2 tsp. salt

1 tsp. freshly ground black pepper

6 to 8 strips lemon peel, piled and sliced into a julienne

3 Tb. chives

2 Tb. red wine vinegar

1 **To make the tartlet dough:** Mix all the ingredients (1½ c. flour, ¾ stick butter, 2 Tb. shortening, 4 Tb. milk, ⅛ tsp. salt, ¼ tsp. sugar) together for a few seconds, then gather the dough together and place on a table. Using the palm of your hand, smear approximately 3 to 4 Tb. of the mixture with each smearing motion, until all the ingredients are homogenized. The recipe makes a short dough, which is ideal for tartlets. Gather the dough together and smear a second time to homogenize well. Refrigerate or roll immediately.

2 The tartlet molds used here are small round ones, approximately 1½ in. across, but you may use small, boat-shaped molds, too. Roll the dough to approximately ⅛-in. thickness. Arrange the little molds on the table, roll the dough onto the rolling pin, and unroll on top of the molds.

3 Use a lump of dough dipped in flour to press the rolled dough into the molds.

4 Roll the rolling pin on top of the molds in different directions to cut the dough. Press the dough farther into the little molds with your fingers. Place in the refrigerator or freezer for 1 hour so the dough is rested before going into the oven. Bake for 10 to 12 minutes in a preheated 425-degree oven, until nicely browned and well-cooked.

5 **To make the peppers:** Arrange the peppers (2 red, 2 green, and 2 yellow) on a broiler tray and place under the broiler approximately 1 to 1½ in. from the heat source. Broil for 12 to 15 minutes, turning the peppers every 3 to 4 minutes, until they blister all around. The green pepper will tend to char more than the yellow, but the skin on all the peppers should blister.

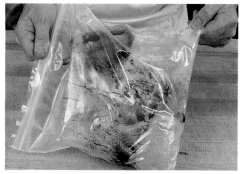

6 Place the peppers into a Ziploc plastic bag and leave for 10 to 15 minutes so the skin on the outside softens and steams, making it easy to remove.

7 Remove the peppers from the bag. They will be limp and soft. Peel off the skin, which should come off very easily. Remove the core, seeds, and stem, and cut the flesh into strips about ⅜ in. wide. Then cut each of the strips into ½-in. pieces. Place in three separate bowls and top each with ½ Tb. (1½ tsp.) chopped garlic, ¼ tsp. each pepper and salt, and 2 Tb. olive oil. Mix well, cover with plastic wrap, and refrigerate until ready to use.

8 When ready to serve, fill each of the tartlet shells with a different colored diced pepper.

11 Cut the pieces of meat into slices weighing approximately ¾ oz. each. The 2 pieces of meat should yield approximately 24 slices. Some pieces will be long and narrow and others will be square.

14 When one plate is ready, cover with plastic wrap and place another finished plate on top. Refrigerate until serving time.

9 The New York strip or shell steak should be completely trimmed of any sinew and fat. Pull the big lump of fat from the front and top to expose meat covered with a thin layer of sinews. Using a knife, remove the sinews.

12 Wet the table and a meat pounder lightly with water so the meat doesn't tear and slide as you pound it. Pound each piece very thin, approximately 3 to 5 in. wide.

15 Chop ½ c. of onions very fine. As the onions are chopped, there is a compound of sulfuric acid released that makes the onions darken and stings your eyes. To eliminate this problem, onions are washed in a sieve under cold water, then placed in a towel and pressed to remove the extra water. The onions will be white and fluffy and will remain so for several days if need be.

Mix the 2 puréed garlic cloves with the ½ c. oil. Drain the 2 to 3 Tb. capers.

10 When the meat is completely trimmed, you will notice a sinew in the center going straight down through the meat. Cut right along the sinew on either side, separating the rectangle of meat into two almost square pieces. The meat should weigh approximately 1¼ lb., and there should be approximately 10 oz. of meat trimmings with a little fat, to be ground into hamburger meat. The remaining 8 to 10 oz. of pure fat can be discarded.

13 Arrange 3 pieces of meat per person on individual plates. This represents about 2¼ oz. of meat per person. The meat should be almost transparent and completely cleaned of fat and sinew.

16 The meat can be arranged on a large platter or individual plates. Sprinkle with the 2 tsp. salt, 1 tsp. pepper, ½ c. chopped onion, 6 to 8 strips of julienne of lemon peel, the garlic oil, and the 3 Tb. chives. This can be done up to 1 hour before serving. At the last moment, sprinkle 2 Tb. wine vinegar on top and serve immediately.

CHICKEN SALAD DANNY

This delightful chicken salad is exceptional because of the way the chicken is poached, a technique that was shown to me by Danny Kaye. The chicken is poached for only 10 minutes, then the pot is removed from the heat and the chicken continues to cook slowly in the hot liquid for 40 minutes longer, which makes the meat moist, flavorful, and tender.

Regardless of the presentation, this salad should be served at room temperature. The chicken will lose half its flavor if served too cold so if you do make it ahead and refrigerate it, bring it back to room temperature before serving.

The red pepper is peeled to make it more tender and flavorful and milder. The roasted pecans with cayenne are a crunchy, savory addition and give a satisfying texture to the salad. They are also excellent as a snack or served with drinks.

This salad can be presented simply (as shown in photograph 5) with basil leaves and pecans around and some wild mushrooms. The fanciful way in which the salad is presented in photographs 6–8, which is easy and fun to do, makes it particularly attractive for a light brunch or a children's birthday party.

Yield: 6 servings

POACHING THE CHICKEN

1 chicken, about 3½ lb. (It should yield 1¼ to 1½ lb. clean meat.)
1 carrot, peeled and halved
1 onion, peeled, stuck with 3 cloves
½ tsp. salt
4 to 5 black peppercorns
2 bay leaves
1 rib celery
2 to 3 sprigs fresh thyme, or ½ tsp. dried

DRIED WILD MUSHROOMS

1 oz. dried wild mushrooms (preferably cèpes)
1½ c. warm water
1 Tb. butter
Dash salt and freshly ground black pepper

CHICKEN SALAD DRESSING

1 clove garlic, peeled, crushed, and chopped (½ tsp.)
¼ tsp. salt
¼ tsp. freshly ground black pepper
1 Tb. Dijon-style mustard
1 Tb. red wine vinegar
1/16 tsp. cayenne pepper
½ tsp. Worcestershire sauce
¼ c. good olive oil, or 3 Tb. peanut oil and 1 Tb. walnut oil

ROASTED PECANS

1 c. pecan halves (about 80)
1 Tb. butter
1 Tb. sugar
¼ tsp. salt
⅛ tsp. cayenne pepper

ADDITIONAL GARNISHES

1 large red pepper
2 hard-cooked eggs
1 bunch chives
12 to 18 basil leaves

1 Place the chicken, breast-side down, in a saucepan with high sides so it fits snugly. Add just enough water to cover (6 to 7 c.) and the halved carrot, onion, ½ tsp. salt, 4 to 5 peppercorns, 2 bay leaves, rib of celery, and 2 to 3 sprigs thyme. Bring to a boil and cook very gently, covered, for 10 minutes. Set aside, still covered, and leave for 40 minutes in the hot broth to continue cooking.

Meanwhile, place the ounce of dried mushrooms in the 1½ c. of warm water to soak for at least 45 minutes to reconstitute them.

2 Remove the chicken from the now lukewarm broth, and set it aside to cool further. The broth can be strained and left to cool before de-fatting. (The mushroom liquid can be added to the broth and the broth refrigerated or frozen for future use in soups or stocks.)

3 **Prepare the red pepper garnish:** Using a vegetable peeler, <u>peel off as much of the red pepper skin as possible.</u>

4 It is difficult to peel in the pleats and recesses of the pepper, so when most of the surface is peeled, cut the pepper into wedges at the pleats, remove the pith, center, and seeds, and <u>peel with a sharp knife the areas of the skin that were inaccessible before the pepper was cut.</u> Cut the pepper into long strips and set aside. Pick the chicken meat off the bones and discard the skin and bones. You should have 1¼ to 1½ lb. of meat. Shred the meat into pieces, following the grain.

5 **For the dressing:** In a bowl, combine the chopped garlic clove, ¼ tsp. each salt and pepper, 1 Tb. each mustard and vinegar, ¹⁄₁₆ tsp. cayenne, and ½ tsp. Worcestershire together with a whisk. Add the ¼ c. oil in one stroke and mix briefly. The dressing should not be homogenized but somewhat separated so it looks glossy on top of the chicken.

To roast the pecans: Cover the pecans with water, bring to a boil, boil 30 seconds, and drain. Heat the 1 Tb. butter in a saucepan, add the pecans, 1 Tb. sugar, ¼ tsp. salt, and ⅛ tsp. cayenne, and cook, tossing the pecans in the pan until they are caramelized and have a dark, glossy color. Set aside to cool.

For the mushrooms: Clean the stems of the drained mushrooms of any dirt and remove tough sections. Cut into slices (if not already sliced) and press to remove excess water. Sauté in the 1 Tb. butter for 1 minute, add a dash of salt and pepper, and set aside to decorate the plates.

Toss the dressing with the chicken and arrange on individual serving plates. Place some diced hard-cooked eggs on top with some chopped chives and basil leaves around the salad, and decorate each plate with the roasted pecans, mushrooms, and red pepper.

6 For another individual presentation, arrange a slice of hard-cooked egg on a plate to simulate the head of a chicken, with two pieces of mushroom cut out to simulate the chicken's beak and pieces of red pepper for the cockscomb and the eye. Next to the head, arrange chicken pieces to begin creating a body.

7 Keep arranging chicken, mushrooms, and red pepper pieces to complete the body. <u>Arrange long pieces of chives on top.</u>

8 Finally, put little leaves of basil alongside the chicken and place pecans on top of the basil to finish the presentation. Serve at room temperature.

RED OAK DUCK SALAD

The cooking technique used in this recipe produces a moist, firm, delicious duck. It is rich enough so that one-fourth of the duck will serve one person.

The salad is seasoned with a pungent dressing made with shallots, garlic, vinegar, and the rendered duck fat, which is quite flavorful. The savory duck fat could, however, be replaced by peanut oil or olive oil, or a mixture of both, alone or in combination with the duck fat.

The red oak leaf salad is flavorful, beautiful, and combines well with the arugula. Any lettuce can be used, depending on the season and personal taste. The scrambled egg garnish should be done at the last moment and the eggs should not be completely cooked but still runny.

The duck can be cooked ahead and kept refrigerated in its own fat. Cook skin-side down again just at serving time to recrisp the skin and warm the duck, and toss the salad with the dressing just before arranging it on the plates so it doesn't wilt.

Yield: 4 servings

1 duck, cleaned, with insides removed (about 4 lb.)
½ tsp. salt
¼ tsp. freshly ground black pepper
SALAD
1 head (about 10 oz.) red oak leaf lettuce
1 bunch arugula (about 2 c. leaves, loose)
DRESSING
1 medium clove garlic, crushed and minced fine (½ tsp.)
1 Tb. chopped shallot
¼ tsp. salt
¼ tsp. freshly ground black pepper
1 Tb. red wine vinegar
3 Tb. duck fat, peanut or olive oil, or a mixture of the oils and the duck fat
1 tsp. light soy sauce
EGG GARNISH
½ tsp. butter
2 eggs, beaten with a fork
Dash salt and freshly ground black pepper

1 Clean out the inside of the duck, removing the package containing the neck, gizzard, and liver. (The liver can be sautéed in some duck fat and eaten on toast and the gizzard and neck reserved with the carcass and wing tips for stock.) Remove the wing tips and cut at the second joint of the wings, leaving the remaining wing section attached to the duck. Set aside the center part of the wing; it will be cooked in this recipe. Remove the extra skin from the neck; it will also be cut into pieces and used in the recipe. To remove the wishbone, lift up what's left of the skin of the neck and run the point of a sharp knife all around the wishbone, which is in the shape of a half moon in the duck.

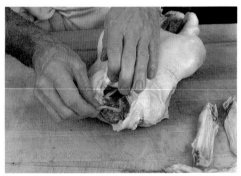

2 Slide your thumb in back of the wishbone to loosen and pry it out.

3 With the duck on its back, cut through the skin and the meat on either side of the breastbone clear through to the bone underneath.

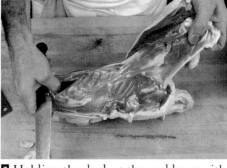

4 To remove the leg, hold the duck by the drumstick high enough off the table so the weight of the bird pushes the breast down. Then cut the skin all around the thigh and around the little "oyster" piece of meat in the back portion of the duck.

7 Holding the duck at the neckbone with one hand, pull with the other hand to remove the breast in one piece from the carcass. Repeat on the other side. You now have 4 pieces of duck, two breasts and two legs.

10 Cut the extra skin and pieces of fat into ¼-in. pieces for cracklings. In the back on the top, left, are the pieces of bone, cut into 1- to 2-in. pieces. Next to them is the extra fat. In front, from left to right, are the two legs, the two breasts with the pieces of wing bones in the center, and, on the right, the two fillets.

5 Grab the leg of the duck at the knee joint and crack it open to expose the joint. Cut through the joint and pull to remove the leg in one piece. Repeat on the other side.

8 The only meat left on the carcass is the two small fillets on either side of the central breastbone. Pull them out.

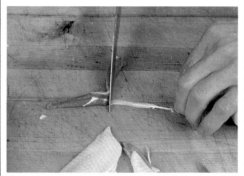

6 To remove the breast, place the bird on its side, lift up the skin at the shoulder, and cut through the joint of the shoulder. (You can determine where to cut by moving the wing bone with one hand and feeling with the other hand to find the joint.)

9 To remove the sinews in each of the fillets, lay them flat on the table and, holding the projecting sinew with your fingertips, scrape the meat from it with the blade of a vertically held knife.

11 Sprinkle the duck pieces with ½ tsp. salt and ¼ tsp. pepper, arrange them skin-side down in a pan (preferably non-stick) large enough to accommodate them in one layer, and place over medium heat. Add the wing pieces and diced fat and skin to the pan. (The bones can be frozen for use in stock.) →

12 Cook the duck for approximately 15 minutes over medium to high heat so it browns well. Most of the fat will melt from the skin on the duck and the extra diced skin and fat, and the duck pieces will be half submerged in the fat. Notice that the duck skin will have shrunk considerably and will be well-browned. Turn the pieces over, reduce the heat to very low, cover the skillet with a lid, and continue cooking for 30 minutes. Steam will develop inside. Remove the pieces of duck to a bowl, pour the clear fat (about 1¼ c.) over them, setting aside the pieces of crackling and the wings. The pieces of duck should be tender and can, at this point, be refrigerated in their own fat.

13 At serving time, remove the duck from the fat, and cook it skin-side down without any fat in a nonstick skillet for approximately 10 minutes, if the duck is still lukewarm, and 12 to 15 minutes if completely cold.

14 **To prepare the salad greens:** Wash the oak leaf lettuce and the arugula and dry thoroughly in a salad spinner. You should have approximately 6 c. of oak leaf and 2 c. of arugula.

To make the salad dressing: Combine the ½ tsp. minced garlic, 1 Tb. chopped shallot, ¼ tsp. each salt and pepper, 1 Tb. vinegar, 3 Tb. duck fat (and/or oil), and 1 tsp. soy sauce, and stir gently. The dressing should not be homogenized but should look separated.

15 Arrange the two salad greens in separate bowls and toss each with some of the dressing.

16 Arrange the salad greens on four individual plates with pieces of duck in the center. Sprinkle pieces of crackling here and there on the salad.

For the egg garnish: At the last moment, heat a skillet for 1 minute, add the ½ tsp. butter and, when hot, the 2 beaten eggs, and stir gently over high heat. Season with salt and pepper. The eggs should not be completely cooked; they should still be runny. Place spoonfuls of the egg around the duck on the salad.

17 The pieces of duck should be lukewarm to warm, the salad at room temperature, and the eggs warm.

2 Pull up the field salad, keeping each individual head attached. Pinch off the bottom of the root on each and wash carefully in cold water. Drain in a salad spinner.

Melt the 1 Tb. butter on top of the stove and, when hot, add the 36 to 40 pecans and a pinch of salt. Toss together and place in a preheated 375-degree oven for 6 to 8 minutes to brown nicely. Set aside. They should be served fresh at room temperature.

SALAD TULIPE

The Salad Tulipe, first created for Sally Darr at her restaurant La Tulipe in New York City, is a flavorful combination of field salad, pecans, goat cheese, pears, and walnut oil dressing. The field or corn salad (*doucette* or *mâche* in French) is planted around the end of August and gets large enough to be ready for picking at the end of November. After the first frost, it becomes sweeter and more tender.

The pears must be ripe – Bartlett, Comice, or Anjou pears are best for this dish. A semihard goat cheese, preferably the small, round variety, is preferable, and the pecan halves should be freshly roasted.

Yield: 6 servings

36 to 40 segments field or corn salad (*mâche*) (6 to 8 pieces per person)
1 Tb. butter
36 to 40 pecan halves (about 6 to 8 per person)
Pinch salt
3 ripe pears (Bartlett, Comice, or Anjou; ½ pear per person)
1 Tb. lemon juice for pears

¾ lb. goat cheese, preferably the small, round, semihard variety

WALNUT DRESSING

1 Tb. sherry vinegar
2 Tb. walnut oil
¼ tsp. salt
¼ tsp. coarsely ground black pepper
1 Tb. peanut or safflower oil

3 Halve the 3 pears lengthwise, core, peel, and cut each into quarters. Sprinkle with lemon juice to prevent discoloration. Cut the goat cheese into small wedges.

For the dressing: Combine the 1 Tb. sherry vinegar, 2 Tb. walnut oil, ¼ tsp. each salt and pepper, and 1 Tb. peanut oil.

1 The field salad as it looks in the garden ready to be picked.

4 Arrange 3 pieces of pear on each plate with pieces of cheese and pecans between. Arrange 4 to 5 heads field salad in the center and sprinkle with approximately 2 tsp. of dressing per plate. Serve immediately.

BRESSANE SALAD

I named this Bressane salad after the place where I was born, Bourg-en-Bresse, the area of France best known for the excellence of its chickens. In this recipe, the skin, gizzard, heart, and liver of chicken are used and the meat reserved for sautéing. Small boiling potatoes and an earthy garlic dressing make a flavorful, inexpensive country salad. The curly endive can be used by itself with the same dressing.

Choose curly endive that is white inside to ensure that it will be tender with a nutty taste. If you grow your own salad, as I do, gather up the outside leaves on the growing plant and tie them around the inside leaves in a bundle like a head of cauliflower. The inside leaves, not then exposed too much to the sun, will grow white because the chlorophyll doesn't develop. Belgian endive is grown in the same way. The white center of the salad has a nutty, crunchy, tender taste, as opposed to the more bitter, tougher green areas. If white curly endive is not available, substitute an escarole or a mixture of romaine and iceberg lettuce.

Pull the skin off the chicken pieces. The chicken meat can be reserved for another meal.

Yield: 6 servings

CRACKLINGS

Skin from 1 chicken or equivalent in
   chicken parts
¼ tsp. salt

6 chicken gizzards
4 chicken livers
12 chicken hearts

CHICKEN INNARDS

3 Tb. butter
¼ tsp. salt
¼ tsp. freshly ground black pepper
½ c. brown stock or demi-glace

2 heads curly endive with the whitest possible center for taste and tenderness
   (about 8 c. loose)
6 small boiling potatoes (¾ lb.)

DRESSING

3 cloves garlic, chopped fine (1½ to
   2 tsp.)
2 Tb. French mustard, Dijon-style
1 Tb. red wine vinegar
¼ tsp. salt
¼ tsp. freshly ground black pepper
2 Tb. olive oil
2 Tb. vegetable oil

1 Spread the chicken skin on a baking sheet. Sprinkle with the ¼ tsp. salt and place in a preheated 400-degree oven for 20 minutes.

2 The skin should be very crisp. If not, cook a little longer. Remove to a plate and set aside. The fat rendered by the chicken skin can be used to sauté potatoes or for stew.

3 To obtain the fleshy part of the gizzard, cut down along the lump of meat, sliding your knife around it to remove it from the skin in one piece. Cut the meat into 2 or 3 slivers. Set aside.

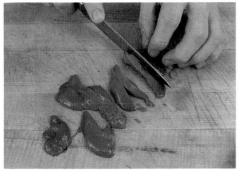

4 Cut away and discard any green areas on the liver and remove any sinews. Cut the liver into slivers about ½ in. wide and set aside.

7 Trim off any green areas, which tend to be tough, and cut the remainder into chunks of approximately 1½ in. Wash in a lot of cold water, lifting the salad up from the water and drying it thoroughly in a salad spinner.

9 At serving time, melt the 3 Tb. butter in a skillet large enough to hold all the chicken innards in one layer. When hot, add the chicken gizzard pieces and sauté for 30 seconds over high heat. Add the heart slivers and sauté for another 15 seconds. Finally, add the liver, ¼ tsp. each salt and pepper, and continue sautéing for about 1½ minutes longer. Add the ½ c. brown stock or demi-glace to the mixture and return just to the boil. Set aside.

In a large bowl, combine the greens with the dressing, tossing well to mix. Add the potatoes, tossing gently to avoid breaking them. Arrange a few slices of potato on each plate with some greens on top. Spoon 1 to 2 Tb. of the chicken innards on top with 1 to 2 Tb. of the juices in the skillet.

5 Cut the heart lengthwise into quarters or thirds and set aside.

8 Cover the 6 potatoes with water in a saucepan and bring to a boil. Boil gently 16 to 18 minutes, until tender. Drain. The potatoes should be lukewarm at serving time. Cut the potatoes (with or without the skin, as you prefer) into ½-in. slices.

For the dressing: Combine the 3 garlic cloves and 2 Tb. mustard, and add the 1 Tb. vinegar, and ¼ tsp. each salt and pepper, mixing well. Add the 2 Tb. each olive and vegetable oils slowly, in a stream, whisking continually to incorporate. Set aside.

6 When buying the salad, try to select endive with a completely white center.

10 Break the crackling into pieces. Sprinkle on top of the salad and serve immediately.

1 When picking the dandelions, use a small paring knife and be sure to cut deeply enough into the ground so as to take most of the roots.

2 Cut off the end of the root as well as the damaged leaves around it, but don't separate the little heads of the greens. If some of the heads are too large, split them in half, but the leaves should not be entirely separated – the part of the root remaining makes the salad more flavorful.

WILD DANDELION SALADE LYONNAISE

Wild dandelion salad is a specialty of our house in the spring. Wild dandelions are much better than the cultivated variety; they taste sweet, nutty, and bitter at the same time. They should be picked in the early spring, when there is not yet a flower or when the flower is still in a bud, and preferably in an area where there are dried leaves or gravel so most of the plant's root is buried and white. This makes a sweeter and more tender dandelion.

Although wild dandelion salad is traditionally made with cooked eggs, croutons rubbed with garlic, and a strong vinaigrette accented with garlic and sometimes anchovy fillets, in my recipe I do it with herring and pigs' feet, as it's prepared in Lyon. Any of the ingredients are optional and can be changed to fit one's own taste.

Pigs' feet, if they are cured, will have a better flavor. The same pigs' feet cure used in the Parsleyed Ham recipe (page 63) can be used here. If not, the pigs' feet can be cooked directly in water to cover for approximately 2½ to 3 hours, until tender, and the meat can be picked off the bones.

Yield: 6 servings

8 oz. dandelion greens, washed and dried
½ cooked pig's foot, chopped* (about 1 c.) (optional)
½ lb. or 1 whole herring, skin and line of bones removed, cut into ⅜-in. dice
8 oz. salt pork, cut into *lardons* ¼ in. thick by 1 in. wide
1 qt. cold water
2 Tb. peanut oil

2 Tb. corn or safflower oil
1 large piece baguette, cut into 24 ¼-in. slices
1 large, peeled clove garlic for rubbing baguette slices

GARLIC VINAIGRETTE

2 cloves garlic, peeled and chopped fine (1 tsp.)
3 Tb. red wine vinegar
½ tsp. freshly ground black pepper
¼ tsp. salt

3 hard-cooked eggs, peeled and cut into wedges

GARNISH

Dandelion flowers

3 Wash in a lot of cold (but not too cold) water, shaking the greens under the water and then lifting them out. Repeat a couple more times to be sure that all sand and dirt inside has been removed. Dry well in a salad spinner.

* Note: Crackling can be substituted; see Bressane Salad (page 90).

4 Pick the meat off the bones of the pig's foot and cut into 1-in. pieces. Pick the skin and bones off the herring and cut into ¼-in. dice. Cut the salt pork into ¼-in.-thick slices about ¾ to 1 in. long called *lardons*. Cover the pieces of salt pork with a quart of cold water, bring to a boil, and cook gently 2 minutes. Rinse in a colander under cold water and drain. Sauté in a skillet with the 2 Tb. peanut oil over medium to high heat, until well-browned and dry, about 8 to 9 minutes. Meanwhile, pour 2 Tb. corn or safflower oil onto a cookie sheet or pizza pan. Tilt to coat the pan with the oil. Cut the baguette into 24 ¼-in.-thick slices and place them flat on the oiled tray.

6 Combine the herring, pig's foot, 1 tsp. chopped garlic, 3 Tb. vinegar, ½ tsp. pepper, and ¼ tsp. salt in a large bowl and, when the *lardons* are browned and very hot, pour them with their fat into the pig's foot mixture. Stir well.

5 Turn the slices over so they are slightly oiled on both sides, and bake in a preheated 400-degree oven for about 7 minutes. They should brown equally on both sides.

When the bread has cooled off a little, rub both sides of each slice with the peeled clove of garlic.

7 When ready to serve, add the dandelion greens, toss briefly, add the croutons and the 3 hard-cooked eggs cut into wedges, and toss again briefly. Decorate the top with dandelion flowers and serve immediately.

SALAD OF FRESH FOIE GRAS NICOLE

Foie gras, or fattened liver, is a delicacy that goes back to the Greeks and Romans. It is usually the liver of a goose or duck that is fattened to reach the creamy, smooth consistency of what we know as fresh foie gras.

Foie gras bought in cans and crocks is usually imported from France and ranges from a mediocre mousse de foie gras, made of trimmings of the liver mixed with other ingredients, to a bloc de foie gras, which is the whole liver, usually studded with truffles. The fresh, uncooked foie gras that I am using was not obtainable in the United States until a few years ago. Ducks and geese are now raised in this country to produce foie gras and it is available in specialty stores. Being expensive and quite rich, a small sliver weighing about 2 oz. is enough for each person. Served lukewarm, it can be combined with an almost endless variety of greens and vegetables.

Yield: 6 servings

12 oz. fresh duck foie gras, preferably cut into 2-oz. slices, each about ¼ in. thick
6 oz. oyster mushrooms, about 1 oz. per person
½ large celeriac, or celery root, peeled and cut into julienne sticks about ⅛ in. wide by 2 in. long
1 large head (or several small) curly endive, very white, washed and dried (about 1 c. per person)
¼ tsp. salt
¼ tsp. freshly ground black pepper
1 Tb. butter
6 Tb. demi-glace (reduced brown stock), or juices from roasted chicken, veal, or beef, warmed (optional)
2 Tb. red wine vinegar

GARNISH AND DECORATION

1 doz. sorrel leaves, stacked and cut into ¼-in. strips
6 pansies (optional)

1 Slice the foie gras into slivers of approximately 2 oz. per person (either 1 or 2 slivers), each about ¼ in. thick. Cut the mushrooms into slices.

2 Peel the half of celeriac. You will notice that the center is often very soft and cottony. With a paring knife, remove the cottony part and discard it. Cut the celeriac into about ⅛-in. slices, stack the slices together, and cut into a julienne about 2 in. long.

Cut the head of curly endive into 2-in. pieces, and wash and dry carefully.

3 At serving time, sprinkle ⅛ tsp. each salt and pepper on the pieces of foie gras, and heat the 1 Tb. butter in a very large skillet or divide it between 2 smaller skillets. When hot, add the foie gras slices and sauté over high heat for about 45 seconds on each side. Remove the foie gras to a plate. You will notice that some of the foie gras has melted so you have more "butter" than originally. Add the celeriac and sauté over high heat for about 1 minute. Add the mushrooms and sauté for an additional minute. Sprinkle with the remaining ⅛ tsp. each salt and pepper and add any of the drippings that may have accumulated around the slices of foie gras on the plate. Finally, add the curly endive and toss very briefly, just enough to coat the salad with the butter.

4 Divide the salad among 6 individual serving plates. Place a slice of foie gras on top, and sprinkle each of the servings with 1 Tb. demi-glace and 1 tsp. red wine vinegar. Garnish with the shredded sorrel and decorate the top, if desired, with a pansy or another edible flower. Serve right away.

TRUFFLES

A truffle is a subterranean mushroom that grows through the root systems of certain trees, in symbiosis with the host tree – primarily oaks, hazelnuts, and elms. The truffle matures in from six to ten years and the precious fungi is usually found by a sow or a trained dog.

Truffles grow from 5 or 6 in. to 1 ft. deep in the ground of the contaminated trees, and efforts to grow them outside the "wild" have not been very successful so far. A good oak tree lives for as long as 50 years and will yield up to 1½ lb. of truffles per year in a good season. A truffle hunter who knows what trees yield truffles will exercise extreme caution, often digging out the truffles at night to keep from being followed.

The regions where truffles grow generally have mild seasons with well-spaced rainfall of at least 25 in. a year. The elevation is usually about 1,000 ft. above sea level and the mineral composition of the soil is very alkaline – always above 7 on the Ph scale.

There are at least 60 species of truffles but only a few are really prized and this is where the confusion arises. People often encounter truffles that have no value; they may look good but they do not have the flavor and the extraordinary pungent smell of the prized species.

Most of the value of the truffle is in the smell rather than the taste. Truffles are often bought fresh, packed in uncooked rice. The rice gets permeated with the fumes of the truffle. Yet, by the time the

rice is cooked, the flavor has, unfortunately, disappeared. Usually, it is better to add truffles at the end or to simmer them (covered with a lid) gently in a sauce so their flavor is retained.

The most sought-after of the black truffles is the Tuber melanosporum, a beautiful reddish truffle that turns a rich black when fully ripened. The inside is a dark gray-black color with the mycelium, or white filament lines, running through it. It has a sweet, powerful fragrance, strong enough so that one fresh truffle placed in a plastic bag with a dozen unshelled eggs permeates the eggs with the truffle taste. An omelet made with these eggs will taste of truffle, even though the truffle itself is not used.

The second best black truffle is the Tuber brumalle, quite flavorful and strongly perfumed. The largest supplier of brumalle truffles is found at the market of Morcillo, Spain, according to Urbani, one of the largest truffle merchants in the world. The inside of the brumalle is brown rather than dark gray-black with the white mycelium.

A third good variety is the Tuber aestevum (meaning "summer truffle"), which develops earlier in the year than the other two varieties. The inside is a lighter brown with white mycelium lines. A summer truffle has less pungency and savor than the other two species mentioned above.

The skin of the black truffle is somewhat coarse and granulated. It is usually removed, chopped fine, and used to flavor pâtés and sauces. The outside of the Tuber aestevum is particularly coarse and tough and any peelings must be chopped very fine to be palatable. The inside of a truffle is usually sliced or placed whole in brioche or in pâté or foie gras.

White truffles are different from black truffles in their fragrance and cannot be compared. The best of the white truffles, considered by many to be the quintessence of all truffles, with the most pungent taste, is the Tuber magnatum. The best of these come from northern Italy, although some good ones are found in the Grenoble area as well as in Provence, France. The best black truffle is said to come from the Perigord, in the southwest of France. Some good ones are also found in Provence and Italy. The white truffle has a more potent scent – some say almost garlicky – than the black fungus. The inside is pale beige streaked with the white lines of the mycelium. The Tuber magnatum, served here with risotto and inside brioche toast as well as in the carpaccio, is grated or thinly sliced (we used a vegetable slicer) and arranged on top of the dish just before serving.

The white truffles of Oregon, the Tuber gibbosum, have a musty, woody, pungent smell. The taste does not compare with the white Tuber magnatum but it, too, will enhance many dishes. The Tuber gibbosum is found in medium, small, or very small sizes (see step 3). The "sand truffle" of North Africa is the famous truffle of antiquity known as hydnon to the Greeks. This Ferfezia arenoria is a white truffle of low quality and little taste. It is sometimes found in New York markets, but even though it is priced much lower than the Tuber magnatum, it's not worth buying.

Canned truffles can be excellent. Try to find cans marked "first cooking" because, like mushrooms, truffles will shrink, and in order to guarantee the avoirdupois on the can, the truffles are cooked first to allow them to shrink and are then placed in a can with some of the cooking juices and cooked a second time. The "first cooking" designation is usually indicative of better quality,

even though weight cannot be guaranteed. Canned truffle peelings are added to sauces and, if of good quality, are well worth the price.

Leftover truffles, either raw or cooked, can be kept in cognac or brandy. The liquor will take on the truffle flavor and can then be used in pâtés or sauces, while the truffles can be chopped and added to pâtés or other dishes. Fresh black truffles freeze better than white, which tend to turn brown and get mushy.

When buying truffles, be sure – if they have not been brushed – to scrape the dirt off them before weighing. Unscrupulous sellers have been known to pack dirt into the holes and uneven surfaces of truffles to add weight to them. Fresh black truffles should have a strong aroma, be plump rather than wrinkled, and be firm and heavy. White truffles should also exude a strong perfume, be beige rather than brown, and be firm and plump.

Truffles spoil fairly rapidly: White truffles can be kept 5 to 6 days, or up to 10 days if wrapped in paper or stored in rice, while black truffles may keep a few days longer but will eventually shrink and spoil. Most of their flavor may spread through the refrigerator unless they are used as soon as possible or placed in oil or brandy or frozen.

Truffles are best served with fast-cooked dishes such as scrambled eggs or omelets, or in potato dishes where the potatoes and truffles form a harmonious, delicate, and flavorful combination.

In my truffles in brioche recipe, a small amount of ground fillet of pork is combined with the truffle to extend it. The truffle salad flavored with walnut oil is also excellent with an extra virgin olive oil. White truffles are at their best with risotto or as a toast of truffle with Parmesan cheese, as well as grated and rolled into carpaccio.

It is worth spending more money for a good truffle than using an inferior quality

canned truffle peeling or a summer truffle, which will be almost tasteless in a dish. If truffles are not available, nothing can replace them. Yet, other mushrooms, such as the Boletus edulis, cèpe (in French), porcini (in Italian), and Horn of Plenty, often available in specialty markets at certain times of the year, can be used in pâtés or other dishes. They are flavorful and black and will look somewhat like truffles.

Carpaccio of White Truffles

Risotto with White Truffles

Black Truffle Salad

White Truffle Brioche Toast

Black Truffles in Brioche with Truffle Sauce

FIVE TRUFFLE RECIPES

IDENTIFYING AND PREPARING TRUFFLES

1 The white Oregon truffle is found in medium or small sizes and ranges from a pale beige to a darker brown. It has a musty, strong, woody aroma. The inside has basically the same color and design as the prized truffle of Italy, the *Tuber magnatum,* on the left.

2 The *Tuber magnatum* should be brushed under lukewarm water to remove any dirt from the crannies and holes on the surface and dried. The surface is smooth and need not be peeled. It should have a dry, strong, pungent aroma. Store, refrigerated, in a plastic bag, embedded in rice, or wrapped in newspaper (which should be changed every day or so). The truffle can also be sliced and kept in oil or brandy.

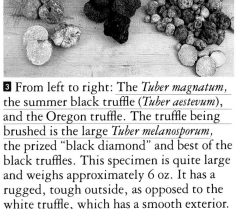

3 From left to right: The *Tuber magnatum,* the summer black truffle (*Tuber aestevum*), and the Oregon truffle. The truffle being brushed is the large *Tuber melanosporum,* the prized "black diamond" and best of the black truffles. This specimen is quite large and weighs approximately 6 oz. It has a rugged, tough outside, as opposed to the white truffle, which has a smooth exterior. →

4 A brushed and cut summer black truffle *Tuber aestevum*. Like the *Tuber brumalle*, it will get darker when cooked. Uncooked, it will have a dark brownish inside with the striation of the white mycelium.

5 The large *Tuber melanosporum,* cut in half. The inside is a dark gray, rather than brown like the summer black truffle.

6 Cut the *Tuber melanosporum* into 4 pieces and trim off the outside skin of each piece.

7 Finely chop the skin, which is tougher. The trimmings can be used in pâtés and sauces.

8 Cooked and canned truffles stored in alcohol. As a result of cooking, they are darker in color than the fresh truffle. Keep them in the refrigerator immersed in brandy. The liquid can be used for flavoring pâtés or sauces.

CARPACCIO OF WHITE TRUFFLES

Yield: 8 servings

1 lb. New York strip steak, completely cleaned of any sinews and fat
1 white truffle (about 1 to 1½ oz.)
¾ tsp. salt
½ tsp. freshly ground black pepper
3 Tb. freshly grated Parmesan cheese
4 Tb. good virgin olive oil

FOR THE CROUTONS

1 Tb. olive oil
12 thin (½ in.) slices baguette

1 Tb. good virgin olive oil
1 Tb. chives

1 The piece of steak should be completely cleaned of any sinews, fat, nerves, etc. Cut the steak into thin slices about ¾ to 1 oz. each. The pieces can be cut in different directions, either with the grain or against it; the New York strip is a tender piece of meat and it doesn't matter how it is cut. Wet a meat pounder and cutting board slightly (to keep the meat from tearing), and pound the slices of meat until they are about ⅛ in. thick and 3 to 4 in. across. Arrange on a plate.

2 Using a conventional cheese grater, grate the truffle.

3 Sprinkle the pieces of the meat with the ¾ tsp. salt and ½ tsp. freshly ground black pepper. Sprinkle each piece with about 1 tsp. of grated truffle, and ½ tsp. each of Parmesan cheese and good virgin olive oil. Fold in the long sides of each piece of meat to create straight sides, and roll up the long way into tubes.

4 **For the croutons:** Oil a cookie sheet with the 1 Tb. olive oil. Lay the 12 slices of baguette on top, press them into the oil, then turn them over. Place in a preheated 400-degree oven for about 8 minutes, until nicely browned. Arrange the carpaccio tubes on a tray, sprinkle with a little (1 Tb.) olive oil and the 1 Tb. chives, surround with the croutons, and serve.

RISOTTO WITH WHITE TRUFFLES

Yield: 4 servings
3 to 4 c. chicken stock
3 Tb. butter
4 Tb. chopped onion
1 c. rice, preferably Arborio rice from the Piedmont
TO FINISH
½ tsp. salt
¼ tsp. freshly ground black pepper
1 Tb. butter
⅓ c. freshly grated Parmesan cheese
2 medium white truffles (about 4 oz.)
½ c. demi-glace (reduced brown stock) or leftover juices from roasted veal or beef

1 Bring the 3 to 4 c. stock to a boil in a saucepan and set aside. Melt the 3 Tb. butter and add the 4 Tb. chopped onion. Cook for about 1 minute, until the onion becomes transparent, and then stir in the 1 c. rice.

Note: 1 c. of roundish kernels of rice will serve about four people as a first course with ½ truffle per person, or 2 medium truffles (about 4 oz.) total.

2 Cook the rice dry with the onion for about 3 to 4 minutes and add 1 c. of the stock and stir it in well. Bring to a boil, cover, and cook for about 2 minutes. The stock should be practically absorbed. Add 1 c. more of the stock, stir, cover, and cook again for approximately 3 to 4 minutes. The stock will be completely

absorbed at this point. Add an additional ½ c. of stock and cook the rice, uncovered, stirring occasionally, until that addition of stock is absorbed. Then, add ½ c. more stock and cook until it is absorbed.

3 Keep adding the stock one tablespoon at a time, stirring often, until the stock is absorbed and the rice is just tender. The rice will cook for a total of 22 to 25 minutes and the object is to have the rice creamy but not mushy. It should be slightly *al dente,* or firm to the bite, in the center.

4 **To finish the rice,** season with the salt and pepper, stir in the 1 Tb. butter and ⅓ c. grated Parmesan cheese, and mix just enough to incorporate. →

5 Arrange the rice on four different plates. Using a vegetable peeler or truffle slicer, slice half of each truffle into thin shavings onto a serving of rice. It should cover the rice completely on top.

6 Use a good demi-glace (reduced brown stock) or well-seasoned, leftover juices from a roast of veal or beef. Place about 1 to 2 Tb. of the juice around the rice. Serve immediately.

BLACK TRUFFLE SALAD

Yield: 6 servings

3 c. loose field salad or <u>mâche</u>, washed and dried
3 c. loose Bibb lettuce, washed and dried
2 c. thin slices from a small zucchini
Sprinkle of salt
3 medium black truffles (about 5 oz.)

DRESSING

1 Tb. walnut oil
2 Tb. peanut oil
1 tsp. wine vinegar
½ tsp. salt
¼ tsp. freshly ground black pepper
1 c. julienne of mushrooms

Extra peanut oil for the top of the salad
Additional freshly ground black pepper

1 Wash and dry the 3 c. field salad, keeping it whole, if possible (see Salad Tulipe, step 2, page 89). Wash and dry the 3 c. Bibb lettuce, making sure not to squeeze and bruise it. Be certain the greens are well-dried either by using a salad spinner or by placing between paper towels to absorb any moisture that might dilute the dressing.

  Arrange the 2 c. sliced zucchini on a baking sheet, sprinkle lightly with salt, and place in a preheated 400-degree oven for 3 to 4 minutes, until slightly softened and wilted.

  Clean and peel the truffles; the skin can be chopped or placed in alcohol for use in sauces. Slice the truffles thin with a vegetable peeler or truffle slicer.

  Combine the oils (1 Tb. walnut and 2 Tb. peanut), 1 tsp. vinegar, ½ tsp. salt, and ¼ tsp. pepper to make the dressing.

2 Just before serving, toss the greens and 1 c. julienne of mushrooms in the dressing and arrange on 6 plates. Arrange a layer of zucchini around the salad and the sliced truffles on top.

3 Sprinkle or brush the truffles lightly with the extra peanut oil and sprinkle with freshly ground pepper. Serve right away.

4 Variation for a more casual serving: Toss the greens and zucchini together, arrange on a plate, and place the sliced truffles at random on top of the salad. Serve immediately.

WHITE TRUFFLE BRIOCHE TOAST

1 brioche, baked in a coffee can (see Black Truffles in Brioche with Truffle Sauce, following recipe), or homemade-type bread

FOR EACH SERVING

2 tsp. freshly grated Parmesan cheese
Dash freshly ground black pepper
2 tsp. first-quality virgin olive oil
About 10 slices white truffle (*Tuber magnatum*)

1 Make a brioche in an empty coffee can according to the recipe for Black Truffles in Brioche with Truffle Sauce, or Brioche Mousseline, page 136. Remove the brioche from the can to cool. When the loaf has cooled to lukewarm, cut into slices approximately ¾ in. thick.

2 For each serving, arrange a slice of brioche on each plate, sprinkle with 1 tsp. Parmesan cheese, some freshly ground black pepper, and 1 tsp. of the olive oil. With a vegetable peeler, shave the white truffle on top. Sprinkle the remaining oil and Parmesan cheese on top and serve immediately.

BLACK TRUFFLES IN BRIOCHE WITH TRUFFLE SAUCE

Yield: 6 servings

BRIOCHE

1 envelope active dry yeast (¼ oz.)
2 Tb. milk (at about 100 degrees)
½ tsp. sugar
1½ c. all-purpose flour
½ c. cake flour
¼ tsp. salt
3 eggs
1¼ sticks butter (5 oz.), softened

TRUFFLE FORCEMEAT

6 oz. tenderloin of pork
1 large black *melanosporum* truffle (about 6 oz.)
¼ tsp. salt
¼ tsp. freshly ground black pepper
1 Tb. cognac
1 Tb. butter
1 Tb. chopped shallot
2 Tb. demi-glace (reduced brown stock)

Egg wash made with 1 egg with half the white removed, beaten

TRUFFLE SAUCE

1 Tb. butter
1½ Tb. chopped carrots
1½ Tb. chopped onion
¼ c. Madeira wine
¾ c. demi-glace (reduced brown stock)
Salt and freshly ground black pepper to taste
¼ c. chopped truffle peelings (from above)

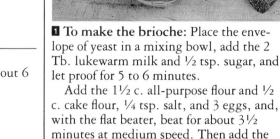

1 To make the brioche: Place the envelope of yeast in a mixing bowl, add the 2 Tb. lukewarm milk and ½ tsp. sugar, and let proof for 5 to 6 minutes.

Add the 1½ c. all-purpose flour and ½ c. cake flour, ¼ tsp. salt, and 3 eggs, and, with the flat beater, beat for about 3½ minutes at medium speed. Then add the 1¼ sticks soft butter and stir on low speed (1 or 2) for about 30 to 40 seconds, just long enough to incorporate most of the butter. Set aside and let rise for 1½ hours in a warm place – 70 to 75 degrees. Break the mixture gently by hand, stirring again so the butter is well-incorporated. At this point, the brioche can be placed in a plastic bag and refrigerated for a few hours or overnight.

To make the forcemeat: Grind the 6 oz. of pork or chop with a knife until fairly fine, and place in a bowl.

Clean the truffle by brushing under lukewarm water. Peel, reserving the peeling for the sauce, and cut the truffle into 4 pieces. Then, with a vegetable peeler, cut the pieces into thin slices directly into the pork. Add the ¼ tsp. each salt and pepper and 1 Tb. cognac.

Heat the 1 Tb. butter and, when hot, add 1 Tb. chopped shallots. Sauté for about 20 seconds and add to the truffle-pork mixture, stirring to incorporate well.

Place the truffle peelings in a mini-chop and process until finely chopped, or chop by hand. Set aside. →

2 Add 2 Tb. of demi-glace (reduced brown stock) to the pork-truffle filling.

3 Butter a cookie sheet and evenly space 6 mounds of brioche dough (about 3 to 4 oz. each) on it. Spread each into a circle about 4 to 5 in. in diameter, and place equal amounts of the pork-truffle mixture, mounding it up, in the center of each circle.

4 Bring the brioche dough back on top of the forcemeat and turn the whole package upside down; it will be sticky. Surround each brioche with a folded strip of buttered aluminum foil to support the sides, folding the aluminum foil at the ends to secure it. Brush the tops with the egg wash, and set aside to rise at room temperature for 30 to 40 minutes.

5 Bake in a preheated 375-degree oven for about 30 minutes. Remove the foil strips.

6 **To make the truffle sauce:** In a saucepan, melt the 1 Tb. butter and add the 1½ Tb. each chopped carrots and onion. Sauté for 1½ to 2 minutes until softened, and add the ¼ c. wine. Cook to reduce until there is only about 1 Tb. of liquid remaining. Add the ¾ c. demi-glace and salt and pepper to taste. Bring to a boil, add the chopped truffle peelings, and return to the boil. Remove from the heat immediately and set aside so the truffles steep in the stock. At serving time, arrange about 2 to 3 Tb. of the sauce on each serving plate and place a truffled brioche on top. Serve immediately. The brioche has been cut open to show the inside.

CAVIAR

Caviar is usually produced from cured sturgeon eggs but increasingly today we find caviar made from salmon and whitefish, as well as lumpfish. Less well known is caviar from trout eggs and gray mullet, and then there is the famous boutargue of Provence.

The largest sturgeon, beluga (not to be confused with the white beluga whale), can measure 16 ft. or more and weigh over 2,000 lb. That means an enormous amount of caviar when you realize the eggs represent approximately 15 to 18 percent of the weight of the sturgeon. And sturgeon has been known to live over 100 years. The Caspian Sea and the Black Sea in Russia have the greatest concentration of sturgeon in the world, but Americans are now producing some caviar from Pacific Northwest sturgeon and from the more plentiful spatula or shovelnose sturgeon from the Mississippi Valley.

The four sturgeon caviars are beluga, which has the largest eggs and is extracted from the largest sturgeon; it is dark to light gray in color and, although the taste is the same, the lighter the color, the higher the price. Osetra (spelled in a variety of ways) has a firm grain, is usually brown or slightly golden; it has a stronger, more assertive flavor than beluga and costs 40 percent less. Sevruga, with the smallest grain and produced from the smallest sturgeon, tends to be softer than beluga and osetra, though many specialists find it the best tasting. It runs about half the price of beluga. Finally, there is pressed caviar, made from sturgeon eggs that are a little overripe and thus tend to break; it has a good, concentrated taste and is a bargain for the caviar lover.

American sturgeon caviar is much like sevruga in size and taste. Salmon caviar is excellent, the best being from the chum or dog salmon; often called "natural" caviar, it has a pale, slightly reddish color, whereas the eggs from coho salmon are a deeper red and are slightly smaller and firmer.

Lumpfish caviar, the most common and lowest grade of caviar, comes from Iceland, Norway, or Denmark and is usually black, red, or golden. Golden caviar from whitefish comes from the Great Lakes and has tiny but tender, flavorful eggs that separate well. It is a good caviar for the price and is becoming more readily available. Although most caviar authorities don't recommend it, I have managed to freeze fresh caviar and have found it as good or better than commercial pasteurized caviar, which is usually mushy and oversalted.

Caviar is best served plain with buckwheat pancakes called blinis, butter, and frozen vodka. Many specialists recommend that a spoon made of something other than metal (mother-of-pearl or crystal) be used to scoop up the caviar. Personally, I have never noticed any difference in taste between caviar eaten with a metal spoon as opposed to a spoon made of mother-of-pearl.

In the recipes here, I have served black caviar in puff paste and on buttered Danish pumpernickel bread. Red caviar or golden whitefish caviar is served in lukewarm, boiled small red potatoes with sour cream, which is a delicious treat. Finally, there is the classic serving of caviar with blinis and frozen vodka.

Caviar with Blinis and Frozen Vodka

Clockwise, from top left: Caviar Canapés, Red or Golden Caviar Potatoes, and Caviar Puffs.

FOUR CAVIAR RECIPES

IDENTIFYING CAVIAR

1 Identifying caviar: The most common types of caviar available. In the top row, from left to right: natural salmon (from the chum), red salmon (from the coho), and whitefish caviar. In the bottom row, from left to right: beluga, osetra, sevruga, and pressed caviar. Notice that the black sturgeon caviar is identified by the color on the lid of the can; blue for beluga, yellow for osetra, green for sevruga, and red/purple for pressed caviar.

2 The best-quality caviars: from left to right, beluga, osetra, and sevruga. Notice the size and color of the beluga and that the osetra is slightly golden/greenish with a very separated grain. The sevruga grains are smaller and a bit lighter in color.

3 The same three caviars displayed on spoons: from left to right, beluga, osetra, and sevruga. Sometimes the color will change from one fish to another, getting lighter or darker depending on the maturity of the eggs, the time of the year it is fished, the length of time it has been kept, the amount of salt in the brine, how long it has been stirred, and so on.

4 The three other types of caviar: from left to right, the red coho, the whitefish, and the natural, from the chum.

5 Served on a plate with mother-of-pearl spoons: from left to right, the red coho, the whitefish, and the natural. Notice that the grains should be whole, soft, and sticking together but not broken.

CAVIAR PUFF

Yield: 24 servings
6 oz. Puff Paste (page 144)
Egg wash made with 1 egg with half the white removed, beaten
3 Tb. butter, softened
8 Tb. black caviar
Sieved yolk of 1 hard-cooked egg

1 Caviar is often served on pieces of toast or pastry shells, which complement its taste. Roll the puff paste into a rectangle about 14 in. long by 6 in. wide, and cut, lengthwise, into 2 strips. Beat the egg wash (1 egg with half the white removed) and brush the pastry with it. Place in the refrigerator or freezer for a few minutes to harden the dough, then cut out pastry ovals with a cutter about 3½ in. long by 1½ in. wide. Arrange on a cookie sheet and bake in a preheated 400-degree oven for 15 to 20 minutes, until nicely browned.

2 After the ovals have cooled a little, use a knife to cut a hole out of the center to create receptacles. Make a paper cone (see "Swimming Swans," page 234, steps 2–6) and fill it with the 3 Tb. soft butter. Pipe a little ring of butter into each pastry receptacle and top with 1 tsp. of caviar. Sprinkle the sieved yolk onto a plate and arrange the caviar puffs on top.

CAVIAR CANAPES

Yield: 12 servings
3 Tb. butter, softened
3 slices hard whole wheat Danish bread
4 Tb. caviar
Dash paprika
Sieved white of 1 hard-cooked egg

1 Spread about 1½ Tb. of the soft butter on the 3 slices of bread and spread the 4 Tb. caviar on top. Cut each bread slice into fourths. Place the remainder of the soft butter in a paper cone (see "Swimming Swans," steps 2–6, page 234), and instead of cutting the cornet straight across at the tip, cut it on the bias on both sides so the tip of the cornet is cut into a **V** shape.

2 In the center of each canape, squeeze out the butter from the cornet. You will notice that the butter will emerge from the cornet in a little leaf shape because of the way the cornet is cut at the tip. Pull up on the cornet to make a tail on each leaf. Make 2 or 3 additional leaves on each canapé and dot the center with a dash of paprika. Arrange the sieved egg white on a serving plate and top with the caviar canapés.

RED OR GOLDEN CAVIAR POTATOES

Yield: 12 servings
1 lb. small red-skinned potatoes (about 12)
4 Tb. sour cream
½ tsp. freshly ground black pepper
12 Tb. red or golden caviar
12 small endive leaves

1 Cover the 1 lb. potatoes with cold water in a saucepan and bring to a boil. Boil gently until tender (about 18 to 20 minutes), then drain the potatoes. Cut a "cap" off each potato, then, using a small melon baller, scoop out a ball of potato flesh from each.

2 Put 1 tsp. of sour cream in each hollowed-out potato, sprinkle with freshly ground black pepper, and top each with 1 Tb. of either the red or golden caviar. Wedge a piece of endive into each potato alongside the mound of caviar (you can do this either before or after you add the caviar), and arrange on a plate. Serve while the potatoes are still slightly warm.

CAVIAR WITH BLINIS AND FROZEN VODKA

Yield: about 24 blinis
1 bottle vodka
FOR THE BLINIS
1½ tsp. active dry yeast
¾ c. lukewarm milk (at about 100 degrees)
½ tsp. sugar
⅓ c. buckwheat flour
¾ c. all-purpose flour
3 eggs
3 Tb. melted butter
⅓ c. sour cream
½ tsp. salt
Peanut or corn oil

Soft butter to fill a small ramekin (about ¾ stick or 3 oz.)
One 14-oz. can beluga caviar
Parsley leaves for decoration

1 The classic accompaniment to caviar and blinis is frozen vodka.

To freeze the vodka: Place the vodka bottle in a tall, narrow plastic container and fill the container up to the neck of the bottle with cold water. Place in the freezer overnight. Sometimes the plastic may crack as the water freezes and expands. When ready to serve, run the container under water to release the block of ice containing the bottle, and unmold.

2 With a screwdriver or sturdy knife, carve the square upper edge of the ice to make it look more like a natural block of ice. After about 1 to 2 hours, as the ice melts a little, it will be smooth and more transparent.

3 **For the blinis:** Combine the 1½ tsp. yeast with the ¾ c. lukewarm milk and ½ tsp. sugar, and proof for 4 to 5 minutes. Add the ⅓ c. buckwheat and ¾ c. all-purpose flour, 3 eggs, and 3 Tb. melted butter.

4 Mix thoroughly with a whisk until smooth, then stir in the ⅓ c. sour cream and ½ tsp. salt and mix well again.

5 Cover the dough and let rise in a warm place (about 70 to 75 degrees) for about 1 hour. At this point, the dough will bubble up and emit a strong, delightful smell of yeast.

8 Arrange the blinis in a flowerlike design in a bowl and place on a starched cloth napkin centered on a dinner plate. Set the vodka and butter alongside. Scoop the beluga caviar gently from the can and into a special serving dish set in ice, and serve.

6 To cook the blinis, heat about 1 Tb. of peanut or corn oil in a large, heavy skillet, preferably nonstick. When hot, pour about 2 Tb. of batter into the skillet for each pancake. Cook over high heat for about 45 seconds to 1 minute on one side (until the top is bubbling), turn, and cook for about 15 to 20 seconds on the other side. Stack the finished pancakes on a plate and continue making more until all the batter is used up.

7 To serve the blinis with the caviar, fill a small crock or container with butter and smooth the top. Using the tines of a fork, draw a design on the surface of the butter and decorate with a few parsley leaves.

FROMAGE BLANC JEAN-VICTOR WITH ROASTED GARLIC

It is good to make fromage blanc a few days ahead so the taste develops and the cheese gets firmer. This recipe makes 2 cheeses that serve about 6 to 8 persons each. If you want to make the traditional coeur à la crème, combine the two batches of cheese, flavor with a dash of sugar, and serve with the double-cream sauce and a garnish of strawberries, raspberries, or any other variety of summer berries. Instead, I have prepared the version my father, Victor, used to make that includes garlic, herbs, salt, and pepper.

Roasted garlic is mild and flavorful and easy to eat when served with tiny demitasse spoons so the cooked cloves can be spooned out and spread on croutons to be eaten with the cheese. Roasted garlic can also be served with game (quail, pheasant, or partridge). Young, fresh garlic, unfortunately only available at certain times of the year, is best

for roasting as it develops a very nutty flavor. Older garlic that is softer and darker tends to get bitter.

The long croutons, made from small French bread loaves or baguettes, are prepared by using a minimal amount of oil and by roasting in the oven, rather than under the broiler. This makes for a very crisp, flavorful crouton containing little fat.

The coral tree, made of scallions and carrot "flowers," looks striking on any buffet table. It goes well with the fromage blanc because the scallions are eaten together with the cheese, garlic, and croutons.

Yield: 2 cheeses, each serving 6–8

1 For the fromage blanc: Using a food mill fitted with the fine screen (rather than a food processor, which will tend to liquefy the cheese too much), strain the 8 oz. each cream cheese, cottage cheese, and ricotta cheese into a bowl.

2 Add the 1 tsp. puréed garlic, ⅓ c. chopped herbs, 1 tsp. each black pepper and salt to the cheeses, and fold in gently with a spatula. Whip the 1½ c. cream until stiff and fold it into the cheese mixture.

3 Cut two 12 × 12-in. squares of single-layer cheesecloth and use them to line two bowls. Scoop half the cheese mixture into each bowl.

4 Bring the corners of the cheesecloth together and tie to make round balls of cheese. Thread a wooden dowel through the knotted corners of the cheesecloth and hang the cheese, refrigerated overnight (or for a few days), over a pot to drain and develop more flavor. If this amount does not fit in your refrigerator, make the cheese in smaller amounts. Or hang it in a cold cellar – 50 degrees or less.

5 **For the crouton sticks:** Cut 3 to 4 small, long, narrow French loaves or baguettes (approximately 6 in. long) into wedges about 1 to 1½ in. thick and spread the 3 Tb. oil on a jelly roll pan. Press the bread wedges onto the pan and turn them over so they are lightly oiled on both sides. Bake in a preheated 400-degree oven for 8 to 10 minutes, until nicely browned all around.

6 **For the roasted garlic:** Remove the excess skin from the outside of the 6 to 8 garlic heads and discard any of the cloves that are damaged. Place the heads in a saucepan with enough water to cover them. Cover with a lid and simmer gently for 10 minutes. Drain and cool the heads.

7 When ready to sauté the garlic, cut off about one-third of the top of the garlic head on the stem side. (The flesh from the top pieces you have cut off can be removed and used in salads or soups.) Sprinkle the head on the cut side with a dash of salt.

8 Heat the 2 Tb. butter and 1 Tb. oil in a saucepan. When hot, place the head of garlic, cut-side down, in the saucepan and cook over low heat, covered (so the garlic develops moisture and doesn't dry out), for approximately 10 minutes. The garlic heads should be nicely browned. Turn the heads over and cook, covered, another 5 to 8 minutes longer, until the garlic is soft and tender throughout.

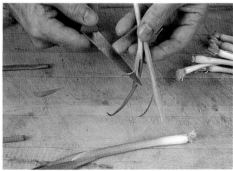

9 **To make the coral trees:** Try to select scallions that have several "branches" or tubes coming out of the stem. Peel the 12 scallions and cut the tops at different heights. With the point of a knife, split the ends of the leaves on each stem to create an open flower effect.

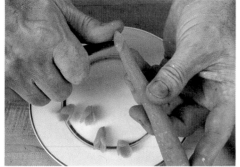

10 To make the carrot flowers: Peel one of the carrots and then sharpen it on the thin end to a point. With a knife or vegetable peeler, cut above the tapered point on four sides to make four flat surfaces around the carrot. With the point of a knife, cut a "petal" out of each flat side, keeping the base of the "flower" still attached to the carrot.

11 Twist the base of the "flower" to make it break free from the carrot. The leftover carrot still has a pointed end with four flat sides on it. Repeat the same technique to make another "flower" and release it in the same way. Repeat until you have as many carrot flowers as you desire (18 to 24 for my recipe). Place the prepared scallions and the "flowers" in cold water or ice water. This will firm up the carrots and make the ends of the scallions curl.

12 To make the vase: Cut off the top third of an acorn squash and spoon out the seeds. At the junction of each section of the squash, cut a little wedge to create a scalloped edge.

13 Press the bulb end of the scallions in a metal florist's frog and place the frog inside the hollowed-out squash. Reserve 1 carrot "flower" for a garnish and insert wooden toothpicks into the base of each remaining "flower" to create a stem.

14 Insert the wooden stems into the open ends of the scallions.

15 Keep filling up the fringed scallion ends to create a beautiful bouquet of coral flowers.

16 To make the double-cream sauce: Whip the 1 c. heavy cream until it just begins to firm up and combine with the 1 c. sour cream and ¼ tsp. each salt and pepper. (This mixture simulates the French "double cream." If you feel it is a little too thick, dilute it by adding 1 or 2 Tb. of water.)

To serve the fromage blanc: Place some of the sauce on a serving dish or pan. (If you serve the sauce on something made of metal – I have used a heart-shaped copper pan – assemble the dish at the last moment as the sauce may pick up a metallic taste and discolor after a while. Invert the cheese into the sauce and carefully remove the cheesecloth.

17 Arrange some of the garlic heads in the sauce surrounding the cheese and garnish the dish with parsley leaves. Decorate the cheese with the reserved carrot "flower" and parsley leaves, and serve with the croutons and the coral bouquet alongside.

18 As a serving variation, if the cheese is to remain longer on a buffet, place the cheese with the sauce in a round ovenware dish and serve the garlic on a separate plate with the croutons on the side.

PLUMS AND CHERRIES IN MOUNTAIN BREW, CHERRIES IN VINEGAR, AND CORNICHONS (SOUR FRENCH GHERKINS) IN VINEGAR

Every year we put up a few preserves at our house, especially during the cherry and plum season. We also grow our own cornichons, the small pickling cucumbers, picking them each morning when they are still very small, and then preparing them in the French style in vinegar with tarragon, pearl onions, and peppercorns.

For the cherries and plums in mountain brew, it is best to use a grain or fruit alcohol, which is almost pure (190 proof), and dilute it with water. The juice of the fruit itself dilutes it further, and, for this reason, the 190-proof alcohol is diluted by one-third, making it about 120-proof. Also, by the time the fruit is macerated in it, the alcohol goes down to regular strength (about 85 proof, depending on the juice in the fruit).

In states where grain alcohol is not sold because of state laws, plain vodka can be substituted and will produce a very satisfactory result, although it will not be quite as strong as the grain alcohol mixture. Prunes can be done in the same manner as the plums and cherries, covering them first with hot water to make them rehydrate a bit

and using the water to dilute the alcohol.

In the plum recipe, I have chosen some firm, juicy, sweet small golden plums called Reine-Claude and red Santa Rosa plums of the same size. For the cherries in vinegar, use firm Bing or other type sweet cherries. The cornichons should, of course, be tiny.

The plums will be ready to consume in about two months, the cherries in about four to five weeks, and the cornichons, although best if eaten between two weeks and seven to eight months after preserving, will keep in the vinegar for as long as two years. The sweet cherries in vinegar are an excellent substitute for the cornichons and their sour taste makes them delicious with pâtés or cold cuts. In France, it is customary to serve fruit in alcohol with some of the juice in a brandy snifter as an after-dinner drink.

Yield: 1 qt. of each

PLUMS IN MOUNTAIN BREW

1¼ lb. medium to small firm, sweet white Reine-Claude or red Santa Rosa plums, or a mixture of both (about 18 to 24 pieces of fruit)
¾ c. corn syrup
¼ c. boiled and cooled water
1 c. 190-proof grain or fruit alcohol, or, if not available, highest proof vodka

CHERRIES IN MOUNTAIN BREW

About 1¼ to 1½ lb. sweet cherries, with stems
½ c. boiled and cooled water
1 c. grain alcohol (see above)
7 Tb. sugar

CHERRIES IN VINEGAR

1¼ to 1½ lb. sweet red cherries, with stems
4 Tb. sugar
1 c. distilled white vinegar (4 to 5 percent acid strength)
½ c. water
⅛ tsp. cayenne pepper

CORNICHONS IN VINEGAR

1 lb. tiny gherkins or pickling cucumbers (about 60 to 70)
2 Tb. kosher-type salt
2 or 3 tarragon sprigs
½ c. tiny pearl onions, peeled
1½ tsp. black peppercorns
1 small hot pepper, if hotness is desired
About 1½ c. distilled vinegar (4 to 5 percent acid strength)

1 **For the Plums in Mountain Brew:** The plums will be more flavorful if pricked all over with a sewing needle. Combine the ¾ c. corn syrup, ¼ c. boiled and cooled water, and 1 c. alcohol in a bowl. Place the plums in a 1-qt. mason jar, tapping the jar on the bottom with the palm of your hand to make the plums fit more tightly in the jar. Add the alcohol mixture to the plums. The liquid should just about cover the plums. Cover tightly with a lid and set aside in a cool place, such as the cellar, for at least two months.

Note: If a grain alcohol is not available, replace it and the boiled and cooled water with about 1½ c. of vodka.

2 **For the Cherries in Mountain Brew:** Trim the stems of the cherries, leaving about ½ in. of stem on each so that the cherries stay firm. There is no need to prick or cook the cherries. Make sure the cherries are dry and place them in a 1-qt. mason jar, filling the jar.

Mix together the ½ c. boiled and cooled water, 1 c. grain alcohol, and 7 Tb. sugar until the sugar is dissolved, and pour the mixture over the cherries in the jar. Cover tightly with a lid and set aside in a cool place for at least 4 to 5 weeks. If grain alcohol is not available, combine the sugar with 1½ c. of vodka with the highest alcohol content available.

For the Cherries in Vinegar: Trim the cherry stems as explained above and place the cherries in a 1-qt. mason jar, tapping

the jar on the bottom to make the cherries fit snugly.

In a bowl, mix together the 4 Tb. sugar, 1 c. distilled white vinegar, ½ c. water, and ⅛ tsp. cayenne pepper. Pour the pickling solution over the cherries, barely covering them. Cover the jar tightly with a lid, and set aside in a cool place for at least 4 to 5 weeks.

3 **For the Cornichons:** If you grow your own cornichons, as we do, pick a few every day, toss them in some salt, and set aside for a few hours or overnight. Then place them in some vinegar, adding a few pickles every day, as they grow, until the jar is filled. The gherkins should be no more than 1½ to 2 in. long and still have the small flowers attached.

Drain and rub the cornichons with a damp paper or other type towel to rub off the prickles or bumps and flowers.

4 Toss and roll the cornichons in the 2 Tb. salt and set them aside for at least 3 hours, but preferably overnight, to cure.

5 Dry each cornichon individually with a paper towel and arrange them in a jar, interspersing them with 2 or 3 tarragon sprigs, ½ c. pearl onions, and 1½ tsp. peppercorns. The small hot pepper is optional.

6 Tap the bottom of the jar with the palm of your hand to move the cornichons and make them fit more tightly, and then fill the jar with 1½ c. vinegar. Cover tightly with a lid. Set aside the sealed jar in a cool place for at least 2 weeks before consuming.

7 The preserves, ready to be stored, from left to right: the Cherries in Mountain Brew, the Cornichons, the red and white Plums in Mountain Brew, and the Cherries in Vinegar.

- COUNTRY FRENCH BREAD AND BAGUETTES
- EPI AND CROWN BREAD WITH
     WHOLE-GRAIN DOUGH
- BLACK PEPPER BREAD WITH WALNUTS
- WHOLE WHEAT BREAD WITH RAISINS
- BREAKFAST ROLLS
- CRANBERRY BREAD
- VEGETABLE BREAD
- CHEESE BREAD
- CROISSANTS AND PAIN AU CHOCOLAT
- BRIOCHE MOUSSELINE

BREADS

Very simple recipes are often deceptive because they are the hardest to make well. From wine, which is fermented grape juice, to cheese (curdled milk), to French bread, made of water, flour, and yeast, mastering these simple, basic techniques entails many years of practice, the proper equipment, and the right conditions to achieve perfection.

When making bread, the professional baker, in addition to his years of knowledge, needs not only the right ingredients and equipment but also temperature and humidity controls; brick-lined ovens are helpful because they give enormous amounts of heat as well as "forced" steam to produce the texture and crust of real French bread. It is important to use a bread flour that is high in gluten. The gluten is the protein part of the flour that gives the elasticity necessary for the bread to develop. A good bread flour has as much as 15 to 16 percent protein.

The thick crust on French bread is usually caused by "forced" steam. The dough is always made with water – milk would produce a softer crust. If a bread collapses, it is likely that it was not kneaded enough, that there was too much water in the dough, or that it rose too quickly. A small amount of yeast and a long rising time result in larger air pockets in the bread and give the finished loaf a "nutty" taste. Some bakers add vitamin C in the form of ascorbic acid to the dough to make the air bubbles hold better and to have stronger dough.

Temperature and humidity are extremely important, and the rising of the dough will vary according to the time of the year and the weather conditions. Sugar, as well as warm temperatures, helps the yeast develop faster. If the bread is made with cold water or the temperature is cold, the bread will rise slowly; if the temperature drops too low, the yeast won't continue to develop.

It is important that the dough be left to rise in an area that is not only fairly warm but also draft-free and moist so that it develops well. A professional proof box is very humid, and I simulate the same conditions by wrapping a cardboard box in a plastic bag (see page 120, step 13). The surface of the dough should remain slightly sticky and wet as it develops. If it becomes too dry on top, a crust forms and the dough doesn't develop properly.

Fresh bakers' yeast, which comes in 0.6-oz. packages, can be used as well as dry yeast, which comes in ¼-oz. (7-g) packages. The fresh and the dry yeast can be used interchangeably.

A dough starter, a <u>levain</u>, can be added to the dough, as shown in the basic French dough, to start the fermentation and give the dough a slightly "nutty," sour taste. It is usually supplemented with yeast. The starter is made by reserving a piece of risen dough and keeping it in a jar filled with water. Refrigerated, it will keep for 7 to 10 days.

To measure the flour in the following recipe, always use a dry measuring cup to scoop the flour directly from the bag, and then level it by hand. This produces a fairly tightly packed cup, and 3 c. of flour will amount to 1 lb. The moisture in flour varies from season to season. Humidity will be absorbed by flour in summer and so the amount of water should be decreased accordingly. It's just the opposite in winter, so then a little more water is sometimes required.

There is something very rewarding about making bread. It is physical, basic work that is comforting and satisfying to most people. Moreover, nothing equals the smell of fresh bread baking in the oven – a yeasty, sweet, filling smell that is almost as satisfying as the taste that follows.

My big, beautiful Country French Bread with cracklings (which can be eliminated or bits of cooked bacon substituted) and the baguettes are made from the same basic French bread dough. For a different look and taste, I have a Black Pepper Bread with Walnuts, which freezes very well and is delicious cut very thin and served, buttered, with oysters or smoked salmon. The <u>Epi</u> and Crown Bread with Whole-Grain Dough is very chewy, wholesome, and, although it toughens a bit the day after it's baked, sliced thin it makes excellent toast. The Whole Wheat Bread with Raisins is sophisticated, freezes well, and is excellent cut into thin slices for sandwiches or breakfast; it is at its best with a sweet Gorgonzola. The Breakfast Rolls, made with milk, are a bit softer and milder than the baguettes and are excellent plain with butter and jam or toasted for breakfast. The Cheese Bread is similar to a light brioche and has, in addition to cheese, diced pears. It is delicious served with fruit, nuts, and cheese.

The recipe for Country French Bread and Baguettes as well as the recipe for <u>Epi</u> and Crown Bread with Whole-Grain Dough is made with a starter. If you have not put away some dough as a starter, make a starter 4 to 5 days ahead by mixing together ¾ c. flour, ½ tsp. yeast, and a dash of sugar and water. Knead, let rise, deflate, and refrigerate in water. If no starter is available, use the same ingredients indicated in the recipes, but increase the yeast by ½ envelope (2½ envelopes instead of 2) and the water by 1½ c. and follow the same recipe.

2 This starter consists of 6 oz. of dough left over from the last time I made French bread and 1½ c. of water. It has been in the refrigerator for 1 week. The water has a slight sour taste, and the dough is very spongy and airy with a sour smell. After the yeast has proofed for 10 minutes, add the starter with its liquid, 7 c. of the flour, and the 1 Tb. salt.

COUNTRY FRENCH BREAD AND BAGUETTES

This beautiful, showy, large country bread can be made, as I have done in this recipe, with the skin of one chicken, cooked in the oven into cracklings, or with small pieces of cooked bacon, or you can bake it plain. The decoration on top makes the loaf attractive; pieces of dough (kept in the refrigerator) are placed on top of the loaf just before the loaf goes into the oven.

A baguette is the traditional long loaf of French bread. In the recipe here, the top is slashed diagonally on one baguette, another has crosses cut into the top, and the third just a line cut down the center. Two baguettes are sprinkled with flour and one with cornmeal. A crunchy, fresh baguette is ideal with any meal, from breakfast to dinner.

Yield: 1 large loaf and 3 baguettes

DOUGH

2¼ c. warm water (95 to 100 degrees)
2 envelopes active dry yeast
1 tsp. sugar
Starter: 6-oz. piece of dough kneaded, risen, and stored with 1½ c. water*
10 c. bread flour (3¼ lb.)
1 Tb. salt

4 Tb. cornmeal
Extra flour for the tops
CRACKLING
Skin from one chicken
⅛ tsp. salt

1 Combine the 2¼ c. water (approximately 95 degrees) with the 2 envelopes of yeast and 1 tsp. sugar, stirring gently just enough to mix, and set aside to proof for 10 minutes.

3 Using the dough hook attachment on the mixer, mix the dough on speed 3 (medium) for about 5 minutes. At this point, the dough will be very elastic but still soft. All the flour is not added at the beginning because the mixer is not strong enough to work a very stiff dough and could become damaged. The 7 c. of flour produce a soft dough, well-kneaded by the machine and with its gluten well-developed.

Note: Although any of these breads can be kneaded by hand, an electric mixer will make your life easier. But you must use a heavy-duty mixer with a dough hook. I use a KitchenAid but any comparable appliance will do the job. You will have to adjust your model to the different speeds I recommend for my mixer. It starts off with "stir," then runs from 1 to 10 speeds, which can be translated as slow, medium, and fast.

*If starter is not available, increase the yeast to 2½ envelopes and the water to 3½ c.

4 With the machine on speed 1, add about 1½ c. flour and mix gently, just enough (approximately 1 minute) to incorporate the flour into the dough. Turn the dough out onto a board with the remaining flour and knead for 5 minutes.

5 Press your hands into the dough, pushing forward, then fold the dough on itself. Press, push, and fold the dough on itself, rotating it each time. Repeat again and again.

6 After about 5 to 8 minutes of kneading, the dough will have absorbed as much flour as it can. All of the flour may be used or some may be left, depending on the humidity. The dough should be very smooth but strong, and it should resist your fingers, when you press them into it, and bounce back.

7 Place the dough in a plastic bowl or other container with a cover (or use plastic wrap), and let rise, covered, in a warm place (70 to 75 degrees) for 2 to 2½ hours.

8 Spread the chicken skin on a cookie sheet and sprinkle it with the ⅛ tsp. salt. Place in a preheated 400-degree oven for 20 minutes, until well-baked and crisp.

9 When risen, the dough should have doubled in volume. Bring the sides of the dough to the center and knead it again in the bowl to deflate it and make it into a ball.

10 To make a starter for future use, cut a piece (approximately 5 to 6 oz.) from the dough and put it in a plastic container with 1½ c. water. Cover and place in the refrigerator. Set aside another 2-oz. piece of dough, covered, in the refrigerator to decorate the loaf after the final rising.

11 Divide the dough: Cut 3 pieces, approximately 12 oz. each, for the baguettes and set aside, covered. With your hands, extend the remaining dough (about 2 to 2¼ lb.) on a floured work surface to form a rectangle about 16 × 10 in. Break up the cracklings and arrange the pieces on top of the dough. →

12 Roll the dough tightly on itself with the cracklings inside and form it into a loaf. Press it into an oval shape approximately 11 in. long by 6 in. wide.

13 Sprinkle 2 Tb. of the cornmeal on a baking sheet and place the loaf on top.

Prepare a proof box by inserting a trimmed cardboard box into a large plastic bag. When the bag is closed, you will have a humid hothouse similar to a professional proof box, which provides the perfect environment for the bread to rise properly. Insert the bread into the proof box, tie it closed, and let rise at room temperature for 1½ hours.

14 Remove the 2-oz. piece of dough from the refrigerator and make strips by rolling the dough with your hand, making one end thicker than the other.

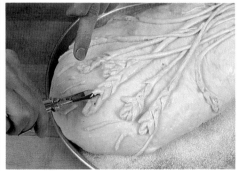

15 Brush the risen loaf with water and arrange the strips of dough on top with the thick part spread out at one end. With scissors, cut into the thick ends of the dough strips to make them resemble wheat stalks.

16 Sprinkle the bread with flour from a sieve and, using a razor blade, cut in between and around the "wheat stalks," making slashes that follow the design.

17 Bake in the center of a preheated 425-degree oven for 50 minutes. During the first 10 minutes of baking, create steam to make the bread develop well by throwing water into the bottom of the oven: At 2- to 3-minute intervals, toss about 2 Tb. of water onto the floor of the oven and repeat two more times — for a total of three times in the first 10 minutes of baking. Remove the bread from the oven. Note how the steam created by tossing water onto the oven floor has helped the bread form a thick crust on top.

18 Let the bread rest for at least 1 hour before cutting into it. The dough should be spongy and well-risen inside with pieces of crackling showing. This bread makes a beautiful centerpiece for a buffet. It is good with earthy things, such as pâté, cheese, salami, or a garlicky salad.

19 **For the baguettes:** Roll the 3 reserved pieces of dough into 18-in. lengths and place on a cookie sheet coated with the remaining 2 Tb. cornmeal. Roll one of the baguettes in the cornmeal so it is coated all around.

22 With a razor blade, score the surface of 1 floured loaf on the diagonal one way. Repeat on the other floured loaf, cutting a second set of lines across, in the opposite direction, to create a crisscross effect. Cut the surface of the loaf coated with cornmeal lengthwise with one long slit.

20 Place the baguettes in the proof box (step 13), and let rise for 1 hour in a warm kitchen (70 to 75 degrees).

23 Bake in the center of a preheated 425-degree oven for 30 minutes. After 1 to 2 minutes, throw 2 Tb. of water in the bottom of the oven to create steam. Repeat 3 to 4 minutes later, and again, a third time, 3 to 4 minutes after that. The loaves should be well-browned and crusty.

21 Remove the baguettes from the home-made proof box and, if they have dried out a little on top (they should still be sticky), brush with water. Sprinkle the two outside loaves with flour. (The center loaf has been rolled in cornmeal.)

EPI AND CROWN BREAD WITH WHOLE-GRAIN DOUGH

The _épi_ — the bread shaped to look like a stalk of wheat — and the crown bread were favorites at the small restaurant my wife and I had in Connecticut. We used to make 30 _épis_ a day. Both are chewy, tough breads with a thick crust and a strong, nutty taste.

Any leftover bread should be placed in a plastic bag to help prevent it from drying out too much. When ready to eat, it can be dampened with water and placed back in the oven for a few minutes to re-crisp. Or, it can be sliced thinly and baked in the oven to make delicious croutons, which will go well with salad, pâtés, or other foods.

Yield: 3 _épis_ and 1 crown

2 c. warm water (95 to 100 degrees)
1 tsp. sugar
2 envelopes active dry yeast
Starter: 6-oz. piece of dough + 1½ c. water*
1 Tb. salt
8 c. bread flour (2½ lb.)
1 c. bran (1½ oz.)
1½ c. cracked wheat (7 oz.)
3 Tb. semolina or Cream of Wheat

1 Combine the 2 c. warm water with the 1 tsp. sugar and 2 envelopes of yeast and set aside for 10 minutes to proof.

Add the starter with its own liquid, the 1 Tb. salt, and 7 c. of the bread flour. Using the dough hook attachment on a mixer (see page 118, step 3), mix the dough on speed 3 (medium) for 5 minutes, until the dough is tight, elastic, and smooth. Add the remaining cup of flour, and mix on speed 1 for 2 minutes longer, until thoroughly incorporated.

2 Turn the dough out onto a table. It should still be fairly soft. Add the cup of bran and 1½ c. cracked wheat, and press the dough into it until the bran and grain are incorporated into the dough.

3 Knead the dough in on itself, pressing it, pushing it, and folding it over, rotating it each time. Continue kneading in the same manner for 5 minutes.

4 All the bran and grain should be incorporated. If the dough is still a bit sticky, knead in 2 to 3 Tb. extra flour until it is strong and springy to the touch and doesn't stick to your fingers anymore.

* If starter is not available, increase the yeast to 2½ envelopes and the water to 3½ c.

5 Place in a bowl, cover, and let rise for 3 hours. The dough should have doubled in size and filled up the bowl. Pull the dough from the sides of the bowl and bring it back toward the center of the bowl, punching it to push out the air. Turn out onto a board.

6 **For the épi:** Cut three pieces of dough (1 lb. each) to make three *épis.* Roll each piece into an 18-in. length. Place on a cookie sheet coated with 1 Tb. of semolina. Using scissors, cut down from the top into the dough, keeping the scissors almost flat and cutting so the "grain of wheat" is almost severed from the "stalk."

7 As it is cut, pick up the tip of the "grain of wheat" and move it to one side of the "stalk ."

8 Cut again in the same way, 1½ in. from the first cut, and move the next "grain of wheat" to the other side of the "stalk." Continue cutting at 1½-in. intervals the length of the loaf, alternating the placement of the "grains of wheat" to create a whole head of wheat with about eight points.

Repeat with the other two *épis.*

Place the loaves in a proof box (see page 120, step 13) for 1½ hours, until doubled in size.

Remove from the proof box, brush with water, sprinkle 1 Tb. of semolina on top, and bake in a preheated 425-degree oven for 30 to 35 minutes, throwing 2 Tb. of water at a time onto the oven floor 3 times (at 2- to 3-minute intervals) during the first 10 minutes of baking.

9 **For the crown:** Knead the remaining 2 lb. of dough into a smooth round. With your thumb, make a hole in the center of the ball of dough.

10 Pressing both thumbs into the center, turn the dough around, stretching and squeezing at the same time to extend and increase the size of the hole in the center, until you have created a ring about 9 in. across with the dough measuring approximately 2 in. wide.

11 Sprinkle the remaining 1 Tb. of the semolina on a baking tray and place the crown loaf on top. Place in the proof box (see page 120, step 13) for 2 hours. Brush with water, sprinkle with flour, and score, slashing the top in a crisscross pattern with a razor blade.

12 Bake in a 425-degree oven for 40 minutes, throwing 2 Tb. of water at a time onto the floor of the oven 3 times (at 2- to 3-minute intervals) during the first 10 minutes of baking. It should be very crusty and nicely browned.

BLACK PEPPER BREAD WITH WALNUTS

This strongly flavored, compact black bread can be kept for days or frozen. It is ideal sliced very thin, buttered, and served with oysters, Salmon Gravlax Evelyn, or Salmon Tartare (page 8). The rye and buckwheat flour could be decreased to produce a lighter bread or increased for denser texture. A small amount of baking powder is added to the dough to help the yeast rise because there is a lack of gluten in the rye and buckwheat flours. The bread will freeze well, provided it is properly wrapped. Defrost slowly under refrigeration for a few hours so it doesn't dry out too much.

Yield: 1 large loaf

2½ cakes fresh yeast (0.6 oz. each), or
   2½ envelopes active dry yeast
2½ c. water, warmed to about
   100 degrees
2 tsp. dark molasses
3½ c. bread flour
2 c. rye flour
1 c. whole-grain buckwheat flour
2 Tb. unsweetened cocoa powder
½ tsp. baking powder
1 tsp. coarsely ground black peppercorns
1 c. broken walnuts
1 Tb. salt

TO BRUSH BREAD

½ tsp. cornstarch mixed with 3 Tb. cold
   water

1 In a KitchenAid mixer bowl (see page 118, step 13), combine the 2½ cakes or envelopes of yeast, ½ c. warm water, and the 2 tsp. molasses, and proof for about 10 to 15 minutes. Meanwhile, combine the 3½ c. bread flour and 2 c. rye flour, 1 c. buckwheat flour, 2 Tb. cocoa powder, and ½ tsp. baking powder (about 6 c. total volume). Add 4 c. of the dry mixture to the yeast mixture with the remaining 2 c. of warm water. (Two cups of the dry mixture are reserved and added to the bowl at the end of the mixing time, because if all the solids were added at the beginning, it would make the dough too stiff to mix.) Mix on speed 3 or 4 with the dough hook for about 5 minutes to develop the gluten.

Combine the 1 tsp. pepper, 1 c. walnuts, and 1 Tb. salt with the reserved dry mixture, add to the mixer bowl, and beat for about 2 minutes on speed 2. Cover with plastic wrap and let proof for 1½ to 2 hours at room temperature. The dough should double in volume.

2 Gently lift and push down on the dough to deflate it. Oil a cookie sheet and lift the dough out of the bowl with your oiled hand (to prevent it from sticking to the dough).

3 Place the dough on the cookie sheet and press it into an oval shape about 12 in. long by 6 in. wide. Place in a proof box (see step 13, page 120) and let rise for 1½ hours at room temperature.

4 Meanwhile, mix the ½ tsp. cornstarch and 3 Tb. water in a small saucepan and bring to a boil, stirring. Set aside.

When the bread has risen, brush with the cornstarch mixture and score the top by pulling a knife gently across its surface to create a stylized wheat design. Place in a preheated 400-degree oven and throw about 2 to 3 Tb. water into the bottom of the oven before you close the door to create some steam. Cook about 10 minutes and again throw 2 to 3 Tb. of water into the bottom of the oven. Continue cooking for another 35 minutes, for a total cooking time of 45 minutes.

5 The bread tastes better after 1 or 2 days and should be thinly sliced and buttered for serving with oysters, smoked salmon, or other fish.

WHOLE WHEAT BREAD WITH RAISINS

This is an ideal bread to do ahead or to take to a party or a picnic. It will cut very well into thin slices, stay moist for several days, and continue to develop more taste. It is excellent served with a rich cheese, such as Gorgonzola or Brie, or made into sandwiches.

Yield: 1 large loaf

2 envelopes active dry yeast
2½ c. warm water (95 to 100 degrees)
⅓ c. honey
4 c. whole wheat flour (1¼ lb.)
2¼ c. bread flour (about 12 oz.)
¾ Tb. salt
1 c. dark raisins
2 Tb. cornmeal

1 Put the 2 envelopes yeast with 2½ c. water (about 95 degrees) and ⅓ c. honey in the bowl of a KitchenAid mixer (see page 118, step 3). Stir gently to mix, and let proof for 10 minutes at room temperature.

Add 3 c. of the whole wheat flour and the 2¼ c. bread flour along with the ¾ Tb. salt. Using the dough hook, mix on speed 3 of the KitchenAid mixer for about 5 minutes. At that point, the dough will be very sticky and elastic but still fairly wet. Add the 1 c. raisins and the rest of the whole wheat flour, and mix about 1 minute on speed 1, just enough to incorporate the flour and raisins into the dough.

Place the dough on a floured board and knead for about 5 minutes with the same folding and pressing technique used in making the *Epi* and Crown Bread, page 122.

2 Lift up the dough and press it in on itself, using 2 to 3 Tb. of additional flour as you knead, until the dough is resilient but doesn't stick to your fingers anymore. It should be a bit softer than the Country Bread (see page 119, step 6) dough. Place the dough back in the mixer bowl, cover with plastic wrap, and let rise at room temperature for 2 hours.

5 Brush with water and sprinkle 1 Tb. of the cornmeal on top. Slash three lines with a razor blade on each half of the top to create a design. Place in a preheated 425-degree oven for 30 minutes, throwing 2 Tb. of water at a time onto the oven floor 3 times at 3- to 4-minute intervals during the first 10 minutes of baking.

After 30 minutes, reduce the heat to 400 degrees, and continue baking another 15 to 20 minutes.

3 At that point, the dough should have at least doubled in volume and should be soft and quite elastic. Pull the dough from the sides of the bowl in toward the center, pressing it in on itself to push out the air.

6 The bread is well-browned and crusty. This loaf will tend to stick to the cookie sheet, so use a spatula to loosen and release it.

4 Turn the dough out onto a board and form into a loaf about 9 in. in diameter by 1¼ in. high. Place on a cookie sheet sprinkled with 1 Tb. cornmeal. Place in a proof box (see step 13, page 120) for 1 to 1½ hours, until well-developed and risen.

The dough should have at least doubled and should be soft. Pull the dough from the sides of the bowl and in toward the center and press it down to extrude the air. Knead a few seconds, until the dough is tightly together again.

Turn the dough onto a floured board and cut into about twelve 2½- to 3-oz. pieces. Roll the dough pieces into small balls by using both hands to press the balls of dough on the table and move them with a circular motion while applying light pressure to create a tight ball. Arrange on a cookie sheet and let rise in a proof box (see step 13, page 120) for 50 to 60 minutes.

Brush with water and form a cross on top by slashing with a razor blade. Place in a preheated 425-degree oven and bake for 20 minutes, until nicely browned. These rolls can be served almost immediately or can be reheated whole or sliced and made into toast.

BREAKFAST ROLLS

Although the dough is divided to make a dozen rolls in the recipe here, it could be formed into 1 large loaf, baguettes, or a crown. This dough, made with milk and a little butter, is softer and more tender than the Country Bread (page 118) and the Epi (page 122) or the Whole Wheat Bread with Raisins (page 125). The rolls can be served for lunch and dinner or sandwiches can be made with them, but they are at their best for breakfast with butter, jam, and coffee or tea.

Yield: 12 rolls

1¼ c. milk
1 envelope active dry yeast
1 Tb. sugar
3 c. (1 lb.) bread flour
3 Tb. butter
½ tsp. salt

Heat the 1¼ c. milk to 95 degrees and place in the bowl of a KitchenAid mixer (see page 118, step 3) with the envelope of yeast and 1 Tb. sugar. Mix gently to combine and let proof for 10 minutes.

Add 2¾ c. of the flour, 3 Tb. butter, and ½ tsp. salt, and mix on speed 3 for approximately 5 minutes.

Place the dough on the table and knead with the remaining ¼ c. of flour, adding a few additional tablespoons of flour if needed. Knead the dough for about 5 minutes, folding it onto itself, and pressing and pushing it to develop the gluten. The dough should be resilient and elastic but softer than the dough for Country Bread (page 118), Epi and Crown Bread (page 122), or Whole Wheat Bread with Raisins (page 125).

Place the dough back in the KitchenAid bowl, cover with plastic wrap, and let rise for 1½ hours at room temperature.

2 Combine the ⅓ c. bran flakes, 3 c. flour, 1 tsp. salt, 2 Tb. sugar, and 1 tsp. each baking powder and baking soda in a bowl. Add the milk-butter mixture and the 2 eggs, and mix until well-combined. Finally, add the 1½ c. cranberries and ½ c. walnuts, and <u>stir just enough to incorporate them into the batter</u>.

3 Butter and flour a 8- or 9-in. springform pan and <u>pack the batter into it</u>. It should come one-half to two-thirds of the way up the sides of the pan.

CRANBERRY BREAD

This cranberry bread is best served with savories. It is excellent with game and rich cheese, such as Gorgonzola or ripe Brie, because the acidity and astringency of the berries cuts the richness of the game or cheese.

Do not over-stir the berries into the mixture. Fold them in just until they are suspended throughout the bread, giving it a beautiful color and texture. Use fresh cranberries because frozen ones will bleed through the cake and the effect and taste will be entirely different.

The bread can be baked in a loaf pan or in a springform pan, as I have done, to give it an unusual shape and different look.

Yield: 10–12 servings

1⅓ c. milk
½ stick butter (2 oz.)
1½ c. cranberries
⅓ c. bran flakes
3 c. flour (1 lb.)
1 tsp. salt
2 Tb. sugar
1 tsp. baking powder
1 tsp. baking soda
2 large eggs
½ c. coarsely chopped walnuts

1 Heat the 1⅓ c. milk until lukewarm and then cut the ½ stick butter into it, stirring until the butter melts. <u>With a knife, coarsely chop the 1½ c. cranberries</u>, or pulse them a few times in the food processor. They should be in good-size pieces.

4 Place the pan on a cookie sheet and bake in a preheated 350-degree oven for approximately 55 minutes to 1 hour, <u>until nicely browned</u> and baked through (until a knife inserted in the center comes out clean).

5 Set aside the cranberry bread for at least 1 to 2 hours to cool completely and firm up inside. Remove from the pan, cut into wedges, and serve. Excellent with cheese and game, any leftover bread is great cut into thin slices and toasted.

VEGETABLE BREAD

This vegetable bread is ideal to serve by itself or for brunch or dinner with fish, meat, or soup. It is attractive and, although my recipe calls for carrots, red peppers, spinach, asparagus, and corn kernels, any type of vegetable one has on hand can be used. It makes an ideal snack or light lunch with cheese and fruit.

Yield: 8 servings

RICH BRAN DOUGH

1 cake fresh yeast (0.6 oz.), or 1 envelope active dry yeast (1 Tb.)
¼ c. milk, warmed to about 100 degrees
½ tsp. sugar
2 c. flour (10 to 11 oz.)
1 tsp. salt
3 eggs
½ c. bran flakes
1 stick butter, softened (¼ lb.)

VEGETABLES

1 small carrot, cut into ¼-in. strips
6 small asparagus spears, peeled
½ medium red pepper, seeded, peeled (see Volume I, Deep-Fried Eggs Julia, page 47), and cut lengthwise into 1- to 1½-in. strips
6 oz. spinach, cleaned
⅓ c. corn kernels
Egg wash made with 1 egg with half the white removed, beaten
1 Tb. fresh bread crumbs

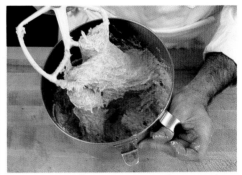

1 Place the cake or envelope of yeast, ¼ c. warm milk, and ½ tsp. sugar in the bowl of a KitchenAid mixer (see page 118, step 3) and proof for about 5 to 6 mintues, until the mixture bubbles on top. Add the 2 c. flour, 1 tsp. salt, 3 eggs, and ½ c. bran flakes, and beat with the flat beater on speed 4 for 3 minutes. Add the stick of butter in pieces and mix on speed 3 for about 30 seconds, just long enough to incorporate the butter. The mixture should be sticky and elastic. Cover with plastic wrap and let rise at room temperature for 1½ to 2 hours (depending on time of year, heat, and humidity), until at least double in bulk. →

2 **For the vegetables:** Place the carrot strips in 1 in. of water in a skillet and boil for about 5 minutes. Add the 6 asparagus spears and pepper strips, cover, and boil about 2 minutes. Then add the spinach and corn, cover, and boil 1 minute longer. Using a slotted spoon, spread the vegetables out in a large pan so they cool quickly.

3 When the dough has risen, push it down gently and place on a floured board. Spread the dough out by patting with a wet hand (to prevent the dough from sticking to it) into a rectangle approximately 11 × 13 in. Arrange the vegetables on top of the dough.

4 Roll the dough with the vegetables inside, using a dough scraper to scrape the dough off the table. It should form an oblong loaf about 12 in. long by 3 in. thick.

5 Butter a baking sheet and place the loaf on it seam-side down. Fold a piece of aluminum foil (about 2½ to 3 ft. long) lengthwise into fourths. Butter the foil and wrap it around the bread, as shown. Tie loosely in place with a piece of string. This will hold the bread in shape, preventing it from spreading out too much on the cookie sheet. Brush with the egg wash and sprinkle with the bread crumbs. Let rise at room temperature for about 30 minutes.

6 Bake in a preheated 400-degree oven for about 20 minutes. Remove the string and the collar and continue cooking 10 minutes longer at the same temperature, for a total of 30 minutes. Let the bread rest for at least 20 to 30 minutes before slicing. Cut the bread into ¾-in.-thick slices.

7 Arrange the bread on a serving plate. Slices can be served as a garnish to meat and fish or served with cheese. If made ahead, refrigerate the loaf and reheat for a few minutes in the oven so it is about room temperature for serving.

2 Butter a 3-qt. charlotte mold and arrange the dough in it. Place in a proof box (see page 120, step 13) and let rise for 1 hour.

Brush with egg wash.

3 Sprinkle with the 1 Tb. oatmeal and slash two lines with a razor blade across the surface of the loaf. Place in the center of a preheated 400-degree oven for 15 minutes, then reduce the heat to 350 degrees and continue cooking for another 20 minutes.

CHEESE BREAD

This delicate bread, made with sharp cheddar cheese and dried pears, is lovely to serve with fresh fruit and nuts and is excellent for brunch. Any leftover bread is good cut into slices and toasted, which brings back the taste of the cheese.

Yield: 1 large loaf

1 c. milk
1 envelope active dry yeast (1 Tb.), or 1 cake fresh yeast (0.6 oz.)
1 tsp. sugar
3 c. bread flour
1 tsp. salt
¾ stick butter
2 eggs
About 6 oz. grated sharp cheddar cheese (about 2 c.)
1 c. ¼-in. pieces dried pears (4 oz.)
Egg wash made with 1 egg with half the white removed, beaten
1 Tb. oatmeal (not the instant kind)

1 Heat the 1 c. milk to about 95 degrees and add the envelope of yeast and 1 tsp. sugar. Combine gently and proof for 10 minutes in the bowl of a KitchenAid mixer (see page 118, step 3).

Add the 3 c. flour, 1 tsp. salt, ¾ stick butter, 2 eggs, and, using the dough hook, beat on speed 3 for about 5 minutes. Add the 2 c. grated cheese and 1 c. diced pear, and mix about 30 seconds to 1 minute, just long enough to incorporate. This dough doesn't require further kneading. Cover the bowl with plastic wrap and let the dough rise at room temperature for 1½ hours.

At that point, the dough will be well-risen. Fold the dough in on itself from the sides toward the center and press to deflate.

4 Remove from the oven and keep in a warm place for 15 to 20 minutes so the dough doesn't soften and the bread collapse on itself. After an hour, the dough should still be warm and can be cut and served. The center should look buttery and have a yeasty, cheesy smell.

3 sticks cold unsalted butter (12 oz.)
1 envelope active dry yeast (1 Tb.), or 1
  cake fresh yeast (0.6 oz.)
1¼ c. warm milk (90 to 100 degrees)
2 tsp. sugar
1 lb. all-purpose unbleached flour (3 c.)
1 tsp. salt
Egg wash made with 1 egg with half the
  white removed, beaten

FOR THE *PAIN AU CHOCOLAT*

3 to 4 oz. bittersweet chocolate*

CROISSANTS AND PAIN AU CHOCOLAT

Croissants are the quintessence of a French breakfast. These flaky rolls served with café-au-lait and jam represent the classic breakfast, or petit déjeuner. Croissants are eaten only for breakfast in France, but in America today they are often served as rolls for lunch or dinner or made into sandwiches with ham or other savory ingredients.

Croissant dough is a cross between Puff Paste (see page 144) and Brioche (see page 136). It is a flaky dough that is rolled and folded like a puff paste but contains yeast. Unlike a classic puff paste, which requires six turns or folds, croissant dough is given only four turns. Because the yeast in it makes the dough rise and break through the layers you have created by folding, too many turns would blend the dough too much and make it lose its flakiness. Croissant dough can be made ahead and frozen, but it should not be frozen for too long, as the yeast in it will eventually die in the freezer.

The croissants here are small (approximately 1½ oz. each), while the ones served with meals or with savory fillings are often as large as 3 oz. It is important that the dough rise in a very moist environment so I use a plastic bag and a cut-out cardboard box to take the place of a proof box. The plastic bag seals in moisture and the card-

board prevents the plastic bag from falling onto and sticking to the croissants. It is especially important to use a proof box in very dry climates; otherwise, instead of rising, the dough tends to form a crust on top that prevents further development. After the croissant is formed, the dough should be moist on top so that the yeast can develop and expand the dough.

The petit pains au chocolat are made by rolling chocolate up in a piece of rectangular croissant dough. The real pain au chocolat that I remember eating as a child was simply a little piece of French baguette or ficelle (thinner than a baguette) that we ate after school with a bar of black chocolate. To this day, partly because of nostalgia, the bread version has more taste and crunchiness to me than the one made with croissant dough. In certain parts of France, bread and chocolate are still a standard snack that French children get when they arrive home from school in the afternoon.

Yield: about 20 small croissants and 8 pains au chocolat

1 Cut each of the 3 sticks of butter into 4 lengthwise slices. Place on a plate and refrigerate. Combine the envelope or cake of yeast with the 1¼ c. milk and 2 tsp. sugar in the bowl of a mixer, and let proof about 10 minutes at room temperature. Add the 3 c. flour and 1 tsp. salt, and mix with the flat beater for about 20 to 30 seconds, just until smooth.

* Bittersweet chocolate is different from bitter chocolate, which is unsweetened chocolate. Although semi-sweet chocolate is slightly sweeter than bittersweet, you can substitute semi-sweet for bittersweet. If you find that you want a slightly less sweet flavor than semi-sweet gives you, for every 8 oz. use 7 oz. semi-sweet and 1 oz. unsweetened.

2 Place the dough on a board, preferably cold, and press down on it with your hands to extend it, using as little flour as possible. The board can be set outside to cool in winter or in the refrigerator. A jelly roll tray filled with ice can also be placed on the board to cool it. It doesn't matter if the dough is crushed at this point since there is no butter in it yet. Roll it out to create a rectangle approximately 18 to 20 in. long by 8 to 10 in. wide and about ¼ in. thick. Arrange the slices of butter, one next to another, on top of two-thirds of the pastry, covering it to within about ¾ to 1 in. from the edge.

3 Lift up the uncovered third of the dough and fold it over the portion of the dough covered with butter. Press the edges so the dough layers stick together.

4 Fold the rectangle in half so that one layer of dough is in the center separated by layers of the butter, which is completely enclosed now. Press the edges so the pastry

layers hold together well. If the dough is not too elastic, the first turn can be completed now: Place the rectangle of dough in front of you so the short side faces you, and roll it out, flouring the bottom and top of it, into a rectangle approximately 18 in. long by 9 in. wide and about ⅜ in. thick. Using a large rolling pin with ball bearings helps.

5 Brush off any excess flour on top of the dough and fold it so the two ends meet in the center.

6 Fold the dough again to create a four-layered piece of dough. (This is called a double turn but, in fact, it represents only one-third more than the single turn, which produced three layers.) Place the dough in a plastic bag and refrigerate for 30 minutes to 1 hour or longer for the dough to "relax." Give the dough another double turn. Refrigerate again and give another double turn (for a total of three double turns). At this point, the dough should be wrapped and allowed to rise. It will rise if placed in the refrigerator or a cool place for 2 to 3 hours, or it can be wrapped loosely and placed in the coldest part of the refrigerator and left overnight.

7 After a few hours (or overnight) in the refrigerator, the dough will have risen.

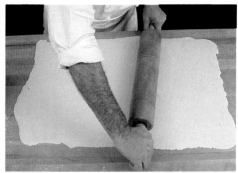

8 On a floured board, roll the dough into a big square about 20 in. by 20 in. and ⅛ in. thick. Be sure to roll in one direction and . . .

9 . . . then in the other direction, extending it from the center forward and backward, then left and right. Avoid going back and forth on the dough, which tends to develop the gluten and gives the dough too much elasticity. Let the dough rest for 8 to 10 minutes on the table (or in the refrigerator on trays) before cutting the croissants, to allow the dough to lose some of the elasticity developed from rolling it out. →

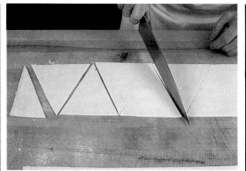

10 Trim the edges and cut the rectangle of dough into 3 strips, each about 6½ in. wide. (Two of the strips will be used to make croissants and one to make *pain au chocolat*.)

Mark each strip into 5-in. segments and cut into triangles weighing approximately 1½ oz. each. Two strips should yield about 20 croissants. (Large croissants are made by cutting a triangle 8 × 8 × 8 in., weighing about 2½ oz.) Brush the triangles lightly with water to help the dough stick together as it is rolled.

11 Roll the triangles of dough from the base, first folding the dough on itself and pressing so it sticks and then . . .

12 . . . rolling with your fingers and the palms of your hands while pressing down and out on the dough to extend it. It should be pressed forward and rolled tightly. Be sure to wet the tip of the triangle, then press or crush it into the croissant so it adheres to the dough underneath.

13 Place the croissants on a cookie sheet lined with parchment and bend the ends forward to create the traditional crescent shape. Notice that the point of the croissant is tucked under.

14 Brush the croissants with water to eliminate any flour left on top and to prevent them from drying out. Insert the tray of croissants into a proof box (see page 120, step 13) and tie the bag closed. Be sure the plastic doesn't touch the croissants and let them rise in a warm place at a temperature of 70 to 75 degrees for about 1½ hours (or less, depending on humidity), until the croissants almost double in size. Brush with egg wash. Place in a preheated 425-degree oven for approximately 15 to 18 minutes. Freeze remaining croissants for later use or repeat the rising and cooking procedures.

15 For the *pain au chocolat*, pieces of chocolate can be used. However, if making a great many, it is better to melt chocolate and spread it on a piece of parchment or wax paper into a strip approximately 3½ in. wide and ⅛ to ¼ in. thick. Refrigerate or cool until it begins to set and then cut into sticks approximately ¾ in. wide by running your knife through it. Allow the chocolate to harden further and, when completely cold, lift the strips of chocolate from the paper. To make a few *pains au chocolat*, just break pieces of chocolate and arrange on the dough.

16 Cut the remaining strip of croissant dough crosswise into pieces 3 in. wide and 5 in. long. Dampen with water and place a piece of chocolate on top along one edge. Roll tightly and place, seam-side down, on a cookie sheet lined with parchment paper. Let rise in the proof box (like the one used to make croissants) for approximately 1 to 1½ hours, depending on the humidity and temperature.

17 Brush with the egg wash and bake in a preheated 400-degree oven for 15 to 20 minutes for the small croissants and the *pain au chocolat* and 20 to 25 minutes for the larger croissants.

BRIOCHE

Brioches are buttery, light breads made from a moist yeast dough. Traditionally a breakfast bread, brioche can also be adapted to encase sausage, goose liver, or game pâtés, although when used this way, the dough is usually made with less butter.

To make a brioche dough, first prepare a sponge, a mixture in which the lower proportion of liquid to flour allows the yeast to develop quickly, giving it a head start before more flour is added. Once the sponge has risen, the eggs, additional flour, and butter are worked into it and, in my recipe, the resulting dough is so light, airy, and buttery that it is referred to as a brioche mousseline. Compared to the usual dough for brioches, a mousseline benefits from slower risings at lower temperatures, and these factors – plus the kneading procedure outlined in the recipe that follows – develop the gluten and make a stronger dough that is better able to absorb the extra butter.

Brioche dough can be made by hand or with an electric mixer with a dough hook. It is then formed in the classic shape (either large or small), in round loaves baked in cylindrical containers, such as cans (ideal for round slices), or in standard loaves. Here I am preparing the brioche dough by hand so that you can see the transformation of the dough, but the mixer would work as well. The time of rising should be reduced when the weather is humid and hot. A cardboard box wrapped in a plastic bag creates a homemade proof box (see page 120, step 13) where brioches and croissants develop perfectly well without forming a crust. Crusting would inhibit the brioches' rising in the oven while baking. After baking, be sure to let the brioches cool in the pans a full hour; if unmolded while still hot, they may collapse in on themselves.

BRIOCHE MOUSSELINE

Yield: about 24 small or 3 large brioches

SPONGE

1 cake fresh yeast (0.6 oz.), or 1 envelope
  active dry yeast (1 T.)
¼ c. sugar
¼ c. water, warm from the tap (100
  degrees)
¾ c. flour (about 3 oz.)
2 Tb. cognac

DOUGH

5 large eggs
2 egg yolks
1 lb. flour (3 c. dipped directly into the
  flour container and leveled off)
1½ tsp. salt
1 lb. unsalted butter (4 sticks), softened
Egg wash made with 1 egg with half the
  white removed, beaten

1 For the sponge, crush the yeast cake and
¼ c. sugar together with a fork until you
have a paste. Add the ¼ c. warm water
and ¾ c. flour, and mix well until
smooth. Mix in the 2 Tb. cognac, cover
with plastic wrap, and let rise at room
temperature (70 to 75 degrees) for 1 hour.

2 To make the dough by hand: In a bowl,
combine the sponge with the 5 eggs, 2
egg yolks, 1 lb. flour, and 1½ tsp. salt.
Dump the mixture out onto a marble or
other smooth surface.

3 Work the dough for 8 to 10 minutes,
lifting it and flipping it back on the table
to create air bubbles inside the dough.
Note: The dough is very sticky.

4 Using both hands, lift the dough . . .

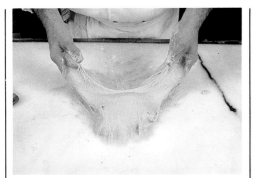

5 . . . and flip it back on itself. After 8 to 10 minutes of beating, the gluten will develop and give strength to the dough.

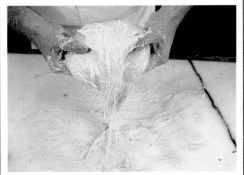

6 The dough should be satiny and elastic and you should be able to pick it up from the table in one mass. This elastic dough will absorb the large quantity of butter required for my recipe.

7 Start adding the soft butter, about ⅓ to ½ stick at a time, squeezing and mixing it with some of the dough. Do not worry if the butter is still visible in the dough.

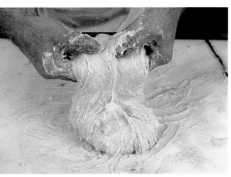

8 Work quickly. The object now is not to develop the gluten in the dough but to combine the butter. Work the whole mixture briefly to combine the butter more thoroughly. Place in a bowl and cover with plastic wrap.

9 Let rise at room temperature for 5 to 6 hours, or until nearly doubled in size. Knead the dough in the bowl gently with your fingers for a few seconds to deflate it, cover it again, and refrigerate overnight, or for about 12 hours. It will develop slowly in the cold. (It can remain in the refrigerator for up to 1 day.) When ready to use, turn the dough out onto a floured table and knead it briefly to press out all the air.

10 To make individual brioches, divide the dough into balls the size of small golf balls (weighing about 2 oz.) and roll each one on the floured table, applying pressure with your hand and moving in a circular motion to give body to the dough. To make the "head," use the side of your hand and saw one end of the dough to form a small lump the size of an olive. Don't go through the dough – it should remain attached to the body of the brioche. Flour the table lightly as necessary to prevent sticking.

11 Pick up each brioche by the "head" and place it in the buttered mold. This method of forming each brioche enables you to save time by doing it in one single, quick motion.

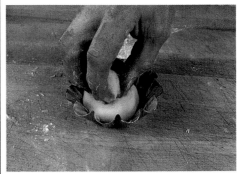

12 Push the "head" down into the brioche. To rise properly, brioche should be in a humid, moist place. Use a cardboard box (a wine box is ideal), cutting off the top and front so a cookie sheet can be slid in and out easily. Put the box into a large garbage bag. Finish forming the remaining brioches and arrange the molds on a cookie sheet. Slip the cookie sheet into the box and close the plastic bag with a twister. Let rise at room temperature for 2½ hours, until barely doubled in bulk.

13 The dough can also be divided into 3 large brioches. To make a large brioche with a "head," knead about 1 lb. (almost one-third) of the dough, reserving a small amount (about 2 oz. – the size of a golf ball) for the head, until smooth, and place in a large, buttered brioche pan or charlotte mold. Make a hole in the center. Roll the reserved, 2-oz. piece of dough so it looks like a pear. Press the pointed end down into the hole on the brioche. The head should sit in the center on top of the brioche dough. Place in the plastic bag to rise for about 3½ hours at room temperature, until barely double in bulk.

14 To make a long tubelike brioche that is an ideal shape for cutting round slices, butter well a 1-lb. coffee can. Press about 1 lb. (almost one-third) of the dough inside (filling about half the can). Tie a buttered collar of aluminum foil around the can that extends about 3 in. above the can. (Make sure it fits in your oven standing up.) Cover with plastic wrap and let rise at room temperature for about 3½ hours, until the dough is almost to the top of the collar of the can. For the brioche loaf, butter a loaf pan. Roll 4 pieces of dough (about 5 oz. each, 1¼ lb. total), pressing them gently into the buttered loaf pan. Proof in the plastic bag for about 3½ hours at room temperature. Brush the brioches gently with the egg wash. The yolk gives a rich brown color and the white makes the glaze shiny.

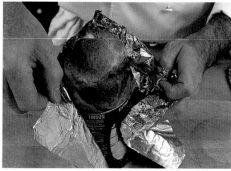

15 Bake in a preheated 350-degree oven for about 25 minutes for the small brioches and 45 to 50 minutes for the large one and for the loaf. Let the brioches (especially the large ones) cool at room temperature for 1 hour before unmolding. Remove the aluminum collar from the loaf in the coffee can.

16 The dough is very light and spongy and may collapse slightly on itself if unmolded while still very hot. Cooked brioche, sliced and unsliced.

ALTERNATE PREPARATION METHODS

TO MAKE WITH A KITCHENAID MIXER
(see page 118, step 3)

Prepare the sponge in the bowl of the mixer. When it has risen, add the 5 eggs, 2 egg yolks, 1 lb. flour, and 1½ tsp. salt, and work with the dough hook for 5 minutes on speed 4. Reduce the speed to slow and add the butter, stick by stick, mixing just long enough to combine. If the butter isn't readily incorporated, finish by hand, but do not worry if the butter is still visible here and there.

TO MAKE WITH A FOOD PROCESSOR

The dough is better made in two batches because, unless you have a professional-size machine, the motor will stop. Make the sponge in a separate bowl. When ready, place half of the sponge with half of the 5 eggs, 1 egg yolk, 1½ c. flour, and ¾ tsp. salt in the bowl of the food processor. Process for about 1 minute and add 2 sticks of butter. Process just long enough to mix in the butter. Repeat with the other half of the ingredients. (The butter can also be added by hand at the end.)

- CLASSIC PUFF PASTE DETREMPE
- PUFF PASTE #2 (FAST PUFF)
- PUFF PASTE #3 (INSTANT PUFF)
- STRAWBERRY NAPOLEON
- FANCY VOL-AU-VENT OF SPICY CHICKEN
- PUFF PASTRIES OF OYSTER AND
  ASPARAGUS
- PUFF ANCHOVY FISH
- CHEESE STRAWS
- BLACK RASPBERRY JAM DARTOIS
- PITHIVIER ALMOND CAKE
- FLAKY RASPBERRY TART
- CRYSTALLIZED PUFF PASTE OF ORANGE
- PUFF PASTE OF STEWED STRAWBERRIES
  AND CREAM
- PEAR IN PUFF AND ALMOND PASTRY
  CREAM
- CHERRY-RASPBERRY PILLOW
- APPLE CRUNCH
- TARTE TATIN
- RHUBARB GALETTE
- BANANA TART LUQUILLO
- EXOTIC CUSTARD FRUIT GALETTE
- LIME AND ORANGE TARTLETS
- CHOCOLATE-ORANGE TART MARTINE
- FRESH RASPBERRY LINZER TORTE
- BLACKBERRY CLAFOUTIS
- ORANGES IN BLACKBERRY SAUCE
- GALETTE DE PEROUGES
- SUGARED PUFF PASTE STICKS
- ZIMFOUR
- DULCET CHOCOLATE SQUARES
- CANDIED LIME AND GRAPEFRUIT PEELS
- CHOCOLATE TRUFFETTES
- FRUITCAKE FINGERS
- CHRISTMAS CAKE CUBES
- GLAZED FRUITS

PUFF PASTE

Puff paste, feuilletage in French after the word feuilles, which means leaves, is a flaky, multilayered dough made with flour, water, and butter in approximately equal proportions. Although it's a rich dough with a large percentage of butter, it is relatively inexpensive, as it can be rolled extremely thin and many things can be made with a pound of puff paste.

First, a dough is made with flour bound with a liquid, usually water but sometimes milk or cream. This elastic, shiny dough is called the détrempe, and you roll it out, place butter on top, and then fold the two together. By rolling and folding the dough several times (six "turns"), you create a multilayered structure consisting of about 1,500 layers of elastic flour dough and butter. You can damage the layers if you let the butter get too soft and squeeze out of the dough or if you roll out the dough without enough flour on your work surface and it starts sticking. But, if the layers are intact when the puff paste is placed in the oven (and thus the layers are all "waterproofed" by the butter), as the water in the basic dough turns into steam, the steam will be held inside and will push the layers up into a "thousand leaves" (mille feuilles).

All-purpose flour (containing about 10 to 11 percent gluten) or pastry flour (about 7 to 8 percent gluten) can be used for puff paste. A few drops of lemon juice added to the dough tend to soften the protein and make the dough less elastic. Yet one needs a fairly strong flour for the puff paste to develop properly. The ultimate goal in making puff paste is to keep the flour dough layers separate from the butter layers. If the butter gets incorporated into the flour dough, the result is ordinary pie dough.

Two problems are likely to arise with puff paste. One, the heat generated by your hands as you work the dough is apt to soften the butter and make it stick. Two, if you overwork the dough, it tends to develop the gluten and the dough becomes so elastic that it can't be rolled out again. The remedy for both problems is the refrigerator. Allowing the dough to rest in the refrigerator hardens the butter, preventing it from sticking, and it also relaxes the gluten and makes the dough easy to roll again.

Puff paste, well-wrapped, freezes beautifully. Left covered in the refrigerator, it can be kept a couple of days, but eventually some of the natural yeast will develop and render the dough a bit sour so it turns darker and becomes unusable.

Puff paste is extremely versatile. It is used in puffed vol-au-vents, which can be served with sugar on top (see Puff Paste of Stewed Strawberries and Cream, page 167, and Pear in Puff and Almond Pastry Cream, page 168) or in plain small or large vol-au-vents (Puff Pastries of Oyster and Asparagus, page 153, and Fancy Vol-au-Vent of Spicy Chicken, page 150). It can also be used in tarts (Flaky Raspberry Tart, page 162) or cakes such as the classic Napoleon (Strawberry Napoleon, page 147) as well as transformed into Cheese Straws, page 157, or Pithivier Almond Cake, page 160.

It is important to use the best possible unsalted butter with the least amount of water in it. When the butter is kneaded or cut, no drops of water should be visible. Making puff paste with vegetable shortening works quite well, too, but the taste doesn't equal that of the puff paste made with butter. Occasionally cream is used instead of water in the basic détrempe mixture, and this makes a tender, light, delicate pastry, richer in butter. Although the classic dough will be made with a pound of flour for a pound of butter, the amount of butter can be decreased to as little as 10 ounces per pound. The amount of water needed ranges from 8 to 14 ounces, depending on the moisture in the flour.

The number of "turns" ranges from four to six. Less butter and fewer "turns" make a dough that is still flaky but not as rich, suited to something like a salmon in crust, where the dough is very thin around the fish and where it should cut without crumbling too much under the knife.

In the recipe that follows, I have done a Classic Puff Paste, allowing the dough to rest between each "turn." Although this dough takes several hours to complete, it requires only a few minutes of work for each "turn" between resting periods.

The second version of the puff paste (Fast Puff) is quicker. The basic flour dough is spread on the table, the butter sliced on top of it, and the flour dough folded on top of the butter. Several "double turns" are given to the dough at once, and it takes no more than 1 hour to make.

Finally, the very fast version, or Instant Puff, is done in 20 minutes and is well-suited for wrapping meat or fish or as the base of a tart. It is a flaky dough that doesn't puff up too much but is still tender.

Puff paste should rise, but the ultimate goal is to have a tender, flaky, and delicate pastry. An overworked pastry will rise but it will be tough.

There are some differences between classic, fast, and instant puff pastes. The greater the amount of butter and the more folds, the more likely it is that the puff paste will puff up and be flaky and tender. Classic or fast puff paste is ideal for making a large vol-au-vent or the Pithivier Almond Cake. The instant puff paste is good for Cheese Straws or for a tart shell as well as for wrapping fish pâté in a crust, because the dough will still be flaky and tender without being too rich.

In making the fast and instant puff pastes, especially, you should put the flour in the freezer to get very cold before you start working in order to reduce the problems of the heat generated by warm hands, which softens the butter. Yet remember that although the butter can be cold, it can't be frozen because it has to be maleable enough to roll out into thin sheets. If the butter is frozen, it will stick through the dough without laminating. The water, however, should be ice cold like the flour.

2 Place the pound of butter with the ¼ c. flour in the bowl of a KitchenAid mixer and, using the whisk, mix until the ingredients are well-homogenized, about 15 to 20 seconds. Using plastic wrap, pat the butter mixture into a 5- to 6-in. square about 1 in. thick on another piece of plastic wrap. Refrigerate for at least 30 minutes along with the flour dough.

Roll out the *détrempe,* using as little flour as possible, into a square about 12 × 12 in. Place the butter mixture at an angle in the center of the dough, positioning it so the corners of the butter face the sides of the *détrempe.*

3 Bring the corners of dough over the butter, overlapping them slightly to encase the butter completely.

THREE WAYS TO MAKE PUFF PASTE

CLASSIC PUFF PASTE DETREMPE

Yield: approximately 2½ lb.
1 lb. all-purpose flour (about 3 c.), very cold (put a bag of flour in the freezer overnight)
¼ stick unsalted butter, at room temperature (2 Tb.)
½ tsp. salt
8 to 9 oz. cold water (depending on humidity)

BUTTER MIXTURE

1 lb. unsalted butter, at room temperature
¼ c. flour

PUFF PASTE #2 (FAST PUFF)

Yield: approximately 2½ lb.
1 lb. very cold all-purpose flour (3 c.)
½ tsp. salt
8 to 9 oz. cold water (depending on humidity)
1 lb. unsalted butter (4 sticks)

PUFF PASTE #3 (INSTANT PUFF)

Yield: approximately 2¼ lb.
1 lb. very cold all-purpose flour (3 c.)
3 sticks unsalted butter (12 oz.)
½ tsp. salt
¼ tsp. lemon juice
8 to 9 oz. cold water (depending on humidity)

1 To make the classic puff paste (for the <u>détrempe</u>): Place the pound of flour, ¼ stick soft butter, ½ tsp. salt, and 8 to 9 oz. cold water in the bowl of a KitchenAid mixer (see step 3, page 118). Using the flat beater, mix on speed 2 for about 45 seconds, until well-combined. Gather the dough together, wrap it in plastic wrap, and place in the refrigerator.

4 Pound the dough gently with a rolling pin to extend it. Then flour the surface of the dough and roll it into a rectangle 20 in. long by 10 in. wide by ⅜ in. thick.

5 Brush the dough to remove any flour from the surface and fold one-third of the dough back onto the rectangle.

6 Bring the remaining single thickness of dough back over the double thickness so the rectangle is folded into thirds like a letter. Brush off any flour as you fold. This is the first "turn." Wrap the dough in plastic wrap or place in a plastic bag in the refrigerator for 30 minutes to let it rest before giving it another turn.

Place the rectangle on the table with the folded side facing you and roll it out again into a rectangle about 20 in. long by 10 in. wide by ⅜ in. thick. Fold again into thirds. This is the second "turn." Re-wrap

and refrigerate again for 30 minutes. Roll again into a 10 × 20-in. rectangle and fold into thirds, again brushing any flour from the center as you fold. If you feel that the dough is well-rested and not elastic at that point, give the dough another "turn" immediately, which will be two "turns" in a row, making a total of four "turns." Let the dough rest again for 30 minutes or longer.

Eventually, give a fifth and sixth "turn," allowing the dough to rest in the refrigerator 30 minutes between each "turn." The finished dough will have six "turns." After the dough has rested, it can be rolled into long, thin rectangles and stacked on a tray with plastic wrap between the rectangles.

After it rests, the dough won't shrink when cut out for *vol-au-vents* or other shapes. The dough can be frozen whole or rolled, cut into shapes, and frozen. To use, defrost the large pieces to roll. The frozen shaped pieces should be placed in the oven frozen for best results.

7 To make the Fast Puff Paste #2: Use cold flour (from the freezer). Since the dough will be worked out very quickly with several "turns" in a row, the cold flour will absorb the heat generated through manipulation and rolling. Place the pound of flour, ½ tsp. salt, and 8 to 9 oz. water in the bowl of a KitchenAid mixer (see page 118, step 3), and mix with the flat beater for about 15 seconds, just enough for the dough to be well-homogenized and hold together.

Place the dough on the table. Cut each of the 4 sticks of unsalted butter into 3 or 4 lengthwise slices.

8 Roll out the *détrempe* into a rectangle approximately 18 in. long by 9 in. wide by ¼ in. thick. Arrange the butter slices over two-thirds of the dough to within ¾ in. of the outside edges.

9 Bring the lower third of the dough (not covered by butter) on top of half of the butter.

10 Bring the remaining third of the buttered dough over the top, creating a sandwich with five alternating layers of dough and butter. Press along the sides to ensure that the dough is glued together. →

11 Pound the dough gently with a rolling pin to start extending it. Then, flour (minimally) the dough and roll it into a rectangle about 9 to 10 in. wide by 20 in. long by ¼ to ⅜ in. thick.

12 Bring each end of the rectangle toward the center so it joins, and roll gently to seal.

13 Fold the dough in half again, creating a four-layer dough rather than the three layers of the classic puff paste shown in photographs 2–6. This is what is called a "double turn." Roll again into a rectangle and give the dough another "double turn." Wrap and refrigerate the dough for at least 30 minutes.

Flour the board and roll the dough again into a 10 × 20-in. rectangle, fold into the center and then in half again (another "double turn"). At that point, if the dough is not too elastic, give it a fourth "double turn." Wrap and refrigerate. After it has rested, the dough will be ready to use.

14 To make Puff Paste #3 (Instant Puff): (Notice that the proportion of butter is less and the flour is very cold.) Place the lb. of cold flour in a bowl and slice the 12 oz. of butter in ⅛-in. slivers on top of it.

15 Add the ½ tsp. salt, ¼ tsp. lemon juice, and 8 to 9 oz. cold water, and mix with a spoon until most of the flour is moist and most of the mixture holds together. Do not over-mix.

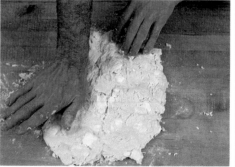

16 Place on a work surface, preferably cold, and spread the dough with the heel of your hand into a coarse rectangle approximately 9 × 12 in.

17 If the dough sticks to the work surface, use a dough scraper to lift it up and fold it into thirds, as indicated in steps 5 and 6.

18 Then flour the dough, pound it, as shown in photographs 4 and 11, to start extending it, and roll the dough again into a rectangle about 9 × 20 in. You can see that the pieces of butter are still quite visible in the center.

19 Fold the dough into a "double turn," making sure to brush the flour from the center. Again, extend the dough to make a rectangle about 8 × 20 in.

20 Roll the dough out for the third time into a rectangle about 8 × 20 in. Notice that the butter is still visible but less and less so. Fold the dough again into a "double turn." At that point, the dough will be quite elastic. Wrap in plastic wrap and place in the refrigerator for at least 1 hour before using. If, after you've let the dough rest in the refrigerator, you want it more flaky, give it another single or double "turn" before using.

Puff paste is used in several of the dishes that follow and any of the three puff paste recipes here can be used, depending on availability.

STRAWBERRY NAPOLEON

The napoleon is the classic puff paste dessert. Unfortunately, it is not often very good in restaurants because the pastry has been put together too far ahead and the cream filling has turned it soggy. The closer it is put together to the time it is served, the better it will be.

You can use any of the three recipes for puff paste as well as leftover trimmings. The dough should not puff up too much but should be very flaky, tender, and cooked until well-done and dark brown. The cake can be stuffed with pastry cream or whipped cream, as done here, or a combination of both. Fruits as well as crushed nuts can be arranged in the center. The top can be decorated with whipped cream or covered with powdered sugar, fondant, or currant jelly as well as crumbs from the cooked puff paste trimmings.

Notice that the bottom of the dough actually becomes the top, as it is the flattest piece. The large, whole strawberries glazed with currant jelly make a beautiful decoration on top and an excellent garnish.

Yield: 6–8 servings

1 lb. Puff Paste (page 144) or puff paste trimmings
2 jars red currant or strawberry jelly (10 oz. each)
2½ c. heavy cream
4 Tb. sugar
1 tsp. vanilla
1 Tb. Kirschwasser
1 tsp. gelatin dissolved in 1½ Tb. hot water (optional)
1 qt. strawberries, stems removed and halved, or cut lengthwise into thirds
Toasted sliced almonds (optional)

GARNISH

12 large strawberries with stems on

1 On a baking tray about 14 × 16 in., roll out the puff paste to a thickness of ⅛ in. to cover the tray. Prick the dough with a fork so it doesn't rise too much during cooking, and place in a preheated 400-degree oven for 25 to 35 minutes. It should be well-crisped and well-done.

While the dough is cooking, melt the 2 ten-ounce jars of jelly. Place in a saucepan over low heat and melt slowly, stirring occasionally. Don't mix with a whisk or stir too much as it tends to get granular. If this happens, strain through a fine strainer. Keep warm by setting in hot water so it is not too liquid, but don't let it cool so much it begins hardening again.

2 When the dough has cooled off, trim the four sides to make a rectangle about 12 in. wide by 14 in. long. Cut lengthwise into three strips, each about 4 in. wide. Reserve the trimmings for decoration.

3 To assemble the cake: Put the 2½ c. cream, 4 Tb. sugar, 1 tsp. vanilla, and 1 Tb. Kirschwasser into a bowl. Whip by hand or with an electric mixer until firm. If the weather is hot and the cream has a tendency to leak, add the 1 tsp. gelatin dissolved in 1½ Tb. water in one stroke to the whipped cream, and mix with a whisk to incorporate. Put the cream in a pastry bag fitted with a ½-in. plain tip. Pipe the cream lengthwise onto one of the pastry strips, making a line of cream on either side and one down the center. Arrange half of the pieces of berries in between the rows of cream and brush the berries with a little currant jelly.

4 Place a second pastry strip on top of the first one (be sure to reserve the nicest strip for the top) and press the second layer down onto the lower layer. Pipe on 3 rows of whipped cream as before. Arrange the remaining berries in between the rows and brush them with currant jelly.

5 Crush some of the trimmings on top, reserving some for pressing around the sides of the napoleon. Toasted sliced almonds could also be placed in the center as well as around the sides.

6 Place the last strip of cooked pastry on top. Be sure to turn it upside down so the top has the smoothest possible surface. Press gently into the other two layers so the mixture adheres well together. Coat the sides and top lightly with the remaining cream.

7 Crush the rest of the puff paste trimmings with your fingers and press the crumbs along the sides of the cake so they stick. The cake is now ready to be served.

8 For a decoration: Wash the large straw-berries and dry with paper towels. (They should be well-dried as any moisture remaining will liquefy the currant jelly.) Dip one at a time into the melted currant jelly.

11 Cut the cake into 1½-in.-thick slices. Place on serving plates with the coated berries and serve immediately.

9 Lift the berries and drain off the excess jelly by scraping the berries gently on the lip of the pan. Place the berries on a cold plate in the refrigerator for at least 10 minutes to set the jelly.

10 Arrange the berries on top of the cake. Lift the cake with two large spatulas and place it on a serving platter.

FANCY VOL-AU-VENT OF SPICY CHICKEN

A large *vol-au-vent* made in the traditional way with a ¼-in.-thick layer of puff paste topped with a border made of another ¼-in.-thick layer to create a receptacle is not done much nowadays. To make it successfully, the puff pastry had to be perfect and the crust, at best, would still remain gooey in the center. But the technique for *vol-au-vent*, as shown here, is so foolproof that you can use any of the puff pastry recipes on page 144, including trimmings.

This large *vol-au-vent* can be shaped as you wish — high or narrow and spread out. It is served filled and garnished with a peppery, spicy chicken, but could be served as well with veal or sweetbreads in a cream sauce. It could also be used for a dessert garnished with a stew of pears with a caramel cream sauce or the stewed strawberries, page 167.

A *vol-au-vent* makes an impressive centerpiece. Each guest is served a portion of the pastry along with the filling and garnish. The pastry can be kept warm in the oven and the filling prepared ahead, but the dish has to be assembled at the last moment because the sauce will soften the *vol-au-vent*

very quickly. It takes only a few minutes to assemble.

Here mushroom caps are carved with a knife for decoration and the stems and bases of the caps used in the dish. But the mushrooms could also be simply cut into halves or quarters.

Yield: 8 servings

About 1 lb. Puff Paste (page 144)
Egg wash made with 1 egg with half the white removed, beaten

SPICY CHICKEN FILLING

8 large, firm white mushrooms (½ lb.)
A 3½-lb. chicken, skin removed and boned out (1½ lb. meat)
1 lb. ripe tomatoes (2 large)
3 Tb. butter
1 Tb. olive oil
1 tsp. salt
⅜ tsp. freshly ground black pepper
2 tsp. chopped garlic
½ c. sliced shallots
3 Tb. red wine vinegar
1 c. dry white wine
½ tsp. cornstarch dissolved in 1 Tb. water
½ c. small Nice olives
A few drops Tabasco sauce
1 Tb. minced chives
1 Tb. chopped fresh tarragon

GARNISH

Chive flowers

1 Roll out a rectangle of pastry approximately 9 to 10 in. wide by 20 in. long and cut it into 2 squares. Arrange 1 square on a cookie sheet lined with parchment paper and brush along the edges of the pastry with water. Place a ball of aluminum foil in the center of the pastry. It should be large enough to cover the center and approximately 2½ to 3 in. high.

Place the second square of pastry on top and press it firmly around the edges so it adheres. You will notice that as you press it along the edges, the top pastry is slightly stretched before being secured by pressing down on it. The air remains inside and the dough doesn't sink around the ball of foil but stands out around it.

2 Use a 9-in. flan ring to mark the circumference of the *vol-au-vent*. Cut out the circle with a knife and set aside the trimmings. Brush the dough with water.

3 Decorate with strips of dough. In my recipe, I have decorated with a long strip of dough that is first wrapped around the center to mark where the lid will be, then spiraled around again a little below, and finished by gathering together a little strip that will look like a flower after it cooks. Finally, I have stuck ovals of dough to the dough strips to create leaves.

4 Brush the *vol-au-vent* with egg wash and, with the point of a knife, mark concentric lines on top to decorate the lid. Make a hole in the center of the lid to enable steam to escape. Then mark each of the leaves to simulate the veins on a leaf.

5 Mark the outside edge of the pastry on a bias, pressing with the back of a knife into the dough to create a decorative edge.

6 Place in a preheated 400-degree oven and bake for approximately 30 minutes, until very crisp and brown.

7 Allow the dough to cool for 5 to 10 minutes and, with a knife, cut the lid off. Squeeze the ball of aluminum foil to make it smaller, then retrieve it. The shell is now ready to be filled.

8 To flute the mushrooms: Hold the blade of a small, sharp knife loosely in your fingers with the cutting edge out. Using your thumb as a pivot, move the blade forward and down in a continuous motion by twisting your wrist. The rotation should be smooth and regular from the center to the bottom of the cap.

9 When the motion is finished, the cutting edge of the blade should have carved a strip out of the mushroom cap. Remove the trimmings and rub the carved cap with a piece of lemon to prevent discoloration. Slice the cap off and cut the rest of the mushroom, including the stem, into a ¼-in. dice. Repeat with the other mushrooms. You should have about 1¾ c. of mushroom pieces.

10 Remove the chicken skin (it can be used in Country French Bread, page 118) and bone out the chicken. You should have approximately 1½ lb. of meat. Cut the meat into 2-in. pieces. Peel and seed the 1 lb. of tomatoes and cut the flesh into a ½-in. dice (yielding about 2 c.). →

PASTRIES & PETITS FOURS

151

11 The filling for this dish doesn't take long to make and shouldn't be started much more than 10 to 15 minutes before serving. Melt the 3 Tb. butter in a saucepan large enough to hold all the chicken in one layer. Add the 1 Tb. olive oil and, when hot, add the chicken pieces and sprinkle with 1 tsp. salt and ⅜ tsp. pepper. Cook about 3 minutes on one side, turn the pieces, and cook about 3 minutes on the other side. With a slotted spoon, remove the pieces of chicken to a dish and cover. They will continue cooking in their own heat and juices.

13 Decorate with the chive flowers, put the lid on, and serve immediately.

12 To the pan drippings, add the 2 tsp. chopped garlic and ½ c. sliced shallots, and sauté for about 15 to 20 seconds. Add the 3 Tb. vinegar, bring to a boil, and cook the vinegar until it is reduced almost completely and the butter starts sizzling again. Then add the 1 c. white wine and bring to a boil. Cook over high heat for 3 to 4 minutes, until the wine is reduced to approximately ⅓ c. Add the mushrooms (both diced and carved caps) and the tomato pieces, cover, bring to a boil, and cook for about 3 to 4 minutes. Add the ½ tsp. cornstarch dissolved in 1 Tb. water, stir, bring to a boil, and add the chicken, ½ c. olives, and a few drops of Tabasco. Return to the boil, cover, and set aside for 1 to 2 minutes.

Warm the *vol-au-vent* in the oven. Add the 1 Tb. each minced chives and chopped tarragon to the chicken, and spoon the mixture into and around the *vol-au-vent*.

PUFF PASTRIES OF OYSTER AND ASPARAGUS

These small puff pastries of oyster and asparagus are ideal as a first course (1 per person) or as a main course (2 per person). The asparagus can be replaced by sticks of zucchini or other types of vegetables. Scallops or shrimp can be substituted for the oysters, and the dish can be served either with shellfish or with vegetables or with a mixture of both, as done in the recipe here.

The puff paste should be well-cooked and crisp, and any of the three puff pastes on page 144, or trimmings, can be used. Notice that the dough will be rolled very thin. The Chinese chili paste with garlic adds a wonderful hot taste to the dish, but if it is unavailable, a few drops of Tabasco can be substituted.

Yield: 6 servings as a main course, 12 servings as a first course

About 1½ lb. Puff Paste (page 144)
Egg wash made with 1 egg with half the white removed, beaten
1½ lb. asparagus (about 24 stalks)
1 c. water
1 stick butter
Salt to taste
1½ doz. large oysters, shucked with juices reserved
1 small clove garlic, peeled and chopped fine (¼ tsp.)
⅛ tsp. freshly ground black pepper
¾ tsp. Chinese chili paste with garlic
2 Tb. lacy dill leaves

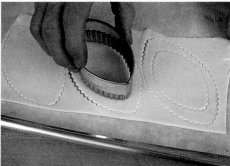

1 Roll the pastry into a very thin rectangle approximately 10 in. wide by 18 in. long and ¹⁄₁₆ to ⅛ in. thick. Brush with egg wash and place in the freezer for 10 minutes to firm up the dough before cutting further.

Cut into 12 ovals approximately 5½ in. long by 3 in. wide with an oval cutter or knife. Then, using a smaller oval cutter or knife, mark smaller ovals inside the larger ones by cutting through the surface of the dough. (These will be the lids of the puff pastries.)

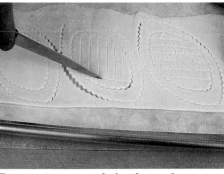

2 With the point of a knife, mark squares inside the lid area to create a design. Place again in the freezer for 5 to 10 minutes to firm up the dough.

Place the ovals on two cookie sheets lined with parchment paper. Bake in a preheated 400-degree oven for 15 to 20 minutes, until well-cooked and crisp. When cooled to lukewarm, cut around the marked area on top of each oval and remove the lid from each. This creates a receptacle, and the lids are placed back on the filling at serving time, like a *vol-au-vent*. Set aside. →

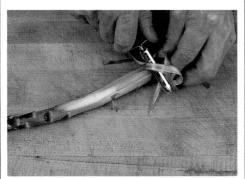

3 **For the asparagus:** Be sure to choose nice, firm asparagus. The tip of the stalk at the top of the picture is opening into tiny flowers and has passed its prime. It won't be as firm as the stalk below, which is tight and plump.

4 In order to use most of the asparagus, some of the stalk has to be peeled where the skin is tough. Holding the asparagus at the end of the stalk, rotate it while you peel with a vegetable peeler (held perpendicular to the stalk), starting somewhat below the tip end and working downward to your fingers at the other end, until the skin is removed all around. The tip, of course, and the upper stalk don't need peeling because they are tender. You can check for tenderness by pressing into the asparagus spear with your nail to see if there is any fiber on top of the skin.

5 Cut away the very end of the asparagus stalk with the trimmings attached and discard. Then, cut each spear about 3 to 4 in. from the tip and slice up into the attached stalk without separating the slices from the tip to create a "fan."

6 The stalk at the tip end of the asparagus has been cut into a "fan" and the remainder of the asparagus stalk can be cut in half, into sticks of about 1½ to 2 in., and then thinly sliced.

The asparagus and the oysters should be cooked simultaneously in two different pans, preferably stainless steel.

To cook the asparagus, place a cup of water in a stainless steel saucepan and bring to a boil. Add the asparagus tips, cover, bring to a boil, and cook about 1 minute. Then add the sliced stems, bring to a boil again, and continue boiling for about 1 minute (about 2 minutes for the tips and 1 minute for the sliced stem pieces). Drain and add 1 Tb. of the butter to the pan and a dash of salt, stirring just until the butter coats the asparagus.

Note: To serve asparagus by itself in the pastry ovals, bring 1 c. of water to a boil, add the asparagus tips, and boil for about 1 minute. Add the asparagus stems, return to the boil, and cook another minute. At that point, there should be only 4 to 5 Tb. remaining. Break ⅓ stick butter into pieces on top, add a dash of salt and pepper, and bring to a strong boil. (The water will mix with the butter and emulsify it, creating a light, creamy sauce.) Fill the little pastry boats with the stems and arrange the tips on top. Replace the puff paste lids and serve immediately.

7 Meanwhile, place the 18 oysters and their juices in a stainless steel saucepan and heat, stirring occasionally. The liquid should barely come to the boil at the edges of the pan. As soon as the frills on the oysters curl, remove them with a slotted spoon and place them in a bowl. Let the cooking juices rest 10 to 15 seconds and then pour gently (leaving any sediment) into a bowl. Discard the sediment and return the juices to the saucepan. Add the ¼ tsp. chopped garlic and reduce over high heat to ⅔ c. Add the ⅛ tsp. pepper and ¾ tsp. chili paste, bring to a boil, and add the remaining butter, piece by piece, while mixing continuously with a whisk. When all the butter is melted, bring the whole mixture to a boil while stirring with a whisk. There is enough liquid in proportion to the butter so that the butter will not "break down," and bringing the mixture to a boil will create an emulsion. As the mixture thickens, remove immediately from the heat, taste, and add salt, if needed, and the 2 Tb. dill. (Remember that the oyster juices may be salty enough so that no additional salt is needed.) Warm up the puff paste receptacles and lids in the oven. Arrange some of the sliced asparagus stems in the bottom of each receptacle, place 2 large oysters on top of the asparagus in each boat, and spoon 1½ to 2 Tb. of sauce over the asparagus and oysters.

8 Place a lid on top of each oval. Arrange 2 tips of asparagus on the side of each plate and serve immediately.

PUFF ANCHOVY FISH

This is a savory that tastes good at the beginning of a meal as well as at the end. It is excellent with cocktails and can also be served as a garnish with a clear soup. The mixture of anchovy fillets, hard-cooked eggs, and chives can be replaced by a purée of shrimp or mushrooms.

Yield: 12 servings

ANCHOVY FILLING

2 eggs
1 can anchovy fillets in oil (2 oz.)
3 Tb. minced chives
¼ tsp. freshly ground black pepper

About 1 lb. Puff Paste (page 144)
Egg wash made with 1 egg with half the
    white removed, beaten

GARNISH

Parsley sprigs

1 Cook the 2 eggs: First place them in a saucepan and cover with warm water from the tap. Bring to a simmer and boil gently for 9 to 10 minutes. Immediately place the eggs in ice cold water and, when just cool enough to handle, crack the shells so the water has a chance to get between the membrane and the egg itself. Allow to cool in the water until completely cold inside and then peel. Put the 1 can of anchovy fillets and their oil with the eggs through a food mill fitted with the fine strainer and purée into a fine paste. Combine the purée with the 3 Tb. chives and ¼ tsp. black pepper. →

2 Roll the pastry to a rectangle about 14 to 15 in. long by about 10 to 12 in. wide with a thickness of approximately 1 in. (The pastry can be any one of the three recipes in this book or puff paste trimmings.) Cut the rectangle lengthwise into 2 strips. Spread the anchovy paste on top of one of the strips, leaving 1 in. of pastry around the filling on all sides.

3 Brush the exposed edges of pastry with cold water and place the other strip of pastry on top, pressing all around the edges to seal. Brush with the egg wash. Place the "sandwich" of anchovies in the freezer for about 10 minutes to firm up the dough.

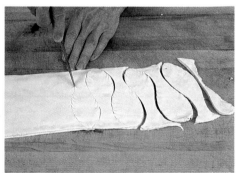

4 Cut continuous fish shapes the width of the pastry, the head of one fish forming the tail of another as the pastry is cut. You should have approximately 12 fish.

5 Place the fish on a tray lined with parchment paper. Mark the head and the eye with the point of a knife and, with a pastry tip, press into the center of the fish bodies to create "scales." Then, mark the tail and fins with a knife and add a piece of dough trimmings to form a "mouth."

6 Place in a preheated 400-degree oven for 20 to 25 minutes, until nicely browned.

7 Arrange the fish on a tray with some fresh parsley sprigs in the center and serve immediately. The fish should still be slightly warm. If done ahead, reheat for a few minutes in a warm oven so they are lukewarm for serving.

CHEESE STRAWS

These little sticks of puff pastry flavored with Parmesan cheese and paprika are ideal to serve as snacks with drinks and are especially good when served with light, clear broth such as consommé or another kind of light soup.

The straws can be cooked straight or twisted, as shown here. They should be eaten fresh. When they are more than a few hours old or when kept overnight, be sure to reheat them in the oven for a few minutes so they get crisp again and have the good taste of fresh butter.

Yield: about 72, half twisted, half plain

½ c. finely grated Parmesan cheese
1 Tb. paprika
Dash cayenne papper
A piece of Puff Paste (any one of the
  3 recipes on page 144, or puff paste
  trimmings), about 12 oz.
Egg wash made with 1 egg with half the
  white removed, beaten

1 Combine the ½ c. Parmesan cheese, 1 Tb. paprika, and dash of cayenne pepper together, and set aside. Roll the puff paste dough into a rectangle approximately 12 × 15 in., with a thickness of about ⅛ in. Brush thoroughly with the egg wash and sprinkle the top with half of the cheese-paprika-pepper mixture.

2 Lift the pastry and turn it over. Brush again with the egg wash and sprinkle with the remaining cheese-paprika-pepper mixture, spreading it so the pastry is well-coated all over. Most of the mixture should adhere on both sides. Fold the dough in half and cut lengthwise into ½-in. strips. You should have about 24 strips.

3 To twist the dough into twisted strips, place one hand at each end of a dough strip and roll one hand toward you and one hand away from you, rolling the pastry under the palm of your hand so it twists.

4 Notice the position of the hands and how the strip of dough has been twisted. Twist about 12 of the strips and reserve the remainder. →

5 Line a tray with a piece of parchment paper that does not extend all the way to the end; there should be about 1 in. of the tray visible at each end. Place the strips of dough about ½ in. apart on the tray and crush the ends of the dough onto the tray beyond the paper at both ends. The object is to make the dough stick to the pan (otherwise it would slide) so that, as it cooks, the strips don't curl and change shape.

6 Place in a preheated 400-degree oven for approximately 12 minutes. The straws should be nicely browned and crisp.

7 Trim away the ends of the pastry with a large knife and cut across the strips to divide them into 3 pieces of approximately 4 in. each.

8 Arrange the plain strips of pastry the same way as the twisted ones on a tray, crushing them at each end onto the tray. Bake at 400 degrees for 12 minutes and, again, cut the strips into 3 pieces.

9 Stack the strips of pastry on two different plates and serve with consommé, other soup, or as a snack or cocktail food.

2 Brush the exposed dough around the jam with water and place the other strip of dough on top, pressing it around the edges so the two pieces adhere well together.

BLACK RASPBERRY JAM DARTOIS

One of the easiest and most delectable desserts made with puff paste is _dartois_, a sandwich of puff paste with jam in the center. Any type of jam can be used or a combination of chocolate and cream called a _ganache_ can be used as a filling.

Like most pastries made with puff paste, this is very good when fresh — at room temperature, just after it has cooled off. Puff paste should not be eaten cold; it is best eaten soon after cooking, when it is very flaky and tender. However, the filling in this particular dessert will not make the pastry soggy, so the _dartois_ could be assembled somewhat ahead of serving. The pieces of crystallized sugar placed on top of the pastry do not melt during cooking and remain intact to give some crunchiness. In addition, as done here, the pastry can be brushed with strained apricot preserves to produce a flavorful and shiny top.

Yield: 6 servings

About ¾ lb. Puff Paste (page 144)
⅓ c. black raspberry jam
Egg wash made with 1 egg with half the white removed, beaten
1 Tb. crystallized sugar
GLAZE

2 to 3 Tb. apricot preserves, melted and strained

1 Roll the pastry into a square about 12 × 12 in. and about ⅛-in. thick. Cut the square into 2 strips, each about 12 × 6 in. Roll 1 strip back onto the rolling pin and unroll it onto a cookie sheet lined with parchment paper. Spread the ⅓ c. raspberry jam down the center of the strip, leaving an inch of dough on all sides.

3 Trim the dough all around, angling it at the corners. The trimmings of dough can be gently pressed into a ball and frozen to be used again for making tarts or at times when you need a flaky dough that doesn't have to puff up too much.

4 Brush the top surface with egg wash and place in the freezer for 5 to 10 minutes so the dough can harden a little. Brush again with the egg wash and mark all around and across the top, using the dull side of a knife. →

5 Sprinkle on the 1 Tb. crystallized sugar, and bake in a preheated 400-degree oven for 20 minutes. The *dartois* should be puffy and golden.

6 Brush the top with the 2 to 3 Tb. melted apricot preserves. Place on a serving tray, cut into 1½-in.-thick slices with a serrated knife, and serve.

PITHIVIER ALMOND CAKE

This famous puff paste almond cake is named after the small town of Pithivier, between Paris and Orléans. Here is the classic cake, with the spiral design on top made with a knife, and the top finished with confectioners' sugar to create a beautiful shine and glaze when baked.

The cake is best eaten when just lukewarm. It is not good cold or after it has been refrigerated because it becomes heavier and more chewy. If there are pieces left over, they should be reheated slightly in the oven before serving. The cake is also excellent served with ice cream. Either of the first two recipes for puff paste, page 144, are best for making this cake.

Yield: 8 servings

ALMOND FILLING
¾ c. whole unskinned almonds
½ c. confectioners' sugar
½ tsp. cornstarch
½ stick butter, softened (4 Tb.)
1 egg
1 Tb. dark rum
½ tsp. vanilla

About 2½ lb. Puff Paste (page 144)
Egg wash made with 1 egg with half the white removed, beaten
GLAZE
Confectioners' sugar

1 For the almond filling: Place the ¾ c. whole unskinned almonds on a cookie sheet in a preheated 400-degree oven and brown for about 12 minutes. Put the toasted almonds, ½ c. confectioners' sugar, and ½ tsp. cornstarch in the bowl of a food processor and process until the mixture is finely ground. Add the ½ stick of butter, 1 egg, 1 Tb. rum, and ½ tsp. vanilla, and process again until smooth. Place in a bowl and, if not using right away, refrigerate. The mixture tends to thicken as it cools in the refrigerator.

Roll the puff paste dough into a large rectangle approximately ¼ in. thick. Using a 10-in. flan ring, mark two circles in the dough.

2 With a sharp knife, cut out the circles. (Don't use the flan ring to cut the dough since it would crush rather than cut the dough, preventing it from rising properly.) Place one of the circles on a cookie sheet lined with parchment paper.

Arrange the almond filling on top, spreading it with a spatula to within 1 in. of the edge of the circle.

3 Moisten the exposed edge of the filled dough with water and place the remaining circle of dough on top. Press around the edge to seal the two dough rounds together. Place the cake in the freezer for 5 to 10 minutes so the dough hardens a little.

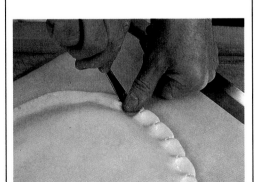

4 Press around the edge with your thumb while notching with a spoon handle to create a design. Press firmly with your thumb to make firm indentations.

5 Brush the top of the cake with the egg wash and, using a knife, mark concentric lines from the outer edge to the center of the cake and make a hole through the dough in the center with the point of a knife.

6 Bake in the 400-degree oven for approximately 30 minutes. Reduce the heat to 375 degrees and, using a sieve, sprinkle the top with confectioners' sugar until nicely coated. Continue cooking for approximately 15 minutes. By that time, the sugar should have melted and created a beautiful glaze. If not, place under the broiler for a few minutes to finish glazing.

7 After cooling for 20 to 30 minutes, cut into wedges and serve lukewarm.

FLAKY RASPBERRY TART

Fresh raspberries are delicious when served on puff paste, provided the puff paste is well-done and very flaky and the raspberries are arranged on top of the pastry no more than 20 to 30 minutes before the tart is served. The closer it is assembled to the moment of serving, the better it will be, so the puff paste won't have time to soften.

The addition of raspberry jam gives a sweetness and an intensity to the berries, and the jelly used on top sets the berries in place and creates a beautiful shine.

The same strip of cooked dough can be garnished with other kinds of fruit, from apricot halves to grapes. Sometimes a layer of pastry cream is put in the bottom and the cooked fruit placed on top and glazed with a preserve.

Yield: 8 servings

About ¾ lb. Puff Paste (page 144)
Egg wash made with 1 egg with half the
    white removed, beaten
½ Tb. confectioners' sugar
4 Tb. black raspberry (or currant or black-
    berry) jam
3 c. fresh raspberries
½ c. currant jelly, melted

1 Roll the dough out very thin (¹⁄₁₆ in.), into a rectangle approximately 9 in. wide by 16 in. long. Trim the sides (the trimmed dough will be about 8½ in. wide by 15 in. long), and place in the freezer for 5 minutes to firm up the dough.

Brush 1 in. along the edges of the dough with water and fold the sides in toward the center of the tart to create a border 1 to 1¼ in. wide. Press into place.

2 The goal is to create a border made of a double layer of dough along the edges. Trim the edges of the dough with a sharp knife so that, instead of being a fold, there are now two layers, one on top of the other.

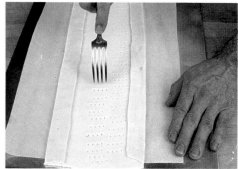

3 Brush the border with the egg wash. Prick the center with a fork to keep it from rising too much.

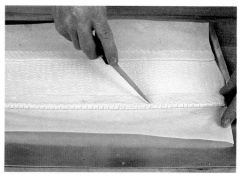

4 With a knife, mark crosswise lines on the border. Create a decorative edge by marking along both sides, and dust the border and the center with the ½ Tb. confectioners' sugar. Let the pastry rest in the freezer for 1 hour so the dough will hold its shape in the oven.

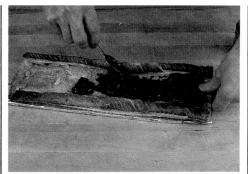

5 Bake in a preheated 400-degree oven for 25 to 30 minutes. Check while baking and, if the top rises too much, crush it down with the back of a spoon. When cold, spread the 4 Tb. jam down the center of the tart between the borders, crushing in the center of the cooked dough to flatten it.

6 Fill the center of the tart with about 1½ c. of the berries. Use any berries here that may be discolored or damaged. Spoon about 2 Tb. of the jelly (see Strawberry Napoleon, page 147, for how to melt the jelly) over the berries and crush them down a little so they soften and mix with the jam and jelly.

7 Arrange the remaining 1½ c. of the best berries on top in neat rows.

8 Allow the remaining melted currant jelly to cool off and thicken slightly. Using a brush, coat the berries with the jelly.

9 Cut the tart into 1½-in.-thick pieces and serve as soon as possible.

CRYSTALLIZED PUFF PASTE OF ORANGE

The crunchy, sugared dough used here provides a perfect contrast to the rich pastry cream and slightly acidic segments of orange. This dessert is at its best when assembled at the last moment.

Yield: 8 servings

RICH PASTRY CREAM

2 egg yolks
3 Tb. sugar
1½ Tb. cornstarch
1 tsp. vanilla
1 c. milk
⅓ stick butter, softened

About 1½ lb. Puff Paste (page 144)
6 Tb. sugar
Egg wash made with 1 egg with half the
  white removed, beaten
6 to 8 large seedless naval oranges

CRYSTALLIZED PEELS OF ORANGES

Skin from 2 oranges (from above)
3 c. water
About ¾ c. sugar

GLAZE

1 c. apricot preserves
¼ c. orange marmalade

GARNISH

Mint sprigs

1 Beat the 2 egg yolks, 3 Tb. sugar, 1½ Tb. cornstarch, and 1 tsp. vanilla together in a bowl for about 30 seconds, until well-mixed. Bring the 1 c. milk to a boil.

2 Pour the boiling milk into the egg yolk mixture while beating with a whisk, then return the mixture to the pan.

3 Bring to a strong boil, stirring—especially around the edges of the base of the pan—so the mixture doesn't scorch as it thickens. Place in a bowl, cover with plastic wrap, and refrigerate until lukewarm.

When lukewarm, whisk in the ⅓ stick soft butter and return to the refrigerator, until cold.

4 Roll the pastry out to ⅛-in. thickness and let it rest for a few minutes so it doesn't shrink too much when cut. Mark 8 rounds with a lid approximately 6 in. across, and cut out the rounds.

5 Line two cookie sheets with parchment paper and sprinkle each with 1 Tb. of the sugar. Place 4 rounds on each tray. With the point of a knife, mark a circle inside each round approximately ¾ in. from the edge. Brush with egg wash and sprinkle 2 Tb. sugar on the 4 rounds on each tray. Place in a preheated 400-degree oven and bake for about 15 minutes, until well-cooked and crispy. If the rounds do not get brown enough, place under the broiler for a few seconds.

8 Cut between the membranes to remove the segments: Cut down close to each membrane with the blade.

11 Lift the peels out with a fork and place them on a tray covered with about ½ c. sugar.

6 With a vegetable peeler, cut approximately 8 strips from the skin of each of 2 oranges and set aside.

9 Twist your knife to lift up the flesh against the next membrane. When all the flesh has been removed, squeeze the membranes over the bowl to release any remaining juice. Set the orange segments and juice aside.

12 Turn the peels in the ½ c. dry sugar, pressing and patting them until they are saturated with sugar on both sides. Set aside for 30 to 40 minutes. (Leftover sugar can be strained and reused when making pastry and leftover syrup can be used to flavor pastry cream or other desserts.)

The crystallized orange peels can be placed in a jar and kept in the refrigerator almost indefinitely. They can be used to decorate cakes, used in a julienne, chopped for use in a pastry cream, or half of each peel can be dipped in melted chocolate and served with drinks as an after-dinner candy. →

7 Peel all the oranges with a sharp knife, moving the knife in a jigsaw motion so all the white pith is removed and the orange is completely nude.

10 **To crystallize the orange peels:** Cover the reserved orange peels with 2 c. cold water and bring to a boil. Boil approximately 30 seconds and drain in a sieve. Rinse the saucepan and place the peels back in the pan with 1 c. of water and ⅓ c. sugar. Bring to a boil and cook for approximately 20 minutes at a gentle boil, until the peels are translucent and the syrup is thick.

PASTRIES & PETITS FOURS

13 At serving time, cut the pastry rounds along the line of the lid and push the crystallized top down into the pastry to create a base that is brown and crisp.

16 Cut 2 pieces of crystallized orange peel in half for each serving and arrange on the plates. Decorate with a sprig of mint and serve.

14 Spread 2 Tb. of the pastry cream in the bottom of each pastry receptacle and arrange the drained orange segments on top.

15 Melt together and strain the 1 c. apricot preserves and ¼ c. orange marmalade. Coat the top of each puff with 1½ to 2 Tb. of the apricot–orange marmalade glaze. Place on individual plates.

PUFF PASTE OF STEWED STRAWBERRIES AND CREAM

The ingredients for this dessert can be prepared ahead, even the puff paste rounds hollowed out, but it should be assembled at the last moment on individual plates so the puff paste does not get soggy.

Yield: 8 servings

About 1½ lb. Puff Paste (page 144)
2 lb. medium strawberries, hulled
⅔ c. sugar
⅓ c. water
¾ c. heavy cream
3 Tb. crème de Cassis (optional)

1 Follow the instructions for Pear in Puff and Almond Pastry Cream, page 168, to make individual crystallized puff paste rounds. Clean the 2 lb. of berries. Leave them whole if they are of medium size. If they are large, cut in halves and set aside.

Make a stew of strawberries: Place the ⅔ c. sugar in a saucepan (preferably stainless steel and large enough to hold all the berries in 1 or 2 layers) with ⅓ c. water. Bring to a boil and cook the sugar to approximately 220 degrees, until it starts getting sticky. Add the berries all at once, bring the mixture back to the boil, and cook about 1 minute, covered. Turn off the heat and let the berries sit for 10 to 15 minutes. At that point, the berries will release their juices and liquefy the sugar syrup, which will turn red and liquid.

2 Drain the berries in a sieve and place the sugar syrup back on the stove. Bring to a boil and cook again for 3 to 4 minutes, bringing it back to 220 to 225 degrees, until reduced to about ½ c. Add the ¾ c. cream and bring to a boil. Combine with the berries and transfer to a shallow bowl. Cool. As the mixture cools, it will thicken.

3 In the Pear in Puff and Almond Pastry Cream recipe, the sugared top of the puff is pushed down into the puff to create a crystallized bottom. In this recipe, the top is removed and used to decorate the top of the berries.

Cut a little round of puff paste from the crystallized lid with a cookie cutter. The trimmings that remain after you have cut out the lid can be pressed back into the bottom of the puff paste shell. →

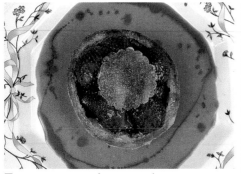

4 Drizzle some of the strawberry cream sauce around the individual plates (it should have thickened as it cooled). Place one of the pastry shells in the center, fill with strawberries and a tablespoon of additional sauce, and top with a pastry cap. If desired, drizzle some crème de Cassis (red currant liqueur) in little drops around the sauce for taste and effect. Serve right away.

PEAR IN PUFF AND ALMOND PASTRY CREAM

This very delicate dessert is great for an elegant party. It should be put together portion by portion at the last moment. If all the ingredients are ready, it doesn't take more than a few seconds to assemble each dessert, and it will be best if done at the last moment so the pastry doesn't get soggy.

Other poached fruit, such as apricots or peaches, or even uncooked fruit, such as bananas or berries, could be used on top of the pastry cream. The time of cooking for poached pears depends on the ripeness of the fruit; it may take from 1 to 2 minutes in a boiling syrup if the pear is ripe, but, on the other hand, a hard pear such as a Seckel or Bosc may take as long as 45 minutes to 1 hour to become tender.

Yield: 8 servings

8 small Bartlett pears (5 to 6 oz. each, 2½ to 3 lb. altogether)
TO POACH THE PEARS

4 c. water
⅔ c. sugar
Skin and juice of 1 large lemon
1 tsp. vanilla
ALMOND PASTRY CREAM

½ c. whole almonds, unskinned (about 3 oz.)
1 c. milk
3 egg yolks
3 Tb. sugar
1½ Tb. cornstarch
1 tsp. vanilla

About 1½ lb. Puff Paste (page 144)
3 Tb. sugar
Egg wash made with 1 egg with half the white removed, beaten

½ c. heavy cream
GLAZE

1½ c. apricot preserves
1 Tb. pear brandy
GARNISH

Mint sprigs

1 Be sure that the pears you buy are all at the same degree of ripeness so they cook uniformly. Peel with a vegetable peeler all around the base of each pear, peeling in a circular motion because the base is round.

2 Where the pear narrows at the neck, peel upward toward the stem, again following the shape of the pear and peeling away strips of skin.

3 Using a melon baller, remove the seeds inside. You will probably need to remove 2 or 3 balls of pear to get all the seeds. The stem should still be attached for decorative reasons.

4 After the pears are completely cleaned, peeled, and hollowed out inside, mix together the 4 c. water, ⅔ c. sugar, juice and yellow skin of one lemon (removed with a vegetable peeler), and 1 tsp. vanilla in a saucepan (preferably stainless steel to prevent discoloration and deep enough so the pears can be submerged in the syrup), and add the pears.

5 You will notice that the pears will float to the top. Anything above the level of the syrup will discolor during cooking, so to keep them down, place a piece of folded paper towel on top of the pears and an inverted plate that fits inside the pot over the towel. This will provide sufficient weight to keep the pears submerged. Bring to a boil, cover with a lid, and boil gently until tender but still slightly firm when pierced with the point of a knife. Let the pears cool in the syrup. (They will continue to cook as they cool.)

6 When the pears are cool, remove the plate and discard the paper towel. Notice that the pears are beautifully white and are now sinking into the syrup. As they cool, the specific gravity of the pears changes, they absorb the syrup, and now, cold, they will sink into the syrup and not discolor.

To toast the almonds: Arrange the ½ c. unskinned almonds on a cookie sheet. Place in a preheated 400-degree oven for 10 to 12 minutes. When cool, grind in a food processor and set aside.

To make the pastry cream: Bring the cup of milk to a boil. Meanwhile, beat the 3 egg yolks, 3 Tb. sugar, 1½ Tb. cornstarch, and 1 tsp. vanilla in a bowl, mixing well with a whisk. Add the hot milk in a stream while whisking (see photograph 2, page 164). Place the mixture back on the stove and bring to a boil, mixing constantly with the whisk—especially around the edges of the base of the pan so the mixture doesn't scorch (see photograph 3, page 164)—until it thickens and boils. Add the ground almonds and set the mixture aside to cool.

7 Roll the dough to a thickness of approximately ³⁄₁₆ to ¼ in. and let it rest, preferably refrigerated, for a few minutes. Use a 4-in. ring or lid to mark the dough and, with a sharp knife, cut it into 8 circles. →

PASTRIES & PETITS FOURS

8 Sprinkle 2 Tb. of the sugar on a cookie sheet lined with parchment paper. Place the 8 rounds of pastry on top and mark a lid ½ in. inside each round with an upside-down measuring cup or the point of a knife. Sprinkle with the remaining 1 Tb. of sugar and bake 15 to 20 minutes in the 400-degree oven.

9 When the dough has cooled for 10 to 15 minutes, cut with the point of a knife into the pastry, following the line you marked before baking, and ease the knife under to remove this top section, leaving the sides intact.

10 After you have released the top, press it down into the pastry shell, baked-side up, so that now the bottom of the shell is golden-brown and crystallized.

11 Beat the ½ c. cream until firm. Add the ½ c. whipped cream to the cold almond cream and mix with a whisk.

12 Drain the pears and dry on paper towels. (The syrup can be placed in a jar and kept in the refrigerator almost forever for use in poaching other fruit.)

Place about 2 Tb. of the almond cream in each pastry receptacle.

13 Strain the 1½ c. apricot preserves through a food mill (a food processor will whip the preserves and make them whitish and full of air bubbles). If the preserves are quite thick, dilute with the 1 Tb. of pear brandy or 1 Tb. of syrup from the pears. Put a little ring of the apricot preserve sauce on a plate and place the filled receptacle on top.

14 Dip the pears into the apricot sauce, rolling them so they are completely coated.

15 Lift the pears out and place each one on top of a filled pastry receptacle. Decorate with a sprig of mint, pushed right into the pear so it holds firmly. Serve immediately.

CHERRY-RASPBERRY PILLOW

This large free-form pie is made with a mixture of cherries and raspberries, but other kinds of fruit could be combined and used instead. The fruits, mixed with a little cornstarch to thicken the juices (and prevent them from leaking) and some preserves for sweetness, are placed uncooked inside the dough.

The pie can be made with a pâte brisée as well as with a puff paste. In fact, if the dessert is to be kept on a buffet table for more than one hour, the pâte brisée would be a better choice since it will keep its crunchiness longer than the puff paste. Although the crystallized sugar on top is not absolutely essential, it gives a nice crispy finish to the dough.

Yield: 8–10 servings

1 lb. Puff Paste (page 144) or *pâte brisée* (page 178 or 180)
1 lb. cherries
⅔ c. cherry preserves, preferably with pieces of fruit
1½ Tb. cornstarch
½ lb. raspberries
2 Tb. butter
Egg wash made with 1 egg with half the white removed, beaten
1 Tb. crystallized sugar
Confectioners' sugar to dust the top

2 To pit, hold a cherry between the thumb and forefinger of one hand so the hole of the stem shows. With the other hand, insert a small, pointed knife into the hole of the stem until you feel the pit. Squeeze the cherry to soften the flesh and loosen the pit with one hand while simultaneously bringing the pit up through the stem opening with the point of the knife. After a bit of practice, this technique works well and the cherries can be pitted quite quickly.

1 Roll the pound of puff paste to a very thin rectangle, about ⅟₁₆ in. thick and 14 in. wide by 22 in. long. Roll the dough up on the rolling pin and unroll it across a cookie sheet so the width of the dough is almost the length of the cookie sheet. Almost half the length of the dough will extend beyond the cookie sheet and will be folded on top of the filling later.

3 Combine the pitted cherries with the ⅔ c. of preserves and the 1½ Tb. cornstarch.

4 Spread the cherry mixture on top of the dough covering the cookie sheet and sprinkle the ½ lb. of raspberries and 2 Tb. butter on top. Brush the edge of the pastry with water and fold the pastry extending beyond the cookie sheet on top of the fruit to encase it. →

5 Press to seal the dough around the edges and trim the corners with a knife. Press gently on the top of the "pillow" to distribute the fruit inside evenly. Brush with the egg wash, and press down with the tines of a fork about 1½ in. all around the pastry to create an edge.

6 Sprinkle the 1 Tb. crystallized sugar on top and mark a crisscross pattern on top of the pastry with the cutting edge of a knife. It's all right if you cut through the dough at certain points because it will allow the steam to escape during cooking.

7 Place in a preheated 400-degree oven for 45 minutes. It may leak slightly, so be sure to move the "pillow" a little on the cookie sheet as it comes out of the oven before the hot liquid has a chance to harden and stick to the pan. Cool to room temperature and sprinkle with confectioners' sugar.

8 At serving time, cut the dessert into segments on a board and arrange on a serving platter. Serve at room temperature.

APPLE CRUNCH

An open-faced tart is the quintessential French dessert, found in the smallest restaurants as well as three-star establishments; it is part of the repertoire of the home cook as well as the professional chef. In Alsace, custard is added to the fruits to hold the pieces together and add richness. Wherever it is made, the tart has one layer of dough underneath and an open top.

My version here is a combination of a French apple tart and American apple pie. There is dough on the bottom and top and the apples are flavored with butter and sugar in the French style. Cinnamon, mace, nutmeg, and other seasonings can be added, if desired.

For the apple crunch to be good, the dough must be rolled extremely thin and the layer of apples inside should be fairly thin. It is cooked at a high temperature for a long time to make it crisp on the bottom as well as on top.

Eat the crunch at room temperature or lukewarm. You can serve it with ice cream or with a dollop of whipped cream or sour cream next to it, and it is also excellent with an aged Cheddar cheese melted on top.

Yield: 8–10 servings

DOUGH

2 c. unbleached cool all-purpose flour*
1½ sticks cold butter
¼ tsp. salt
1 tsp. sugar
½ c. ice cold water

1½ lb. large Rome Beauty apples (about 4 to 5 apples)
2½ Tb. butter
1½ Tb. sugar
Egg wash made with 1 egg with half the white removed, beaten

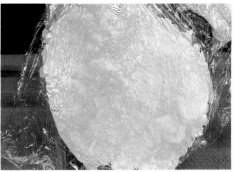

1 Place the 2 c. flour in the bowl of a KitchenAid mixer (see page 118, step 3). Cut the 1½ sticks of cold butter into slivers and add them along with the ¼ tsp. salt and 1 tsp. sugar. Using speed 3 or 4, mix for about 45 seconds to 1 minute. The pieces of butter should still be visible. Add the ½ c. cold water and mix for another 20 seconds or so, until the mixture just holds together. Divide the dough in half and place each piece on a sheet of plastic wrap. Cover each with second pieces of plastic wrap and flatten the two pieces of dough with your hand. Then, roll them out with a rolling pin between the plastic wrap pieces so they will cool faster. <u>Traces of butter are still visible throughout the dough.</u> Refrigerate for 30 minutes before finishing the rolling.

2 Remove the plastic wrap, and place the dough on a floured board. Roll one piece of the dough very thin – less than ⅛ in. – into an oval approximately 17 to 18 in. long by 13 in. wide. <u>Roll outward from the center in all directions</u>; going back and forth over the dough with the rolling pin tends to toughen it. Use a little flour to help in the rolling. Roll the dough back on the rolling pin and unroll onto a large cookie sheet. →

* Note: In areas of the country where it is very warm, the flour can be placed in the freezer for an hour or so beforehand to cool.

3 Peel, halve, and core the 1½ lb. of apples. Cut in thin slices, then cut the slices in halves or thirds and arrange on the rolled pastry to within about 1 in. of the edge.

4 Fold the edge of the pastry back onto the apples. Be sure there are no holes around the sides of the pastry; if you see any, patch with a piece of dough. Dot the top with the 2½ Tb. butter and sprinkle the 1½ Tb. sugar over the apples. Brush the edge of the dough with water.

5 Using flour, roll the remaining piece of dough until it is ⅛ in. thick and the size of the bottom layer. Roll back onto the rolling pin and . . .

6 . . . unroll on top of the apple-filled dough. Press around the edge so the top layer of dough adheres to the bottom layer, trimming any excess dough from the top layer. Brush off the top to get rid of any flour and then brush the top with the egg wash. Place the pie in the freezer for 10 to 15 minutes to harden the dough on top.

7 Cut a design on top. (Holes are necessary to allow steam to escape.) Cut a long, curved stem with some leaves on the sides and cutouts at the end to indicate flowers. The dough, hardened in the freezer, is easy to cut. Otherwise, it would be mushy.

8 Place in a preheated 400-degree oven for 45 to 55 minutes, until nicely crisp on the top and bottom. If you should detect a leak while the pie is cooking, lift gently, patch with a piece of aluminum foil, and continue cooking.

9 Cut into thin wedges and serve at room temperature or lukewarm alone or with the cream served with the Galette de Pérouges, page 195.

TARTE TATIN

Tarte tatin is the famous upside-down, caramelized apple tart created many years ago by two sisters called the demoiselles Tatin. It is an example of a dish that originated in the home kitchen, became a regional specialty, and eventually made its way into most of the great restaurants.

There are many variations on the original concoction. In my version, I cook the apples with the skins on to give a crustier, chewier texture. Dried currants (although regular dried raisins could be substituted), slivered almonds, and dried apricots help fill the holes between the large segments of apple and give taste as well as texture to the tart. Additional apples on top of the large apple segments make the dish thicker and create a flat surface for the pastry to sit on, which results in a nicer shape when unmolded.

The extra caramel added at the end can be omitted for a tarter dish. The tart should be served at room temperature or slightly warm. If done ahead, it is best to keep it in the skillet, as shown in photograph 12. Then, at serving time, put it back in a hot oven or on top of the stove over medium heat for a few minutes to warm slightly and melt the sugar so the mixture unmolds easily.

Yield: 8–10 servings

PATE BRISEE

1 c. flour (about 5½ oz.)
¾ stick butter (3 oz.)
⅛ tsp. salt
½ tsp. sugar
¼ c. ice cold water

FILLING

¼ c. sugar
5 Tb. butter
1 Tb. lemon juice
4 lb. Golden Delicious apples (about 10)
¼ c. slivered almonds
½ c. sliced dried apricots
⅓ c. dried currants
¾ c. water
2 Tb. butter

TO GLAZE THE DOUGH

2 tsp. sugar

CARAMEL GLAZE (optional)

3 Tb. sugar
1 Tb. water
1 tsp. butter

GARNISH

1 c. heavy cream

1 Although the dough can be made by hand, a mixer with the flat beater attachment does the job well and easily. In the summer, it is a good idea to keep the flour in the freezer and the butter refrigerated until ready to add since it is important in a *pâte brisée* to mix all the ingredients together quickly to keep the gluten from developing too much. The butter should remain visible in the dough—not blend into it. The butter will melt during the baking and develop some of the flakiness you find in a puff paste.

Put the 1 c. flour in the mixer bowl and cut the ¾ stick butter into ¼-in.-thick slivers, letting them fall into the flour.

2 Add the ⅛ tsp. salt and ½ tsp. sugar and, using the flat beater, mix on speed 2 (of a KitchenAid mixer—see page 118, step 3) or low speed for about 45 seconds to 1 minute. At that point, pieces of butter should still be visible in the dough. Add the ¼ c. cold water and mix on low speed for about 20 seconds, just until the mixture starts gathering together. Note the texture of the dough as you turn it out onto a large piece of plastic wrap. →

■3 Cover the dough with another piece of wrap the same size. Roll the dough out between the plastic sheets. (If you were to roll it out on the table at this point, the softness of the butter would make it necessary to use a great amount of flour to prevent the butter from sticking, and this would tend to make the dough tough.) The pieces of butter are still visible in the dough through the plastic. Place in the refrigerator for 10 to 15 minutes while preparing the apples. The dough is only partially rolled out—it is still too thick to use.

■4 Put the ¼ c. sugar, 5 Tb. of butter, and 1 Tb. lemon juice in a 12-in. skillet (preferably nonstick). Remove the cores from the apples at the stem end and at the opposite end, using your thumb as a pivot and rotating the tip of a sharp paring knife as you cut into the apple. Split the apples in half, and remove the cores from the centers with the same circular cutting motion. Then, cut again into quarters.

■5 Heat the sugar, butter, and lemon juice in the skillet, and cook until it becomes caramel—3 to 4 minutes. Add the ¼ c. slivered almonds and cook for 10 to 15 seconds. Remove from the heat.

■6 Arrange the apple quarters on top of the caramel, placing them skin-side down in one layer, making two concentric rows with a piece of apple in the center. You will use about 6 to 7 of the apples, 20 to 25 pieces.

■7 Sprinkle the ½ c. apricots and ⅓ c. currants on top. Slice the remainder of the apples thin (you will have approximately 4½ to 5 c.) and add to the skillet to fill it completely.

■8 Add the ¾ c. water, bring the mixture to a boil, cover, and boil gently 10 minutes. The object here is to soften the apples so they sink down and form a flat surface. Remove the lid and continue cooking on top of the stove over medium heat for about 7 to 8 minutes, until there is no visible liquid when you incline the pan slightly. This indicates that most of the moisture has been boiled away and what remain are the sugar and butter, which are beginning to caramelize.

■9 Remove the dough from the plastic wrap and place it on the board. Sprinkle with a little flour and roll very thin (no more than ⅛ in.).

■10 Trim the edge and fold it in on itself to form an edge that is a little thicker all around.

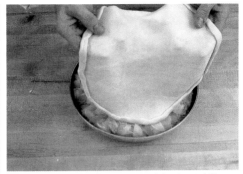

11 Dot the top of the tart with the 2 Tb. butter, broken into pieces, and place the circle of dough on top. Press it down with your hand so it lies completely flat. Pierce with a fork all over and sprinkle with the 2 tsp. sugar, which will caramelize on the dough during cooking.

13 Either at serving time or before, invert the apples onto a serving platter after first shaking the pan gently to make sure the apple mass has loosened.

12 If the handle of your skillet is plastic, wrap it with several layers of aluminum foil to protect it, and place in a preheated 400-degree oven for 45 minutes. To see if the juices are caramelized, incline the pan. If any visible juices remain, place back over heat on top of the stove for 3 to 4 minutes, until you see that the boiling juices have turned into caramel throughout and the top is a solid mass when the tart is moved.

14 To make an extra glaze (which is optional), heat the 3 Tb. sugar, 1 Tb. water, and 1 tsp. butter in a skillet until the mixture turns a light caramel color. Immediately, using a brush or spoon, coat the surface of the apples. This coating of caramel will last for a few hours but will eventually melt down.

15 Beat the 1 c. heavy cream until firm but not too stiff to use as a garnish. No sugar is needed since the apples are sweet. Cut the pie into wedges and serve immediately with a good tablespoon of whipped cream per serving.

1 To make the dough in the food processor, the butter should be very cold and cut into small pieces. Place the 1½ c. flour, ¼ tsp. salt, and 1½ sticks of butter in the food processor and process for about 5 seconds. The butter should still be in pieces. Add the ⅓ c. cold water and process about 5 seconds more, just enough for the dough to start gathering together. The little pieces of butter should still be visible in the dough. <u>Remove the dough from the processor and gather it into a ball.</u> Refrigerate or use immediately.

RHUBARB GALETTE

For this large country-style galette the dough is rolled very thin, from 1/16 to ⅛ in. Any type of fruit can be placed in the center, then the edge of the dough is folded over the fruit, and the resulting galette is baked in a hot oven.

The edges of the dough are left rough, just as they are when you have finished rolling out the dough, giving the tart an unpolished, country look. For any fruits that tend to produce a lot of liquid when cooked—such as plums, rhubarb, grapes, and the like—spread a mixture of ground almonds, flour, and sugar on the dough before adding the fruit, as explained here, to absorb the liquid released by the fruit during cooking and to prevent it from running out through the dough onto the tray and into the oven.

Select rhubarb that is red and ripe. You will notice that, depending on the time of the summer when it is picked, it will be more or less tart so the amount of sugar may have to be increased or decreased. Even when ripe, the rhubarb will make a fairly tart galette. Do not use any rhubarb leaves, since they are toxic.

Yield: 8–10 servings

PROCESSOR PATE BRISEE

1½ c. flour (about 8 oz.)
¼ tsp. salt
1½ sticks cold butter, cut into pieces (6 oz.)
⅓ c. ice cold water

FILLING

2½ lb. rhubarb
⅓ c. sugar
3 Tb. butter

BOTTOM MIXTURE

3 Tb. ground almonds
3 Tb. flour
¼ c. sugar

GLAZE

Mixture of ¾ c. apricot and raspberry or plum preserves, strained together

2 Roll the dough out into a large oval less than ⅛ in. thick. It will be approximately 18 to 19 in. long by 16 in. wide. Tiny pieces of butter should still be visible in the dough at this point. Transfer the dough to a cookie sheet, rolling it up on the rolling pin and unrolling it onto the sheet, and refrigerate it while you prepare the bottom mixture and filling.

3 Cut the 2½ lb. of rhubarb into 2- to 2½-in. pieces and, if the ribs are large, split them in half the long way.

4 Combine the 3 Tb. ground almonds, 3 Tb. flour, and ¼ c. sugar, and spread the mixture out on the dough to within approximately 2 in. of the edge.

5 Place the rhubarb pieces casually in the center of the dough or arrange them in a more orderly fashion. Fold the edges of the dough up over the fruit to create a border of about 2 in., and sprinkle with the ⅓ c. sugar and 3 Tb. butter. Some of the sugar should be sprinkled on the border of dough.

6 Place the *galette* in a preheated 400-degree oven for 1 hour. The dough should be very crunchy, well-cooked, and brown and the fruit in the center very soft. If any of the juices have leaked through the dough onto the tray, be sure to slide a knife underneath and move the pie slightly while it is still hot because the juices will harden and the pie stick to the tray as it cools.

7 Spoon the glaze (¾ c. apricot and raspberry or plum preserves, strained together) over the top of the *galette* and spread it with a spoon or brush. Spread some of the glaze on the dough border. Cut into wedges and serve at room temperature as is or with a little whipped cream.

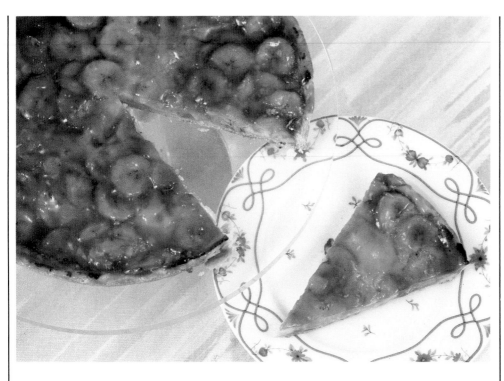

BANANA TART LUQUILLO

This banana tart is made with a banana-flavored filling combined with pastry cream. It is then cooked and glazed with a guava jelly (although another jelly or preserve, preferably from an exotic fruit, could be substituted).

The pâte brisée is different from the one used for the Apple Crunch (page 173), as the dough here is completely blended through the fraisage technique (step 2). This produces a more tender crust with a bit less flakiness than the pâte brisée on page 178.

Like most tarts, this one is best eaten at room temperature, as it tends to harden too much when cold and the flavors of the different components are not as sharp.

The bananas, sautéed with butter and lemon juice, could be eaten by themselves or flambéed with dark rum and served with ice cream or crêpes.

Yield: 8 servings

PATE BRISEE

1¼ c. flour
1 stick butter
1 tsp. sugar
⅛ tsp. salt
2 Tb. ice cold water

BANANA FILLING

2 Tb. butter
⅓ c. sugar
⅓ c. lime juice
1½ lb. bananas (about 4), cut into slices (about 2½ c.)

PASTRY CREAM

1 c. milk
1 egg + 1 egg yolk
4 tsp. cornstarch
¼ c. sugar
½ tsp. vanilla
2 Tb. butter

GLAZE

½ c. guava jelly, or another tropical fruit jelly or preserve

1 **For the pâte brisée:** In a mixing bowl, combine the 1¼ c. flour, 1 stick butter, 1 tsp. sugar, ⅛ tsp. salt, and 2 Tb. ice cold water together, and crush with your fingers until the mixture is crumbly.

2 Place the dough on the table and, using the technique called *fraisage,* smear about ¼ c. forward with the palm of your hand to blend it thoroughly. Repeat until the whole mixture has been blended. One additional *fraisage* of the dough should be sufficient, but if the ingredients are not quite blended, gather the dough together again into a ball and repeat the *fraisage.*

3 On a lightly floured board, roll the dough (from the center out in every direction) into a circle approximately ⅛ in. thick and 14 in. in diameter.

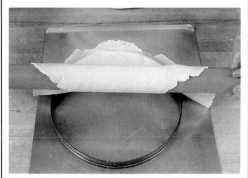

4 Brush any excess flour from the top of the dough, then roll it up on a rolling pin. Unroll over a 10-in. ring placed in the center of a cookie sheet and brush off any excess flour from the top. Note that the top of the dough at this point was table-side down in step 3. So by rolling and unrolling the dough over the rolling pin you are able to remove the excess flour from both sides.

5 Lift up the dough hanging over the sides of the ring and ease it gently into the ring; it is important not to stretch it or it will shrink more during cooking. Push additional dough all around into the rim to create a thicker edge.

6 Roll the rolling pin over the edge of the ring, pressing down and rolling in one direction and then the other to cut the dough evenly. Remove excess dough and reserve it, refrigerated or frozen, for future use.

7 With your thumb and index finger, press on the dough around the edge to create a border. Then, with your thumb, roll a small amount of the dough over the rim of the ring all around, pressing it gently to anchor the shell and hold it in place so it won't collapse on itself during cooking. (When this technique is used, it is not necessary to line the shell with paper and weight it.) Prick the bottom of the dough with a fork and place in a preheated 400-degree oven for approximately 15 to 20 minutes, until lightly browned.

8 **To make the banana filling:** Put the 2 Tb. butter and ⅓ c. each sugar and lime juice in a skillet, and cook until the mixture forms a caramel (about 8 to 10 minutes).

9 When the caramel takes on a pale blond color, add the 4 sliced bananas and sauté gently in the caramel for 3 to 4 minutes.

10 The dough should be nicely browned and have shrunk just slightly from the edges. →

PASTRIES & PETITS FOURS

181

11 To prepare the pastry cream: Heat the 1 c. milk in a saucepan until it comes to a boil. With a whisk, combine the egg, egg yolk, 4 tsp. cornstarch, ¼ c. sugar, and ½ tsp. vanilla in a bowl, mixing until smooth. Whisk in the boiling milk, mix well, and return to the saucepan. Place over medium to high heat, stirring constantly with a whisk so it doesn't burn, and cook until it comes to a strong boil and thickens. Cool for about 10 minutes, then add the 2 Tb. butter and mix well.

Pour the pastry cream into the pastry shell, spreading it to an equal thickness all around.

13 Remove from the oven and let the tart rest for about 15 to 20 minutes until cooled, then scrape off any overhang of dough that holds the tart to the ring.

16 At serving time, slide the tart onto a serving platter and cut it into wedges. Serve at room temperature.

14 Remove the ring.

12 Pour the caramelized bananas on top and stir gently to mix the bananas coarsely with the pastry cream. Smooth the top and bake in the 400-degree oven for 30 minutes.

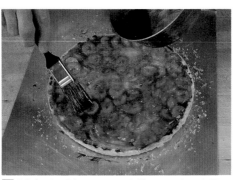

15 Melt the ½ c. guava jelly or other jelly or preserve if it is not soft. Brush the top of the tart with the jelly.

EXOTIC CUSTARD FRUIT GALETTE

This open tart is called a <u>galette</u> because it is cooked free-form and the dough is very thin with its edge folded on itself to create a border. The sweet dough, cooked like a large cookie, will keep well and can be baked up to one day ahead. It can be filled at the last moment with pastry cream and fruit, fruit and jam, or custard cream and jam.

This exotic fruit <u>galette</u> is made with tropical fruits such as feijoa (a very flavorful, almost perfumy fruit that tastes of pineapples and berries), as well as papaya, kiwi, mango, pineapple, banana, and pomegranate seeds, which decorate the top.

The sweet pastry dough is delicate and soft, but it works well if plastic wrap is used when it is rolled out. The dough can be made into small cookies as well as used as a shell for light custard tart recipes (see Lime and Orange Tartlets, page 186).

Yield: 8–10 servings

SWEET PASTRY DOUGH

1½ c. all-purpose flour
¾ c. cake flour
2 sticks butter, softened (½ lb.)
1 egg yolk
¼ c. confectioners' sugar
1 Tb. milk

CARAMEL

½ c. granulated sugar
2 Tb. water

TROPICAL FRUIT FILLING

About ½ mango
About 1 feijoa
About ½ papaya
About ½ kiwi
About 1 banana
About ¼ pineapple
About 3 Tb. pomegranate seeds

PASTRY CREAM

1 c. milk
1 egg + 1 egg yolk
1 tsp. vanilla
¼ c. granulated sugar
2 Tb. cornstarch
2 Tb. butter, softened
1 Tb. rum

GLAZE

½ c. apricot preserves
1 Tb. rum

1 **To make the sweet pastry dough:** Place the 1½ c. all-purpose and ¾ c. cake flour in a mixing bowl, add the 2 sticks of butter (cut into ½-in. pieces), and <u>crush lightly with your hands</u> until the butter is in pea-size pieces.

2 Add the egg yolk, ¼ c. confectioners' sugar, and 1 Tb. milk, and continue crushing the mixture, until most of the butter has been incorporated into the flour and the mixture holds together well.

3 Place the dough on a board and, using the technique called *fraisage*, smear the dough forward, about ¼ c. at a time, pressing it with the palm of your hand to blend it completely. It should be smooth and the same color throughout. If not, repeat the *fraisage* technique once or twice more, until all the ingredients are well-blended. →

183

4 Place the dough on a piece of plastic wrap, cover it with another piece of plastic wrap, and roll it out with a rolling pin into a circle approximately 14 in. in diameter and ⅛ in. thick.

5 Remove the piece of plastic wrap from the top of the dough and invert the dough onto a cookie sheet. Peel off the remaining piece of plastic wrap.

6 Trim the edges of the *galette*, if necessary, to make it uniformly round and fold the edge in on itself to create a border about ½ in. thick.

7 Roll the edge of the dough again on itself all around to make it approximately ½ in. high. Try to keep the circle round and equal all around.

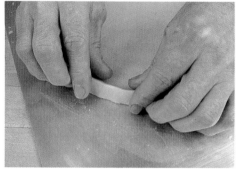

8 Then press the edge of the dough with your fingers, tapering it to a point at the top and keeping the base thick. The shape of the border will prevent it from collapsing on itself during cooking.

9 To decorate the border, use the thumb and forefinger of one hand to pinch the dough while pressing on it with the index finger of the other hand, repeating the pattern at even intervals all around the edge.

10 Put the pastry shell in a preheated 375-degree oven and bake for 25 minutes, until cooked through and well-browned.

11 **To make the caramel:** In a saucepan, combine the ½ c. granulated sugar and 2 Tb. water, and place over medium heat for 8 to 10 minutes, until the mixture turns a caramel color. Pour some of the caramel on the dough and, using a brush made of bristles (not nylon), spread it over the surface of the pastry shell to create a very thin layer. This can be done a few hours ahead; the purpose is for the caramel, which won't melt, to seal the dough and thus prevent the pastry cream from softening it for at least a couple of hours.

12 Peel and slice the mango, cutting directly into the pit and removing long strips of the flesh.

13 Peel and cut the feijoa and the other fruit into thin slices.

14 The pastry cream can be prepared up to one day ahead.

To make the pastry cream: Bring the 1 c. milk to a boil. Whisk the egg, egg yolk, 1 tsp. vanilla, ¼ c. granulated sugar, and 2 Tb. cornstarch together in a bowl. Add the boiling milk, put the mixture back in the saucepan, and bring to a boil, stirring with the whisk to prevent scorching. Boil a few seconds and remove from the heat. When lukewarm, add the 2 Tb. butter and 1 Tb. rum and mix well. Not more than 1 hour before serving, spread the pastry cream on top of the caramelized dough.

15 Arrange the fruit in a pattern of your choosing on top of the pastry cream.

16 For the glaze: Strain the ½ c. apricot preserves through a food mill or a sieve. (Any pieces of apricot that do not go through can be placed back in the jar to be eaten with the rest of the preserves.) Add the tablespoon of rum. Using a spoon, spread the surface of the fruit with the glaze.

17 Then, using a brush, continue spreading the glaze so the fruit is coated evenly.

18 Sprinkle the 3 Tb. pomegranate seeds on top of the *galette*. The tart should be assembled no more than 1 hour before serving. After 1 hour or so, the pastry cream will melt the caramel layer underneath. The tart should be consumed when the caramel layer is partially melted but still slightly crunchy.

19 To serve the fruit and pastry cream without the dough shell: Spread approximately 2 Tb. of pastry cream on individual serving platters, arrange the fruit on top, glaze with the apricot-rum mixture, sprinkle with a few pomegranate seeds, and serve.

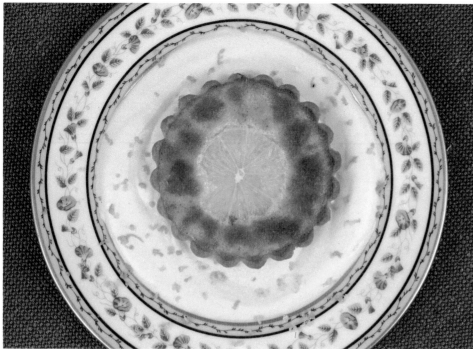

LIME AND ORANGE TARTLETS

These lime-and-orange-flavored pastries are easy to serve as individual tartlets, but this dessert can also be made into a large tart.

The tartlets are served with a cognac sauce here, but they can be served plain, if preferred. Lemon, grapefruit, or a citrus fruit mixture can be substituted for the lime and orange in the recipe here.

The lime slices are added to the tarts when they are half set so the slices don't sink into the filling. They can also be placed on the tartlets after they are cooked; then the tartlets are sprinkled with confectioners' sugar and placed under the broiler for a couple of minutes until some of the sugar melts to produce a marblelike surface.

Yield: 12 tartlets

SWEET PASTRY DOUGH
(see page 183 for ingredients)

FILLING

4 strips orange peel
6 to 8 strips lime peel
2 whole eggs + 4 egg yolks
1 tsp. cornstarch
⅓ c. granulated sugar
Juice of 2 limes and 1 orange, mixed (½ c.)
12 slices of lime (peeling removed)

COGNAC SAUCE

1 egg yolk
⅓ c. confectioners' sugar
3 Tb. cognac
1 c. heavy cream

GARNISH

Grated orange rind

1 **Make and roll out the sweet pastry dough** according to the instructions in the recipe for Exotic Custard Fruit Galette (see page 183, steps 1–3). Use plastic wrap to roll out the dough in order to avoid using too much flour. The dough should be approximately ⅛ in. thick. (The small tartlet pans are approximately 3 in. in diameter by ½ in. thick.)

Remove the piece of plastic wrap from the top of the dough and reverse the dough (supporting it with the other piece of plastic wrap) on top of the lined-up molds. Peel off the remaining piece of plastic wrap and use it to press the dough lightly into the molds.

2 Using a rolling pin, roll directly on top of the molds so the dough is cut around the top edge of the molds.

3 Remove the extra dough and, after sprinkling your fingers with flour so they won't stick, press the dough firmly into each mold so it adheres well to the bottom and sides. The dough will be quite thin.

4 To prevent the dough from collapsing while cooking, line each of the molds with wax paper or aluminum foil and fill with weights (rice or lead pellets). Or, if you have enough extra molds, place one directly on top of each pastry-lined mold and press it down to hold the dough in position during cooking. Arrange on a cookie sheet and bake in a preheated 375-degree oven for 10 minutes. By then, the dough will be set. Remove the empty molds (or weight-filled aluminum foil or wax paper) and continue to bake the pastry for about 5 minutes longer (15 minutes total), or until the dough is almost cooked. Since the filling is liquid and could run out, patch any cracks in the cooked dough with little pieces of raw dough, smearing it into place with your thumb to seal the pastry.

6 Place the 2 whole eggs, 4 egg yolks, 1 tsp. cornstarch, ⅓ c. granulated sugar, ground orange and lime peel, and combined juices of 2 limes and 1 orange in the bowl of a food processor, and process until well-mixed. Pour into a bowl. Using a spoon, fill each of the small tartlet shells with the mixture (about 3 Tb. per shell).

8 **To make the cognac sauce:** Combine the egg yolk and ⅓ c. confectioners' sugar in a bowl, and work the mixture with a whisk for about 1 minute to lighten it. Add the 3 Tb. cognac. Whip the 1 c. cream until it holds a firm peak, and add the cognac–egg yolk mixture to it. Mix well.

5 **For the filling:** With a vegetable peeler, remove 4 strips of orange peel and 6 to 8 strips of lime peel. Chop coarse and place in a mini-chop or coffee grinder. Chop until very fine, almost like a powder.

7 Place the tartlets in a preheated 375-degree oven for 5 minutes. Meanwhile, peel a lime, removing the white pith and baring the fruit. Cut the lime into 12 very thin slices and place one slice in the center of each partially baked tartlet. Continue cooking for 10 minutes (for a total of 15 minutes). Remove from the oven and let cool slightly before unmolding.

9 Unmold the little tartlets and let cool to room temperature. Spoon some of the sauce onto each serving plate. Grate a little orange rind on top of the sauce for flavor as well as color.

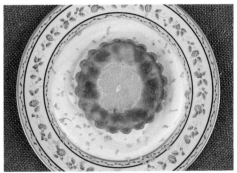

10 Place a tartlet in the center of each prepared plate and serve immediately.

CHOCOLATE-ORANGE TART MARTINE

This tasty chocolate-orange tart is made with a sweet dough that is first baked blind. There is only a thin layer of custard in the tart and that will cook fast. Therefore, unless the dough is precooked, either the custard will be overcooked or the dough undercooked.

The garnish of candied orange peel, pieces of chocolate, and almond slivers can be varied. Raspberry preserves as well as raisins can be used instead of orange peel, and other nuts can be substituted for the almonds, or nuts may be omitted entirely.

Although the tart can be done ahead, the filling (especially the chocolate) gets too hard if the tart is refrigerated. It should be brought back to room temperature either by removing it from the refrigerator an hour or so before serving or by placing it in a hot oven for 4 to 5 minutes; the flavor is better and the chocolate remains creamy when it is not too cold.

Individual tartlets are perhaps more practical to serve at a buffet or large party than the larger tart featured here, and you can adapt the recipe to the small molds.

Yield: 8 servings

SWEET DOUGH

1½ c. flour (about 8 oz.)
2 Tb. sugar
1¼ sticks butter (5 oz.)
1 egg yolk
1 Tb. milk

CANDIED ORANGE PEEL (page 165)

12 peels from 1 large orange
⅓ c. water
½ c. sugar

⅓ c. toasted slivered almonds
3 oz. bittersweet or semi-sweet chocolate, cut into ½-in. pieces (see page 132)

CUSTARD FILLING

1 whole egg + 1 egg yolk
1½ c. heavy cream
Cooking syrup from the orange peel

Confectioners' sugar for dusting the tart

1 To make the dough: Put the 1½ c. flour with the 2 Tb. sugar and the cut-up 1¼ sticks butter in the bowl of a mixer fitted with a flat beater. Mix until most of the butter is incorporated, then add the egg yolk and 1 Tb. milk and mix at low speed just until the dough forms a ball.

2 Gently roll out the dough on a floured board, being careful not to press too hard because it is soft and delicate. Roll out to a circle approximately 12 in. in diameter. The dough should be about ⅛ in. thick.

3 Roll the dough up onto the rolling pin and then gently unroll it over a 10-in. quiche pan with a removable bottom.

4 Lift the hanging dough on the outside of the rim and ease it gently into the quiche pan so the dough isn't stretched but fits properly in the pan. To create a nice border, lift some of the extra dough and press it with your thumb to anchor it to the edge of the pan.

5 Using the rolling pin, roll in one direction and then the other over the pan to trim the dough. Remove the excess.

6 Using your thumb and forefinger, press all around the edge of the dough to even out the border and push it slightly above the rim of the pan.

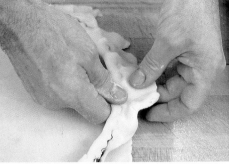

7 Line the dough with parchment paper and weight it for cooking. (The paper and weight will keep the dough flat during cooking and prevent it from collapsing on itself.)

First, fold the paper into thin triangles, and measure the radius of the pan with the paper, taking into account that the paper should be large enough to extend up the sides of the pan by at least 1 in. beyond the rim. Cut the paper.

8 With scissors, fringe the triangle by cutting into it at close intervals to a depth of 1 in. all along the outer edge. This will help the paper sit properly on top of the dough.

9 Open the fringed paper, center it over the dough, and press to make it adhere well to the dough. Fill with fairly heavy weights – either special lead weights designed specifically for this purpose or pebbles. Bake in a preheated 375-degree oven for approximately 20 minutes. Remove the weights and the paper and place the tart shell back in the oven for 10 minutes, until the dough begins to brown lightly inside.

While the dough is cooking, **prepare the candied orange peel:** Use ⅓ c. water and ½ c. sugar and follow the recipe for crystallized peels of orange in Crystallized Puff Paste of Orange (page 165), stopping at the end of step 10. Set aside the peels in the syrup.

10 **For the filling:** Sprinkle the ⅓ c. toasted slivered almonds over the bottom of the precooked shell. Lift the candied orange peels out of the syrup (reserving the syrup) and arrange them on top of the almonds. →

11 Sprinkle the 3 oz. chocolate, cut into ½-in. pieces, into the shell with the almonds and orange peel.

14 Let cool to lukewarm or room temperature. Dust with confectioners' sugar, cut into wedges, and serve immediately.

12 Combine the whole egg and egg yolk, beating them well with a whisk. Add the 1½ c. heavy cream and the syrup from the orange peels, and whisk until blended. Pour the mixture into the shell.

13 Place the tart on a cookie sheet and bake in the center of a preheated 400-degree oven for 20 minutes, until the custard is well-set and the dough brown.

2 To be sure there are no seeds left, strain the purée through a sieve, <u>banging the rim of the sieve with a spatula or your hand to make the seeds bounce and allow the clear liquid to go through.</u> Then, press the seeds to extract any remaining liquid. (See Blackberry Clafoutis, steps 6–8, page 194.) The yield should be about 1⅓ c. If you have more, boil the purée to reduce it to this amount.

FRESH RASPBERRY LINZER TORTE

This fresh raspberry linzer torte is made from a very rich dough that is difficult to roll out in the usual way but easy to spread out with your hands alone or with the help of plastic wrap.

A standard linzer torte is made with raspberry preserve only. However, I find that by the time the preserve has reduced as a result of baking, it often tastes and looks like raspberry "leather" — too sweet and too concentrated. So my dessert is made with fresh or frozen unsweetened raspberry purée mixed with some raspberry preserves. The taste of raspberries is more intense, the color nicer, and the texture softer than in the traditional version.

This cake can be done ahead and will keep well overnight, covered and refrigerated. But it should be removed from the refrigerator early enough so it is not served ice cold. It may even be placed in a hot oven for a few moments to bring it back to room temperature and restore its flavor.

Yield: 8–10 servings

FILLING

1 twelve-ounce package unsweetened frozen raspberries, or 12 oz. fresh raspberries
⅔ c. raspberry preserves

LINZER DOUGH

1½ c. flour
¾ c. slivered almonds
¼ c. sugar
¼ tsp. powdered mace
¼ tsp. powdered cinnamon
1 tsp. vanilla
1½ sticks butter, cut into pieces (6 oz.)
3 egg yolks

Confectioners' sugar for dusting the cake

1 For the filling: Purée the fresh or defrosted unsweetened frozen raspberries along with the raspberry preserves <u>through the fine screen of a food mill.</u>

3 For the linzer dough: Put the 1½ c. flour, ¾ c. slivered almonds, ¼ c. sugar, ¼ tsp. each mace and cinnamon, and 1 tsp. vanilla in the bowl of a food processor and process until the almonds are finely ground. (They will be almost as fine as the flour.) Add the 1½ sticks butter (cut into pieces) and the 3 egg yolks, and pulse the motor of the processor about 10 times, until the mixture just begins to hold together. Turn the dough out onto the table and smear it with your hands, pressing it forward in the technique of the *fraisage* (step 2, page 180), until the dough is thoroughly mixed.

Place two-thirds of the dough on a large cookie sheet, cover with a piece of plastic wrap, and, with a rolling pin, <u>roll it out to a thickness of ¼ in.</u> →

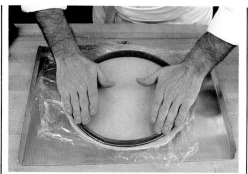

4 Using a 10- to 11-in. flan ring, press through the plastic to cut a circle on the dough.

5 Remove the plastic wrap and the trimmings around the rim.

6 Fit the flan ring around the disk of dough. Make some of the extra dough into rolls about ¾ in. thick and place them all around the inside of the ring to create a border.

7 Press on the border of dough, sealing it to the disk of dough beneath and extending it slightly above the rim of the ring.

8 Pour the raspberry mixture into the shell. Using a little extra flour, roll the remaining dough into ropes about the thickness of a pencil. Place one of the ropes across the center of the torte and arrange four additional ropes parallel to it.

9 Then, arrange five ropes going in the other direction across the top of the torte.

10 Fold the extended border of dough back on top of the ropes and filling.

11 Bake in the center of a preheated 375-degree oven for approximately 45 minutes. Remove from the oven and immediately sprinkle some confectioners' sugar on top. If the sugar is added while the jam is still bubbling, any that touches the filling will melt and only the sugar on the dough will remain.

12 Serve the linzer torte at room temperature, cut into wedges.

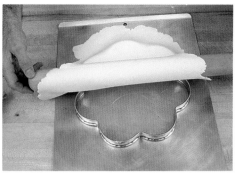

2 Unroll the dough onto a ring or pie form set on a cookie sheet. I am using a scalloped ring, which gives the tart a nice design, although the ring could be rectangular, square, or round. Lift up the hanging dough to ease it gently into the ring and press it so it adheres to the cookie sheet underneath and the inside of the ring without being stretched.

3 Lift up the hanging dough so that you can press additional dough onto the metal ring. You want to create a little border of thicker dough all around to contain the filling and give a more attractive look to the shell.

4 Roll your rolling pin across the top of the metal ring one way and then the other to cut the dough, crisscrossing so that the dough is cut uniformly all around. →

BLACKBERRY CLAFOUTIS

A traditional <u>clafoutis</u> is a mixture of fruit (usually cherries), eggs, cream, milk, and flour that is baked and often served with a custard cream. The recipe here is made of blackberry purée and eggs baked in a light cream cheese dough that has been partially precooked. It should be served at room temperature, as it would be runny if served too hot. The surface can either be glazed, as in this recipe, with a translucent jam (apricot as well as raspberry) or sprinkled with confectioners' sugar.

Yield: 8 servings

CREAM CHEESE DOUGH

1 c. flour (about 5½ oz.)
½ stick butter (2 oz.)
4 oz. cream cheese, at room temperature

BLACKBERRY SAUCE

Yield: about 3 c.
1¼ lb. fresh or frozen unsweetened blackberries (about 1¾ c. purée)
1 twelve-ounce jar blackberry jam or preserves (preferably seedless)

FILLING

3 Tb. slivered almonds
2 eggs
3 c. blackberry sauce (from above)
1 Tb. raspberry brandy

GLAZE

⅓ c. strained apricot, raspberry, or peach jam or preserves, or a mixture of apricot and berry jam or preserves

Extra blackberries for decoration

1 **To make the cream cheese dough:** Place the cup of flour and ½ stick butter, cut in pieces, into the bowl of a food processor, and process for about 10 to 15 seconds. Then add the 4 oz. of cream cheese in pieces and process approximately 10 seconds more, until the mixture forms a ball. The dough can be made ahead and refrigerated or used immediately.

To roll, flour a board lightly and roll the dough out very thin (⅛ in. thick) into a circle. Roll it back onto the rolling pin.

5 Pinch the extra border of dough all around to make it even and nice looking. A decorative edge can be created with a dough crimper (a small metal pincher with teeth that creates a ridged edge). To use the crimper, hold the dough on the insides of the ring with the index finger of one hand and crimp the outside edge with the other hand. Place a piece of parchment paper or aluminum foil inside the pastry shell and weight it with special metal weights, pebbles, or rice. (See page 189, steps 7–9, on arranging the paper inside.) Then place in a preheated 375-degree oven for approximately 15 to 20 minutes to pre-bake the dough. While the shell is baking, prepare the blackberry sauce.

6 For the blackberry sauce: Place the 1¼ lb. of fresh or frozen unsweetened blackberries that have been thawed with the 12-oz. jar of blackberry jam in a food mill fitted with the finest screen, and strain the mixture. Most of the seeds will be removed through this straining.

7 To remove any remaining seeds, strain the sauce again. Place it in a sieve with a medium mesh and bang the top edge of the sieve with a spatula or the palm of your hand so that the seeds jump up and most of the liquid goes through. It is a mistake to press the mixture immediately with a rubber spatula as any seeds in it will clog the holes.

8 When most of the sauce has strained through the sieve, press on the mixture left in the strainer with a rubber spatula to obtain the extra remaining sauce. Clean off the bottom of the strainer to retrieve any extra sauce and discard the seeds. (The seeds can also be placed in vinegar to lend flavor.)

9 For the filling: Brown the 3 Tb. slivered almonds on a cookie sheet in a preheated 400-degree oven for 6 to 7 minutes, until lightly browned. Beat the 2 eggs with a fork and combine with the 3 c. of blackberry sauce and the 1 Tb. raspberry brandy. Pour into the dough shell. Sprinkle the almonds on top and place in a 375-degree oven for about 25 to 30 minutes, until set. The dough will shrink slightly, making the ring easy to lift off.

10 Coat the top of the *clafoutis* with the glaze (⅓ c. strained apricot or peach jam or preserves, or a mixture of apricot and berry jam or preserves), using a spoon or brush to apply it. Cut into wedges and serve with extra blackberries on the side.

ORANGES IN BLACKBERRY SAUCE

The blackberry sauce in the preceding recipe can be prepared several days ahead and even frozen (like a sherbet) and then melted again for use as a sauce. It can also be used to make this fast, easy, attractive dessert. One large orange per person should be enough. The oranges should be seedless, juicy, and sweet.
Yield: 6 servings

6 large, seedless oranges
1½ c. blackberry sauce (page 194)
6 mint sprigs
1 brioche (page 136), optional, or cookies

1 With a vegetable peeler, peel the rind from one of the six oranges. Pile up the strips of rind and cut them into a fine julienne. Set aside. Peel the rest of the oranges with a sharp knife, cutting closely all around so that the pith as well as the rind is removed and the oranges are completely nude. Cut the orange flesh from the attached segments (see Crystallized Puff Paste of Orange, page 165, steps 8–9). Squeeze the remaining membrane to extract the juice and reserve it for another recipe.

2 Place about 4 Tb. of the blackberry sauce on each of 6 plates. Arrange orange segments in a wheel design in the center of the sauce and place the julienne of orange around the edge of the sauce to form a border. Garnish the center with mint and serve immediately with a slice of lukewarm brioche or cookies.

GALETTE DE PEROUGES

This galette is a specialty of a small town named Pérouges, located between Lyon and Bourg-en-Bresse, where I was born. I serve this thin, crusty, and buttery cake with prunes poached in port wine and whipped heavy cream mixed with sour cream. This is a delightful combination of flavors that makes an interesting and unusual dessert. Poached apricots can also be used instead of prunes.

The galette is best when served fresh and still slightly warm, soon after it comes out of the oven. If allowed to cool off, it can be reheated slightly in the oven before serving. The prunes should be cool but not ice cold and should be served with the whipped cream on the same plate.
Yield: 8 servings

POACHED PRUNES

1 c. boiling water
1½ c. good port wine
1 lb. large unpitted prunes (about 36)
1 tsp. potato starch dissolved in 1 Tb. prune juice

DOUGH

1 cake fresh yeast (0.6 oz.), or 1 envelope active dry yeast (1 Tb.)
¼ c. milk, warmed to about 100 degrees
½ tsp. sugar
2 c. flour
¼ tsp. salt
3 eggs
1 stick + 2 Tb. butter, softened

GALETTE TOPPING

3 Tb. melted butter
4 Tb. sugar

SAUCE

1 c. heavy cream
1 c. sour cream

1 Pour the 1 c. boiling water and 1 c. of the wine on top of the 1 lb. prunes. Cover with plastic wrap and let soak 24 hours. Drain off the juice (approximately 1 c.), place in a saucepan, and bring to a boil. Add the 1 tsp. potato starch dissolved in 1 Tb. prune juice, and return to the boil. Reduce by boiling down to 1 c. if the yield is more. Pour back over the prunes with the remaining ½ c. port and cool.

2 Place the cake or envelope of yeast, ¼ c. milk, and ½ tsp. sugar in a mixer bowl and let proof for 5 to 6 minutes, until the yeast develops. Add the 2 c. flour, ¼ tsp. salt, and 3 eggs, and beat with the flat beater on medium speed for about 3 minutes. Add the stick plus 2 Tb. of softened butter and mix approximately 30 seconds, just long enough for the butter to be incorporated. Cover with plastic wrap and let proof at room temperature for 1½ to 2 hours. It should double in bulk. Break the dough gently by kneading it briefly. Butter a baking sheet and place the dough on it. Wet your hand (to prevent it from sticking) and spread the dough into a rectangular shape about 12 × 15 in., with rounded corners, approximately ¼ to ⅜ in. thick.

3 Brush the top of the dough rectangle with the 3 Tb. melted butter, and sprinkle it with the 4 Tb. sugar. Some of the sugar will be absorbed by the melted butter while some will form a crust on top. Let proof at room temperature for about 20 to 25 minutes.

4 Place in a preheated 425-degree oven for 15 minutes, until nicely browned.

5 Whip the 1 c. of cream until soft peaks form. Fold in the 1 c. of sour cream. There is no sweetener added to the cream because the prunes and *galette* are sweet enough. If desired, however, some sugar can be added. Serve a crunchy wedge of the lukewarm pastry per person with some prunes and cream.

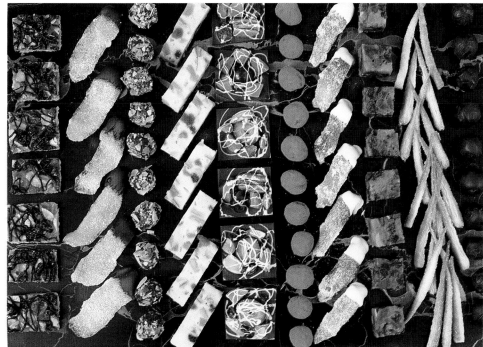

An arrangement of all the petits fours. From left to right: Zimfour, Candied Grapefruit Peel, Cognac-Almond Truffles, Fruitcake Fingers, Dulcet Chocolate Squares, Orange Truffles, Candied Lime Peel, Christmas Cake Cubes, Sugared Puff Paste Sticks, and Coffee-Rum Truffles.

AN ASSORTMENT OF PETITS FOURS

SUGARED PUFF PASTE STICKS

Traditional "pig's ear" cookies are made with pieces of puff paste that are dredged in sugar, then rolled up from either end, and cut into slices. After they have baked, the cookies emerge looking like what the French call palmier (palm trees) and the English call "pig's ears."

The same dough, rolled in sugar and cut into little strips, will bake much faster and become even crispier and more caramelized than "pig's ears." They make a nice contrast on a tray of petits fours and are easy to make. Any of the puff paste recipes (page 144) or trimmings can be used.

Yield: about 70–80 sticks

8 oz. Puff Paste (page 144)
½ c. sugar

1 Sprinkle about ¼ c. of the sugar on a board and roll out the puff pastry. Reserve 1 Tb. of the remaining ¼ c. sugar for use later, and sprinkle the rest on top of the pastry. Turn it over and roll it out again so both sides are well-coated with the sugar. The finished pastry rectangle should measure about 10 × 16 in.

2 Cut the rectangle lengthwise into two strips and stack one on top of the other. The sugar coating will prevent their sticking. Cut the pastry into thin wedges or strips approximately 3½ to 4 in. long and ⅜ in. wide.

3 Separate the strips and arrange them on a cookie tray lined with parchment paper. They can be fairly close together as they tend to shrink a little during cooking. Sprinkle with the reserved 1 Tb. sugar.

4 Bake in a preheated 400-degree oven for 10 minutes, until well-crisped and brown. Arrange on a tray as part of a cookie assortment.

ZIMFOUR

These petits fours, a recipe of Gloria Zimmerman's, are often made at our house. They freeze well and will keep, covered, in the refrigerator or in a cool place for several days. They are made here in the form of an open tart and could be served as such cut into wedges with, perhaps, some whipped cream or a fruit salad.

The cookie dough can be used for different kinds of tarts and the julienne of orange (similar to the candied orange julienne in the Frozen Citrus Soufflé, page 271) can be added to creams, soufflés, or cakes. The decorative lines of chocolate on top could be made with white chocolate or a mixture of bittersweet and white rather than the plain bittersweet I have used.

In the filling, pieces of dried figs or apricots could be substituted for the golden raisins.

Yield: 16–20 Zimfour

COOKIE DOUGH

1 c. flour (about 5½ oz.)
½ stick butter (2 oz.)
1½ Tb. sugar
1 egg yolk mixed with 1 tsp. vanilla and 1½ Tb. cold water

JULIENNE OF ORANGE

Peels of 2 oranges, cut into julienne
2½ c. water
⅓ c. sugar

ZIMFOUR FILLING

⅓ stick butter
⅓ c. golden raisins
½ c. sliced almonds
2 Tb. cream

GARNISH

2 Tb. bittersweet chocolate (see page 132), melted

1 **For the cookie dough:** Put the 1 c. flour, ½ stick butter, and 1½ Tb. sugar in the bowl of a food processor and process for about 10 seconds. Add the egg yolk mixed with 1 tsp. vanilla and 1½ Tb. water and process another 8 to 10 seconds, until the mixture forms a ball. Remove and wrap the ball of dough until ready to roll out or roll it out immediately.

2 Roll out the dough between two sheets of plastic wrap until it is a very thin rectangle a little larger than 9 in. wide by 12 in. long. Remove the sheet of plastic wrap from the top of the dough, and invert it with its plastic wrap liner onto a cookie sheet. (The dough is rich enough that it won't stick, so it is not necessary to line the cookie sheet with parchment paper or rub it with butter.)

3 Remove the second sheet of plastic wrap. If need be, the dough can be rolled on the cookie sheet at this point to make it a little thinner. The dough can be trimmed and patched to make a finished rectangle of 9 × 12 in.

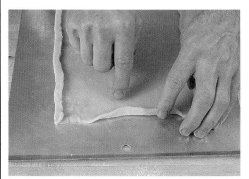

4 Make a border all around the edge by rolling the dough onto itself and pinching it to make it pointed on top. Bake the rectangular shell in a preheated 400-degree oven for about 15 to 20 minutes, until the dough is set and just begins to brown slightly.

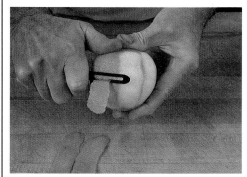

5 Meanwhile, peel 2 oranges to obtain about 15 strips of peel from both.

6 Pile up the strips, one on top of the other, and cut into a fine julienne (yielding about ½ c.). Place the julienned peel in a saucepan with 2 c. of the cold water and bring the water to a boil. Boil for about 10 seconds, drain through a sieve, and wash the peel under cold water. Rinse the cooking pan and return the orange peel to it with ½ c. water and ⅓ c. sugar.

7 Bring the mixture to a boil and cook for about 6 minutes. By then, the liquid should be reduced to a fairly heavy syrup and the julienne should be soft and translucent.

8 **For the filling:** To the orange-peel mixture in the pan, add the ⅓ stick butter, ⅓ c. golden raisins, ½ c. sliced almonds, and 2 Tb. cream, and stir to mix well. Spread the mixture over the precooked dough rectangle on the cookie sheet and place in the 400-degree oven to cook for another 10 to 12 minutes, until the dough is well-cooked and the filling brown on top.

9 Pour the melted bittersweet chocolate into a cornet (see "Swimming Swans," page 234, steps 2–6). Fold down the top of the cornet, cut it at the tip, and drizzle the chocolate over the Zimfour to form a chocolate lattice on top.

10 Cut the Zimfour into about 16 to 20 squares and serve. (To serve as petits fours, see page 197.)

DULCET CHOCOLATE SQUARES

These little squares of chocolate with fresh fruit, dried fruit, or almonds embedded in them are fanciful and are always welcome after dinner. They can be made into very colorful combinations with different fruits. The nut-chocolate combination works well and so does the tart dried apricot and chocolate mixture.

Vary the color and the taste with white chocolate, milk chocolate, and bittersweet chocolate. Instead of making one layer of the fruit-nut mixture over the chocolate base, as I have done, you can build one or two more layers of fruits and nuts, drizzling melted chocolate over them to act as a glue with a final layer of fruit and nuts on top.

The chocolate is cut into squares with a knife when it has just set – before it gets too hard. It can also be cut into rounds with a cookie cutter or into little strips. Dulcet Chocolate Squares are a welcome addition to the petits fours tray (see page 197).

Yield: about 18–20 squares

12 dark raisins
12 golden raisins
1 or 2 strawberries
8 to 10 pecans
8 to 10 almonds
1 to 2 pieces dried apricot
About 6 oz. bittersweet or semi-sweet
    chocolate (see page 132)
1 Tb. white chocolate (optional)

1 Assemble all the fruits and nuts you will need – dark and golden raisins, strawberries, nuts, and apricot pieces. The nuts can be toasted or not, but toasted almonds and walnuts will have more taste. Melt the 6 oz. chocolate over hot water, then pour 2 lines (about 16 in. long) of bittersweet chocolate onto wax or parchment paper.

2 With a spatula, spread the chocolate out so each strip is about 2 in. wide and no more than ⅛ in. thick. If you wish, put the white chocolate in a paper cornet (see "Swimming Swans," page 234, steps 2–6) and pipe it in circles the length of one of the strips.

3 Before the chocolate hardens, embed a combination of dried fruit, fresh fruit, nuts, and so forth, the length of the strips.

4 To make it a bit more fanciful, sprinkle the fruit and nuts with a drizzling of white chocolate from the cornet. Refrigerate until well-set but not too hard, so the strips can be cut.

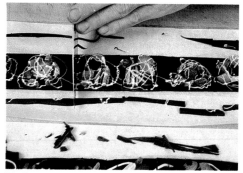

5 If the chocolate is too hard and brittle to cut, leave at room temperature to soften somewhat. Trim the sides and cut the strips into squares. Refrigerate until serving time or freeze. At serving time, decorate a cookie tray with the Dulcet Chocolate Squares and other cookies (see page 197).

CANDIED LIME AND GRAPEFRUIT PEELS

Candied lime and grapefruit peels are easy to make and they can be used in so many ways: chopped and mixed into pastry cream, cut into a julienne to decorate cakes and soufflés, as well as diced and combined with other dried fruits (such as raisins and apricots) to be soaked in rum and cognac, and then added to a fruitcake. They can also be served plain or, as shown here, with one of the tips of each candied grapefruit peel dipped in melted bittersweet chocolate and one of the tips of each lime peel dipped in white chocolate.
Yield: 24

1 to 2 large, very green limes
1 large, bright-skinned grapefruit
3 c. cold water

FOR THE PEELS OF EACH FRUIT

1 c. sugar
1½ c. water

2 c. sugar, to roll the peels in
About 2 oz. bittersweet chocolate (see page 132), melted, for dipping
About 2 oz. white chocolate, melted, for dipping

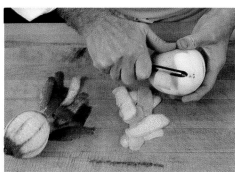

1 Using a vegetable peeler, <u>cut about 12 strips of peel</u> from each large lime and grapefruit. (Strips cut with a peeler will be thin and thus cook quite quickly.) Place the strips in a pan with 3 c. cold water. Bring to a strong boil over high heat, boil 15 seconds, then drain and wash under cold water. Put the lime and grapefruit peels in separate pans, and add ½ c. sugar and ¾ c. water to each pan. (They should not be cooked together, as their flavors tend to blend.) Bring the liquid in each pan to a boil, and cook over medium to high heat. Cook the lime peel for about 6 minutes, until the syrup gets thicker and the lime skin begins to get transparent.

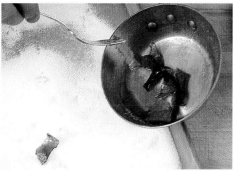

2 Using a fork, lift out the strips of lime peel and place them on a cookie sheet <u>coated with the 2 c. sugar. Turn the peels, pressing down on them so the sugar adheres to both sides, then arrange them on a plate.</u>

3 The grapefruit peels will take a little longer to cook, about 8 to 10 minutes total. When transparent, <u>lift them out of the syrup with a fork and place in the sugar.</u>

4 Turn the peels in the sugar, <u>pressing them so they are well-coated on both sides with the sugar.</u> Arrange on the plate with the lime peels and set aside for 30 minutes. If they are not to be used right away, place them in a plastic container with a tight-fitting lid so they don't dry out. They can be stored like this in the refrigerator for weeks.

5 **Chocolate peels:** Dip the tip of each grapefruit peel into about 2 oz. melted bittersweet chocolate, and arrange on a cookie sheet lined with parchment paper.

6 Dip the lime peels into about 2 oz. <u>melted white chocolate, and arrange them</u> on the cookie sheet with the grapefruit peels. Refrigerate until the chocolate hardens.

CHOCOLATE TRUFFETTES

These small chocolate truffles, or truffettes, freeze quite well and can be made ahead. Many of the chocolate truffles on the market have a soft and creamy interior and it is impossible to keep them for more than a few days, but these have a firm consistency that lasts.

The basic mixture can be flavored differently. I have used three flavor combinations: orange and Grand Marnier, coffee and rum, and cognac and almond.

Each variety has a different coating, which makes the flavors easy to identify. One is dusted with bitter cocoa powder, another is rolled in roasted sliced almonds, and the third is coated with melted chocolate.

Chocolate truffles can also be flavored with a praline paste, which is a mixture of caramelized sugar and almonds, or vanilla, as well as cinnamon or bourbon. Other coatings – from white chocolate to shaved chocolate – can be used, and the mixture can be shaped into squares as well as sticks.

These truffles are part of the petits fours tray that is shown on page 197.

Yield: about 60–70 truffettes about the size of a large cherry

BASE MIXTURE

½ lb. bittersweet or semi-sweet chocolate (see page 132)
½ stick butter (2 oz.)
2 egg yolks

ORANGE TRUFFLES

1 tsp. grated orange rind
1 Tb. Grand Marnier
Cocoa powder for dusting

COFFEE-RUM TRUFFLES

2 tsp. coffee extract (pages 255, 256)
2 tsp. rum
3 to 4 oz. bittersweet chocolate, for coating

COGNAC-ALMOND TRUFFLES

1 Tb. cognac
¾ c. sliced almonds

1 Put the ½ lb. bittersweet chocolate in a saucepan and melt over hot water. Add the ½ stick butter and stir with a whisk until smooth and glossy.

2 Add the 2 egg yolks and whisk. The mixture will thicken and lose some of its shine.

3 Divide the mixture among three different bowls. To one of the bowls, add the 1 tsp. orange rind and 1 Tb. Grand Marnier, and mix well. To a second bowl, add the 2 tsp. each coffee extract and rum, and stir to mix thoroughly. To the chocolate mixture in the remaining bowl, add the 1 Tb. cognac and mix well. After the addition of liquid to each of the bowls, the chocolate may become shiny again or it may remain dull; either way is fine. Refrigerate the bowls until the chocolate mixture hardens.

4 When the chocolate mixtures are very hard, make truffettes, one batch at a time, by scooping out teaspoonfuls and placing them on a cookie sheet lined with wax or parchment paper.

5 Take each of the little chocolate balls and roll between the palms of your hands to round them, making them look like a real truffle that might be found underground.

6 For the orange truffles: Place the orange-flavored truffles on a plate dusted generously with cocoa powder and shake the plate so they roll in the powder and are coated on all sides. Set aside.

7 **For the cognac-almond truffles:**
Arrange the ¾ c. almonds on a cookie
sheet and place in a preheated 400-degree
oven to brown for 8 to 10 minutes. When
the almonds are cool, press the balls of
cognac-flavored truffles into them, crushing the nuts slightly and embedding them
into the truffles to coat them on the outside.

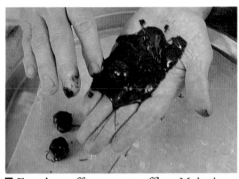

8 **For the coffee-rum truffles:** Melt the
3 to 4 oz. chocolate in a double boiler and,
when cool enough to handle, pour about 2
Tb. of it into the palm of one hand. Roll
the coffee-rum truffles one by one in the
chocolate in your hand until well-coated
and place them on a cookie sheet lined
with wax paper. Refrigerate until the outside chocolate has hardened.

9 The assortment of truffles is ready to be
arranged for serving with the other petits
fours, page 197.

FRUITCAKE FINGERS

*This colorful petit four is made with leftover
fruitcake (page 276) that is cut into little strips
and soaked with cognac syrup.*
Yield: 12 fingers
2 slices (each 1 in. thick) of leftover fruitcake, page 276
COGNAC SYRUP

1 Tb. cognac
½ Tb. water
2 tsp. sugar

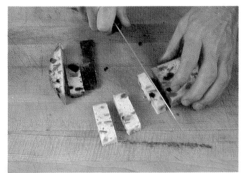

1 Trim the slices of leftover cake and
cut them into strips about 2 in. long by
½ in. wide.

2 In a small bowl, mix the 1 Tb. cognac,
½ Tb. water, and 2 tsp. sugar until the
sugar is dissolved. Using a brush, saturate
the cake fingers with the syrup. (See page
197 for Fruitcake Fingers on the finished
petits fours tray.)

CHRISTMAS CAKE CUBES

*This recipe uses leftover English Christmas
Pudding, which is cut into cubes and soaked
with a dark rum syrup. It makes a nice contrast
and a good addition to the petits fours tray.*
Yield: 12 cubes
2 slices (each about 1 in. thick) of leftover
   English Christmas Pudding (page 278)
RUM SYRUP

1 Tb. dark rum
2 tsp. water
2 tsp. sugar

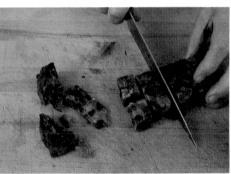

1 Cut leftover English Christmas Pudding
into 1-in. cubes.

2 In a small bowl, mix together the 1 Tb.
rum and 2 tsp. each water and sugar until
the sugar is dissolved, and brush it on the
cubes until they are well-soaked. Arrange
on a petits fours tray (see page 197).

GLAZED FRUITS

Dried fruits, such as apricots, figs, dates, and prunes, can be filled with marzipan (tinted with food coloring) and dipped into a white caramel, a sugar cooked to approximately 310 degrees, or what is called the "break" or "crack" stage. The fruits should be coated while the sugar is very hot so the syrup, which tends to thicken while it cools, is not too thick and so does not form too heavy a layer around the fruit. To remove some of the excess caramel, the dipped fruits can be rubbed gently along the side of the pan before being placed on an oiled tray.

Dried fruits will hold better than, for example, glazed strawberries (see pages 149 and 213) because fresh fruits tend to release their juices, which eventually melt the sugar shell around them. Since the dried fruits used here with marzipan don't release any juices, they keep better. Serve them at the end of a meal, perhaps with petits fours, or use them to decorate a Croquembouche (page 237) or other cakes, such as the St. Honoré (page 239).

2 oz. marzipan
3 to 4 drops red food coloring
3 to 4 drops green food coloring
12 small Mission figs
12 dried apricots

CARAMEL

1 c. sugar
3 Tb. water
A dash cream of tartar or a few drops
    lemon juice or vinegar (optional)

1 Mix half the marzipan with a few drops of red food coloring and the other half with a few drops of green food coloring. Open the fruit and stuff with little pieces of the tinted marzipan. Re-form the fruit around the stuffing so it holds well.

2 Secure each of the stuffed fruits with a toothpick so that they will be easier to dip into the sugar.

For the caramel: In a saucepan (preferably a "sugar pan," which is an unlined copper pan specially designed to cook sugar), place the 1 c. sugar and 3 Tb. water, stirring just enough to wet the sugar. Unlined copper tends to acidify the sugar, and acid helps prevent crystallization (when the sugar forms into cloudy lumps). If a sugar pan is not available, a dash of cream of tartar (tartaric acid) or a few drops of lemon juice (citric acid) or vinegar (acetic acid) will achieve the same result.

Heat the mixture to a boil, cover, and continue cooking for about 30 seconds to melt any crystals of sugar that may have collected around the sides of the pan above the boiling syrup. (The steam created by covering the pan will do this.) Remove the cover and cook, without stirring, to 310 to 320 degrees, which is the hard-crack stage. Remove the pan from the heat. Holding each piece of fruit by the toothpick, dip it into the caramel, lifting and dragging it along the side of the pan to eliminate the excess syrup, and place on an oiled baking sheet.

3 When the sugar is set (10 to 15 minutes), remove the toothpicks by twisting and pulling, and arrange the stuffed fruit attractively on a platter. Serve when ready.

(CONTINUED)

- PEAR BROWN BETTY WITH PEAR SAUCE
- CREPE FRANGIPANE WITH TANGERINE
  SAUCE
- PRALINE-CHOCOLATE PARADIS
- CHOCOLATE GOURMAND
- CHOCOLATE GOBLETS WITH ESPRESSO ICE
  CREAM OR COINTREAU STRAWBERRIES
- NOUGATINE SHELL WITH CHOCOLATE
  GOURMAND OR CHANTILLY
- COFFEE-RUM CARAMEL CUSTARD WITH
  LIME TUILE COOKIES
- CREME BRULEE WITH VERBENA

VANILLA-BOURBON GENOISE

A genoise is a basic sponge cake. In order that it be light and of an even consistency, room-temperature eggs are beaten with sugar at high speed; there is no baking powder in a genoise. The addition of melted butter improves the flavor but tends to deflate the batter. To compensate for this, I beat the egg mixture longer than usual so that, by the time everything is incorporated, the texture will be correct.

As must be evident by now, the key to a good genoise is its texture. If the egg mixture is underbeaten, the cake will not be moist enough. Excessive overbeating, on the other hand, makes the batter too fluffy, which means the cake will be dry and crumbly when cooled. And if the flour is not properly folded into the mixture, the cake will be gooey and heavy. Once the cook knows the pitfalls to avoid, however, the process is fairly straightforward, and, although the sponge cake can be made by hand, an electric mixer is ideal for the job. A genoise is unusually versatile, lending itself to an enormous variety of pairings with creams, custards, fruits, and syrups. My vanilla-bourbon genoise is sprinkled with a light syrup and spread with a delicate butter-cream, then decorated with a fine stream of chocolate and a ribbon of buttercream — but your own fancy may suggest other designs.

There are many different buttercreams. The traditional mixture is an emulsion of egg yolks and cooked syrup with butter added. It is also made with boiled frosting and butter or pastry cream and butter, confectioners' sugar and butter, as well as the fine, delicate version here, which is made of custard cream and butter.

Yield: 10–12 servings

GENOISE

4 extra-large eggs + 1 egg yolk
⅓ c. sugar
1½ tsp. vanilla
¾ c. flour (dip the cup directly into the flour bin to measure)
½ stick butter, melted (2 oz.)

BOURBON SYRUP

3 Tb. warm water from the tap
1 tsp. vanilla
2 Tb. sugar
3 Tb. bourbon

VANILLA-BOURBON BUTTERCREAM

¼ c. heavy cream
1 c. milk
3 egg yolks
⅓ c. sugar
2 tsp. vanilla
2 Tb. bourbon
2½ sticks unsalted butter, at room temperature (10 oz.)

---

1 small piece (about 1 Tb.) bittersweet chocolate (see page 132)
¼ tsp. vegetable oil

1 Butter and flour a 10-in.-diameter by 2-in.-deep aluminum cake pan. Put the 4 eggs, 1 yolk, ⅓ c. sugar, and 1½ tsp. vanilla in the bowl of a KitchenAid mixer. Pass the bowl a few times over a flame, beating the mixture until it is about body temperature; or mix over hot water. (When you dip your finger in, you should not feel any change in temperature.) Beat on speed 6 for 8 minutes; the mixture should have quadrupled in volume. It may develop faster or slower depending on the quality of the eggs.

2 Sift the ¾ c. flour directly on top of the cake mixture and fold gently until well-combined. Note that I have secured the bowl by placing it in a heavy saucepan to keep it steady while folding. →

3 Add the ½ stick tepid melted butter, sprinkling it on top of the batter and gently folding it in. If poured in too quickly, the butter will sink to the bottom of the bowl. Butter will tend to break down the mixture so do not over-fold and be gentle. Pour into the prepared cake pan, place on a cookie sheet in a preheated 350-degree oven, and bake for 25 to 30 minutes.

Meanwhile make the bourbon syrup: Mix the 3 Tb. warm water, 1 tsp. vanilla, 2 Tb. sugar, and 3 Tb. bourbon together until smooth. Set aside.

When done, the cake should be nicely browned and the sides should shrink slightly from the edge of the pan. Remove from the oven and keep in a warm place for 15 to 20 minutes before unmolding. Unmold on a wire rack. When cool, place in a plastic bag and refrigerate.

4 The delicate part of making a custard is to keep the eggs from scrambling. Pour the ¼ c. cream into a bowl with a fine sieve handy; the custard will be strained through the sieve into the cold cream, which will stop further cooking and prevent curdling. Pour the 1 c. milk into a saucepan and bring to a boil. Put the 3 egg yolks and ⅓ c. sugar in a bowl, and beat with a whisk for about 1 minute, until fluffy and pale yellow. Combine the boiling milk with the yolk-sugar mixture. Pour the custard into the saucepan and return it to medium heat, stirring continuously with a spoon, until it reaches about 180 degrees and thickens. Strain immediately through the sieve into the cold cream and mix well. Add the 2 tsp. vanilla.

5 Let cool to tepid. Add the 2 Tb. bourbon. The custard should be just thick enough to coat the spoon. A finger run across the coated spoon will leave a mark, as shown.

6 Meanwhile, beat the 10 oz. butter with a whisk until fluffy and soft. Start adding the custard cream to it, ¼ c. at a time, beating after each addition until smooth and fluffy. Keep adding until all the custard cream is combined with the butter. Hold at room temperature until ready to use.

7 **To build the cake:** First measure and cut a piece of cardboard the size of the bottom of the cake pan. Using a long serrated knife, slice the cake into 3 horizontal layers. As you slice, keep the blade level and rotate the cake. The blade should not be removed from the cake until the cutting is complete.

8 If you find the cutting technique difficult to master, use guides such as these spatula handles about ⅜ to ½ in. thick. Place the cake in between. The blade of the knife should be long enough to go through the cake and rest on both guides. Start by cutting the first layer from the top of the cake, then placing it on the cardboard upside down. The top of the genoise is now the bottom layer of the cake. Brush with bourbon syrup. Spread a thin layer of buttercream on top.

9 Add the second layer.

10 Brush with syrup before coating with buttercream. Place the third layer on top (the bottom of the cake is now the top), brush with remaining syrup, and coat with buttercream on top, spreading it as smoothly as you can with a long, thin metal spatula.

11 Holding the cake up (it will be secure on the cardboard), spread buttercream as smoothly as possible all around the sides.

12 Melt the 1 Tb. bittersweet chocolate and add ¼ tsp. vegetable oil to it. Make a cornet (see "Swimming Swans," page 234, steps 2–6) and pour the chocolate into it. Cut off the tip and draw a design to your liking on top.

13 Fill a pastry bag fitted with a fluted tip with the remaining buttercream, and pipe a pattern all around the edge of the cake. Refrigerate until serving time. (If the cake is to be kept for several hours, cover it with plastic wrap, after the buttercream has set, to prevent the cake from absorbing the flavor of other foods in the refrigerator.) Cut into wedges and serve.

STRAWBERRY FONDANT VALENTINE

Tasty and pretty, this heart-shaped dessert is ideal for St. Valentine's Day, and the strawberries announce the coming of spring. The same batter could be made into a large cake (a 9-in. pan in a round or heart shape) and the inside filled with strawberry jam and cream. In winter, fill it with orange marmalade and orange sections and serve it with an orange sauce. Any kind of fruit can be used, according to the season.

It takes only a couple of minutes to make the pink fondant, but it should be used within an hour or so of preparation. Otherwise, cover it with plastic wrap so it doesn't get hard on top. Strawberries can also be dipped in the fondant and used as a garnish. However, I have chosen to glaze the strawberries with cooked sugar.

For glazing, use ripe strawberries, preferably with stems so you can hold them easily as you dip them into the extremely hot sugar (between 310 and 320 degrees). Be sure the berries are dry so they do not splatter, and proceed with caution.

If the berries are ripe and the sugar is used right away while it is very hot and thin, the shell of sugar crusted around the berries will be thin. The hot sugar will partially cook the ripe berries. Within 15 to 20 minutes, the berries will release some juice, which will begin to melt the shell of

sugar, so the glazing cannot be done more than 1 hour before serving. The riper the berries, the faster the moisture is released. The right time to serve the berries is when the sugar shell is partially melted so that it is very thin and close to breaking open and the berries will be lukewarm, juicy, and a bit soft inside as you bite into them. If hard, unripe berries are used, the sugar remains thick and the berries dry and hard. Glazed berries can be served with after-dinner drinks as well as used to decorate cakes or cold soufflés.

Yield: 8–10 hearts

CAKE BATTER

3 eggs, separated
¾ c. sugar
1 tsp. vanilla
¼ c. vegetable oil
½ c. cake flour
½ c. all-purpose flour
1 tsp. baking powder
½ c. milk

FAST PINK FONDANT

2 Tb. warm water from the tap
1 Tb. corn syrup
3 to 4 drops red food coloring
2 c. confectioners' sugar

STRAWBERRY FILLER

½ c. strawberry jam or preserves
2 c. sliced strawberries
1 c. heavy cream
2 Tb. sugar

CARAMEL-GLAZED STRAWBERRIES

1½ c. sugar
½ c. cool water
6 to 8 drops lemon juice (optional)
12 very large, ripe strawberries with
    stems

STRAWBERRY SAUCE

2 c. hulled and cleaned strawberries
½ c. strawberry jam
1 Tb. cognac

GARNISH

Small pansies or other edible flowers for
    decoration

1 **For the cake batter:** Mix the 3 egg yolks, ¾ c. sugar, and 1 tsp. vanilla together with a whisk in a mixing bowl. Add the ¼ c. oil, whisking to incorporate. Mix together the ½ c. each cake and all-purpose flour and 1 tsp. baking powder, and add to the bowl, mixing well with the whisk. Add the ½ c. milk and mix with the whisk for 20 to 30 seconds so that the mixture is smooth and light.

2 Beat the 3 egg whites with a whisk or an electric beater until stiff but not dry. Mix one-third of the whites into the batter with a whisk to lighten it and then, using a spatula, fold in the remainder of the whites until well-incorporated.

3 Butter and flour the little heart-shaped molds (each with a capacity of approximately ½ to ¾ c.). Place approximately ⅓ c. of the batter in each mold, filling them three-fourths full.

4 Bake the molds in a preheated 325-degree oven for approximately 35 minutes and cool for 10 to 15 minutes before unmolding. Unmold and let cool completely on a rack. (At this point, the cakes can be placed in airtight containers and kept for a few days or frozen.)

5 If the heart batter has run over slightly and the cakes are irregular in shape, trim them to make them neat and split each one in half horizontally to make two layers.

For the fondant: Mix together the 2 Tb. warm water, 1 Tb. corn syrup, and 3 to 4 drops food coloring. Put the 2 c. confectioners' sugar in a bowl and add the water–corn syrup mixture to it. Stir with a whisk until well-mixed and then beat with the whisk for approximately 20 to 30 seconds, until very smooth. Depending on the moisture in the sugar, you may need slightly more water (approximately ½ tsp.). Or, if the fondant is too thin, add a little sugar. Arrange half the hearts on a wire rack and spread a good tablespoon of the fondant on each cake so a little of it runs down the sides. This can be done ahead so the fondant dries slightly and remains shiny.

6 **For the strawberry filler:** On the cut halves of each heart, spread 1 Tb. of the jam and arrange 3 to 4 Tb. of the sliced berries on top, pressing them into the jam.

Whip the 1 c. cream with the 2 Tb. sugar until stiff. Place in a pastry bag with a plain ½-in. tip and pipe some cream on top of the cut berries. Place a fondant-covered cake layer on top of each.

7 **To glaze the berries:** Put the 1½ c. sugar and ½ c. cool water in a small saucepan, preferably unlined copper, and stir just enough to wet the sugar and create a syrup. Then cook over medium to high heat until a candy thermometer registers between 310 and 320 degrees (hard-crack). This will take approximately 15 minutes after the mixture comes to a boil. (The unlined copper sugar pan tends to prevent the sugar from crystallizing. If unavailable, add 6 to 8 drops of lemon juice to the syrup when it is almost cooked to prevent crystallization.)

Oil a tray very lightly. If the 12 strawberries are not clean, wash them gently and dry them thoroughly.

Put the pan containing the boiling hot sugar syrup on a pot holder and tip it. Dip the strawberries, one at a time, into the hot syrup, making sure that each berry is completely submerged so that it is coated all around. Lift the berries out of the syrup and drag them lightly over the lip of the pan to remove excess syrup.

9 **For the strawberry sauce:** Cut the 2 c. of strawberries into pieces. Place the berries in a food processor along with the ½ c. strawberry jam and 1 Tb. cognac. Process until smooth. (No straining is necessary.)

At serving time, place a layer of the sauce on a serving platter. Arrange some of the heart cakes on top and the glazed strawberries decoratively around them. Decorate with small pansies or other edible flowers and serve immediately.

10 For an intimate St. Valentine's Day meal or a tête-à-tête dinner, place 2 hearts on top of some sauce on a small oval platter and arrange glazed berries around them. Serve immediately.

8 Set the coated berries on the oiled tray. The sugar will harden around them. Set aside until serving time.

BLACK AND RED CURRANT CAKE

Because there is a law prohibiting their cultivation in the United States, black currants are not available fresh in any market. However, black currant preserves are readily available, and red currants are available fresh in summer at farms as well as certain specialty stores. These small, juicy, acidic berries should always be strained because they are full of seeds.

This cake is a delightful summer treat with its beautiful color and slightly tart taste. It can easily be made several days ahead and should rest at least 4 to 5 hours for the Bavarian mixture to set well before being unmolded and cut.

Notice that the sponge cake is trimmed after cooking so the currant filling covers the outside and the recessed cake is actually encased inside. The currant filling could be served by itself like a Bavarian cream or with a garnish of whipped cream, and the sponge cake can be used almost anytime a cake is called for.

Yield: 10–12 servings

SPONGE CAKE BATTER

3 eggs, separated
¾ c. sugar
1 tsp. vanilla
¼ c. corn or safflower oil
½ c. cake flour
½ c. all-purpose flour
1 tsp. baking powder
½ c. milk

CURRANT FILLING

1½ lb. fresh red currants (about 2 c. strained)
4 egg yolks
½ c. sugar
¼ c. cold water
2 envelopes gelatin (about 1½ Tb.)
4 Tb. water
3 egg whites
2 Tb. sugar

FINISHING THE CAKE

2 Tb. raspberry brandy
⅓ c. black currant preserves, preferably with pieces of the fruit
¼ c. currants for top of cake
¼ c. currant jelly, melted

FOR DECORATION

1 c. heavy cream
1 Tb. sugar
¼ c. fresh currants with stems attached

1 **For the cake batter:** Mix the 3 egg yolks, ¾ c. sugar, and 1 tsp. vanilla together with a whisk in a mixing bowl. Add the ¼ c. oil and mix just enough to incorporate. Mix the ½ c. each cake and all-purpose flour and 1 tsp. baking powder together, then add to the bowl along with ¼ c. of the milk, mixing well with the whisk. Then add the remaining ¼ c. milk and beat with the whisk for 20 to 30 seconds, until the mixture is smooth and light.

Beat the 3 egg whites with a whisk or an electric beater until stiff but not dry. Mix one-third of the whites into the batter with the whisk to lighten the mixture and, using a spatula, fold in the remainder of the whites until well-incorporated. (See Strawberry Fondant Valentine, page 212, steps 1–2.)

Butter and flour a 10-in. springform cake pan about 2 in. high and pour the batter into it. Place on a cookie sheet and bake in a preheated 325-degree oven for 40 to 45 minutes. Let the cake cool for 20 to 25 minutes, and then unmold it onto a wire rack. Let cool further while making the filling.

2 Strain the currants through a food mill fitted with the smallest screen and then, if there are still seeds in the purée, strain it again through a sieve (see straining technique, Blackberry Clafoutis, page 194, steps 7–8).

3 Place the 4 egg yolks in a mixer fitted with a whisk beater. Put the ½ c. sugar with the ¼ c. cold water in a saucepan and stir just enough to dissolve the sugar. Place on the stove, bring to a boil, and cook for about 4 to 5 minutes, until the mixture will spin a thread (about 230 degrees on a candy thermometer). <u>Pour the hot syrup into the yolks slowly while beating at low speed.</u> Increase the speed to high and continue beating on medium to high speed for about 10 minutes.

5 Beat the 3 egg whites until stiff, add the 2 Tb. of sugar, and beat again for about 30 seconds to incorporate the sugar into the whites. Spoon about one-fourth to one-third of the egg whites into the red currant mixture and mix with a whisk. <u>Using a rubber spatula, gently fold the rest of the egg whites into the red currant purée.</u>

When the cake is cool, trim it all around with a knife or scissors to make it approximately 9 in. in diameter, and then cut it in half horizontally to make two layers.

7 Line the bottom and sides of the spring-form pan used for baking the cake with parchment paper, oiling the paper on one side and placing the oiled side against the pan so the paper adheres well. Place the cake layer with the preserves on the bottom in the center of the pan. There should be about ½ in. of space all around between the cake and the pan. <u>Spread about half the currant filling on top and around the sides.</u>

4 <u>The mixture should be thick and creamy.</u> Meanwhile, combine the 2 envelopes of gelatin with the 4 Tb. of cold water and let set until the gelatin absorbs the water. Melt the softened gelatin over low heat and, when the gelatin is well-melted, add it to the 2 c. of red currant purée, mixing well with a whisk. Now combine that currant-gelatin purée with the egg yolk–sugar mixture, mixing it with a whisk.

6 Sprinkle one layer of the cake with 1 Tb. of the raspberry brandy and <u>spread the ⅓ c. black currant preserves on top.</u>

8 Place the other cake layer on top of the filling and push down on it gently to embed it in the filling. Sprinkle the cake with the remaining tablespoon of raspberry brandy and <u>spread the remaining currant filling on top.</u>

9 <u>Sprinkle the ¼ c. of currants on top of the cake</u> and refrigerate for at least 1 to 2 hours until the filling is set.

10 Melt the ¼ c. currant jelly slowly over low heat, mixing it only occasionally. When it is liquid, place over ice cold water and stir until it begins to thicken. Pour it on top of the cake and spread it all around. Place the cake back in the refrigerator for at least 2 hours.

At this point, remove the springform sides, then slide the cake onto a serving plate.

13 To serve, cut wedges of the cake and place on individual plates. Decorate with some of the fresh currants and a little dab of whipped cream and serve immediately.

11 Remove the parchment paper from around the cake. It can be left on underneath.

12 Whip the 1 c. heavy cream and 1 Tb. sugar until the cream is firm, and place it in a pastry bag fitted with a star tip. Decorate the outside of the cake with the cream and arrange the ¼ c. fresh currants, still attached to their stems, around the outside of the platter.

CHOCOLATE YULE LOG WITH MINT LEAVES

This is a stunning dessert for a Christmas or fall party. It is made up of several procedures that can be used as independent recipes.

The jelly roll cake is filled with a chocolate pastry cream (but you could fill it with a buttercream, whipped cream, or jam instead). A rich rum chocolate glaze (a ganache) coats the jelly roll, and, finally, chocolate "bark" is placed around the cake to enclose it. The chocolate roll looks like the stump of a tree and is usually served without the chocolate "bark." Mint leaves and other kinds of larger leaves are pressed into the "bark"—some just for effect, but the mint leaves complement the taste of the chocolate so you don't need to remove them before serving.

Refrigerate the cake until serving time after covering it well with plastic wrap because the chocolate tends to absorb tastes from other foods in the refrigerator. After a few moments on the buffet, the chocolate "bark" will soften just enough that it can be cut into pieces with the point of a sharp knife as the cake is sliced. This cake, with-

out the "bark," freezes well, provided it is properly wrapped and not kept frozen for more than a couple of weeks. Defrost under refrigeration.

Yield: 10–12 servings

JELLY ROLL CAKE

8 eggs, separated
⅔ c. granulated sugar
1 tsp. vanilla
⅔ c. flour

CHOCOLATE PASTRY CREAM FILLING

3 egg yolks
⅓ c. granulated sugar
2 Tb. cornstarch
1 tsp. vanilla
1½ c. milk
5 oz. bittersweet or semi-sweet chocolate (see page 132), broken into pieces

RUM-CHOCOLATE GANACHE OR GLAZE

About 4 oz. (½ c. melted) bittersweet or semi-sweet chocolate
½ c. heavy cream
1 Tb. dark rum

CHOCOLATE BARK WITH LEAVES

12 oz. bittersweet chocolate
12 to 15 mint leaves + extra larger leaves for imprint

DECORATIONS

Confectioners' sugar for dusting cake
Autumn leaves or holly

1 **To make the jelly roll cake:** Beat the 8 egg yolks, ⅔ c. sugar, and 1 tsp. vanilla together for about 1 minute, until very fluffy and smooth. Then add the ⅔ c. flour and mix well with a whisk until smooth.

Beat the 8 egg whites by hand or with an electric mixer until firm. Pour the egg yolk mixture on top of the whites.

2 Fold the yolks gently into the whites to retain most of the volume.

3 Butter a parchment paper–lined jelly roll pan 12 × 16 in. (See paper buttering technique, Chocolate Cloud Cake, page 222, steps 4–6.) Spread the cake batter on the paper, making it of equal thickness all over.

4 Bake in a preheated 350-degree oven for approximately 13 minutes. The cake will be puffy when removed from the oven. It will deflate and shrink slightly as it cools but will still remain quite soft and pliable.

5 For the chocolate pastry cream filling: Beat the 3 egg yolks, ⅓ c. sugar, 2 Tb. cornstarch, and 1 tsp. vanilla together with a whisk. Meanwhile, bring the 1½ c. milk to a boil. Pour the boiling milk into the egg yolk mixture, stirring, then return it to the saucepan. Bring to a boil, stirring with a whisk so the pastry cream doesn't stick and burn on the bottom. Boil for about 10 seconds. Remove from the heat. The mixture will be quite thick.

6 Add the chocolate pieces to the saucepan and stir gently with a whisk to help melt the chocolate. After 5 minutes, stir again.

7 The mixture should be very smooth. Transfer to a bowl, cover, and refrigerate.

8 Slide a spatula under the cooled cake and remove it to a board with the parchment paper underneath still intact. When the chocolate pastry cream is cold, spread it on the top of the cake – the part exposed in the oven – which has visible cracks.

9 Using the paper lining underneath, lift up the cake and begin to roll it on itself.

10 Keep rolling, still using the paper, until the jelly roll is rolled up tightly.

11 The pastry cream is now completely enclosed in the cake roll. Roll the cake up in the same parchment paper and refrigerate it for up to a day or so.

12 To finish the yule log, remove the paper and place the cake on a serving platter. Cut off both ends of the log at an angle. These pieces will be used to simulate stumps on the log.

To make the rum-chocolate ganache: Melt the 4 oz. bittersweet chocolate in a double boiler. Place the ½ c. cream and 1 Tb. rum in a bowl and, when the chocolate is melted, add it and beat with a whisk for 15 to 30 seconds, until the mixture lightens slightly in color and becomes about the consistency of a buttercream. Do not over-whisk because incorporating too much air will whiten the *ganache* and make it set too hard as it cools. If this should happen, remelt slightly and beat again.

13 Using a spatula, coat the whole cake with a thin layer of the *ganache*.

14 Place the two end pieces of cake on top to simulate tree stumps.

15 Continue coating the cake and stumps with the *ganache*. When thoroughly coated, draw the tines of a fork through the soft *ganache* to create a bark design. Using the point of a knife, make circular designs on top of the stumps and at either end of the log to simulate the design on a tree. At this point, the cake can be refrigerated. When cold, cover loosely with plastic wrap. It is usually served as this point.

16 For a more elaborate serving variation, chocolate bark can be added.

For the chocolate bark: Melt the 12 oz. bittersweet chocolate in a double boiler and pour a strip of it about the length of the cake onto parchment or wax paper.

17 With a narrow, flexible spatula, spread the chocolate to a thickness of about ⅛ in., smearing the chocolate out at intervals to make a jagged edge along the length on one side to simulate broken pieces of bark.

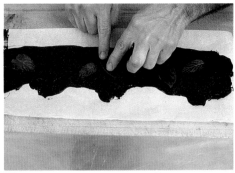

18 While the chocolate is still warm, press the mint leaves and larger leaves into the surface. The mint leaves will be left in the chocolate and the larger leaves removed at serving time.

19 Press another strip of parchment paper on top of the chocolate and turn the package over onto a tray so the side with the leaves is touching the tray. Refrigerate. Repeat to make a strip of chocolate bark for the other side of the cake.

20 When the chocolate bark has hardened, remove the layer of paper from the top. The chocolate should have curled up a little at each end, which at this point will help it fit the contour of the cake. →

21 Cut through the chocolate and paper along the straighter side to trim it to a clean edge.

22 Place the chocolate (still attached to the paper), straight-edge down, alongside the cake, pressing it lightly against the cake. If the coating of the cake is still somewhat soft the bark strips will stick to it. (The bark can be made ahead and arranged around the cake before it is refrigerated.) The heat of your hand pressing against the paper may soften the chocolate slightly and make it adhere better to the cake. Peel off the paper.

23 Remove the larger leaves from both strips of the chocolate bark; they will have left leaf imprints in the chocolate, which was the desired effect. Leave the mint leaves in place.

24 Sprinkle a very light dusting of confectioners' sugar on the log to simulate snow.

25 Arrange fall leaves or holly around the cake, cut into slices, and serve.

CHOCOLATE CLOUD CAKE

This Chocolate Cloud Cake is make from a flour-free, light chocolate roulade, almost like the base mixture of a soufflé. Layers of chocolate cookie dough give a crunchy texture to the cake, which is flavored with whipped cream, cognac, and bitter orange marmalade. The marmalade could be replaced by raspberry, boysenberry, or apricot preserves, if you wish.

The cake freezes well if it is properly wrapped and is not kept frozen for too long. It should be defrosted slowly under refrigeration before serving.

The chocolate cookie dough is delicate and brittle. The only seasoning in it is the bittersweet chocolate, and, if you were to use it instead as a shell for a tart or for cookies, some sugar (about ⅓ c.) should be added to it.

Yield: 10–12 servings

CHOCOLATE ROULADE

⅓ c. coffee extract (see pages 255, 256)
½ c. granulated sugar
6 eggs, separated
8 oz. bittersweet or semi-sweet chocolate
   (see page 132)

CHOCOLATE COOKIE DOUGH

2 oz. bittersweet or semi-sweet chocolate
5 Tb. water
2½ c. flour
1½ sticks butter, softened (6 oz.)

WHIPPED CREAM MIXTURE

1 envelope gelatin (about ¾ Tb.)
¼ c. water
2 c. heavy cream
3 Tb. cognac
3 Tb. granulated sugar

1 c. bitter orange marmalade

CHOCOLATE GLAZE

5 oz. bittersweet or semi-sweet chocolate
½ c. confectioners' sugar
3 Tb. butter
3 Tb. water

1 c. mixture of almonds and hazelnuts, toasted in the oven about 12 minutes at 400 degrees

1 For the chocolate roulade: Combine the ⅓ c. coffee extract with the ½ c. sugar and boil for 1½ to 2 minutes, until syrupy and somewhat sticky. Put the 6 egg yolks in the mixer bowl and, with the beater on low speed, pour the coffee syrup on top of them. When blended, mix at high speed for about 10 minutes. The mixture should be thick and creamy.

2 Melt the 8 oz. bittersweet chocolate in a double boiler, then add it to the coffee–egg yolk mixture.

3 Whip the 6 egg whites until firm and add them to the chocolate–coffee–egg yolk mixture, folding in gently. →

4 To line a jelly roll pan (16 × 12 in.) with parchment paper, first cut a rectangular piece of parchment paper a little larger than the pan and butter half of it. Fold the buttered half of the paper onto the unbuttered half.

5 With a knife, make a 1-in. slit in both of the open corners of the folded paper, open the paper up, and place it buttered-side down in a jelly roll pan, pressing it very lightly (there's just enough butter to grease the pan slightly). Lift the paper and turn it over in the pan. It will adhere well now.

6 The paper will overlap at the corners where it has been cut, making it fit better in the pan.

7 Spread the chocolate roulade batter evenly in the pan.

8 Bake in a preheated 350-degree oven for about 13 minutes, <u>until the cake is nicely set and puffy.</u> Set aside to cool.

9 For the chocolate cookie dough: Melt the 2 oz. bittersweet chocolate with the 5 Tb. water. Put the 2½ c. flour in the bowl of a mixer with the 1½ sticks soft butter and, using the flat beater, start mixing on low speed. When most of the butter is incorporated, add the melted chocolate and mix on low speed just until the batter holds together. <u>Place the ball of dough on a large cookie sheet</u> (14 × 17 in.).

10 With a piece of plastic wrap extended over it, <u>roll the dough out with a rolling pin into a rectangle approximately 12 × 16 in.</u>

11 <u>Remove the plastic wrap.</u> The dough should be no more than about ⅛ in. thick. Bake in a preheated 400-degree oven for about 15 minutes, until just cooked.

12 Trim the dough all around the edges, reserving the trimmings, and <u>cut the rectangle into two halves, each 10 in. long by 7 to 7½ in. wide.</u>

13 **For the whipped cream mixture:** Put the 1 envelope gelatin in a bowl with ¼ c. water, and set the bowl in a skillet filled with water. Heat the water and stir the gelatin with a spatula until it is completely dissolved.

Combine the 2 c. cream and 3 Tb. each cognac and sugar in a bowl, and beat until firm. Add the hot, dissolved gelatin in one stroke while stirring quickly with a whisk to incorporate it smoothly into the mixture.

Unmold the cake with its baking paper still intact. Cut it in half with scissors, cutting right through the cake and the paper. Trim the sides to form two rectangles the same size as the cookie dough (about 10 in. long by 7½ in. wide). Cut out a piece of cardboard the same size and cover it with aluminum foil. Place a piece of the cookie dough on top of the cardboard and, using a long spatula, coat it with ½ c. of the bitter orange marmalade. Place about one-third of the cream mixture on top of the marmalade and spread it gently over the surface.

14 Turn one of the cake rectangles over, place it on top of the cream, and peel off the paper. Spread another one-third of the cream on top, smoothing it to the edges.

15 Slide the second cookie dough rectangle on top, spread it with the remaining ½ c. bitter orange marmalade and then the rest of the cream.

16 Place the other half of the cake, turned upside down, on top of the cream and peel off the paper. Press gently to level the cake.

Prepare the chocolate glaze: Put the 5 oz. bittersweet chocolate, ½ c. confectioners' sugar, and 3 Tb. each butter and water in a saucepan or in a double boiler, and stir gently over low heat until the mixture is melted and smooth. The chocolate glaze is fairly thick but still thin enough to coat the cake. Cool until tepid and, if too thick to spread on the cake, add 1 Tb. water and mix until smooth.

17 With a large spatula, spread the glaze lightly on top and around the sides of the cake until well-coated. Process the 1 c. mixture of almonds and hazelnuts in the food processor until finely chopped, then press them on the top and sides of the cake to make them adhere. Refrigerate until cold and then cover the cake tightly with plastic wrap so it doesn't pick up any other food tastes in the refrigerator or freezer. The cake can be frozen at this point.

18 At serving time, remove the cake from the cardboard, cut it in half and then into individual portions, and serve right away.

CHOCOLATE-WHISKEY-PRUNE CAKE

This very rich chocolate cake should be baked in a 10- to 12-in. cake pan so it will be approximately 1 in. thick, which makes it easy to cut into small portions. It can be baked in a quiche pan lined with parchment paper as well as in a cake pan. It is baked at a fairly low temperature for a short time so it doesn't get dry and over-cooked; in fact, the center of the cake should be a bit wet after it is cooked. Cut the cake into small wedges and serve with whipped cream to lighten it.

The caramelized pecans used as a decoration add a nice look to the cake but are not absolutely necessary. The sprig of fresh mint in the center can be cut into a julienne and sprinkled on the whole cake or on individual portions. The prunes can be omitted or replaced by raisins or diced dried apricots and the bourbon replaced by rum or cognac.

The cake should not be served ice cold but at room temperature, at which point the texture is softer and the taste more flavorful. If refrigerated, bring to room temperature before serving.

Yield: 12 servings

CAKE BATTER

1 c. diced prunes
⅓ c. bourbon whiskey mixed with 1 Tb. water
1 c. hazelnuts (about 5 to 6 oz.)
2 Tb. cornstarch
6 eggs
12 oz. bittersweet or semi-sweet chocolate (see page 132), melted
⅓ c. granulated sugar
3 sticks butter, at room temperature (12 oz.)

CARAMELIZED PECAN GARNISH

⅓ c. granulated sugar
12 pecan halves

About 1 tsp. confectioners' sugar for dusting the cake
A few mint sprigs for decoration
1 c. heavy cream

1 **For the cake:** Cut the 1 c. prunes into a ¼-in. dice and place them with the ⅓ c. bourbon and 1 Tb. water in a bowl to macerate for a few hours.

Arrange the 1 c. hazelnuts on a baking sheet and place in a preheated 400-degree oven for approximately 12 minutes, until nicely browned. It is not necessary to remove the skin afterward. Put the hazelnuts with the 2 Tb. cornstarch in a food processor and process until reduced to a fine powder. Add the 6 eggs and process until well-mixed.

Meanwhile, mix the 12 oz. melted chocolate, ⅓ c. sugar, and 3 sticks soft butter together, and beat well with a whisk. Finally, add the hazelnut-and-egg mixture to the chocolate mixture along with the prunes and bourbon, and stir gently until well-incorporated.

2 Butter half of a square piece of parchment paper. Fold the unbuttered side of the paper onto the buttered side and press together to make a square.

3 Fold the square into smaller and smaller triangles.

4 Holding the paper triangle as shown, measure the radius of a round cake pan 10 to 12 in. in diameter and cut the paper so it will fit exactly in the pan.

5 Place the paper buttered-side down in the pan and, as soon as it touches the pan firmly, turn it over so the buttered side is up. The paper is buttered on both sides now and will adhere well to the bottom of the pan and not stick to the batter.

Pour the batter into the pan, set the pan on a pizza pan or cookie sheet, and place it in a preheated 325-degree oven for 20 to 30 minutes, until the cake is set but still slightly wet in the center.

6 **To make the caramelized pecans:** Place the ⅓ c. sugar over medium heat and stir until the sugar starts melting. It will probably crystallize, forming into lumps. Continue to cook it.

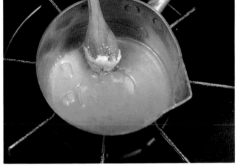

7 Most of the sugar is melted, although there are still some lumps visible. As the sugar continues to cook and starts to reach caramel temperature (about 318 to 320 degrees), the lumps will melt.

8 Very lightly oil a small tray. When the caramel has turned a rich brown color, add the 12 pecan halves and turn them so they are coated with the caramel. With a fork, lift the pecans one by one out of the caramel and deposit them on the oiled tray. The caramel will harden within a few minutes. When hard and cool, trim around the pecans with scissors to remove any rough projections or excess caramel.

9 At serving time, unmold the cake onto a serving platter and peel off the paper.

10 Fold the paper into a thin triangle again and cut it in half crosswise, creating a small round circle at the pointed end.

11 Center the circle on top of the cake and . . . →

12 . . . dust the top of the cake with 1 tsp. confectioners' sugar.

13 Carefully remove and discard the paper circle and arrange the caramelized pecans around the perimeter of the cake.

14 Place a sprig of mint in the center of the cake. Whip the 1 c. cream until soft peaks form. Serve little wedges of the cake with a dollop of the whipped cream decorated with a sprig of mint.

CHOCOLATE-CHERRY CAKE

This rich, luscious chocolate-cherry cake made with fresh cherries is wonderful for a birthday party. It can be made ahead — at least through frosting (step 15) — and will keep a few days this way in the refrigerator. Be sure, however, that after the frosting has hardened, the cake is covered with plastic wrap so it doesn't pick up any tastes in the refrigerator. It is quite rich and will go a long way.

The cherry filling, made with cooked cherries, gelatin, and cream, can be served by itself as a Bavarian cream. The cherry garnishes — cherries dipped in currant jelly or in egg white and sugar — make a nice presentation and could be served instead of petits fours with after-dinner drinks.

The chocolate glaze is a <u>ganache</u>, made of chocolate and heavy cream, and it is used in three different ways. Some is hardened and used as a coating (steps 11 and 12), some is left as liquid and used as a glaze (steps 13, 14, and 15), and, finally, the glaze is allowed to harden and used as a buttercream for the top decoration (steps 18 and 19).

Yield: 10–12 servings

CAKE BATTER

9 oz. bittersweet or semi-sweet chocolate (see page 132)
2 sticks butter (½ lb.)
7 eggs, separated
1 c. all-purpose flour
2 Tb. baking powder
⅓ c. granulated sugar

CHERRY FILLING

1 lb. fresh cherries, pitted (for cherry-pitting technique, see Cherry-Raspberry Pillow, page 171, step 2)
½ c. + 2 Tb. granulated sugar
¼ c. water
1½ envelopes gelatin (about 1 Tb.)
2 Tb. cold water
¼ c. cherry preserves
4 Tb. Kirschwasser
2 c. heavy cream
2 Tb. warm water from the tap

COATING AND GLAZE

12 oz. bittersweet or semi-sweet chocolate, cut into pieces
1½ c. heavy cream

CHERRY GARNISHES

½ c. currant jelly, melted
36 cherries with stems
1 egg white
1 c. confectioners' sugar

Nasturtium blossoms for decoration (optional)

1 For the cake batter: Combine the 9 oz. bittersweet chocolate and ½ lb. butter, and melt together over low heat or over hot water in a bowl. Add the 7 egg yolks to the chocolate mixture and mix with a whisk. The mixture will thicken.

2 Mix the 1 c. flour with 2 Tb. baking powder and add to the chocolate mixture. Stir in with a whisk. Beat the 7 egg whites with a whisk or an electric beater until stiff, add the ⅓ c. granulated sugar, and beat for another 10 to 15 seconds to incorporate the sugar. Add about one-third of the egg whites to the chocolate mixture and mix it well with a whisk to lighten the batter.

3 Fold in the remaining egg whites with a spatula until well-incorporated.

4 Butter a springform pan 10 in. in diameter and 2 in. high, and pour the cake mixture into the pan. Place on a pizza pan or cookie sheet in the center of a preheated 350-degree oven for approximately 50 minutes, until cooked and well-set.

5 Let the cake cool at room temperature for at least 30 minutes, then unmold it from the springform. Invert onto a wire rack, remove the base of the pan, and allow to cool completely.

6 For the cherry filling: Combine the 1 lb. pitted cherries with ½ c. of the granulated sugar and ¼ c. water in a saucepan, and bring to a boil, covered. Boil about 1 minute, then drain the cherries, reserving the juice. Boil the juice to reduce it to ¾ c.

Moisten the 1½ envelopes gelatin with 2 Tb. cold water, and when the water has been absorbed by the gelatin, add it to the reduced cherry juice, heat, and stir until well-mixed. Add the ¼ c. cherry preserves and 2 Tb. of the Kirschwasser to the mixture, and set it aside.

Whip the 2 c. cream until it forms soft peaks, and when the cherry mixture has reached room temperature, combine it with the whipped cream. Place in the refrigerator for at least 30 minutes before using it, to allow it to firm up somewhat.

7 Slice the chocolate cake in half horizontally, then split each half again to make 4 layers. (For cake-slicing technique, see Vanilla-Bourbon Genoise, page 210, steps 7–8.) Mix the remaining 2 Tb. Kirschwasser with the remaining 2 Tb. granulated sugar and 2 Tb. warm water to make a syrup.

Cut a round piece of cardboard the size of the cake and place one of the cake layers on top, reserving the bottom layer of the cake (the flattest layer) for the top. Brush some of the Kirschwasser syrup on the cake layer positioned on the cardboard. Spread one-third of the cherry-cream mixture on top. →

8 Place a second layer of the cake on top. If you feel you might have a problem transferring the thin layers onto the cake, use the base of a quiche pan as a spatula to slide the layer onto the cake. Moisten with the Kirschwasser syrup and spread another third of the cherry-cream mixture on top.

9 Add a third layer of cake, moisten it with the Kirschwasser syrup, and spread the remaining cherry-cream mixture on top. Add the remaining layer of cake, moisten with the rest of the Kirschwasser syrup, and smooth out the cherry-cream mixture between the layers. Set aside in the refrigerator for a while.

10 **To make the coating and glaze:** While the cake is in the refrigerator, heat the 12 oz. of bittersweet chocolate with the 1½ c. cream until hot and smooth. Pour about 1 to 1¼ c. of the mixture into a bowl and refrigerate over ice water to harden slightly; set the remainder aside on top of a warm stove so it remains liquid.

As the refrigerated chocolate hardens, whip it with a whisk for a few seconds to lighten it with air. It will lose its shine and get a bit lighter in color.

11 When the cool chocolate is of spreading consistency, lift up the cake, holding it with one hand on the cardboard underneath, and spread some of the chocolate on the outside of the cake, sealing the cherry mixture inside and coating it thinly.

12 Coat the top of the cake with the remainder of the chocolate in the bowl. Notice there is just a thin layer of chocolate on the cake at this point, just enough to make the top and sides smooth. Place the cake in the refrigerator for at least 1 hour so the coating hardens to the proper consistency.

13 If the chocolate you have set aside on the stove has thickened too much, add 1 or 2 Tb. warm water to it. It should be of spreading consistency and barely tepid to the touch. Remove the cake from the refrigerator and place it on a wire rack over a tray or a clean Formica or marble surface so you can retrieve the chocolate drippings. Pour the chocolate coating on top.

14 Spread the chocolate with a long metal spatula so it coats the top and runs down the sides of the cake. Use the spatula to spread the chocolate on the sides where they are not covered. This glazing should be done quickly so the chocolate doesn't have time to harden before the cake is coated uniformly all around.

15 Shake the chocolate cake while still on the rack to smooth the sides and top further. Then lift the cake up and with your finger clean the edge where it sits on the cardboard. Refrigerate the cake.

Scrape up the chocolate drippings and place them in a bowl with any leftover chocolate coating and allow it to harden slightly, stirring it gently with a spatula occasionally. This will be used to decorate the top.

16 To coat the cherries with currant jelly: Melt the ½ c. currant jelly over low heat or over hot water in a double boiler. It should be brought almost to a boil before stirring gently to ensure that it is melted uniformly. Keep at room temperature or over cold water, stirring occasionally, until it starts to cool and thicken.

Cut off only the tips of the stems of 36 large round cherries and be certain the cherries are dry.

Coat half the cherries by holding them by the stem and dipping them into the slightly thickened currant jelly. Lift the cherries from the jelly, place on a cold plate, and refrigerate.

17 To coat the cherries with egg white: Hold the remaining cherries by their stems, dip them in the egg white so they are just lightly wet all around, and then roll in the 1 c. confectioners' sugar to coat the outside. Place on a plate and refrigerate to harden the coating.

18 To finish the cake, work the remaining chocolate (about ⅓ c.) to a soft consistency and place in a pastry bag fitted with a star tip. Pipe a design on top of the cake with the chocolate. Place 2 fresh nasturtiums in the chocolate design for a vivid decoration.

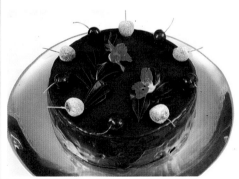

19 Decorate the cake with some of the glazed cherries, alternating the currant jelly–glazed cherries and egg white–sugar–glazed cherries. Serve additional glazed cherries on the side.

20 Serve the cake cold in thin wedges because it is very rich.

PROFITEROLES WITH CHOCOLATE SAUCE

Pâte à choux, also called choux paste or cream puff dough, has innumerable uses in the kitchen, for basic cooking as well as desserts. A few desserts requiring choux paste are the profiteroles, here, the St. Honoré Cake (page 239), the "Swimming Swans" (page 233), the Croquembouche (page 237), and the Paris-Brest Cake (page 242). With the addition of cheese, choux paste can be transformed into gnocchi, pike dumplings (see Volume I, Pike Quenelles and Chicken Liver Timbale Merret, pages 102–04), or mixed with mashed potatoes and fried to make dauphine potatoes. Because of its great versatility, it is always available in a professional kitchen.

Each cup of flour, obtained by dipping a measuring cup directly into the flour bin and leveling it, will weigh 5 to 5½ oz. and require 4 or 5 eggs, depending on size. If the pâte à choux is too thick, the pastry will tend to open up too much as it bakes; on the other hand, if it is too soft, it will have a tendency to sink on the cookie sheet and not rise properly.

For any cake made of pâte à choux, be careful of air-conditioning. If, after emerging beautifully puffy from the oven, the choux is exposed to cool air drafts or high humidity, it will have a tendency to collapse because of the moisture inside the pastry. To prevent this, when the choux is almost finished cooking, open the door of the oven and continue cooking with the oven door held slightly ajar (close it over a large metal spoon, for example), or shut the oven off, open its door, and allow the choux to cool off slowly in the still warm oven so that the moisture inside the pastry can escape. Do not leave the choux in the oven too long, however, or it will dry out.

Another way to release the moisture trapped in the hot choux is to remove the pastry from the oven and cut off the top of it so the moisture can escape. The choux should hold its shape but be tender and moist to the bite.

Sometimes the soft dough on the inside is removed before the choux is stuffed, but this is purely a matter of taste. I enjoy the soft dough inside and prefer to leave it.

This classic recipe for choux paste will be referred to over and over again in the recipes that follow, from St. Honoré Cake to the

Paris-Brest Cake. Basic choux paste can be made with milk or water. Water tends to produce a slightly drier dough, which makes it a good choice if you live in an area where it is humid.

Yield: 36 profiteroles, 9–12 servings

BASIC CHOUX PASTE

1 c. milk or water
⅓ stick butter (about 1½ oz.)
⅛ tsp. salt
¼ tsp. granulated sugar
1 c. flour, scooped up and leveled (about 5 to 5½ oz.)
4 or 5 large eggs
Egg wash made with 1 egg with half the white removed, beaten

PASTRY BUTTERCREAM (for 3 c.)

4 large egg yolks
⅓ c. granulated sugar
3 Tb. potato starch
1½ c. milk
2 sticks butter (½ lb.)

CHOCOLATE SAUCE

8 oz. bittersweet or semi-sweet chocolate (see page 132)
2 c. milk
3 Tb. granulated sugar
3 egg yolks

FOR THE DECORATION

1 Tb. pastry buttercream (from above)
1 Tb. milk
Confectioners' sugar

1 For the choux paste: Combine the cup of milk, ⅓ stick butter, ⅛ tsp. salt, and ¼ tsp. granulated sugar in a saucepan, and bring to a boil. The 1 c. flour does not have to be sifted unless there are little lumps in it. If lumps (sometimes a result of humidity in the summer) are visible, measure out the flour (dipping the cup into the flour and leveling it off) and sift into a bowl. (After sifting, the cup will probably measure 1 c. + 2 Tb., as the sifting will tend to aerate and lighten the flour.) As soon as the mixture in the saucepan comes to a boil, remove it from the stove and add the flour in one stroke. (Otherwise, the mixture will tend to lump.)

2 Using a sturdy wood or metal spoon, stir the mixture fast so it gathers together.

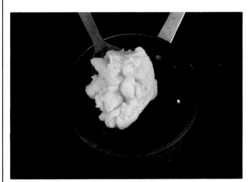

3 Place the mixture back on the stove. It should now come away from the sides of the pan. After stirring for about 30 seconds over medium heat, it should collect into one soft lump almost the texture of modeling clay.

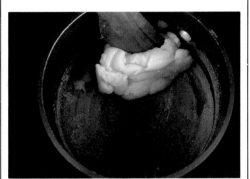

4 Continue cooking about 1 to 1½ minutes, still stirring, until the bottom of the pan is white and cakey. This indicates that the dough has dried a little more, which makes it smoother and stronger.

5 Transfer the dough to a bowl to mix by hand or do it in a mixer. Add 1 egg to the mixture and stir with a wooden spoon. At this point, the dough forms into lumps and it seems it will not hold together. Keep stirring and it will tighten. When this occurs, add another egg and stir until it tightens again. Add the remaining 2 or 3 eggs, one at a time, stirring after each addition until incorporated.

6 The dough should be very smooth but not too soft so it holds its shape. Four or five large eggs are enough.

7 Butter and flour a cookie sheet, using very little of both ingredients. (If too much butter and flour are used, the dough will tend to lift as you pull up on the pastry bag to release it.)

Place the dough in a pastry bag fitted with a star or plain tip. Squeeze out about 1 Tb. of pastry for each profiterole, moving the bag in a circular motion to make a swirl. The mounds of dough should be about 1 to 1½ in. apart on the sheet.

Using a brush, gently dab the tops of the dough mounds with the egg wash to flatten the "tail." (The small amount of egg white in the wash will give a nice shine to the puff and the egg yolk will guarantee a deeper and darker glaze.)

8 Place in a preheated 450-degree oven for 30 minutes. You will notice that most of the design disappears as the choux inflates during baking. Turn the oven off and prop the door open a little with a wooden spoon. Let the choux remain in the oven for about 30 minutes so it dries out and most of the internal moisture escapes. If not to be used immediately, the puffs will keep for a few days stored in a tin box after they have cooled completely. They can also be packed and frozen. →

9 For the pastry buttercream: Combine the 4 egg yolks, ⅓ c. granulated sugar, and 3 Tb. potato starch in a bowl, and mix for about 1 minute, until well-blended and smooth. Bring the 1½ c. milk to a boil in a saucepan and add it to the mixture, stirring.

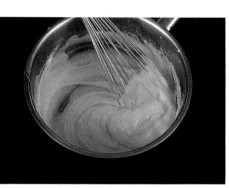

10 Place the mixture back on the stove and bring to a strong boil, mixing with the whisk. Be sure to get the whisk around the edges of the pot, where the mixture will tend to stick. Boil for a few seconds, remove from the stove, cover with plastic wrap, and set aside to cool. Or, to cool more quickly, place the pan in a bowl of ice and water. Set aside 1 Tb. of the mixture for decoration.

11 Put the 2 sticks of butter in the bowl of an electric mixer and whip for about 2 minutes, until fluffy and about the texture of the pastry buttercream. When the pastry cream is at room temperature or slightly tepid, add it to the whipped butter, and whip together over medium-high heat for about 45 seconds to 1 minute, until well-combined and fluffy.

12 Cut off the tops of the profiteroles about one-third of the way down. Fill up a pastry bag fitted with a fluted tip and pipe about 1 to 2 Tb. of the pastry buttercream mixture into each of the pastries.

13 Using a small cookie cutter, cut the lids of the profiteroles to make uniformly round circles and put them back on top of the buttercream.

14 For the chocolate sauce: Combine the 8 oz. chocolate, 2 c. milk, and 3 Tb. granulated sugar in a saucepan, and bring to a boil. Beat the 3 egg yolks in a bowl, and when the chocolate mixture is boiling, pour it in a steady stream into the egg yolks, mixing continuously with a whisk. The hot chocolate will cook the egg yolks. Strain the sauce through a fine strainer and cool.

15 For the decoration: Combine the 1 Tb. of reserved pastry buttercream with the 1 Tb. of milk. It should have the consistency of heavy syrup. Using a piece of wax paper, make a cornet (see "Swimming Swans," page 234, steps 2–6). Place the cornet in a glass so it stands upright, pour the cream-milk mixture into it, and fold or twist at the top to enclose the filling. Cut the cornet at the tip just enough to create a small opening.

16 Place about 3 Tb. of the chocolate sauce on each dessert plate and dot with the decorating mixture all around the edge.

17 Drag the point of a knife through each dot slightly to create a white "tail" or "heart" in the chocolate.

18 Dust the profiteroles with confectioners' sugar and place three in the middle of the chocolate sauce for each serving. Serve immediately.

"SWIMMING SWANS"

Creating swans of choux paste is easy, and they make a striking dessert. For large parties, the swan bodies can be stuffed with raspberry preserves and ice cream and frozen. Better yet, little balls of ice cream can be molded ahead, placed on a tray, and frozen, ready to be inserted into the bodies of the swans at the last minute.

An individual choux swan with the raspberry sauce underneath is attractive by itself, or several can be served together on one plate. The addition of the caramel "cage" (steps 18–21), placed on top of the birds, fits in with the concept and makes for a striking presentation. Small, individual "cages" can also be made to fit over individual servings.

Yield: 12 swans

BASIC CHOUX PASTE

½ c. milk
½ c. flour
1 Tb. + 1 tsp. butter
Dash salt
⅛ tsp. granulated sugar
2 to 3 large eggs
Egg wash made with 1 egg with half the white removed, beaten

RASPBERRY SAUCE

12 oz. fresh raspberries, or 1 twelve-ounce package frozen unsweetened raspberries, thawed
1 c. raspberry preserves
1 Tb. raspberry brandy

CHOUX FILLER

4 Tb. black raspberry jam (about 1 tsp. for each swan)
1 pt. vanilla ice cream (see page 280)

DECORATION

1 c. heavy cream
1 Tb. confectioners' sugar
1 Tb. Grand Marnier

CARAMEL FOR CAGE

1 c. granulated sugar
3 Tb. water

Confectioners' sugar for dusting the swans
A few flowers for decoration

1 Make the choux paste according to instructions in Profiteroles with Chocolate Sauce, page 230, steps 1–6. Very lightly butter and flour a cookie sheet. Place the choux paste in a pastry bag fitted with a ½-in. plain tip and squeeze out the paste in teardrop shapes to resemble the bodies of swans, as shown: Press or squeeze without moving the bag to create the main part of the body and then stop squeezing and pull to create a tail.

2 To make a paper cone or cornet, which is needed to create the neck and head of the swan, cut a piece of parchment or wax paper into a right-angle triangle shape about 8½ × 8½ × 12 in.

3 Fold the triangle at the center of the larger side, overlapping the ends to form a cone. Do not worry if the point is not very tight.

4 Keep twisting the paper around to double it. The tip of the cone is still not tight. To make a needle-size opening at the tip, place your thumbs on the inside and your fingers on the outside of the cone, and slide your thumbs down and your fingers up so the paper slides and the tip tighten into a fine point.

5 Still holding your fingers in place (so the paper doesn't unroll), fold the outer edge of the paper inside the cone to secure it.

6 The paper cone is now ready to be filled.

7 Place about 3 to 4 Tb. of the choux paste into the paper cone and cut the tip to enable you to squeeze out enough paste to create the heads and necks of the swans. First, make a small round for the head and continue "drawing" and squeezing the dough out to shape the curved neck of the swan. Then press the tip of the paper cornet on the cookie sheet so that when it is lifted, the dough adheres to the surface of the cookie sheet rather than sticking to the cornet.

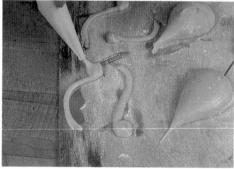

8 To make the beak, stick the end of the cornet (or you could use the point of a knife) into the heads of the swans and draw up enough dough to create a beak. (An alternative way of creating the beak is to insert an almond slice in the head as shown in photograph 17.) Brush the swan heads and bodies with the egg wash and place in a preheated 350-degree oven for 20 minutes.

9 Open the door and, without removing the tray from the oven (if possible), remove the heads and necks (which will be cooked) with a spatula and place them on a tray. Continue cooking the bodies for another 15 minutes (35 minutes total), then turn off the oven, open the door, and insert a spoon (see Profiteroles with Chocolate Sauce, page 231, step 8) to hold the door slightly ajar. Leave the swan bodies in the oven for another 20 to 25 minutes so the steam inside them has a chance to escape and the swans hold their shapes well.

10 Cut a lid off each of the swan bodies. Notice that the cut is made on an angle so that less is taken from the narrow tail.

11 Cut the lids in half lengthwise. These two lid pieces will be placed back on the swan bodies later to create the wings of the swans.

12 To make the raspberry sauce: Place the 12 oz. of raspberries with the 1 c. preserves in the food processor and process until smooth. Pour through a fairly coarse strainer. At first, do not press on the seeds with a spatula while straining the sauce as this tends to plug the holes of the strainer. Instead, bang on the rim of the strainer with a wooden spoon or spatula to make the mixture jump, thus keeping the little seeds from clogging the holes of the strainer and allowing most of the liquid to go through. Finally, to extract any remaining liquid, press on the seeds. Add the 1 Tb. raspberry brandy to the strained sauce.

Combine the 1 c. cream, 1 Tb. confectioners' sugar, and 1 Tb. Grand Marnier in a bowl, and whip by hand or with a mixer, until firm. Place in a pastry bag fitted with a star tip.

13 At serving time, place a teaspoon of black raspberry jam in the bottom of each swan body. Then scoop approximately 3 Tb. of vanilla ice cream on top.

14 Pipe some whipped cream (about 3 Tb.) on top of the ice cream in each of the swan bodies.

15 Position the wings on each side of a swan body and position a neck in the center so it is held firmly in the whipped cream. Dust the swans with confectioners' sugar.

16 Place about 3 Tb. of raspberry sauce on a serving platter and position a swan in the center. Serve immediately. →

17 As an alternative way of serving, place about 1 c. of the raspberry sauce on a large platter and arrange the swans on top so they face one another.

19 Swirl some interconnecting caramel lines into the open spaces between the crossed lines on top. Make several circles in the center on top to strengthen the construction and continue spooning the caramel to create a design and hold the lines together.

21 Place the cage on top of the swans. Add a few fresh flowers, inserting them into the "iron work" of the cage for a more striking effect, and serve.

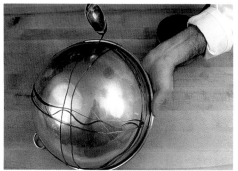

18 To make the serving platter even fancier, a caramel cage can be placed on top of the swans.

    For the caramel cage: Combine the 1 c. granulated sugar and 3 Tb. water in a saucepan, and cook on top of the stove until the mixture turns a caramel color. Then remove the pot and place in cold water for 10 to 15 seconds, stirring to cool the mixture and thicken the caramel (it should be fairly thick for making the cage).

    To make the cage, oil an inverted copper or stainless steel bowl. (The copper bowl is nice because it has a rounded bottom rather than a flat base.) To make a caramel cage successfully, follow the principles of good construction; i.e., don't splatter the caramel indiscriminately all around the mold but first go from one side to the other to create supporting "beams" across. Drizzle a few rings around the bottom, rotating the bowl to form a base for the cage and to hold the beams together.

20 After it cools and sets on the mold for at least 10 to 15 minutes, lift off the cage by pushing it up in a couple of places on one side. The pushing will be registered on the other side and the entire cage can be easily removed from the oiled mold.

CROQUEMBOUCHE

Croquembouche, as the name indicates in French (croque, "to crunch" and bouche, "mouth"), is a cake built of choux held together with a caramel. Very large croquembouche are made in a special mold for wedding cakes and are usually decorated with an almond brittle and flowers made of marzipan.

The scaled-down version here can be made easily and quickly. Because it is narrow and not too tall, the cream is placed in the hollow center instead of stuffing each of the choux. When choux are stuffed (see St. Honoré Cake, page 239), they become heavier and it is harder for them to stick together. The tops of the light, unstuffed choux below are glazed with caramel and built free-hand into a small pyramid. The inside of the cake is brushed with apricot jam (or, if you prefer, chocolate or currant jelly) and filled with sweetened whipped cream.

Yield: 8–10 servings

CHOUX PASTE

1 c. milk
⅓ stick butter
⅛ tsp. salt
¼ tsp. granulated sugar
1 c. flour
4 or 5 large eggs

CARAMEL

1 c. granulated sugar
3 Tb. water

DECORATION

Small silver balls, crystallized violets, or
    other decoration

FILLING

2 Tb. apricot jam
2 c. heavy cream
2 Tb. confectioners' sugar
1 Tb. Kirschwasser

Flower to decorate top (optional)

1 Prepare the choux recipe, following mixing instructions for choux in Profiteroles with Chocolate Sauce, page 230. Pipe out rounds of choux approximately 1½ Tb. each, as explained for St. Honoré Cake, page 240, step 6. The recipe should yield about 18 choux.

Bake in a preheated 375-degree oven for 30 minutes, turn off the oven, prop open the oven door, and let the choux remain in the oven for 20 to 30 minutes to allow moisture trapped inside to escape.

For the caramel: Mix the 1 c. granulated sugar and 3 Tb. water together in a saucepan (see explanation in Glazed Fruits recipe, page 204, step 2), and cook over medium heat until the mixture turns a light amber-caramel color. Remove from the heat, place on a pot holder, and, holding each choux at the base, dip the top into the caramel, scraping the pastry against the edge of the pan to remove any excess. Immediately, before the caramel hardens, sprinkle a few silver balls (available at supermarkets), crystallized violets, or other attractive decorations onto the top of each choux. Place on a tray.

2 When all the choux have been glazed, halve two or three of them and place a bit of caramel along the sides of each piece. Arrange cut-side down in a circle to form a "crown" for the base of the cake. Stick the point of a knife into the caramel and drizzle a little of the caramel between the choux halves. Hold them together firmly for a few seconds until the caramel hardens and the choux adhere.

3 Start building the croquembouche by dipping one side of each choux into the caramel and placing it, caramel-edge down, onto the choux beneath to hold it in place. With the point of a knife, paint a little caramel between the choux when needed to make them stick together. Hold each layer in place for a few seconds, until the caramel hardens and the choux hold firmly before moving to the next layer.

4 Continue building. My croquembouche is made of about 18 choux. Place the last choux on top, drizzling on additional caramel as needed (but using only the minimum amount required) to hold the structure together.

5 Wait for about 5 minutes; the croquembouche will hold together. Place it upside down in a tall, narrow pot so that it is held securely in place. Using a long brush, coat the inside with 2 Tb. apricot jam or other preserves.

6 For the filling: Beat the 2 c. cream, 2 Tb. confectioners' sugar, and 1 Tb. Kirschwasser in the bowl of an electric mixer until firm, then place in a pastry bag fitted with a star tip. Fill the inside of the cake with most of the cream.

7 Turn the croquembouche right-side up onto a plate. Pipe the remainder of the whipped cream around the base as a decoration, and, if desired, add a flower to decorate the top. Serve, if you wish, with stuffed Glazed Fruits, page 204.

The cake is traditionally cut by starting at the top. The first layer can be cut with scissors or a knife to separate it from the structure. Afterward individual choux can be broken off and served with a spoonful of the whipped cream from inside.

ST. HONORE CAKE

St. Honoré is the patron saint of pastry chefs and this cake, named after him, is centuries old. For a different look, I place a piece of dough on top of the choux, the same dough that is used as a bottom for the cake, to make "caps" for the choux. The glazing of the tops of the caps as well as the crushed pistachio garnish gives a nice finish to the cake. The few "angel hairs" or strings of caramel on top look nice but must be added at the last moment. The finer the threads of sugar, the faster they will melt, and these little lines of caramel won't last more than 15 to 20 minutes.

Yield: 10–12 servings

SWEET PASTRY DOUGH

1 c. flour
¾ stick butter (3 oz.)
3 Tb. confectioners' sugar
1½ to 2 Tb. milk

PATE A CHOUX

1 c. milk
⅓ stick butter
⅛ tsp. salt
¼ tsp. granulated sugar
1 c. flour
4 or 5 large eggs
Egg wash made with 1 egg with half the
   white removed, beaten

ST. HONORE CREAM

1½ c. milk
2 egg yolks
1 whole egg
2 tsp. vanilla
4½ tsp. flour
½ c. granulated sugar
2 c. cold heavy cream
2 Tb. granulated sugar
2 Tb. Cointreau

DECORATION

3 Tb. shelled pistachio nuts

CARAMEL

½ c. granulated sugar
2 Tb. water

1 **To make the sweet pastry dough:**
Place the 1 c. flour, ¾ stick butter, 3 Tb. confectioners' sugar, and 1½ to 2 Tb. milk together on a board and, using a pastry scraper and your fingers, break it into a granulated mixture. Gather the dough together and crush it with the palm of your hand in a technique called *fraisage*. (See technique for sweet dough, page 180, step 2.)

2 The dough is quite soft. Place it on a piece of plastic wrap and position another piece of plastic wrap on top. Roll the dough to a thickness of approximately ⅛ in.

3 Remove the piece of plastic wrap from the top and invert the dough onto a cookie sheet. Peel away the other piece of plastic wrap. (The dough, with a sheet of plastic wrap on the top only, could also be rolled out directly on the cookie sheet.)

approximately 2 in. in diameter. Notice that the pastry bag is held at an angle and the tip is practically touching the cookie sheet. Without moving the bag, press on it with the palm of your hand until you have squeezed out the right amount of dough. Then, stop pressing and quickly lift the bag up. There will be a little "tail" of dough left on each mound, which will be covered up later.

4 Use a 9- or 10-in. flan ring or lid as a pattern and cut the dough into a circle. Prick the bottom. Reserve the trimmings. Fill a pastry bag fitted with a ½-in. plain tip with choux paste (see Profiteroles with Chocolate Sauce, pages 230–1, steps 1–6, for detailed instructions on making choux paste). Pipe two strips of dough, one next to the other, around the edge of the sweet pastry dough circle.

9 Remove from the oven. Cut off the tops immediately (to let the hot, moist air inside the choux escape), removing the round of sweet pastry dough and about the upper third of each choux.

7 Roll the sweet pastry dough trimmings out into a strip about 20 in. long, and, with a cookie cutter, cut about 12 small rounds approximately the same size (2 in.) as the choux mounds.

5 Flatten the circles of choux paste with a spatula or knife until 1½ in. wide and not much thicker than the dough underneath. Place in a preheated 375-degree oven and bake for 20 minutes. Remove from the oven.

8 Place a round of dough on top of each choux and press gently to flatten it over the "tail." Brush the sweet pastry dough tops with the egg wash and place in the 375-degree oven for 30 minutes. Then open the door of the oven slightly and let the choux cool with the oven turned off for another 15 to 20 minutes.

10 **For the St. Honoré cream:** Bring the 1½ c. milk to a boil. Meanwhile, in a bowl, mix the 2 egg yolks, 1 whole egg, 2 tsp. vanilla, 4½ tsp. flour, and ½ c. granulated sugar until combined. When the milk is boiling, combine with the egg mixture, place back on the stove, and bring to a boil, stirring constantly with the whisk, especially around the edges of the pan, to keep the mixture from scorching (see instructions for preparing pastry buttercream in the recipe for Profiteroles with Chocolate Sauce, page 232, steps 9–11). Cool until tepid.

Whip the 2 c. cold cream with the 2 Tb. each granulated sugar and Cointreau in a large mixing bowl until firm but not stiff. Add about one-fourth to one-third of the whipped cream to the pastry cream, mixing with a whisk until well-combined.

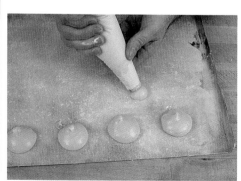

6 Butter and lightly flour a cookie sheet. Pipe choux paste mounds of approximately 1½ Tb. each in rows about 1½ in. apart. There should be about 12 mounds, each

11 Gently fold in the remaining whipped cream with a spatula until it is well-combined with the pastry cream.

14 Sometimes the caramel runs down along the sides of the caps. With scissors, trim off any big lumps of sugar around the edges.

17 Place the lids back on top of the cream-filled choux bases and place one filled choux in the center. If you have any caramel left and the cake is to be served soon, with a spoon drizzle little lines of caramel on top of the cream-filled center.

12 Crush the 3 Tb. shelled pistachios with a meat pounder or with the bottom of a pan, and set aside to use for decoration.

15 Dip the base of each choux lightly into the caramel and arrange, one next to another, around the base of the cake. The caramel should secure the choux to the ring.

18 The St. Honoré, ready to be served. Cut in between each choux to serve wedges that contain a piece of the sweet pastry on the bottom, one choux, and some of the cream in the center.

13 **For the caramel:** Mix the ½ c. granulated sugar and 2 Tb. water in a saucepan, and cook until it reaches the caramel stage. Immediately, place the pan on the counter on a pot holder and dip each of the choux caps into the caramel, letting the excess drip off and then scraping each choux lightly against the side of the pan so there is just a thin layer of caramel on each cap. Before the caramel sets, sprinkle a little of the crushed pistachios on top of each cap.

16 Place the St. Honoré cream in a large pastry bag fitted with a star tip. Fill up the choux bases all around and fill the center of the cake with cream, piping a design on top with the cream to make it more attractive.

PARIS-BREST CAKE

A Paris-Brest looks like a wheel and was named after a famous bicycle race from Paris to Brest, a town in Brittany. Traditionally, the big ring of choux paste is covered with almonds and stuffed with cream. However, in the recipe here, I have made a crushed almond praline powder and covered it with a rich mixture made of pastry cream, butter, and whipped cream. The praline, which is coarsely crushed in a mortar here, could be ground finer and used with ice cream and pastry cream as well as custard cream.

To make it easier to cut the cake at the table, the lid is pre-cut into sections and placed back on top of the cream-filled base. So at serving time it is easy to insert the knife and remove portions without having the cake collapse on itself.

If you make the cake ahead and refrigerate it a few hours, be sure to lightly cover it with a piece of plastic wrap so that it won't pick up other flavors.

Yield: about 12 servings

BASIC CHOUX PASTE

1 c. milk
⅓ stick butter
⅛ tsp. salt
¼ tsp. granulated sugar
1 c. flour
4 to 5 large eggs
Egg wash made with 1 egg with half the white removed, beaten
1 Tb. slivered almonds

PRALINE

½ c. granulated sugar
¾ c. whole almonds

RICH FILLING CREAM

¾ c. milk
2 large egg yolks
3 Tb. granulated sugar
1½ Tb. potato starch
1 stick butter (¼ lb.)
2 c. heavy cream
2 Tb. dark rum
2 Tb. granulated sugar

Confectioners' sugar for dusting

1 Prepare the choux paste dough (for techniques, see Profiteroles with Chocolate Sauce, pages 230–1, steps 1–6).

Butter and lightly dust a large cookie sheet, then, using a pot lid or flan ring as a guide, mark a circle in the flour. Fit a pastry bag with a ¾-in. plain tip and fill it with the choux paste. Holding the pastry bag about 1½ to 2 in. above the cookie sheet, pipe out a circle of choux paste by moving the bag forward and letting the paste fall gently from the bag along the circle outline in the flour. Make two additional circles, one inside the first ring and one on top, balanced between the two rings below. Notice that I have started and ended the three rings at different places to give added strength to the pastry; if all three started and ended at the same place, the cake would crack there.

2 Brush the circle with egg wash. The rings will tend to push together when you brush. Dip the fork in the egg wash and run it around the circle to make lines simulating the bark of a tree.

3 Place 1 Tb. slivered almonds on top of the cake.

4 Bake in a preheated 375-degree oven for 25 minutes. Reduce the heat to 350 degrees and cook for another 30 minutes. Shut the oven off, open the door, and hold it open with a spoon so it is slightly ajar. Let the cake cool in the oven 20 to 30 minutes to let the moisture escape. It should be nicely brown and hold its shape.

5 To make the praline: Place the ½ c. granulated sugar in a saucepan, preferably a stainless steel or unlined copper pan. Cook over medium to high heat, stirring occasionally. This will be a dry sugar caramel (no liquid added), which makes a very hard caramel. Stir the sugar as it melts. As the melting sugar is stirred into the dry sugar, the mixture often crystallizes, making it hard to stir. Keep cooking the sugar until most of the pieces of crystallized sugar melt.

6 When the mixture is a light amber color (with some crystallized sugar still visible in it), add the ¾ c. whole almonds. Keep cooking on top of the stove. Don't worry if the mixture sets into large lumps. Continue cooking; the sugar pieces will eventually melt and the almonds will separate from the sugar, which will turn a rich caramel color.

7 At that point, pour the mixture onto an oiled tray, spreading it slightly to help it cool.

8 When cold, you can lift the almond sugar from the oiled tray in one block. Break into pieces, place them in a mortar, then pound with a pestle to form a crumbly consistency. (See step 10 for texture.)

9 To remove the lid from the Paris-Brest, insert a knife horizontally into the cake about one-third of the way down from the top, and cut all the way around to release the lid in one piece.

10 Sprinkle the crushed praline into the bottom half of the cake.

To make the rich filling cream: Follow the instructions for making the pastry buttercream in the recipe for Profiteroles with Chocolate Sauce, page 232, steps 9–11, using half the quantity shown there. Combine the 2 c. heavy cream with the 2 Tb. each dark rum and granulated sugar, and whip until stiff. Using a whisk, combine about one-third of the whipped cream with the rich filling cream at room temperature, mixing until smooth. Fold the remainder of the whipped cream into the mixture with a rubber spatula. Spoon into a pastry bag fitted with a star tip and fill the center of the cake with whipped cream, squeezing it out on top of the crushed praline. →

11 Cut the lid of the Paris-Brest into as many portions as you want to serve (from 12 to 18).

12 Rearrange the pieces side by side on top of the cake to re-form the lid. Dust with confectioners' sugar.

13 Thrust a knife through the lid at the separations, then cut down through the cake to divide it into servings. Serve.

RUM BABAS WITH PEACHES

Baba and savarin (the next recipe) use the same dough, but babas are cooked in a different size and shape. After baking, both the baba and savarin can be wrapped and frozen until serving time.

Because babas as well as the savarin have a dry, airy texture, they are soaked in a syrup, often flavored with rum, before serving. Other alcohol can be substituted for the rum as well as vanilla extract for a nonalcoholic dessert.

The yeast dough will develop differently, depending on whether it is humid or dry, cold or hot, and the rising time may have to be adjusted 10 to 15 minutes one way or the other, based on climatic conditions.

The babas are served here with poached peaches, coated on top at serving time with a little of the reduced syrup.

The tiny babas (step 4) are made in thimblelike cups (holding about 3 Tb.) that are filled halfway with the batter. They can be served with fruit or used as decoration.

Yield: 10–12 babas

BABA DOUGH
½ envelope active dry yeast (⅛ oz.)
½ c. milk, heated to 100 degrees
1 tsp. granulated sugar
2 c. flour (about 10 to 12 oz.)
3 eggs
½ tsp. salt
1 oz. raisins (¼ c.)
¾ stick butter, at room temperature (6 Tb.)
Egg wash made with 1 egg with half the white removed, beaten

POACHED PEACHES
See Custard Wheat Cake with Peaches, page 302

SYRUP
¾ c. granulated sugar
1½ c. warm tap water
1 tsp. vanilla

2 Tb. dark rum

BABA GLAZE
1 Tb. dark rum
½ c. confectioners' sugar

GARNISHES
12 candied violets
1 c. heavy cream whipped with 1 Tb. granulated sugar

1 **For the baba dough:** Put the ½ envelope yeast with the ½ c. warm milk and the 1 tsp. granulated sugar in the bowl of a mixer. Proof for about 5 minutes, until the mixture bubbles on top.

2 Add the 2 c. flour, 3 eggs, and ½ tsp. salt, and beat approximately 3 minutes with the flat beater on medium speed. The dough should be very elastic. Then, add the ¼ c. raisins and the ¾ stick butter, and beat at the same speed for approximately 1 minute to incorporate. Don't worry if some pieces of the butter are still visible at this point. Cover the dough or batter with a towel or plastic wrap, and let rise at room temperature (about 70 to 75 degrees) for about 1 hour. Meanwhile, cook the peaches according to the recipe in Custard Wheat Cake with Peaches, page 303, step 9.

3 Stir the batter gently to push the air out. Butter the baba molds (½- to ¾-c. capacity) and fill half full with the batter.

4 For tiny babas, use thimble cups with a capacity of 3 Tb. Butter the cups and fill them one-half full with the baba mixture. Set aside in a warm place (70 to 75 degrees) away from any draft, and let the larger babas rise for about 30 to 40 minutes and the smaller ones for approximately 20 minutes. Brush the top of the risen babas with the egg wash, and bake them on a cookie sheet in a preheated 375-degree oven, about 12 minutes for the tiny babas and about 20 minutes for the larger ones.

5 Let the babas cool for 15 to 20 minutes and then remove them from the molds. At this point, they can be allowed to cool completely, placed in airtight wrapping, and frozen.

6 **To make the syrup:** Mix the ¾ c. granulated sugar, 1½ c. warm tap water, and 1 tsp. vanilla together until the sugar is completely dissolved. Place the babas in a gratin dish so they are fairly snug, one against the other, and pour the syrup (about 2 c.) over them. Let the babas soak in the syrup for 20 minutes or so, turning them occasionally so they absorb as much syrup as they can. The syrup may not be completely absorbed after this amount of time; push a knife through a baba, and if the center is soft, you can assume that the syrup has penetrated into the middle of the babas. If still hard, soak longer.

7 For our recipe, cut the larger babas in half lengthwise and brush the surfaces of each half with the dark rum, using a total of 2 Tb.

For the glaze: Combine the 1 Tb. of dark rum with the ½ c. confectioners' sugar in a bowl, and mix until smooth. Brush the outside surface of each half baba with the glaze and decorate with a little piece of candied violet.

8 Place two baba halves on each serving plate with peach halves on either side. Coat each of the peaches with about ½ Tb. of the peach syrup. Mound some of the whipped cream in the center, decorate it with a candied violet, and serve right away.

2 Brush the top of the savarin with the egg wash, place on a cookie sheet, and bake in a preheated 375-degree oven for approximately 35 minutes.

BOURBON APRICOT SAVARIN WITH FRUIT

This savarin is made with the same mixture as used for the babas (see Rum Babas with Peaches, page 244) but is done in a ring form that produces a large, beautiful dessert that can be brought to the table and cut.

The savarin is garnished with a fresh fruit bound with apricot preserves and flavored with bourbon, but it can be served just with whipped cream. The top of the savarin is glazed with an apricot preserve mixture that is also flavored with bourbon.

Yield: 10–12 servings

SAVARIN

Baba recipe in Rum Babas with Peaches (page 245, steps 1–2)
Egg wash made with 1 egg with half the white removed, beaten

SYRUP

¾ c. sugar
1½ c. warm tap water
1 tsp. vanilla

2 Tb. bourbon
½ c. strained apricot preserves
¼ c. almond slices, toasted
Extra raisins for decoration

SAVARIN FRUIT GARNISH

2 Tb. bourbon
2 ripe peaches, diced (1½ c.)
1 c. sliced strawberries

⅓ c. blueberries
⅓ c. apricot preserves

WHIPPED CREAM CENTER

1½ c. heavy cream
2 Tb. sugar

1 Follow the recipe for Rum Babas with Peaches (steps 1 and 2) to make the savarin dough. Butter a 4-c. savarin mold and spread the dough in it, filling the mold one-third to one-half full. Proof at room temperature (70 to 75 degrees) away from any drafts for approximately 1 hour.

3 Let cool in the mold for at least 30 minutes and unmold. Place on a round gratin dish slightly larger than the savarin.

4 Combine the ¾ c. sugar, 1½ c. warm water, and 1 tsp. vanilla, pour the syrup over the savarin, and let it soak for 30 minutes, turning it occasionally or basting it with the syrup so most of the syrup is absorbed. Plunge a knife into the cake to make sure that it is moistened in the center. When the syrup has been sufficiently absorbed throughout the savarin, place it on a rack to drain and then on a plate. Brush first with the 2 Tb. bourbon and then with the ½ c. strained apricot preserves to make it shiny all over.

5 Arrange the ¼ c. of sliced toasted almonds in a flower design on top, pushing them into the preserves so they adhere to the cake. Use raisins as the flower centers.

6 For the savarin fruits garnish: Combine the 2 Tb. bourbon with the 2 diced peaches, 1 c. sliced strawberries, ⅓ c. each blueberries and apricot preserves, and mix well.

Whip the 1½ c. cream with the 2 Tb. sugar until stiff.

Arrange the savarin on a large platter with the fruit garnish around it and inside the hollow center. Pile the whipped cream on top of the fruit in the center, piping it from a pastry bag fitted with a star tip. Decorate the cream in the center with a few pieces of fruit and serve immediately.

CARAMEL SNOW EGGS

Snow eggs, <u>oeufs à la neige</u> in French, are the archetypical French dessert, served in starred restaurants as well as at family dinners. Bathed with a custard cream (crème anglaise), they are usually coated with caramel.

The eggs are made with a light meringue mixture and poached in milk or water. They can be formed with a pastry bag or a large spoon, as well as with an ice cream scoop, which is easy and gives the eggs a roundish, uniform shape. When the snow eggs are poached in milk, the liquid is traditionally used to make the custard cream. However, I find that the milk tends to reduce during the poaching and gets too much of a cooked taste. Moreover, eggs poached in water have a cleaner look and are more tender than eggs poached in milk.

It is important that the temperature of the poaching water does not rise above 180 degrees and that the eggs are poached only a few minutes on each side. If they boil in the cooking liquid, they will expand and deflate as they cool, becoming rubbery.

When the caramel is sprinkled on the eggs in thin threads, it tends to melt faster than when applied in large spoonfuls, which will last for at least 2 to 3 hours. Snow eggs can be poached a few hours ahead of serving and

the custard cream can also be made ahead. The dessert should not be assembled more than a couple of hours before serving or the caramel will have melted by serving time.

The eggs could be served instead with raspberry or coffee sauce, and nuts can be added to the egg whites, as done in the Almond Floating Islands, page 250, step 4. Spices such as cinnamon or nutmeg can also be added to the sugar.

Yield: 8 servings

CUSTARD CREAM

½ c. heavy cream
1 tsp. cornstarch
1½ c. milk
6 egg yolks
⅓ c. sugar
1 tsp. vanilla

LIGHT MERINGUE MIXTURE

6 egg whites
¾ c. sugar

CARAMEL

½ c. sugar
2 Tb. water

1 To make the custard cream: Put the ½ c. cream in a bowl and set a fine strainer on top. In a saucepan, mix the 1 tsp. cornstarch with the 1½ c. milk, and bring to a boil. Meanwhile, with a whisk, mix the 6 egg yolks and ⅓ c. sugar together in a bowl, and beat until smooth, about 30 seconds to 1 minute. Pour in the boiling milk, then return the mixture to the saucepan and stir with a wooden spoon over medium heat until it thickens (at about 180 degrees). The foam created from beating the egg yolks and sugar will disappear when the custard has reached 180 degrees and the mixture will thicken. Immediately pour it into the cold cream through the fine strainer (to catch any curdled bits); this will lower the temperature of the custard mixture and prevent it from curdling further. The custard should coat the spoon. Add the 1 tsp. vanilla, cover, and cool. (See Vanilla-Bourbon Genoise, page 210, steps 4–5.)

2 Place a fairly large saucepan with at least 1½ to 2 in. of water in it on the stove, and bring the water to approximately 175 to 180 degrees.

For the light meringue mixture: Beat the 6 egg whites by hand with a whisk or in a mixer, until stiff. When firm, sprinkle the ¾ c. sugar quickly (in 5 to 10 seconds) onto the whites while continuing to beat, and beat for another 10 seconds, just long enough to incorporate the sugar. Using a round ice cream scoop that holds approximately ⅓ to ½ c., scoop up a portion of the meringue, filling the scoop completely, and smooth the top with your fingers to round it.

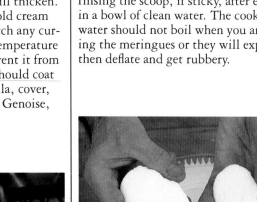

3 Drop balls of meringue one by one (you should have 6 to 8) into the hot water, rinsing the scoop, if sticky, after each use in a bowl of clean water. The cooking water should not boil when you are poaching the meringues or they will expand and then deflate and get rubbery.

4 Cook the meringue balls approximately 3 minutes on one side and, sliding a slotted spoon underneath, turn them over and cook them for 3 minutes on the other side. Remove to a paper towel with the slotted spoon. The meringue balls can be made ahead to this point and cooled. To check whether the meringue is cooked, cut one ball in half and press on the cut surface. It should have a spongy texture.

5 To make the caramel: Combine the ½ c. sugar and 2 Tb. water in a saucepan. Mix together just enough to moisten the sugar and place over medium heat until the mixture boils. Keep boiling without stirring or shaking the pan until the mixture becomes caramel-colored (12 to 15 minutes). Remove the caramel from the heat, resting it for a few minutes so it will thicken a little.

Pour the custard cream into a serving platter and arrange the meringue "eggs" on top. Drizzle a spoonful of caramel on top of each "egg."

6 For individual servings, spoon approximately 1½ oz. of custard cream on each plate and serve with one of the "eggs." For a serving variation, a caramel cage (see "Swimming Swans," page 236, steps 18–20) can be made, using a small bowl as a mold, and placed on top of an individual serving of the caramel snow eggs.

ALMOND FLOATING ISLANDS

Floating islands are similar to snow eggs (page 247), but are baked in the oven in a <u>*bain marie*</u> *(double boiler). Here they are demonstrated in individual portions, although the dessert can be made in a large soufflé mold. The recipe uses small glass containers with about a 1 ½-c. capacity as well as small oval ceramic or porcelain dishes (used for jellied eggs) with about a 1-c. capacity.*

The bottom of the molds is coated with a caramel finished with butter to keep it a bit softer. The filled molds are then cooked in a double boiler. Some of the caramel adheres to the bottom of the dishes when the floating islands are unmolded, but some of it drips down over the desserts to mix with the custard sauce.

The rum custard sauce is made with fewer egg yolks than traditionally called for in a custard cream. The milk, cornstarch, and sugar mixture is brought to a rolling boil and poured directly on top of the yolks. Because of the small proportion of egg yolks

to milk, the temperature of the mixture rises to 180 degrees, ensuring that the lecithin in the egg yolks will thicken. The sauce doesn't need further cooking and is strained to eliminate any curdled pieces. The sauce here is flavored with rum but could also be flavored with cognac, bourbon, or vanilla.

Floating islands can be cooked a day or so ahead and kept, covered, in the refrigerator so the tops don't get rubbery. Covering also keeps the dessert moist, making it easier to unmold. When left uncovered, the sugar hardens around the edge of the molds and makes the floating islands difficult to unmold.

Yield: 8 servings

RUM CUSTARD SAUCE

1½ c. milk
2 tsp. cornstarch
⅓ c. sugar
3 egg yolks
½ c. cold heavy cream
1 tsp. vanilla
3 Tb. dark rum

BUTTER CARAMEL

½ c. sugar
4 Tb. water
2½ Tb. butter

6 egg whites
½ c. sugar
½ c. toasted slivered almonds, chopped coarse

DECORATION

Toasted almond slivers

1 **For the rum custard sauce:** In a saucepan, combine the 1½ c. milk, 2 tsp. cornstarch, and half the ⅓ c. sugar, stirring occasionally. Meanwhile, in a bowl combine the rest of the sugar and the 3 egg yolks, stirring well with a whisk. When the milk-cornstarch-sugar mixture comes to a strong boil, pour it all at once into the yolks and mix thoroughly with a whisk.

2 The quantity of boiling milk as compared to the quantity of egg yolk is such that the egg yolk will be cooked by the hot milk and not require further cooking. Strain the mixture immediately through a fine strainer into a bowl and add the ½ c. cold cream. When lukewarm, add the 1 tsp. vanilla and 3 Tb. rum. Set aside until serving time. →

3 **For the butter caramel:** Combine the ½ c. sugar with 3 Tb. of the water just enough to moisten the sugar. Place over medium heat, bring to a boil, and cook, without shaking or moving the pan, until the mixture turns caramel-colored (12 to 15 minutes). When caramelized, remove from the stove, add the 2½ Tb. butter and remaining 1 Tb. water, and stir well, until combined. Pour 2 Tb. of the caramel into the bottom of 8 individual molds with a capacity of 1 to 1½ c. Let the caramel cool and harden, then butter lightly around the sides of the molds.

5 Place the meringue mixture in a pastry bag without a tip and squeeze it into the caramelized molds.

8 When cool, the individual desserts can be covered with plastic wrap and refrigerated. They will keep for up to 2 days. At serving time, place about 3 to 4 Tb. of the rum custard sauce on individual serving plates, unmold the small floating islands on top, letting whatever caramel that comes out drip over them. Decorate with some extra toasted almond slivers and serve immediately.

6 Tap the molds on a pot holder set on the table so there are no air bubbles in the center of the meringue.

4 Beat the 6 egg whites until very firm. Sprinkle the ½ c. sugar quickly (in 5 to 10 seconds) on top while beating at high speed with the whisk, and continue beating for another 10 seconds. Fold in the ½ c. almonds.

7 Arrange the molds in a pan surrounded by lukewarm tap water. Place in a preheated 350-degree oven for 25 to 30 minutes, until well-set in the center and puffy. Remove from the water and let cool.

ORANGE VACHERIN JEANNETTE

This striking dessert is easy to make. It is prepared ahead and frozen. Because of the sugar content, the meringue doesn't harden in the freezer but the cream between the meringue layers does. The finished dessert holds well and is easy to slice.

The sugar is added to the beaten egg whites fairly quickly and the mixture is whipped only a few seconds after the addition of the sugar, which can still be felt granulated in the finished mixture. This produces a brittle, dry, and tender meringue. The meringue is cooked slowly, until dry, brittle, and slightly beige in color. The whipped cream is flavored with Grand Marnier and the grated peel of orange. The flavoring can be changed and ice cream can also be spread on the meringue with the whipped cream before freezing.

Candied violets or other candied flowers or fruits enhance the look of the dessert considerably. The raspberries are added mostly for color. Embedding them in the cream before freezing assures that they will not fall off, but they don't taste as good as fresh berries and are added mostly for aesthetic reasons. Extra fresh, unfrozen berries can be added to the plates at the last moment and served with the cake.

After the cake has been in the freezer for 5 to 6 hours and is hard on top, wrap it securely with plastic wrap and aluminum foil so it doesn't pick up freezer tastes or get freezer burn. It can be kept frozen for a few weeks.

Yield: 8–10 servings

MERINGUE MIXTURE

5 egg whites
1¼ c. sugar

ORANGE CREAM FILLING

4 c. heavy cream
¼ c. sugar
2 Tb. Grand Marnier
Skin of 1 orange, grated, or removed with a vegetable peeler and chopped fine (1½ Tb.)

DECORATION

Candied violets
12 raspberries, or other berries or fruit

1 For the meringue: Beat the 5 egg whites until firm and add the 1¼ c. sugar quickly (in no more than 10 seconds). Keep beating for another 15 seconds on high speed to incorporate the sugar. Place the mixture in a pastry bag fitted with a large (¾-in.) plain tip. Butter a piece of parchment paper and place it buttered-side down on a cookie sheet. Lift the paper and turn it over. (This butters the cookie sheet slightly and the paper adheres to it very well.)

With the pastry bag, make the outline of 2 rectangles approximately 4 to 4½ in. wide by 15 in. long.

2 Continue filling the inside of the rectangles with the meringue. If there is any meringue left, pipe 2 or 3 oval meringues alongside the rectangles.

3 With a spatula or a large knife, smooth the tops of the rectangles to make them solid and smooth. Place in a preheated 200-degree oven for 3 to 3½ hours. (Cook a little longer in humid weather.)

4 The meringue should be dry, brittle, well-cooked, and may have a slightly beige color underneath. Slide it off the paper – it will come off easily.

5 **To make the orange cream filling:** Combine the 4 c. heavy cream with the ¼ c. sugar, 2 Tb. Grand Marnier, and the grated or chopped orange rind, and beat until firm. Trim the meringue rectangles carefully to smooth the edges and reserve the trimmings. Cut a piece of cardboard to fit under the vacherin and wrap it with aluminum foil. The cardboard can be used to transport the cake and the cake can be frozen on top of the cardboard and then removed from it at the last moment before serving. (The cake can also be left on the cardboard for serving.)

6 Place one of the trimmed meringue rectangles, smooth-side down, on the foil-covered cardboard. Spread about a 1-in.-thick layer of the orange cream on top.

7 Crumble the extra meringue ovals on top of the orange cream filling along with the trimmings from the rectangles.

8 Place the second rectangle of meringue upside down on top so the smooth side of the meringue is visible. Spread a thin layer of orange cream filling on top and around the sides of the cake.

9 Place the remaining orange cream filling in a pastry bag fitted with a fluted tip and pipe rows of the filling the length of the vacherin, making the design according to your fancy.

10 Decorate along the base and sides of the vacherin.

11 Decorate the top and the sides with candied violets, and embed some raspberries in the cream. Place in the freezer without covering for 5 to 6 hours, until completely frozen inside. It can be served immediately at this point or wrapped (so it doesn't pick up other food tastes) and returned to the freezer, where it will keep for several weeks.

12 If frozen for only 5 to 6 hours, serve directly from the freezer. If frozen for several days, move it from the freezer into the refrigerator for about 30 minutes before serving to make it easier to slice. Serve it on individual plates from the cardboard or slide the whole cake off the cardboard and onto a platter for serving. Cut into 1-in. slices and serve with additional fresh berries, or other fruit, if desired.

MONT-BLANC MICHEL

This meringue–chestnut cream cake is made in several steps, and a number of basic recipes are involved. All the basic recipes can be used in other combinations or on their own: the meringue, the chestnut-chocolate-rum cream (a turinois, which is usually molded in a loaf pan, sliced cold, and served with a vanilla sauce), and, finally, the glazed chestnuts, which can be stored in a jar with cognac or rum and used to garnish cakes or flavor pastry cream.

The meringue can be done several days ahead and kept in an airtight container so moisture doesn't soften it. The chestnut-chocolate-rum cream can also be made ahead, but for use in this recipe, it will need softening again to make it pliable enough to squeeze through a pastry bag.

Yield: 10–12 servings

1½ lb. large, fresh chestnuts
6 c. cold water

GLAZED CHESTNUTS

1 c. cooked chestnut pieces (from above)
½ c. granulated sugar
1 tsp. vanilla
½ c. water

CHESTNUT-CHOCOLATE-RUM CREAM

Remaining cooked chestnuts (about 1 lb.)
1 stick butter (¼ lb.)
⅓ c. granulated sugar

2 Tb. rum
½ lb. bittersweet chocolate (see page 132), melted

MERINGUE

5 egg whites
1¼ c. granulated sugar

WHIPPED CREAM FOR GARNISH

1½ c. heavy cream
2 Tb. confectioners' sugar
2 Tb. rum

DECORATION

Crystallized violets

1 **To peel the chestnuts:** Score the 1½ lb. of chestnuts with a knife by cutting right through the skin the entire length of each side (both outer shell and inside membrane). This makes them easier to peel later on. Do not roast the chestnuts in one large batch because the peel will come off more easily if removed while the chestnuts are quite warm; instead, arrange half the chestnuts on a baking sheet and roast in a preheated 400-degree oven for about 10 to 12 minutes. You will notice at that point that the nut will start to burst out at the slit, indicating that the chestnut is ready to be peeled. Peel by pulling them apart, removing the outer skin as well as the inner membrane at the same time. Roast and peel the remainder of the chestnuts.

2 **To cook the chestnuts:** Put the chestnuts in a saucepan with 6 c. of cold water. Bring to a boil and cook over medium heat for about 45 minutes. Remove from the heat and let steep in the hot water for about 30 minutes, then drain while still warm. →

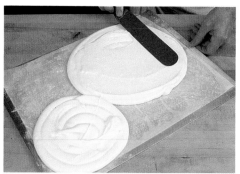

3 **For the glazed chestnuts:** Place 1 c. of the larger cooked chestnut pieces in a saucepan with the ½ c. sugar, 1 tsp. vanilla, and ½ c. water. Bring to a boil and simmer for about 12 to 15 minutes.

4 The chestnuts are ready when they are glazed and most of the liquid has evaporated, leaving only some heavy syrup. Stir as little as possible to avoid breaking the chestnuts further. At this point, they can be placed in a jar, covered with rum or cognac, or left plain, and used, when you want, to flavor sauces or garnish cakes.

5 **For the chestnut-chocolate-rum cream:** Push the remainder of the chestnuts through a food mill fitted with a fine screen. You should have about 1 lb. of chestnut purée.

6 Put the chestnut purée in the bowl of a food processor with the 1 stick butter, ⅓ c. sugar, and 2 Tb. rum, and process for about 30 to 45 seconds, until smooth and light. Add the ½ lb. melted chocolate and stir just enough to mix lightly. Pour into a bowl and stir with a spatula to finish mixing. Set aside.

7 **To make the meringue:** Beat the 5 egg whites until stiff. Add the 1¼ c. sugar in a stream, still beating on high speed until it is incorporated. This should not take more than 10 to 15 seconds because the sugar should not be completely melted into the egg whites.

Butter a piece of parchment paper cut to fit a cookie sheet. Place it buttered-side down on the sheet, then turn it over and press with your hands to make it adhere to the sheet. The residue of butter on the sheet will hold the paper firmly in place and it will lie flat. Flour the paper lightly and mark it with a 10- to 10½-in. ring and a 6-in. ring to create two circles. Place the meringue in a large pastry bag fitted with a large (about ¾-in.) plain tip and pipe out a large circle of meringue and then a smaller one, following the markings.

8 Fill the first circle and then the second with meringue, and smooth the surface of each of them with a spatula.

9 Place the meringues in a preheated 200-degree oven for at least 3 hours. At this point, they should lift easily from the paper. Trim each circle to make it uniformly round.

10 **To assemble the cake:** Put the chestnut-chocolate-rum cream mixture into a pastry bag fitted with a star tip. Pipe some into the center of the larger meringue disk to form a circle about the size of the smaller meringue round. Spread it to a thickness of ¼ to ½ in.

11 Place the smaller meringue on top of the chestnut-chocolate-rum cream disk and pipe mounds of the cream around the edge of the larger meringue.

12 For the whipped cream garnish: Whip the 1½ c. cream with the 2 Tb. confectioners' sugar and 2 Tb. rum until stiff. Spoon into a pastry bag fitted with a star tip, and decorate around the edge of the meringue by piping mounds of the whipped cream between the mounds of chestnut-chocolate-rum cream.

13 Finish decorating the cake by piping additional mounds of the chestnut-chocolate-rum cream and whipped cream on top of the cake. Arrange crystallized violets and glazed chestnuts on the cake to complete the dessert. Cut into wedges to serve. If refrigerated, cover lightly with plastic wrap to prevent it from picking up tastes from other refrigerated foods.

MOCHA SUCCESS CAKE

This Mocha Success Cake is made with a very rich mocha buttercream and a crisp hazelnut meringue mixture. The hazelnut meringue is spread out thin so the meringue dries in the oven and becomes crunchy. By the time the cake is assembled, the meringue may have softened slightly. Although in the recipe below the meringue is fairly crisp, some cooks like the layer of hazelnut meringue softer and closer to a sponge cake in texture. If you like it that way, wrap the cooked layer of dough in plastic wrap and refrigerate it overnight or longer before assembling the cake.

The cake freezes well, provided it is well-wrapped and not kept frozen for more than 1 or 2 weeks. The espresso coffee extract is excellent when made with freshly ground espresso coffee and boiling water. It gives an intensity and true taste of coffee to the buttercream.

The chocolate-covered coffee beans are store-bought. There are two varieties: pieces of chocolate shaped like coffee beans, and actual roasted coffee beans covered with chocolate. Choose the one you prefer, or you can make your own.

This is an ideal cake for a buffet because it keeps its texture and retains its excellent taste for hours.

Yield: 10–12 servings

COFFEE EXTRACT OR CONCENTRATE (for ½ c. extract)
¾ c. water
⅓ c. espresso coffee

MOCHA BUTTERCREAM
½ c. coffee extract (from above)
⅓ c. sugar
3 egg yolks
3 sticks butter, softened (12 oz.)

HAZELNUT MERINGUE
1½ c. hazelnuts
2 Tb. cornstarch
¾ c. sugar
7 egg whites

RUM-FLAVORED WHIPPED CREAM
1½ c. heavy cream
2 Tb. rum
2 Tb. sugar

GARNISHES
1½ c. sliced almonds
12 chocolate-covered coffee beans

1 **To make the coffee extract:** Bring the ¾ c. of water barely to a boil, and add the ⅓ c. espresso (preferably freshly ground) to it in one stroke. Stir with a spoon for 1 to 2 seconds, cover with a lid, and set aside off the heat for 3 to 4 minutes to steep. Strain through paper towels. This will yield approximately ½ c. of extract or concentrate.

2 **For the mocha buttercream:** Combine the ½ c. of coffee extract with the ⅓ c. sugar, and bring to a rolling boil. Boil for approximately 2 minutes, until the syrup starts to get sticky. Beat the 3 egg yolks in the bowl of a mixer on low speed, using the whisk attachment. While the machine is running, pour the syrup into the yolks and beat for 8 to 10 minutes. The mixture should have quadrupled in volume and become smooth and creamy. This is the base of the buttercream.

In another bowl, break the 3 sticks of soft butter into pieces and beat with a whisk by hand or machine for about 1 minute to make the butter soft and light, about the same texture as the egg yolk–coffee mixture.

Combine the egg yolk–coffee mixture with the butter. If the butter tends to curdle at this point (it is a question of temperature), place the bowl over a gas flame or dip it in hot water for a few seconds to start melting the mixture. Then stir with a whisk and the mixture will become smooth. Set aside.

3 **To make the hazelnut meringue:** Brown the 1½ c. hazelnuts on a cookie sheet in a preheated 400-degree oven for approximately 12 minutes. Then wrap them in a towel and rub them to remove some of the skin, but don't worry if you don't get all the skin off. Put the hazelnuts and 2 Tb. cornstarch in the bowl of a food processor and process until powdered, about 20 seconds. Add the ¾ c. sugar and process for another 10 seconds. Beat the 7 egg whites by hand or with a mixer until stiff. Add the hazelnut-sugar-cornstarch mixture and fold it gently into the whites, taking care not to over-mix.

4 Generously butter and flour a large cookie sheet. Spread the meringue mixture out onto the sheet to form a rectangle approximately 17 in. long by 14 in. wide. The batter should be approximately ⅜ to ½ in. thick. Bake in a preheated 375-degree oven for 20 to 25 minutes, until nicely browned and cooked.

5 Run a knife under the meringue as it comes out of the oven to loosen it from the baking sheet. Be sure to do this while the meringue is hot because as it cools it becomes brittle and dry and will be difficult to remove from the tray intact.

6 Transfer the cooked meringue (still pliable and soft since it is hot) to a wire rack and cool thoroughly.

7 The meringue is now dry. Trim the sides to make a rectangle and reserve the trimmings. Cut the rectangle in half lengthwise to make two rectangles approximately 12 in. long by 7 to 7½ in. wide. Cut out a piece of cardboard the same size and cover it with aluminum foil. The cake will be constructed on the cardboard and removed from it for serving.

8 Place one of the rectangles on the cardboard. Spread a thin layer of the buttercream over it.

9 Spoon the remaining buttercream into a pastry bag fitted with a ½-in. plain tip. Make a border and a line down the center of the meringue with the buttercream.

10 **For the rum-flavored cream:** Combine the 1½ c. cream, 2 Tb. rum, and 2 Tb. sugar in a mixing bowl, and whip until stiff. Place the whipped cream in the two cavities created inside the buttercream borders.

11 Crumble the reserved cake trimmings on top of the cream.

12 Place the other meringue rectangle, smooth-side up, on top and press lightly so it adheres well.

13 Use the rest of the buttercream to cover the top and sides of the cake.

14 Arrange the 1½ c. sliced almonds on a baking tray and place in a preheated 400-degree oven for approximately 8 to 10 minutes, until lightly browned. Let cool. Then, lift up the cake, holding it by its cardboard base, and press the almonds all around the sides and on top of the cake. Decorate with the 12 chocolate-covered coffee beans. Cover and refrigerate until serving time.

15 At serving time, slide a spatula or a knife blade under the cake and slide it from the cardboard to a platter or a cutting board. Cut into wedges and serve.

VOLCANO SURPRISE

Baked Alaska is called an "omelette Nor-wégienne" in French when made in the oval shape of an omelet. However, this dessert is done in a conical shape to emulate a volcano, hence its name. The top is adorned with a hollowed-out half lemon that is filled (as soon as it comes out of the oven) with warm brandy, which is ignited, and the dessert is brought flaming to the table. The lemon mousseline cake used here to hold the ice cream in the center can be replaced with a standard genoise or a sponge or pound cake, as well as with ladyfingers.

The light meringue mixture on top is made with egg whites, sugar, egg yolks, and vanilla. The classic baked Alaska tends to be too sweet; adding egg yolks and using less sugar makes a delicate, tender, and beautiful dessert.

The dessert bakes quickly, in approximately 10 to 12 minutes, and should be brought to the table as it comes out of the oven. Although the egg whites should be beaten at the last moment, the ice cream and cake can be assembled ahead and kept covered in the freezer.

Yield: 10–12 servings

LEMON MOUSSELINE CAKE

6 eggs, separated
½ c. granulated sugar
2 tsp. grated lemon rind
1 tsp. vanilla
½ c. potato starch (3 to 3½ oz.)
¼ c. flour

VOLCANO FILLING

1 qt. vanilla ice cream (see page 280)
3 Tb. cognac

LIGHT MERINGUE MIXTURE

8 egg whites
4 egg yolks, beaten with a fork
½ tsp. vanilla
1 c. granulated sugar
1 Tb. confectioners' sugar for dusting

FOR THE FLAMES

½ lemon, hollowed out (use the shell)
⅓ c. warm cognac

1 The lemon mousseline cake, which can be used in other ways, can be made a day or two ahead and stored in a plastic bag to keep it moist.

To make the lemon mousseline cake: Put the 6 egg yolks, ½ c. sugar, 2 tsp. grated lemon rind, and 1 tsp. vanilla together, and <u>mix well with a whisk until smooth and thick.</u>

2 Add the ½ c. potato starch and ¼ c. flour, and mix with a whisk.

3 Beat the 6 egg whites until firm. Add about one-third of the egg whites to the egg yolk–potato starch mixture, and mix with a whisk to lighten the batter. Fold the remainder of the egg whites into the batter.

4 Pour the batter into a buttered 9-in. springform pan.

5 Bake on a cookie sheet in a preheated 350-degree oven for approximately 35 minutes. The cake is nice and puffy as it comes out of the oven. Let cool in the pan in a warm place. The cake will shrink slightly but remain moist and spongy inside.

6 **Prepare the base of the volcano surprise:** Butter the center of an ovenproof tray and slice the cake horizontally into four layers (see Vanilla-Bourbon Genoise, page 210, steps 7–8).

7 Place one of the cake layers on the buttered tray. Spoon the quart of vanilla ice cream onto the bottom cake layer, mounding it in the center, and smooth with a spatula.

8 Cover the top of the ice cream mound completely with a layer of cake to protect the filling entirely. (Leftover cake can be frozen for future use.)

9 Sprinkle the 3 Tb. of cognac over the second layer of cake. At this point, these two layers can be placed in the freezer while you prepare the rest of the dessert.

10 **For the light meringue mixture:** Beat the 8 egg whites until firm. Meanwhile, in a separate bowl, combine the 4 egg yolks with the ½ tsp. vanilla. When the egg whites are firm, add the 1 c. sugar fairly quickly (it should not take more than about 10 seconds) and continue beating with the whisk for another 15 to 20 seconds to incorporate it. Gently fold the egg yolk–vanilla mixture into the egg whites with a spatula.

11 Place some of this meringue on top of the ice cream cake, smoothing and mounding it into a conical shape.

12 You should have approximately a 1-in. thickness of meringue on the cake, with the meringue higher on the center. Spoon the rest of the meringue into a pastry bag fitted with a fluted tip and make a spiral decoration all around the bottom of the "volcano."

13 Continue decorating the cake as illustrated with the remaining light meringue mixture.

14 Embed the hollowed-out half lemon shell in the center on top and sprinkle the cake with the 1 Tb. confectioners' sugar. Work quickly so the ice cream and the meringue mixture remain firm. Place in a preheated 400-degree oven for 12 to 15 minutes.

15 The meringue should be nicely browned and just set inside. As soon as the cake comes out of the oven, pour the ⅓ c. of warm cognac into the lemon shell and ignite it. Bring the dessert to the table immediately.

16 Spoon the flaming cognac on the cake. Using a spoon, scoop up some of the meringue, cake, and ice cream onto individual plates.

RUM CREME ANGLAISE

1 c. heavy cream
1 c. milk
2 tsp. cornstarch
2 egg yolks
1 tsp. vanilla
¼ c. confectioners' sugar
1 Tb. dark rum

COFFEE EXTRACT

½ c. milk
¼ c. finely ground French roast coffee

SOUFFLE MIXTURE

⅓ c. coffee extract (from above)
4 oz. bittersweet or semi-sweet chocolate
  (see page 132)
4 egg yolks
6 egg whites
¼ c. granulated sugar
1 Tb. butter (for buttering mold)
Extra granulated sugar (for coating mold)
Confectioners' sugar (for dusting soufflés)

CHOCOLATE ESPRESSO SOUFFLE

This chocolate soufflé flavored with a concentrated espresso extract has an intense taste. It is made without any flour, because the chocolate gives sufficient body to the soufflé.

Most soufflés can be prepared up to 1 hour ahead and placed in the soufflé mold ready to cook. Small soufflés are the easiest to make, since they tend to rise straight, cook quickly, do not break, and can be served right in their molds.

The recipe here makes enough for 8. It can be prepared either in one large soufflé mold (6 to 8 c.), two 1-qt. soufflé molds, four or five 1–1½-c. soufflé molds, or eight to ten ½-c. soufflé molds.

The soufflé can be cooled, allowed to deflate (it should not sink below the level of the amount originally placed in the mold), covered, refrigerated, and unmolded the next day to be served cold, dusted with bitter cocoa powder and accompanied by the same rum sauce. This makes a light but dense-tasting dessert.

The rum sauce is made with only two egg yolks (remaining from the whites used in the soufflé). Since the lecithin in the egg yolks is not enough of a thickening agent to give the sauce proper viscosity, a bit of cornstarch is added to the milk and cream, which is brought to a boil to ensure that the cornstarch cooks and thickens the liquid. Then the boiling liquid is poured directly into the cold egg yolks and the 180-degree temperature is enough for the lecithin in the egg yolks to thicken, so that you don't have to cook the sauce. This is a very fast version of custard cream and can be done only when the proportion of egg yolks to liquid is small. For a more conventional custard cream, 3 egg yolks per cup of liquid are usually called for and the custard has to be brought to 180 degrees.

Yield: 6–8 servings

1 For the rum crème anglaise: In a saucepan, combine the 1 c. each cream and milk and 2 tsp. cornstarch, and bring to a strong boil. Meanwhile, beat the 2 egg yolks, 1 tsp. vanilla, and ¼ c. confectioners' sugar in a bowl, working with a whisk until very smooth. Then pour the boiling liquid in one stroke on top of the egg yolk mixture.

2 The mixture will thicken as you are pouring the hot liquid in. Mix quickly with the whisk and continue whisking for 5 to 6 seconds after adding the hot liquid, then strain immediately through a very fine strainer. Refrigerate and, when the mixture has cooled, add the 1 Tb. dark rum.

3 **For the coffee extract:** Bring the ½ c. milk to a boil, then add the ¼ c. coffee and stir. Remove from the heat, cover, and let steep for 2 to 3 minutes. Strain the mixture through paper towels. You should have approximately ⅓ c. of very strong coffee extract.

For the soufflé: Combine the coffee extract with the 4 oz. chocolate, and stir over moderate heat with a whisk until the chocolate has completely melted and the mixture is smooth. Add the 4 egg yolks, and stir with the whisk. You will notice that the chocolate mixture will thicken at this point. Whip the 6 egg whites until firm, add the ¼ c. granulated sugar, and continue beating for 5 to 10 seconds to incorporate the sugar.

4 Add about one-fourth of the egg white mixture to the chocolate and mix well with a whisk.

5 With a spatula, fold the rest of the egg whites into the chocolate mixture.

6 Butter and sugar two 1-qt. soufflé molds and fill each with the soufflé mixture.

7 For another variation, butter and sugar ½-c. soufflé molds and the 1½-c. soufflé mold, and fill them with the chocolate mixture.

Arrange the soufflé molds on a cookie sheet and bake in a preheated 400-degree oven 10 minutes for the small soufflés, about 13 to 15 minutes for the 1½-c. mold, and 18 to 20 minutes for the 1-qt. soufflé mold, until set but still wet inside.

8 While the soufflés are in the oven, arrange 3 to 4 Tb. of the rum crème anglaise on each individual serving plate.

9 When the soufflés are done, sprinkle the tops with confectioners' sugar.

10 One way of serving the small individual soufflés is to place them, still in their molds, directly in the middle of the sauce and serve them immediately. Each person scoops a bit of the sauce from his plate, pours it on the soufflé, and eats from the mold.

11 A second variation is to unmold the soufflé onto a large spatula or spoon and turn it back onto an individual serving plate that has been coated with some of the sauce.

12 The unmolded soufflé is now ready to be served.

13 Dust the top of the 1-qt. soufflé with confectioners' sugar as soon as it comes out of the oven.

14 Serve the soufflé immediately, spooning portions onto individual plates coated with about ¼ c. of the rum crème anglaise.

RASPBERRY AND BLUEBERRY SOUFFLE

A soufflé is always a beautiful way to finish an elegant dinner, but it requires work at the last moment, which is not always possible. However, the soufflé mixture in the recipe here can be prepared up through step 9 and placed in the refrigerator for up to an hour before cooking. Furthermore, this soufflé can be cooked 1 day or so ahead, unmolded, and served cold with a raspberry sauce. The cold version has an even stronger berry taste than the hot one. The fresh blueberries folded into the mixture before cooking enhance the look as well as the taste of the soufflé. Do not use frozen blueberries because they will run and discolor the whole soufflé during cooking.

As shown in photograph 10, the soufflé sometimes splits a little in the center while cooking. Although it may not have as professional a look when this happens, it doesn't change the taste. The larger the soufflé, the more it will have a tendency to split. Therefore, smaller soufflés will usually hold their shape better and be easier to serve.

Yield: 8 servings

SOUFFLE MIXTURE

¾ lb. fresh or frozen unsweetened raspberries (to make about 1 c. raspberry purée, unsweetened)
3 egg yolks
½ c. granulated sugar
2 Tb. flour
¾ c. milk
6 egg whites
¾ c. fresh blueberries
1 Tb. butter (for buttering mold)
Extra granulated sugar (for coating the mold)

RASPBERRY SAUCE

¾ lb. fresh or frozen unsweetened raspberries, thawed
½ c. raspberry jam or preserves, preferably seedless, strained
1 Tb. raspberry brandy

Confectioners' sugar to dust top of soufflé

1 Strain the 1½ lb. fresh or frozen raspberries for the soufflé and the raspberry sauce through a food mill and then through a sieve, using the technique explained in the Blackberry Clafoutis recipe, page 194, steps 6–8. Set 1 c. of the purée aside for the sauce and reserve 1 c. for the filling of the soufflé.

2 For the soufflé: Combine the 3 egg yolks with ¼ c. of the granulated sugar and the 2 Tb. flour, and mix with a whisk until smooth. Bring the ¾ c. milk to a boil and combine with the egg yolk mixture. Place back on the stove, bring to a boil, and boil until the mixture thickens. Set aside.

3 Put 1 c. of raspberry purée in a saucepan and cook on top of the stove to concentrate the flavor and reduce to about ⅓ c. Combine with the egg yolk mixture.

4 Beat the 6 egg whites until stiff, using a whisk or an electric mixer. When stiff, add the remaining ¼ c. granulated sugar and beat for another 15 to 20 seconds. Add one-fourth to one-third of the beaten whites to the egg yolk–raspberry mixture and mix with a whisk to incorporate.

5 Add that mixture to the remainder of the beaten whites, and fold with a large spatula until well-mixed.

6 Sprinkle the ¾ c. blueberries on top and fold them in, mixing lightly.

7 Butter and sugar a 6-c. soufflé mold and pour the mixture into it. The mold should be completely filled.

8 Smooth the top and mark lines by gently pressing the edge of a long cake spatula into the top of the mixture and then raising the spatula to leave a line on top. Make lines at 1½-in. intervals all along the surface. Then mark in the other direction, creating crisscrossing lines.

9 Run the tip of your thumb all around the outside of the soufflé to make a clean edge and make the mixture pull back slightly from the rim of the bowl.

10 Place in a preheated 360- to 375-degree oven for approximately 30 minutes. While the soufflé is in the oven, **make the raspberry sauce:** Combine the reserved cup of unsweetened raspberry purée with the ½ c. strained raspberry jam or preserves and the 1 Tb. raspberry brandy, and mix well until smooth.

When the soufflé is removed from the oven, it should be puffed up and cooked inside. Sprinkle it with confectioners' sugar.

11 Spread 2 to 3 Tb. of the sauce on each plate and, at the table, spoon a nice portion of the soufflé into the center. Serve immediately.

Or serve the soufflé cold. Let it deflate slowly at room temperature for 45 minutes to 1 hour, then cover it with plastic wrap and refrigerate for a few hours or, preferably, overnight.

12 Unmold the cold soufflé on a serving platter. It will slide out of the mold easily.

13 Coat the unmolded soufflé with the raspberry sauce and decorate the top with fresh raspberries and blueberries.

14 Place some sauce on each individual plate, cut the soufflé into wedges, and serve on top of the sauce as a light, cold pudding.

APRICOT AND PISTACHIO SOUFFLE

This intensely flavored apricot and pistachio soufflé is made from dried apricots (cooked in water and made into a purée), egg whites, and crushed pistachios. The corn syrup in the apricot purée sweetens the mixture and holds it together well during cooking. The use of corn syrup in soufflés tends to prevent cracking.

The soufflé mixture can be made a couple of hours ahead of cooking and placed in the soufflé mold so it is ready to go into the oven. The smaller the soufflé, the more equally it rises and the less likely it is to crack open.

Although this soufflé is served hot in the recipe here, it can be cooled, unmolded, and served with the sauce.

Yield: 6 servings (1 six-cup soufflé mold)

½ lb. dried apricot halves
2 c. water
⅓ c. corn syrup

½ c. pistachios, crushed
1 tsp. butter (for buttering mold)
2 Tb. granulated sugar (for coating mold)
5 egg whites (¾ c.)
WHIPPED CREAM GARNISH
1 c. cream
2 Tb. confectioners' sugar
1 tsp. vanilla

Confectioners' sugar to dust top of soufflé

1 Place the ½ lb. of dried apricots in a saucepan with the 2 c. of water. Bring to a boil and simmer gently for 25 minutes. Most of the moisture should be gone. Drain in a sieve and place the apricots in the bowl of a food processor with the ⅓ c. corn syrup, and process until puréed.

Peel the ½ c. of pistachios so only the green of the nut is visible, and crack them in a mortar with a pestle or by pressing with the underside of a saucepan so each nut is broken into two or three pieces.

2 Coat a 6-c. soufflé mold with the 1 tsp. butter and sprinkle the 2 Tb. granulated sugar inside to cover the entire surface. Beat the 5 egg whites until stiff. Using a whisk, mix approximately one-third of the beaten whites into the apricot mixture.

3 Add the rest of the beaten egg whites to the mixture with ⅓ c. of the crushed pistachios, and fold in gently and quickly with a rubber spatula. This should not take more than 20 to 25 seconds. Reserve the extra pistachios for use as a garnish.

4 Place the mixture in the prepared soufflé mold. Smooth the top with a spatula, then holding the spatula on edge, press it gently into the top of the soufflé to form lines and create a crisscross pattern. Run your finger all around the mold to clean the edge and recess it slightly.

5 Place on a tray and bake in a preheated 375-degree oven for 20 to 25 minutes. It should be well-set in the center and nicely browned.

6 While the soufflé is cooking, **make the whipped cream garnish:** Combine the 1 c. cream, 2 Tb. confectioners' sugar, and 1 tsp. vanilla, and whip lightly. It should still be slightly liquid, soft and creamy. Spread 1 or 2 spoonfuls of the cream on each individual plate, spread it out on the plate, and sprinkle it with some of the reserved pistachios. Dust the soufflé with confectioners' sugar as it emerges from the oven, and spoon onto the prepared plates. Serve immediately.

Note: This soufflé can also be cooled, unmolded, and served with the whipped cream.

CARAMEL LIME SOUFFLE WITH LIME SAUCE

This soufflé is made ahead, at least five hours before serving but preferably the day before, then unmolded and served cold with the lime sauce. It can also be served hot (step 7) with the same sauce.

The soufflé mold is first lined with caramel and the soufflé is cooked in a double boiler. Soufflés cooked in this manner will tend to rise evenly without cracking and hold their height for 15 to 20 minutes after they come out of the oven. But, unless the mold is lined with caramel, as is done in this recipe, a soufflé baked in a water bath will be wet and white around the sides. It will not have the golden exterior of a regular soufflé that is cooked dry in the oven. The chocolate soufflé, however (page 261), can be cooked in a water bath because chocolate tends to get doughy and, since its exterior is dark anyway, does not require any browning during cooking.

The cold caramel lime soufflé makes a delicate, light, cold dessert that is delicious with the lime sauce.

Yield: 8–10 servings

CARAMEL

2 c. sugar
½ c. water

LIME SAUCE

⅓ c. lime juice
1 Tb. water
Half the caramel recipe from above
2 Tb. Grand Marnier

SOUFFLE MIXTURE

5 egg yolks
¼ c. sugar
2 Tb. cornstarch
1 tsp. vanilla
Grated peel of 1 lime (1½ tsp.)
1¼ c. milk
6 egg whites

1 To make the caramel: Combine the 2 c. sugar and ½ c. water in a saucepan and stir gently, just enough to moisten the sugar. Bring to a boil and cook over high heat without stirring or shaking the pan, until the mixture turns a golden caramel color, approximately 10 to 12 minutes. Pour about half the caramel into a 6-c. soufflé mold.

2 Incline the mold on its side, holding it over a cookie sheet to catch any caramel drippings and, using a bristle brush (not nylon), turn the mold and brush the caramel onto the sides as it flows, until the sides of the mold are completely coated. Work quickly so you can finish coating the mold before the caramel hardens.

To make the lime sauce: Add the ⅓ c. lime juice and 1 Tb. water to the remaining caramel and bring the mixture to a boil, stirring. Set aside to cool.

3 For the soufflé: Place the 5 egg yolks in a bowl with the ¼ c. sugar, 2 Tb. cornstarch, 1 tsp. vanilla, and 1½ tsp. grated lime peel, and mix well with a whisk. Bring the 1¼ c. milk to a boil and combine with the egg yolk mixture. Pour into a saucepan and bring to a boil, stirring with the whisk, especially around the bottom edge of the saucepan to prevent the mixture from scorching. As soon as it comes to a boil (it should be thick and smooth), remove from the heat.

Beat the 6 egg whites until firm and add one-fourth to one-third of them to the egg yolk mixture, mixing them in well with the whisk to lighten the mixture.

4 Add the soufflé base, now lightened by the addition of the egg whites, to the rest of the beaten egg whites and fold in with a spatula. Work quickly to prevent the mixture from getting grainy. It should not take more than 20 to 30 seconds.

5 Pour the mixture into the caramel-lined mold. It should fill the mold.

6 Place the mold in a pan and surround it with lukewarm water. Place in a preheated 350-degree oven for 1 hour 10 minutes.

7 When it emerges from the oven, the soufflé should have risen at least a couple of inches above the mold and be brown on top. It will hold its shape for about 15 to 20 minutes and can be served hot with the lime sauce.

8 To serve the soufflé cold, allow it to cool overnight or at least 5 to 6 hours in the refrigerator, covered (so the edge of the soufflé mold doesn't dry out and get sticky from the sugar, thus causing the soufflé to stick to the sides; if covered, the soufflé will develop moisture and the outside will stay moist). The soufflé will sink down but should not sink below its original volume before baking.

Pull the sides of the soufflé toward its center to loosen it all around.

9 Stir the 2 Tb. Grand Marnier into the caramel-lime sauce. The sauce should be about the thickness of heavy syrup.

10 Unmold the soufflé; it will slide out easily onto a serving platter. Coat with some of the sauce.

11 Cut the soufflé into wedges and serve with additional sauce.

ORANGE SOUFFLE SURPRISE

Orange Soufflé Surprise is made of orange sherbet that has been spooned into an orange shell, covered with a light layer of soufflé, then baked briefly just before it is to be served.

Most of the parts can be prepared ahead: The orange skin shell as well as the sherbet should be frozen in advance. The soufflé mixture, however, should be prepared at the last minute.

The soufflé mixture is made only of egg whites, sugar, and the orange rind for flavor. Because it does not have a pastry cream base, it cooks very quickly and holds its shape very well (for 5 to 10 minutes before deflating). It could also be baked alone as an ordinary soufflé and served with a tangerine sauce (see Crêpe Frangipane with Tangerine Sauce, page 312).

In the sherbet mixture, there is—in addition to the orange juice, lemon juice, sugar, and orange marmalade—an egg white that has been just slightly beaten until frothy. This gives more volume to the sherbet and makes it milder and smoother. The orange sherbet could, of course, be served by itself as a separate dessert or in the orange skin receptacle with some whipped cream and a julienne of orange skin on top.

When the sherbet is served with the soufflé mixture, it should be kept frozen until the

last moment so it can go into the oven on a bed of ice without melting. If, however, you are planning to serve the sherbet on its own, remove it from the freezer and refrigerate for 10 to 15 minutes to soften a little before serving.

Yield: 6 servings

ORANGE SHERBET

6 large bright-skinned oranges
¼ c. orange marmalade
2 Tb. lemon juice
¼ c. granulated sugar
1 egg white

ORANGE SOUFFLE

4 egg whites
½ c. granulated sugar
2 Tb. grated orange rind (from oranges above)

Confectioners' sugar to dust soufflé tops

1 With a vegetable peeler, remove strips from about the top third of the oranges on the navel side. Put the strips in a mini-chop and process them to make about 2 Tb. of grated orange rind. (If a mini-chop is not available, do not remove strips of orange peel. Instead, grate enough of the skin from the top third of the oranges with a grater to make 2 Tb.)

2 Cut off the tops of the oranges to the level where they have been peeled or grated and trim the base of each slightly so it stands solidly. Using a spoon, remove (and reserve) the insides of the oranges to create receptacles. Also remove the orange flesh and juice from the orange tops and reserve, discarding the pith and remaining skin.

3 Push the orange flesh through a food mill; you should have about 3 c. of juice. Place the orange shells in the freezer to harden.

4 **For the orange sherbet:** Add the ¼ c. marmalade to the 3 c. of extracted orange juice along with the 2 Tb. lemon juice and ¼ c. granulated sugar. Whip the egg white with a whisk until just frothy but still liquid and add it to the orange juice mixture.

5 Place in an ice cream freezer and freeze according to the manufacturer's instructions. The mixture should expand in volume, get lighter in color, and be smooth and creamy. Transfer to a mixing bowl and place in the freezer for a couple of hours. When the sherbet has set and the shells are frozen, fill the shells to within ½ in. of the top with the sherbet and return the filled shells to the freezer until serving time.

6 At serving time, place the filled frozen shells on top of little rings or tartlet molds arranged in a roasting pan so they sit squarely and do not roll while cooking. Pack in ice with a little water around them.

7 **For the soufflé:** Beat the 4 egg whites until firm. Mix the ½ c. granulated sugar and 2 Tb. orange rind together and, when the egg whites are firm, add the sugar and rind to them and continue to beat for 10 more seconds, until well-mixed. Transfer to a pastry bag fitted with a fluted tip and pipe rosettes of the soufflé mixture on top of the sherbet in the shells.

8 Place the filled oranges with the ice around them (to keep the sherbet from melting) in a preheated 400-degree oven, and bake for about 7 minutes, until the soufflé on top is puffy and nicely browned. Dust the soufflé tops with confectioners' sugar as soon as you have taken the pan out of the oven.

9 Serve immediately alone or with Lime Tuile Cookies (page 326, steps 7–8), either on serving plates or in sherbet glasses to steady the oranges and make them easier to eat.

FROZEN CITRUS SOUFFLE

A frozen soufflé is a variety of ice cream presented in a soufflé dish with enough of the mixture extending above the rim of the mold to make it look as if it has been cooking and rising in the oven.

This frozen soufflé could be done with the juice and rind of either lemons, oranges, or limes. Here I have mixed the rinds and juices of different citrus fruits, added the fresh ladyfingers, and flavored the dessert with cognac and Grand Marnier. Cognac is added to the soufflé mixture, and Grand Marnier is used to moisten the ladyfingers, which would otherwise get hard and dry as they freeze. The alcohol keeps them moist inside the soufflé, even when it is frozen.

This dessert must be made a day ahead since it should be frozen for at least 10 to 12 hours. After it is frozen, it should be covered tightly with plastic wrap so it doesn't pick up any tastes or dehydrate in the freezer.

The candied julienne of orange peel is flavorful and attractive on top of the soufflé. It can also be used to garnish a hot orange soufflé or an orange cake. Notice that only part of the soufflé mixture is used initially to fill up the mold. When that gets hard in the freezer, the remainder is placed on top inside the collar. This two-step procedure prevents the mixture from running between the paper and the mold.

Yield: 10–12 servings

LADYFINGERS

3 eggs, separated
⅓ c. granulated sugar
⅔ c. flour (measured by dipping the measuring cup into the flour and leveling the cup)
1 tsp. vanilla
1 tsp. butter + 1 Tb. flour for preparing cookie sheet
½ c. confectioners' sugar to sprinkle on top of the ladyfingers
⅓ c. Grand Marnier

SOUFFLE MIXTURE

1 lemon
1 lime
1 orange
½ c. granulated sugar
4 egg yolks
⅓ c. cognac
3 c. heavy cream
2 Tb. granulated sugar

CANDIED ORANGE JULIENNE

8 strips of orange peel from a bright skinned orange, cut with a vegetable peeler so only the surface of the rind is removed

2 c. water
⅓ c. granulated sugar
⅓ c. water
1 c. granulated sugar for lining tray to
    coat julienne

Unsweetened cocoa powder for dusting top
    of soufflé

1 **To make the ladyfingers:** Whip the 3 egg whites in a mixer or by hand (as done above) until they form a firm but creamy peak on the end of a whisk. Add the ⅓ c. granulated sugar all at once and beat for another 5 to 6 seconds to incorporate.

2 Sift the ⅔ c. flour directly onto the egg whites, folding it in gently as you sift.

3 Combine the 3 egg yolks and 1 tsp. vanilla, and fold them gently into the egg white mixture.

4 Fit a 16- to 18-in. pastry bag (preferably made of plastic) with a plain tip with a ¾-in. opening. To prevent the batter from running out through the tip as you fill the bag, twist it just above the tip and push the twisted section into the tip. This will hold the batter back until you're ready to begin using the bag.

5 Fold the cuff of the pastry bag back onto itself to a depth of 1½ to 2 in. so the inside of the bag near the opening is not smeared with the batter. Spoon the batter into the bag.

6 Unfold the edge of the bag and pleat the top like an accordion to close the batter in.

7 To use the bag, hold the pleated end in the hollow between your thumb and finger.

8 Notice the position of your hands when using the bag: The index finger and thumb of one hand hold the bag firmly closed while the lower part of the hand presses on the bag to release the filling. The bag is held near the tip with the other hand to direct the flow from the tip.

9 Butter and flour a large cookie sheet and squeeze out the batter, holding the tip 2 in. above the tray so the batter flows gently from the bag onto the tray. Move the bag backward slowly as you are pressing until a ladyfinger 6 in. long by 1¼ in. wide is formed.

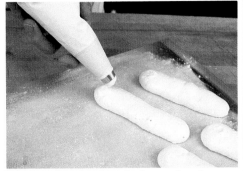

10 To make sure that the batter breaks cleanly from the ladyfingers, stop pressing on the bag as you reach the end of each ladyfinger and lift up the bag abruptly to break the "tail" of the batter. Continue making the ladyfingers. The batter will yield approximately 12 ladyfingers.

11 Sprinkle the ladyfingers generously with the ½ c. confectioners' sugar. Wait about 1½ minutes, until some of the sugar has been absorbed into the batter, and then sprinkle with sugar again. The sugar will create a light crust on top of the ladyfingers as they are cooking.

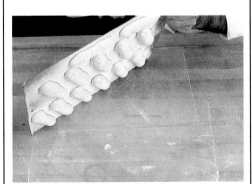

12 Remove the excess sugar that falls around the ladyfingers on the tray by turning the tray upside down over a piece of wax paper on the counter and . . .

13 . . . tapping the back of the tray gently with a knife or spoon. Most of the excess sugar will fall onto the wax paper and can be retrieved. The ladyfingers will not fall off the baking tray as the whole procedure takes only a few seconds. However, the timid cook can leave the sugar around the ladyfingers.

14 Bake the ladyfingers in the center of a preheated 325- to 350-degree oven for approximately 15 minutes, until cooked and light brown on top. Let cool at room temperature in a draft-free place. Then remove the ladyfingers from the tray. At this point, they can be stored in a plastic box with a tight-fitting lid so no humidity gets to them. They can also be wrapped securely and frozen.

15 **To make the soufflé mixture:** With a vegetable peeler, cut 5 strips of peel each from a lemon, lime, and orange. Be sure to remove only the surface of the skin since that is where most of the essential oil is located.

16 Cut the strips into pieces and place in the bowl of a mini-chop or coffee grinder. Reduce to a powder. (If such equipment is not available, do not remove strips of orange peel. Instead, grate enough skin from a whole orange to get approximately 1 Tb. of rind. Repeat with the lemon and lime.)

17 Squeeze the juice of the lemon, lime, and orange into a bowl. Put the ½ c. granulated sugar, powdered or grated citrus peel, and ½ c. of mixed lemon, lime, and orange juice in a saucepan, and bring to a boil. Cook to the thread stage (about 230 degrees), which should take approximately 5 minutes of boiling. →

18 Put the 4 egg yolks in the bowl of a mixer with the whisk attached. While the mixer is running at slow speed, add a little of the fruit syrup in a stream and then turn up the mixer speed to incorporate the syrup. Repeat until all the syrup is used. If the syrup is added at high speed, it splatters around the bowl. If all of it is added at once at slow speed, it may curdle the egg yolks. When all the syrup has been incorporated, beat the mixture on high speed for approximately 8 to 10 minutes. It should be quite thick and have at least tripled in volume. Add the ⅓ c. cognac and stir to incorporate.

19 The texture of the mixture should still be creamy and thick.

20 Sprinkle 6 to 7 ladyfingers with the ⅓ c. Grand Marnier.
    Whip the 3 c. cream with the 2 Tb. of sugar.

21 Fold the whipped cream into the egg yolk mixture.

22 Place about one-third of the soufflé mixture in the soufflé dish. Then break half of the soaked ladyfingers into pieces and embed them in the soufflé mixture. Place another third of soufflé mixture on top, just enough to fill the mold. Place the mold in the freezer for 2 to 3 hours, until the mixture hardens, and refrigerate the remainder of the mixture in the bowl.

23 When the mixture in the soufflé dish is hard on top, fold a length of aluminum foil, long enough to go around the dish easily, into thirds (it should be approximately 6 in. wide), wrap the foil securely around the mold, and tie it in place with string.

24 Combine the remaining soaked ladyfingers, broken into pieces, with the remaining soufflé mixture and spoon it on top of the frozen soufflé, piling it up to fill the collar. Place in the freezer overnight or until hard, and then cover the top with plastic wrap so the soufflé doesn't pick up any tastes from other foods. At this point, it can be kept in the freezer for several days.

25 **For the candied orange peel:** Pile up the 8 strips of orange peel and cut into a fine julienne. Put the julienne in a saucepan with the 2 c. water and bring to a boil. As soon as it boils, drain through a strainer, and wash the julienne under cold water. Rinse the pan and return the julienne to the pan with the ⅓ c. each sugar and water. Bring to a boil and cook, boiling gently, until the syrup starts thickening, about 6 to 8 minutes. At this point, the syrup should be practically to the softball stage (about 240 degrees).

26 You will notice here that the syrup is fairly heavy and the julienne of candied orange is almost transparent. Lift the julienne out of the syrup with a fork and place it on a tray lined with granulated sugar.

27 With your finger or a fork, spread the julienne strips out to separate them and coat them individually with the sugar. At this point, they can be placed in a jar or plastic bag and kept in the refrigerator for weeks.

28 At serving time, remove the collar from the soufflé and smooth the top.

29 Sprinkle the top of the soufflé with unsweetened cocoa powder so it looks like the browned top of an oven-baked soufflé.

30 For an additional effect, draw criss-crossing lines across the top of the soufflé.

31 Arrange a ring of candied orange rind around the soufflé.

32 If the soufflé has been frozen for several days, it may have become very hard. Move it from the freezer to the refrigerator for about 30 minutes before serving so it softens slightly. To serve the soufflé, cut in wedges, slicing down with a knife only to the top of the soufflé dish, and serve by scooping out the wedges. When the top of the soufflé has been served, sprinkle the remainder with cocoa powder and extra orange rind, and serve by scooping out portions with a spoon.

CHRISTMAS FRUITCAKE

This Christmas fruitcake can be made without the mixture of dried and candied fruit to produce a very rich pound cake. However, the dried and candied fruit greatly enhance the cake and make it a festive Christmas or holiday season dessert. You can also cut the cake into tiny pieces and use them for petits fours (see Fruitcake Fingers, page 203).

The candied peels are homemade: an easy, inexpensive procedure that gives you better quality candied peels than you can get commercially. A mixture of the peels and dried fruits will keep almost indefinitely if covered with rum and stored in a jar in the refrigerator. They can be added to soufflés as well as to cakes or fruit salads.

The cake is cooked slowly for a long time, until completely set inside. When cool, it should be wrapped in plastic and stored in an airtight container. It can also be frozen.

Yield: 1 large loaf

CANDIED PEELS

1 grapefruit
1 tangerine
1 lime
1 lemon
6 c. cold water
¾ c. sugar
1½ c. water

DRIED FRUIT

½ c. diced (¼-in.) dried apricots
⅓ c. diced (¼-in.) dried pears
⅓ c. diced (¼-in.) dried peaches
⅓ c. raisins
⅓ c. dark rum

CAKE

2½ sticks butter, softened (10 oz.)
1 c. sugar
5 eggs
3 Tb. orange juice
¼ tsp. salt
2 c. all-purpose flour (about 10 to 12 oz.)
½ c. cake flour

1 For the candied peels: The peels include not only the colored parts of the skin but the pith as well. Cut wedges through grapefruit or other citrus fruits, pull the skin away from the fruit, and dice into ¼-in. pieces. (The fruit can be used for juice or in salads.) You may also use the peel that is left over from squeezing oranges or grapefruits in the morning.

2 Place the diced fruit peels in 3 c. of cold water, bring to a boil, and cook over high heat for about 1 minute, then drain in a colander and wash the pieces for a few seconds under cold water. Rinse the saucepan with cold water, return the diced fruit peel to the saucepan, and add another 3 c. of water. Repeat the boiling, draining, and washing procedure, and wash the saucepan again. This blanching process is intended to remove the bitterness from the peel. Finally, place the diced peel back in the saucepan with the ¾ c. sugar and 1½ c. water and cook about 15 minutes, until most of the moisture is reduced to a very syrupy liquid.

3 Dice the ½ c. dried apricots, ⅓ c. each dried pears and dried peaches, add them to the ⅓ c. raisins, and combine with the candied peels and syrup. Mix in the ⅓ c. dark rum. At this point, the mixture can be placed in a jar and kept, refrigerated, almost indefinitely.

5 Cut a strip of parchment paper long enough to fit the length of a loaf pan and extend 1½ in. beyond it at either end. (This makes it easy to unmold the cake after baking.) Butter the paper and the mold, bottom and sides, and position the paper in the mold, pressing to make it adhere to the bottom and sides at either end. Pour the batter into the prepared pan and smooth the top with a spatula.

7 Allow the cake to cool in the pan. When cool, wrap in plastic wrap and/or aluminum foil and keep either frozen or in the refrigerator. At serving time, cut into ½-in. slices and serve. This cake is a nice accompaniment to cream custard but can be served alone or with fruit and nuts.

4 To make the cake: In the bowl of a mixer, combine the 2½ sticks soft butter and 1 c. sugar. Add the 5 eggs, 3 Tb. orange juice, ¼ tsp. salt, 2 c. all-purpose flour, and ½ c. cake flour, and beat with the flat beater just enough to incorporate. Add the mixture of candied and dried fruit, and fold them in gently with a spatula.

6 Place the loaf pan on a cookie sheet and bake in a preheated 350-degree oven for approximately 45 minutes. Reduce the heat to 325 degrees and cook for another 60 to 70 minutes, until completely set inside.

ENGLISH CHRISTMAS PUDDING

This compact, intensely flavorful pudding can be made weeks ahead and kept, tightly wrapped, in the refrigerator. Although this recipe is for one cake made in a 4- to 6-c. bowl, the recipe can be tripled to make several puddings, as the British do before Christmas, to use as gifts and serve to friends during the holiday season.

As the cake ages it will develop more flavor. The hard sauce recipe as well as the syrup recipe for the top is enough for one cake. As shown with the petits fours (page 197), the Christmas pudding can also be cut into 1-in. cubes, soaked with syrup and alcohol (rum or cognac), and served as petits fours for an after-dinner treat.

The spice seasonings as well as the dried fruit can be varied according to what is available and what your own personal tastes are.

Yield: 8–10 servings

2 oz. beef suet (white fat from steak can be used)
2 slices white bread
¾ c. flour (about 3½ to 4 oz.)
2 eggs
½ c. dark rum
1 Tb. lemon rind
1 Tb. orange rind
2 Tb. orange juice
2 Tb. lemon juice
½ tsp. ground allspice
¼ tsp. ground cinnamon
⅛ tsp. ground cloves
2 tsp. vanilla
¼ c. light brown sugar
½ c. dark raisins
½ c. golden raisins
⅓ c. diced (¼-in.) dried apricots
½ c. diced (¼-in.) dried apple
⅓ c. diced (¼-in.) prunes
⅓ c. diced (¼-in.) dried pears
⅓ c. diced (¼-in.) dried peaches
½ c. pieces (¼-in.) walnuts

SOAKING SYRUP

2 Tb. confectioners' sugar
2 Tb. cognac
1 Tb. lemon juice

HARD SAUCE

1½ sticks butter
½ c. confectioners' sugar
¼ c. cognac

1 **For the pudding:** Cut the suet into ½-in. pieces and place it in the bowl of a food processor with the white bread and flour. Process until the fat is well ground and the mixture is smooth. Add the eggs, rum, lemon and orange rind and juice, allspice, cinnamon, cloves, vanilla, and brown sugar to the mixture in the processor and process until well-homogenized. Place the mixture in a mixing bowl, add the remaining pudding ingredients, and stir to mix well. Cover with a piece of plastic wrap and refrigerate for a few hours or overnight so it develops flavor. It can also be placed directly in the bowl in which it will be cooked. At cooking time, pack the pudding (if you haven't already done so) into a 4- or 5-c. roundish, high-sided mold.

2 Using a piece of plastic wrap, press down on the pudding to pack it tightly into the bowl and to eliminate any air bubbles.

3 Leaving the plastic wrap in place on top of the pudding, wrap the bowl completely with aluminum foil to seal it, and place it in a pot that is large enough to contain it completely. Pour lukewarm tap water around the mold so it comes approximately three-fourths of the way up the sides of the bowl.

5 Unmold the pudding onto a piece of plastic wrap. It should slide out of the bowl easily. Wrap tightly in the plastic wrap and refrigerate (it will keep for several weeks) or freeze.

7 **Prepare the hard sauce:** Put the 1½ sticks butter, ½ c. confectioners' sugar, and ¼ c. cognac in the bowl of a food processor, process until smooth, and spoon into a serving dish. Arrange the pudding on an attractive serving platter with some holly around it to make it festive, and serve with a dollop of hard sauce on top. Pour extra sauce around the platter.

4 Place the pot over high heat and bring the water to a boil, then reduce the heat to very low, cover the pot with a lid, and simmer the pudding for about 5 hours. The water should not boil; it should be maintained at a heat of 180 to 190 degrees. If the water evaporates during cooking, replenish occasionally to keep it at the appropriate level.

When cooked, remove the aluminum foil from around the mold and the plastic wrap from the top. The internal temperature of the pudding should be 180 degrees.

6 At serving time, place the cake back in the bowl in which it was cooked, cover it with plastic wrap and aluminum foil, and steam it again in the same manner for about 1 hour, until warm in the center. Mix the 2 Tb. each confectioners' sugar and cognac with the 1 Tb. lemon juice, stirring until smooth. Unmold the cake and brush it with the syrup to flavor it.

1 **For the vanilla ice cream:** Break the 2 or 3 vanilla beans, place them in a small coffee or spice grinder or mini-chop, and pulverize them into a powder. If the vanilla-bean mixture is still a bit soft and gooey, add some of the sugar from the recipe to the mini-chop so that it grinds into a fine powder.

2 Place the 2 c. milk and 1 c. of the cream in a saucepan, and bring to a boil. Place the remaining 2 c. cold cream in a large bowl. Mix the 4 egg yolks, 1 whole egg, 1 Tb. vanilla, 1 c. sugar, and the powdered vanilla with a whisk. Combine with the boiling milk and cream, and place the mixture back over the heat just long enough for it to thicken, which will occur when it reaches approximately 180 degrees. Do not over-cook the mixture or it will tend to curdle. As soon as the mixture thickens, pour it into the cold cream, which will cool it and prevent it from cooking further and curdling. Combine well.

VANILLA ICE CREAM IN NETTY CUPS WITH SPICY CHERRIES IN WINE

This rich vanilla ice cream made with fresh vanilla beans is distinctive in taste and has a luscious texture. Although it can be served by itself, the crunchy texture and nutty taste of the cookie cup is quite complementary.

The quantity of dough needed for each cup is approximately 1½ Tb. If the cups are made ahead, be sure to store them carefully in a tightly sealed container to keep them from getting soggy.

The cherries are cooked in red wine and spices with port wine and cognac added. They make an excellent dessert by themselves with a little sour cream and a slice of pound cake (see Cinnamon Lemon Cake, page 286, step 6). In my recipe, they make a great addition to the ice cream. The cherries will keep in a jar, refrigerated, for weeks.

Yield: 8 netty cups

VANILLA ICE CREAM

Yield: 10–12 servings
2 to 3 vanilla beans, depending on size
2 c. milk
3 c. heavy cream
4 egg yolks
1 egg
1 Tb. vanilla
1 c. sugar

SPICY CHERRIES IN WINE

Yield: 10 servings
3 lb. large Bing or sweet cherries, pitted
¾ c. sugar
½ tsp. cinnamon
⅛ tsp. ground allspice
⅛ tsp. ground nutmeg
⅛ tsp. ground cloves
Dash cayenne pepper
1 Tb. vanilla
1½ c. dry red wine
1½ tsp. cornstarch dissolved in 1 Tb. water
¼ c. sweet port wine
¼ c. good cognac

NETTY CUPS
See Summer Cornet Susie, page 307

3 Place the mixture in an ice cream maker and make according to the manufacturer's instructions. (It should take from 30 to 45 minutes.) Then tightly pack the ice cream in a bowl or other container, and place it in the freezer, covered, until serving time.

4 **For the spicy cherries in wine:** Place the 3 lb. pitted Bing cherries, ¾ c. sugar, ½ tsp. cinnamon, ⅛ tsp. each allspice, nutmeg, and cloves, dash cayenne, 1 Tb. vanilla, and 1½ c. dry red wine in a large saucepan, preferably stainless steel. Bring the mixture to a boil and cook for 2 to 3 minutes, covered. Let cool, still covered, until lukewarm. Strain off the juice (approximately 2 to 3 c.), and reduce it to 1¼ c. Add the 1½ tsp. cornstarch dissolved in 1 Tb. water to the juice and bring to a boil. Pour over the cherries. When the cherries are lukewarm, add the ¼ c. port wine and ¼ c. cognac, and mix well. At this point, the mixture can be poured into a jar and refrigerated.

5 The cherries in wine should be served very cold. Place 2 to 3 Tb. of the cherry and juice mixture on each serving plate.

6 Place a netty cup in the center of each plate and fill with a ball of the vanilla ice cream. Top with a cherry, spoon a little juice over the ice cream, and serve immediately.

RASPBERRY SHERBET WITH BLACKBERRY SAUCE

Sherbet made with only fresh fruit and jam or sugar brings forth the truest flavor of the fruit. Raspberries, strawberries, blackberries, and the like lend themselves well to this kind of summer sherbet. The raspberry sherbet filled with fresh blackberries here is served with both raspberry and blackberry sauce. The reverse could be made, i.e., a blackberry sherbet filled with the raspberries.

Raspberry and blackberry preserves are used to sweeten the mixture and intensify the fruit taste of the sherbet and the sauce. Buy seedless jam or preserves, if available, eliminating the need to strain and remove the little seeds that make a sherbet unpleasant to eat.

The sherbet can be made in a conventional ice cream maker following the manufacturer's instructions or, as I have done here, by freezing the purée, then emulsifying it in the food processor and freezing it again. This process can be repeated several times to produce a creamier and whiter mixture. If emulsified too much, however, the berry flavor will tend to be less intense. Notice that the sherbet is stuffed with fresh berries only just before serving so the berries inside are not frozen when the dessert is served.

The way the sauces are arranged on the plates is striking and you could use the same technique with different colored sauces, such as vanilla and chocolate, to create the same effect.

Yield: 8 servings

RASPBERRY SAUCE

Yield: 4½–5 c.
2 lb. fresh or unsweetened frozen raspberries
1¾ c. raspberry jam or preserves, preferably seedless

RASPBERRY SHERBET

3 c. raspberry sauce (from above)
2 Tb. corn syrup
1¼ c. cold water

TO FINISH THE DISH

1½ c. blackberry sauce (see Blackberry Clafoutis, page 194)
1½ c. raspberry sauce (from above)
1 lb. fresh blackberries or loganberries

1 **For the raspberry sauce:** Push the 2 Tb. fresh or frozen (thawed) unsweetened raspberries with the 1¾ c. raspberry jam through a food mill fitted with a fine screen and then through a sieve to remove any remaining seeds, following the technique explained in Blackberry Clafoutis, page 194, steps 6–8. You should have about 4½ to 5 c. Set aside 1½ c. of the sauce for finishing the dish.

For the raspberry sherbet: Combine the remaining 3 c. of raspberry sauce with the 2 Tb. corn syrup and 1¼ c. water. Place in a stainless steel bowl and freeze for 3 to 4 hours. When frozen but not too hard, break or mash the mixture into pieces, place in the food processor and emulsify in several batches or all together, depending on the size of your food processor, until the sherbet becomes creamy and lighter in color. It should not be processed more than about 1 minute. By then, it will have liquefied a little. Place back in the stainless steel bowl and then in the freezer again. A few hours later, repeat this procedure to make the mixture a little creamier, then put back in the freezer for a few hours or overnight.

To make the sherbet receptacles, line 1-c. Pyrex (or other) bowls with plastic wrap and place a sizable scoop of sherbet inside each. With a spoon, press on the center of the scoop to hollow it out and push the sherbet up around the sides of the bowl.

2 Fold the plastic wrap inside the sherbet receptacles and place in the freezer for a few hours until hard. (This can be done several days ahead.)

3 If you prefer to serve the raspberry sherbet simply with the sauce, shape it into balls ahead of time. Wrap in plastic wrap and put back in the freezer. It will be quick and easy to serve this way at the last moment.

4 At serving time, place approximately 1 to 2 Tb. of the blackberry sauce in the center of eight very flat serving plates. Using the bowl of a small spoon, push some sauce to the sides of the plates to create a design.

5 Gently pour teaspoons of the raspberry sauce in the spaces left between the blackberry sauce projections to create a design of alternating colored sauces. The sauces will not run into one another for at least 30 minutes if you do this carefully.

6 Remove the frozen sherbet receptacles from the freezer and pull back the plastic wrap to expose the center. Fill with 6 to 8 blackberries, invert, and remove the plastic wrap.

7 Place the inverted sherbet cups carefully in the center of the plates containing the two sauces and decorate the top of each with a blackberry. Serve immediately. The opened dessert shows the blackberries stuffed inside.

GRAPEFRUIT GRANITE

A granité is a mixture of coarsely frozen fruits and fruit juice that is served in the middle of an elaborate meal to clear the palate. It is not as sweet or smooth as a sherbet and is not made in a standard ice cream maker or emulsified in a food processor. It is simply frozen and the granulated pieces are served like fruit ice. At serving time, a splash of brandy or other alcohol is usually poured on top. Granité should be slightly acidic to do its job of cleaning the palate and inciting the diner to eat more.

If left in a slushy form, grapefruit granité makes an excellent summer drink served with tequila, gin, or vodka. The addition of a little grenadine syrup gives it a beautiful color and a nice taste.

Yield: 6–8 servings

4 large grapefruit (preferably thin-
    skinned, juicy, and pink-fleshed),
    about 1 lb.
1 Tb. grenadine syrup
¼ c. honey
¼ c. sugar

GARNISHES

3 or 4 Tb. vodka or gin
Fresh mint sprigs

1 Clean the surface of the grapefruits with warm water and dry thoroughly. Using a vegetable peeler, peel about 8 to 10 strips from the skin of one of the grapefruits, then cut it up coarse. Place the pieces of skin in a mini-chop and process to make about 1 Tb. of grated rind. Set aside. (A conventional grater can also be used, in which case do not remove the peel and be sure to grate only the surface, where most of the taste and essential oils are located.)

2 Cut the grapefruit in half and use a juicer to extract as much juice as possible.

3 Scoop up about ⅓ c. grapefruit pulp, avoiding the seeds and membrane, and add to the juice. The yield of juice and pulp should be about 4½ c.

4 Add the chopped or grated rind, 1 Tb. grenadine syrup, ¼ c. each honey and sugar to the juice and pulp, and mix well. Any seeds or membrane still remaining in the mixture will tend to float to the surface and should be spooned out at this point.

Put the mixture in the freezer and freeze until slushy, then stir it gently. Place back in the freezer and stir occasionally so it freezes evenly throughout.

5 Store the granité in the freezer to make sure that it remains firm. If made several days ahead, remove the granité from the freezer and refrigerate for 15 to 20 minutes before serving to soften it a little. Using a spoon or an ice cream scoop, form the granité into balls and place them in individual serving dishes. Garnish each with a spoonful of vodka or gin and a sprig of mint, and serve immediately.

CABERNET SAUVIGNON PLUMS WITH WINE PLUM SHERBET AND CINNAMON LEMON CAKE

In this recipe, the plums are poached in a spicy wine mixture. The strong syrup of the poaching liquid is reduced further to concentrate the taste. The plums can be served by themselves in the syrup without removing their skins, although peeling them makes for a more attractive presentation.

In the recipe that follows, the plum cooking juices, with the addition of extra wine and water, are made into a sherbet. This sherbet is somewhat granular, what is called in French granités, *which is a water-fruit frozen ice with a strong flavor of the fruit and the wine.*

The cinnamon lemon cake is a dense pound cake, ideal to serve with the plums because it absorbs their juice well. It could also be served with the Stew of Red Summer Fruits, page 298, or other fruit desserts.

After the plums have been poached, they will keep in their juice in a tightly closed container in the refrigerator for several days.

Yield: 8–10 servings

FOR POACHING THE PLUMS

10 large Blackfriar plums (about 3 lb.)
3 c. (1 bottle) red cabernet sauvignon wine
1 c. sugar
1/16 tsp. cayenne pepper
1/2 tsp. cinnamon
1/16 tsp. powdered cloves

Lemon rind (for plum "leaves")

SHERBET

2 c. plum juice (from above)
1 c. red cabernet sauvignon wine
1/4 c. red plum preserves
1 1/2 c. ice cold water

CINNAMON LEMON CAKE

2 sticks unsalted butter, at room temperature (8 oz.)
2 c. sugar
3 Tb. grated lemon rind
1 Tb. lemon juice
1/2 tsp. cinnamon
5 eggs
3/4 c. milk
3 c. cake flour (about 13 oz.)
1 Tb. baking powder
1 Tb. butter
1/2 c. sliced almonds to coat the cake pan

1 To poach the plums: Combine the 3 lb. of plums, 3 c. wine, 1 c. sugar, 1/16 tsp. cayenne, 1/2 tsp. cinnamon, and 1/16 tsp. cloves in a saucepan (preferably stainless steel) so the plums fit snugly in one layer, and bring to a boil. Cover and boil gently until the plums are just tender (not mushy); it may take from 8 to 15 minutes, depending on the ripeness of the fruit. Let the plums cool, covered, in the cooking liquid for at least 1 to 2 hours, until lukewarm.

2 Lift the plums out of the juice and place them in a gratin dish. At this point, the skin can be removed. There should be approximately 4 c. of plum juice. Set aside 2 c. of the juice for the sherbet. Bring the other 2 c. of juice to a boil and reduce it to 1 c.

3 Pour the reduced juice over the plums. Cover with plastic wrap and refrigerate until serving time.

4 For the sherbet: Combine the 2 c. of reserved plum juice with the 1 c. of cabernet sauvignon wine and the 1/4 c. red plum preserves, and bring the mixture to a boil. Boil for approximately 1 minute. (If not boiled, there will be too much alcohol in the wine and the mixture will not freeze well.) Add the 1 1/2 c. ice cold water to the mixture and cool. Place in an ice cream freezer and freeze according to the manufacturer's instructions or prepare it according to the recipe for Raspberry Sherbet, pages 282–3, steps 1–2.

5 When the sherbet is hard and set, scoop it into balls (in preparation for a large party) ahead of time, arrange the balls on a paper-lined tray, cover with plastic wrap, and place them back in the freezer so they are ready to serve.

6 Make the cake: Combine the 2 sticks butter, 2 c. sugar, 3 Tb. lemon rind, 1 Tb. lemon juice, and 1/2 tsp. cinnamon in a large bowl. Whisk until smooth and creamy (about 1 minute). Add the 5 eggs and mix well. Add the 3/4 c. milk and the 3 c. cake flour sifted with 1 Tb. baking powder, and mix until smooth. Do not over-mix.

Butter generously a 9-in. springform pan that is 2 1/2 in. deep, and press the 1/2 c. almonds around the bottom and sides, coating the inside of the pan. Pour the batter into the cake pan, place the pan on a cookie sheet, and bake in a preheated 350-degree oven for 1 1/2 hours, until well-browned and completely set inside. Let cool for 20 minutes before unmolding. Present it upside down so the almonds show.

7 When the cake has cooled, cut it in half and then into long slices. Cut the slices in half.

8 With a vegetable peeler, peel strips of lemon rind and make leaves for the plums. With a knife, cut oval shapes from the strips to simulate leaves (see page 304, step 15, for illustration). Arrange approximately 2 Tb. of the sauce from the plums on each serving plate. Place a ball of sherbet and a plum on each of the plates and stand a slice of cake on end between them. Make an incision in the top of each of the plums and insert a leaf. In our picture, the plum is cut to show the inside. This dessert should be served immediately with a spoon or a knife and fork.

CARAMELIZED APPLE LOAF

This is a delicious autumn or winter dessert and it can be made several days ahead. The caramelized apple loaf is molded in a narrow loaf mold until set, but it could also be made in individual molds. Only part of the skin is removed from the apples. The skin left on gives some chewiness and texture to the mixture.

A portion of the caramelized apples is strained, combined with cream, sour cream, milk, and Calvados. Some of that mixture is used as a sauce with the cake and some of it is frozen into an apple ice cream. The apple loaf, ice cream, and sauce are served together.

The same idea could be applied to pears or other fruits. The stems of the apples, sprinkled with lemon juice to prevent discoloration, are used as a decoration.

The cake should be made one day ahead so it has time to set in the refrigerator, which makes it easier to unmold.

Yield: 8 servings

5 lb. Golden Delicious apples (about 12)
1 Tb. lemon juice to sprinkle on apple stems
1 stick butter (¼ lb.)
Grated rind and juice of 1 lime (about 1 tsp. rind and ⅓ c. juice)
½ c. sugar

APPLE CREAM SAUCE AND APPLE ICE CREAM

Apple purée (one-third of the cooked apple mixture)
1 c. heavy cream
1 c. sour cream
1½ c. milk
¼ c. sugar
2 Tb. Calvados or applejack, for the sauce only

DECORATIONS

6 lime rind peelings for leaves
1 to 2 tsp. grated lime rind, for sprinkling on sauce
Apple stems (reserved from apples above)

1 With the point of a small paring knife, remove the stems from the 5 lb. of apples in one piece, using your thumb as a pivot. Sprinkle the stems with the 1 Tb. of lemon juice, rolling them in the juice and setting them aside.

2 With a vegetable peeler, remove one wide strip of peel from around the middle of each of the 12 apples. Using a knife, remove the base of the core with the same pivot motion used in step 1.

3 Cut the partially peeled apples in half and, again, using the same pivot motion, remove the cores and seeds from the apple centers. Cut each apple half into thirds.

4 Melt the stick of butter in two saucepans (both preferably nonstick). When the butter is hot, add the apples, half to each saucepan, and sprinkle with the grated rind and juice of a lime and the ½ c. sugar. Cover and cook over medium to high heat for 20 to 30 minutes, until the apples are soft and caramelized and there is basically no liquid left in the saucepans. Push about one-third of the mixture through a food mill fitted with the fine screen. Add any pieces of apple and skin that haven't gone through the food mill to the other apples.

5 Line a narrow (preferably porcelain or enamel) loaf pan (ours was a 6-c. pâté mold) with a strip of parchment paper to make unmolding easy later.

6 Pack the remaining cooked apples in the mold, pressing them well with a spoon so they are tight. Cover with plastic wrap, pressing the wrap lightly on the surface of the apples, and refrigerate to cool for a few hours or even several days.

For the apple cream sauce and ice cream: Meanwhile, put the puréed apples in the bowl of a food processor, add the 1 c. each heavy cream and sour cream, 1½ c. milk, and ¼ c. sugar, and process until puréed. You should have about 4½ to 5 c. Set 2 c. of this mixture aside for the sauce and add the 2 Tb. Calvados to it.

Place the remaining 2½ to 3 c. of the mixture in an ice cream freezer and make ice cream according to the manufacturer's instructions. When the ice cream is firm, place it in the freezer until hard, and then, using an ice cream scoop, make 8 ice cream balls. Place the balls on a tray, cover with plastic wrap, and freeze.

7 At serving time, unmold the apple loaf onto a serving platter and remove the paper. Make a small hole in the top of each ice cream ball and embed an apple stem in the hole to simulate an apple.

8 Pour some of the apple cream sauce around the cake. Place the ice cream apples on top of the sauce, decorating them and the cake with lime peelings cut to resemble leaves. Sprinkle 1 to 2 tsp. grated lime rind on the sauce for color as well as taste, and serve immediately, bringing the whole platter to the table or preparing individual plates for serving.

POACHED APRICOTS WITH SOUR CREAM RIBBON

Large, firm, ripe apricots are best for this recipe and they are usually available in the market only in full summer. The apricots can be served with the Cinnamon Lemon Cake (page 286), brioche (page 136), as well as your favorite cookie. They could also be served without the raspberry sauce, with only the reduced syrup.

Ripe apricots will cook very fast — in 1 to 2 minutes — and should be allowed to cool in the cooking syrup. The skin will not slip off the apricots after cooking and they are served with it on. Apricots can be poached several days ahead and kept, refrigerated, in their own syrup in a sealed container.

Yield: 8 servings

POACHING THE FRUIT

8 large, firm, ripe apricots (about 1½ lb.)
Skin of 1 lemon
½ c. sugar
2 c. water

FINISHING THE DISH

1 c. raspberry sauce (see Raspberry Sherbet, page 282)
1 c. sour cream, diluted with 2 Tb. water and mixed with 1 Tb. sugar
Lime rind, cut into leaves (see Custard Wheat Cake with Peaches, page 304, step 15)

1 Place the apricots in a saucepan (preferably stainless steel) so they fit snugly in one layer. Using a vegetable peeler, remove the skin of the lemon and add it to the fruit along with the ½ c. sugar and 2 c. water. Cover, bring to a boil, and cook gently for 1 or 2 minutes, until the fruit feels tender when pierced with the point of a knife. Set the apricots aside in the cooking liquid until lukewarm.

Remove the fruit from the liquid and boil the liquid down to reduce it to ½ c. Pour the reduced liquid over the fruit. At this point, the apricots can be stored, covered, in the refrigerator, for several days.

→

2 At serving time, spoon enough raspberry sauce onto a serving platter to cover the bottom of the platter. Place the sour cream mixture in a pastry bag fitted with a tip with the smallest possible opening (no bigger than the lead of a pencil) or into a paper cornet (see "Swimming Swans," page 234, steps 2–6), and cut the tip off it. Pipe a swirled design around the edge of the plate to create a decorative border. Remove the apricots from their liquid and arrange them in the center of the plate. Drizzle a little raspberry sauce on top of the apricots and decorate with lime leaves. (See Custard Wheat Cake with Peaches, page 304, for instructions on making and attaching leaves.) Serve with additional raspberry sauce on the side and pound cake, brioche, or cookies.

POACHED PEARS IN CITRUS JUICE LAUREN WITH HOME CAKE

The time of cooking and amount of sugar used to poach fruit are dependent on the ripeness of the fruit as well as the type of fruit used. The Bosc is a long-cooking pear, which in my recipe is cooked in 30 minutes, although it sometimes takes longer for the pears to get tender. If using a Comice, Bartlett, or William, the time of cooking will have to be shortened so the pear doesn't cook into a mush.

Cook the pears in a pot (preferably stainless steel) that will accommodate them snugly — the cooking liquid should cover them completely. Pears will tend to oxidize and change color after peeling, so they are immediately placed in the cooking liquid with the juice of citrus fruit to prevent discoloration and to flavor the fruit.

At the beginning of cooking, the pears, being light, will float to the top of the cooking liquid, and the part of the pear that is out of the liquid will oxidize and turn black. To prevent this, place a piece of folded paper towel on top of the pears with an inverted plate that will fit inside the pot on top of the towel to weight down the pears and keep them completely immersed. Cook the pears covered. During cooking, the pears absorb the syrup and become heavier and, therefore, sink into the syrup as they cool.

They will not discolor beyond this point.

This dessert can be made several days ahead and kept refrigerated and covered so the pears do not absorb the flavors of other foods.

The home cake, shown in steps 6 and 7, can be cooked in a coffee can, or in a standard loaf pan. This traditional pound cake can be served with most ice creams or poached fruit desserts.

Yield: 6 servings

FOR THE PEARS

1 large lemon
1 large lime
½ c. sugar
5 c. water
2½ lb. Bosc pears (about 6)
2 Tb. pear brandy

HOME CAKE

1½ c. all-purpose flour (½ lb.)
1½ tsp. baking powder
½ c. sugar
2 eggs
⅓ c. milk
1 stick butter, melted (½ c.)
1 tsp. vanilla

GARNISH

6 mint sprigs

1 For the pears: Peel the lemon and lime with a vegetable peeler (you should have about 8 or 9 strips from each), and put the strips in a saucepan. Squeeze the lemon and lime to extract the juice (you should have approximately ½ c. of the combined juices), and add that to the saucepan with the ½ c. of sugar and 5 c. of water.

2 Peel the pears. The round base should be peeled in a circular motion, going around the entire base, and following the shape of the fruit.

3 The upper part or neck of the pear is peeled vertically, following the long, narrow shape of the neck.

4 To make a decorative "cap" for the pears: Peel each pear from the stem down with a vegetable peeler, leaving some of the skin at the top. Peel strips of the skin to create a scalloped design in the remaining skin.

5 With a melon baller or a small measuring spoon, scoop all the seeds from the fruit. Hollowing out the inside will shorten the time of cooking and make the pear easier to eat.

6 Place the pears in the syrup. Arrange a piece of folded paper towel on top so it covers the whole surface and position an inverted plate so that it fits on top to hold the pears under the surface of the liquid. Bring to a boil, cover with a lid, and simmer gently for about 30 minutes, or until tender when pierced with the point of a knife. Cool, covered, in the liquid.

7 To make the home cake: Mix together the 1½ c. flour, 1½ tsp. baking powder, and ½ c. sugar in a bowl. Add the 2 eggs, ⅓ c. milk, ½ c. melted butter, and 1 tsp. vanilla. Stir with a whisk until completely smooth. Pour the batter into a clean, buttered 1-lb. coffee can. It should fill the can about halfway.

8 Put the can on a cookie sheet and bake in a preheated 350-degree oven for about 50 minutes, until well-set in the center. (If baking the cake in a loaf pan, where the batter is spread out more, it will cook in about 35 minutes.) Let cool, then unmold. At this point, the cake can be wrapped in plastic wrap and stored at room temperature or frozen for future use.
→

9 When the pears are cold, transfer them to a plate and return the cooking liquid to the stove with the peels of lemon and lime. Bring to a boil and boil to reduce to 1 c. Let cool and add the 2 Tb. pear brandy. Arrange the pears in a serving dish that is fairly deep. Pour the reduced juices over the pears.

10 Arrange some of the slices of lime and lemon peel (they will be slightly candied) attractively on and around the pears and decorate with sprigs of fresh mint to simulate pear leaves. Cut the cake into ½-in. slices and serve with the pears.

POACHED WHITE PEACHES WITH ALMOND LEAVES AND CHOCOLATE OATMEAL COOKIES

Unfortunately, white peaches are not always available in all parts of the country. They are very delicate, with a velvety skin and a pale white juicy flesh. There are several species of white peaches, freestone as well as clingstone. They bruise easily and can spoil faster than yellow peaches but have an intense flavor and juiciness and are at their best when ripe from the tree. In order for the peaches to peel easily, they should be ripe and at room temperature when poached. The riper they are, the more easily the skin will come off.

The time of cooking and the amount of sugar added to the cooking liquid will depend on the ripeness of the fruit. The skin, left on the fruit during cooking, will tend to transfer its color to the flesh. When the color of the skin is red-purple, it turns the whole peach a luscious pastel color. After the peaches have been poached and cooled in the syrup, they can be peeled and stored with their syrup in the refrigerator for at least a week.

Almond paste, available in most markets, can be shaped into small animals or flowers and used for decoration. Here it is fashioned into leaves to make the dessert a bit more sophisticated.

The oatmeal cookies, which can be coated with chocolate or left plain, are always welcome and can be served with any type of poached fruit or other desserts. They will remain crisp if they are stored in an airtight container.

Yield: 8–10 servings

FOR POACHING THE PEACHES

1½ c. granulated sugar
5 c. water
Rind of 1 lemon
Juice of 1 lemon (about 2 to 3 Tb.)
10 white peaches (about 3½ to 4 lb.)

CHOCOLATE OATMEAL COOKIES

Yield: about 18
1 stick butter
¼ c. granulated sugar
1 tsp. baking powder
⅔ c. flour
1 c. oatmeal (not quick-cooking)
⅓ c. dried currants (tiny raisins)
4 oz. bittersweet or semi-sweet chocolate (see page 132)

FOR ALMOND PASTE LEAVES

½ lb. almond paste
Confectioners' sugar (to stiffen paste, if
    needed)
Egg white (to soften paste, if needed)
Green food coloring

1 For poaching the peaches: Combine
the 1½ c. granulated sugar, 5 c. water,
and the rind and juice of 1 lemon in a
saucepan, and bring to a boil. Add the
peaches to the boiling syrup.

2 Cover and boil gently for 5 to 12 minutes, depending on the ripeness of the
peaches, until the fruit is tender; it should
resist only slightly when pricked – do not
over-cook.

3 Let the peaches cool in the syrup until
they reach room temperature, then peel.
The skin should slide off easily and will
have transferred its color onto the flesh of
the peach. Reduce the peach juice to 1 c.
of heavy syrup by boiling it down. Then
arrange the peaches in a gratin dish and
strain the syrup over them. Cover tightly
with plastic wrap and refrigerate.

4 For the chocolate oatmeal cookies:
Put the 1 stick butter, ¼ c. sugar, 1 tsp.
baking powder, and ⅔ c. flour in a food
processor and process for 5 to 10 seconds,
until the mixture forms a ball. Place on a
chopping board and add the 1 c. oatmeal
and ⅓ c. currants, mashing the mixture
together to combine.

5 Use a heavy aluminum cookie sheet. (It
is not necessary to oil or butter it.) With
your fingers, roll about 1 Tb. dough at a
time into logs and place them on the
cookie sheet 1 in. or so apart. Press down
slightly to flatten. Bake in a preheated
400-degree oven for 18 to 20 minutes,
until nicely browned.

6 Melt the 4 oz. bittersweet chocolate in
the top of double boiler until smooth and,
using a little spatula or knife, spread some
chocolate (approximately 1 tsp.) on the
underside of each cookie. Place the cookies, chocolate-side down, on a cookie sheet
lined with parchment or wax paper, and
press on them firmly so the chocolate
becomes very flat and smooth.

7 Refrigerate the cookies for a while, or
place them in the freezer for a few minutes
so the chocolate hardens. Peel the paper
from the cookies – it will come off easily.

8 Another alternative is to coat the flat
side of one cookie with chocolate, and then
press it against the flat side of another
cookie to create a sandwich.
  When the cookies are prepared, place
them in an airtight container so they don't
get soggy. →

9 **For the almond paste leaves:** Place the ½ lb. almond paste on a board. If it tends to be a bit soft, add a few spoonfuls of confectioners' sugar and knead to tighten the paste. If, on the other hand, it is too stiff, soften it with ½ tsp. of egg white, kneading until malleable. Add a few drops of green food coloring to the paste and mix thoroughly to color it evenly.

12 At serving time, arrange the peaches in an attractive, preferably glass, serving dish (I have used a shallow glass bowl) and spoon some syrup on top. Pierce the center of each peach on top with a knife, and stick the stems and almond leaves in the incisions. Serve the peaches with the oatmeal cookies.

10 Sprinkle confectioners' sugar on a board and roll out the almond paste to a thickness of approximately ⅛ in. With a knife, cut long, narrow ovals to simulate the leaves of peaches.

11 With a knife, mark the "veins" of the leaves on each side and place them, slightly twisted, on a plate so they dry in that position.

Roll out little strings of almond paste and cut them to resemble stems. If possible, let the almond paste leaves and stems dry for a couple of hours at room temperature to harden and hold their shape.

RED FRUIT–SOAKED CAKE

The combination of sweet, acidic berries, a dense sponge cake, fruit brandy, and good jam makes this dessert a great summer treat. It is best prepared 2 or 3 days ahead so the fruit purée has a chance to soak the cake well. A pound cake or sponge cake can be used as well as a variety of different red berries (cherries, blackberries, raspberries, strawberries, red currants, boysenberries, and so on), depending on availability. In the winter, berries that are frozen, preferably without sugar, can be substituted.

The sponge cake can be served, if need be, a few hours after assembly, but it will keep for 5 or 6 days in the refrigerator. It is also good filled with buttercream or pastry cream. It may be used as a standard cake, and it freezes quite well.

Yield: 10–12 servings

SPONGE CAKE

2 c. flour (about 10 oz.)
1¼ c. sugar
2 tsp. baking powder
6 eggs, separated
½ c. safflower or corn oil
¾ c. milk
2 tsp. vanilla

RED FRUIT PUREE

1½ c. blackberries
1½ c. strawberries
1 c. red currants, stemmed
½ lb. sweet cherries
1½ c. raspberries
8 oz. raspberry preserves
12 oz. black raspberry or blackberry jam
⅓ c. fruit brandy (such as framboise or Kirschwasser) or cognac

CUSTARD SAUCE WITH GELATIN

2 egg yolks
¼ c. sugar mixed with 1 tsp. gelatin
1 tsp. vanilla
1 c. milk
1 c. heavy cream

GARNISH

Mint sprigs

1 To prepare the cake, combine the 2 c. flour, 1¼ c. sugar, and 2 tsp. baking powder in a bowl. Meanwhile, beat the 6 egg whites until stiff. Add the 6 egg yolks, ½ c. oil, ¾ c. milk, and 2 tsp. vanilla to the dry ingredients in the bowl. Mix with a spatula until smooth.

2 With a spatula, combine the egg whites with the batter.

3 Butter and flour a round cake pan approximately 9 in. in diameter and 3 in. deep. Pour the batter into the prepared pan. Place on a cookie sheet and bake in a preheated 325-degree oven for about 70 minutes. →

4 The cake is baked and all puffed up. Let it cool in the pan 30 minutes at room temperature. It will shrink slightly from the edge of the pan and can then be unmolded.

5 A summer assortment of red berries, from left to right: strawberries and cherries in front and raspberries, red currants, and blackberries in the back.

6 To pit the cherries, insert the point of a small knife at the hole of the stem and, at the same time, squeeze the cherry with the fingers to loosen the pit. Lift out the pit with the point of the knife.

7 Put the berries, currants, and pitted cherries in a food processor, and process until puréed. Add the raspberry preserves and jam, and process a few seconds until smooth. Push the mixture through a food mill to remove most of the seeds. You should have 4–5 c. of fruit purée.

8 Trim the brown crust from the top, bottom, and sides of the cake, and process the trimmings in a food processor to make crumbs. (This will be used in the center of the cake.)

9 Use a 3-qt. rounded mold for the cake. To aid in the unmolding, cut 2 strips of parchment paper, butter them on one side, and place in a crisscross pattern buttered-side down in the mold, so they stick to it. The projecting ends of these strips can be pulled to remove the cake from the inverted mold. Cut the cake into ⅜- to ½-in. slices, and place the first slice in the bottom of the mold, pressing to make it conform well to the mold. It will fold and probably break on each side. Cut the pieces at the breaks. Do not worry if the cracks show; by the time the cake is soaked with the fruit, they will not be visible.

10 Cut other pieces of cake to fit, so the entire inside of the bowl is lined.

11 The sides and bottom of the bowl are now lined with the cake.

12 Sprinkle 1 Tb. of brandy on the cake. Add about 1 c. of the fruit purée and the cake trimmings.

13 Add 1 c. of the crumbs and more cake trimmings, crumbs, and fruit purée with sprinklings of the fruit brandy in between, until the inside of the cake is full. Approximately half of the fruit purée (about 2 to 2½ c.) will be used inside the cake and the other half will be served with the cake.

14 Cut the last slice of cake to make a lid so it fits the inside, pressing it in place. Sprinkle again with fruit brandy and cover tightly with plastic wrap. Place in the refrigerator for 24 hours. It will take at least 24 hours for the fruit purée to soak through the cake.

15 To make the custard sauce: Put the 2 egg yolks in a bowl, add the mixture of ¼ c. sugar and 1 tsp. gelatin and the 1 tsp. vanilla. Mix well with a whisk for approximately 1 minute, until the mixture lightens in color and gets fluffy.

Meanwhile, bring the 1 c. milk to a boil. When it boils, add it to the egg yolk mixture. Put the custard back in the saucepan and return it to the stove over medium heat. Cook, stirring gently, for about 1 minute, until the custard thickens. It should reach approximately 180 degrees, at which time the egg yolks will thicken. If over-cooked, the egg yolks may scramble.

Strain the custard immediately through a very fine strainer into a cold bowl. (The strainer will pick up any scrambling that may have occurred.) Place in the refrigerator and stir occasionally until it begins to set.

16 Beat the cup of cream until firm and fold into the custard, which should be between tepid and body temperature but not yet set. If allowed to set too much, the cream will not incorporate properly. On the other hand, if the whipped cream is added while the custard is still hot, it will liquefy. Cover the custard sauce with plastic wrap and refrigerate for at least a few hours.

17 Strain the remaining red sauce through a fine strainer. (There will still be little pieces of seeds that have gone through the food mill. As a serving sauce, it is smoother and more attractive when pushed through a fine strainer.) Add the remaining brandy (about 2 Tb.) to the sauce.

Unmold the cake onto a serving dish with sides high enough to contain the sauces. Arrange some of the white custard sauce around the cake and pour some of the fruit sauce over the cake.

18 The red sauce will run down and begin to mix with the white sauce. With the point of a knife, draw the red sauce into the white sauce, and vice versa, to create a design.

19 Decorate the top of the cake with a few sprigs of mint and serve in slices with extra custard and red fruit sauce.

STEW OF RED SUMMER FRUITS

This tasty hodgepodge of stewed red summer fruits can also be done in winter with fruits such as bananas, apples, and oranges. After the fruits are cooked and the juices reduced, the mixture will keep in the refrigerator for several days; in fact, the dish improves after one day, as the juices will thicken slightly and the flavor of the fruit becomes more intense.

The addition of basil lends a delightful fragrance and a slightly licorice taste to the stew. It is excellent served with a brioche (page 136) or the Cinnamon Lemon Cake (page 286). It could also be served with ice cream or crème fraîche.

The ripe fruits are cooked very briefly so they keep their shape. However, the amount of cooking time may have to be changed slightly, depending on the ripeness of the fruits – perhaps increased by ½ minute or so for firmer, less ripe fruits.

Yield: 8–10 servings

STEWED FRUIT MIXTURE

1 Tb. grated orange rind
⅓ c. fresh orange juice
1 c. dry white wine
1 c. cream or syrup of cassis
¼ c. strawberry jam

1 lb. firm, red Santa Rosa plums (about 10)
1 lb. Bing cherries, washed
1 large sprig fresh basil (6 to 8 leaves)
1 lb. seedless Red Flame grapes, washed
1 lb. blueberries, washed
1 lb. strawberries, washed, hulled, and cut into wedges

SAUCE AND GARNISH

1 pt. sour cream
2 Tb. sugar
4 Tb. water
1 brioche (see page 136), optional

DECORATION

Mint leaves with flowers, if available

1 Place the 1 Tb. of orange rind and ⅓ c. orange juice, 1 c. white wine, 1 c. cream of cassis, and ¼ c. strawberry jam in a saucepan, and bring to a boil. Boil for about 1 minute. Wash the pound of plums, cut them into wedges, and remove the pits.

2 Add the plums along with the pound of cherries to the boiling liquid.

3 Add a sprig of basil to the pot. Place the mixture back on the stove, bring to a strong boil, and boil for about 1 minute.

4 With a slotted spoon or a skimmer, remove the fruit from the boiling liquid and place it in a bowl. Put the basil back in the cooking liquid with the pound of grapes. Return to the boil and cook 30 seconds.

5 Transfer the grapes from the poaching liquid to the fruit in the bowl and place the pound of blueberries and pound of strawberries in the saucepan with the basil. Return the mixture barely to the boil, remove the fruit, and add it to the fruit in the bowl. Drain as much juice from around the fruit as you can and add it to the saucepan.

6 You should have approximately 3 c. of juice. Boil it down to reduce it to 2 c. and pour the reduction on top of the fruit (with the basil) and cool. When cool, remove and discard the basil.

7 For the sauce: At serving time, combine the 1 pt. sour cream and 2 Tb. sugar with 4 Tb. water, and mix until just slightly liquid. Place approximately 2 Tb. of the juices from the fruit on each plate. Swirl about 1 Tb. of the sour cream in a design in the juice, using a spoon or the point of a knife.

8 Spoon the fruit into the center of the plate, arranging it attractively. Decorate with the mint flowers and leaves, and serve, if you wish, with a lukewarm wedge of brioche. Serve immediately.

FRUIT SALAD AMBROSIA IN MELON SWAN

This flavorful fruit salad is made with fresh as well as dried fruits that have been macerated in a sweet-sour sauce made of honey, lemon juice, rind of citrus fruit, and Kirschwasser. The acid in the lemon juice keeps the fruit from discoloring.

The sauce can be made ahead and the dried fruit prepared and combined with the sauce and kept in the refrigerator, ready to be added to the fresh fruit an hour or so before serving. The sauce and dried fruit mixture will keep several weeks in the refrigerator. Most of the fresh fruits will hold their shape and color in the sauce for a few hours, but delicate fruits, such as raspberries, tend to break down and should be added just before the salad is served.

The mixture of fruit used should be changed according to what's available in the market and your own personal taste. Look for different flavors in the fruit as well as different textures and colors. Remember, too, that even though pineapples, apples, pears, and bananas may look different before they are peeled, their flesh is basically the same color.

The salad, which can also be served in individual dishes, is good with Cinnamon Lemon Cake (page 286) or with another pound cake. For a special party, it can be presented in a melon carved into the shape of a swan, as done here.

Yield: 8–10 servings

FRUIT MACERATING SAUCE

3 strips lemon rind
3 strips lime rind
3 strips orange rind
⅓ c. honey
⅓ c. lemon juice
¼ c. apricot preserves
2 Tb. Kirschwasser

DRY FRUIT MIXTURE

¼ c. dark raisins
⅓ c. sliced (¼-in.) dried apricot halves
8 pitted prunes, cut into ½-in. slices
2 dried peach halves, cut into ½-in. strips

FRESH FRUIT MIXTURE

1 pineapple (to make 1½ c. pineapple pieces)
1½ c. sliced mixture of papaya and mango
1 banana, sliced
1 c. pitted cherries
1 c. seedless grapes
½ persimmon, peeled and cut into wedges
1 kiwi, cut into small wedges
1 large, ripe honeydew melon, for decorative receptacle
2 c. honeydew melon balls, from melon above
½ c. raspberries

1 For the fruit macerating sauce: Pile up 3 strips each of lemon, lime, and orange rind (peeled with a vegetable peeler) and cut into a fine julienne. You should have approximately 2 Tb. of the combined julienned rinds.

2 In a bowl, combine the rind with ⅓ c. each honey and lemon juice, ¼ c. apricot preserves, and 2 Tb. Kirschwasser. This makes a nice base for the fruit mixture.

3 Add the dried fruit mixture (¼ c. raisins, ⅓ c. apricot slices, 8 sliced pitted prunes, and 2 peach halves, cut into strips) to the macerating sauce. This mixture can be made ahead and stored in a jar in the refrigerator.

6 Add the 1½ c. sliced papaya and mango mixture, the sliced banana, the 1 c. each of pitted cherries and seedless grapes, the wedges of persimmon and kiwi, and mix well.

9 Cut on each side of the neck, then, going around the back of the melon on both sides, create the tips of the wings.

4 **For the fresh fruit:** Cut the pineapple into halves and then wedges. Cut off the top of each wedge – the central woody core of the fruit – and then cut the flesh to separate it from the rind.

7 **To prepare the honeydew melon:** Using the point of a knife, draw an oval shape to outline the inside of the neck of the swan. Cut the inside curve of the neck.

10 Turn the melon around. Cut down from the tip of one wing around to the other side to create a roundish space between the wings.

5 With the pineapple wedges still on the rind, cut into little slices about ½ in. thick and add to the mixture in the bowl.

8 Cut around the outside, following the same shape to create the neck and head of the swan.

11 Pry out the top piece of the melon, leaving the cutout swan in one piece.
→

CAKES, SOUFFLES & DESSERTS

12 With a melon baller, remove 2 to 3 c. of melon balls from the inside of the swan and add them to the salad. With a large spoon, scoop out the remainder of the flesh in the swan to create a hollow receptacle, and cut away the flesh behind the neck and head to make it thinner, being careful not to cut away too much at the base of the neck so it holds its shape. The extra flesh can be reserved for another use.

13 At the end of each wing, cut thin wedges to create feathers.

14 Make a hole in the head for the eye and fill it with a piece of raisin or any dark-colored fruit to simulate an eye, then cut a little wedge for the mouth. Fold the ½ c. raspberries into the salad in the bowl, fill the swan with the fruit salad and juice, and serve.

CUSTARD WHEAT CAKE WITH PEACHES

This custard wheat cake is light and tender in texture and delicate in taste. It makes a stunning presentation when surrounded by poached fruit. The decorating technique of piping chocolate on top to make the outline of a design, then filling in the pattern with colored peach preserves, of course, can be used to decorate other cakes and desserts.

The recipe here uses Cream of Wheat, but you could use semolina, tapioca, or farina instead to make this very elegant dessert. Notice that only a small amount of the starch is used, which is enough to give the cake the proper texture. The custard can be made several days ahead. However, if you do make it ahead, use a Pyrex or nonmetallic mold; the cake would tend to discolor after a while if left to set in a metal savarin mold, as I have used. After the custard is made and has set, it can be placed upside down on a serving plate and stored this way until ready to unmold (actually it will make unmolding easier).

The poached pears can be served on their own with, perhaps, a slice of pound cake (see Cinnamon Lemon Cake, page 286) for a delightful dessert. Or serve as I have indicated for Poached White Peaches, page 292.

Yield: 10–12 servings

WHEAT CAKE

2 tsp. grated lime rind
3 egg yolks
½ c. granulated sugar
1 envelope gelatin (about ¾ Tb.)
1 tsp. vanilla
1½ c. milk
3 Tb. instant Cream of Wheat
1½ c. heavy cream

POACHING THE PEACHES

1½ c. granulated sugar
5 c. water
Rind and juice of 1 lemon (2 to 3 Tb.)
8 peaches (about 5 oz. each)

PEACH SAUCE

1½ c. peach jam or preserves, strained
2 Tb. cognac
Extra juices from the cooking of the peaches

DECORATION

3 Tb. peach preserves, strained
Red, green, and yellow food coloring
1 Tb. melted bittersweet or semi-sweet chocolate (see page 132)
Rind of 1 lime

WHIPPED CREAM GARNISH

1 c. heavy cream
1 Tb. confectioners' sugar
1 candied violet

1 In a bowl, mix together the 2 tsp. lime rind, 3 egg yolks, ½ c. granulated sugar, 1 envelope gelatin, and 1 tsp. vanilla with a whisk. Bring the 1½ c. milk to a boil in a saucepan, add the 3 Tb. Cream of Wheat, and return the mixture to the boil, stirring constantly until it thickens, about 2 to 3 minutes. Combine with the egg yolk mixture, whisking to incorporate.

2 Place back on the stove and bring to a boil, stirring. The mixture will thicken slightly. Put the batter in a bowl and let cool to room temperature. In the meantime, whip the 1½ c. heavy cream until it holds a soft peak.

3 When the Cream of Wheat mixture is about at room temperature or slightly tepid, fold in the cream.

Note: If the Cream of Wheat mixture is allowed to set too long, it will become hard, and folding in the cream will be difficult. If this should occur, reheat it to soften. On the other hand, if the whipped cream is added to the mixture while still boiling hot, the whipped cream will melt.

4 Lightly oil a savarin mold with safflower or corn oil. Pour the cake mixture into the mold, filling it, and smooth the top.

5 To cover the mold, make a ring out of parchment or wax paper: Fold a square piece of paper large enough to cover the mold into fourths.

6 From the point, which has no opening, fold the paper into a triangle.

7 Continue folding the paper onto itself in the same way, making narrower and narrower triangles.

8 Measure the radius of the mold starting from the center and cut off the folded paper at the place marked by the outer edge of the mold.

9 Holding the paper over the mold again, cut out the center by cutting through the paper at the inner edge of the mold (when opened you will have a paper ring). Cover the mold with the ring and refrigerate for a few hours or overnight, until set.

Meanwhile, **cook the peaches:** Combine the 1½ c. granulated sugar, 5 c. water, and the rind and juice of 1 lemon in a saucepan, and bring the mixture to a boil. Add the peaches, cover, return to the boil, lower the heat, and continue to cook, covered, over low heat for 6 to 10 minutes, depending on the ripeness of the peaches, until the peaches are tender.

10 Let the peaches cool until lukewarm in the syrup, then remove them and reduce the syrup to approximately 2 c. by boiling it down. Combine again with the peaches.

Note: The skin of the peaches can be removed now or later. If the skin is left on and the peaches are stored in the syrup, the skin color will tend to seep into the flesh of the peaches, giving them a nice color. If the skin of the peaches does not slide off easily, peel with a vegetable peeler to remove it.

11 **To make the peach sauce:** Combine the 1½ c. peach jam, 2 Tb. cognac, and a few tablespoons of reduced syrup from the peaches to make the mixture of spreading consistency. The remaining syrup can be reserved for poaching other fruits.

Remove the paper ring from the top of the mold, turn the mold over onto a serving platter, and unmold the cake. You may have to shake the mold or cover it with a towel dipped in warm water to get the cake to unmold.

12 Make 4 little cornets of parchment or wax paper (see "Swimming Swans," page 234, steps 2–6).

Place 1 Tb. of strained peach jam in each of three small containers. Add one or two drops of red color to one, green to a second, and yellow to the third.

Melt approximately 1 oz. of bittersweet chocolate over hot water and pour it into one of the cornets.

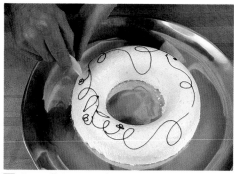

13 Cut off the tip of the cornet containing the melted chocolate and create a freehand design, drawing with the chocolate to make a long stem, ivy leaves, and flower outlines.

14 Spoon the three colored jams into each of the remaining cornets, and cut the tips from them. Gently press the jams into the chocolate outlines, filling in the leaves and flowers to create a stained-glass-window effect with the different colors.

15 Using a vegetable peeler, remove strips of rind from a lime. With a knife, cut oval shapes from the strips to simulate leaves.

16 At serving time, whip the cup of cream and 1 Tb. confectioners' sugar together until the cream is firm. Place in a pastry bag fitted with a star tip and decorate the center of the cake with the whipped cream. Place a candied violet on top. Arrange the peaches around the cake, and coat them with the peach sauce. Make little incisions on the tops of the peaches with a sharp knife, and insert the lime rind leaves. Serve immediately.

1 To make the dough: Break the 7 oz. (about 12) graham crackers and place them in a food processor with the ¾ stick butter, 1 tsp. cinnamon, 1 Tb. lemon juice, and 1 tsp. grated lemon rind. Process for a few seconds, until the dough comes together. Remove from the food processor and line the bottom of a 9-in. cake pan that is 3 in. deep.

2 Reserve approximately half the dough for the sides of the pan. Press a piece of plastic wrap on top of the remaining dough on the pan base and roll to spread it. It should be very thin, approximately ⅛ in. thick.

3 Trim the dough around the edge of the pan bottom with your fingers. Reassemble the pan and press the remainder of the dough up around the inside of the pan so it comes up about 1 to 2 in. This border of dough on the sides doesn't have to be exactly the same height all around; it can vary a little to lend an interesting design to the side of the cake. →

ROLAND CHEESECAKE WITH BLUEBERRY-CURRANT SAUCE

Cheesecake is a popular dessert at our house and is certainly the favorite of my brother, Roland. When he visits from France, we have a cheesecake ready to welcome him and to start his vacation in the proper mood.

Although the cheesecake should be made the day before serving so it has time to rest and set, it should not be served ice cold from the refrigerator. If done ahead and refrigerated, it should be brought back to room temperature for serving because it is moister and more flavorful this way.

If baked in a cake pan with a removable bottom, as done here, the cake can remain on the pan base and be placed as such on a serving platter. This prevents damage to the platter when the cake is cut. Although the cake is baked in a cracker crumb crust here, it can be made without any crust.

The sauce, made with strained apricot preserves, is flavored with cognac, but rum as well as whiskey could be used. The cake is very attractive and colorful with its garnish of currants and blueberries, but other summer berries could be used in the same way, depending on availability.

Yield: 12 servings

CHEESECAKE DOUGH

About 12 graham crackers (7 oz.)
¾ stick butter (3 oz.)
1 tsp. cinnamon
1 Tb. lemon juice
1 tsp. grated lemon rind

FILLING

1¾ lb. cream cheese, at room temperature
1 c. sugar
1 c. sour cream
2 Tb. lemon juice
1 Tb. grated lemon rind
2 tsp. vanilla
4 large eggs

SAUCE

2 c. apricot preserves
2 Tb. cognac
1 to 2 Tb. water (depending on viscosity of jam)
1 c. red currants
1 c. blueberries

4 For the filling: In a mixer bowl, put the 1¾ lb. cream cheese (at room temperature), 1 c. each sugar and sour cream, 2 Tb. lemon juice, and 1 Tb. lemon rind, and mix with the wire whisk at medium speed until smooth. Add the 2 tsp. vanilla and 2 of the eggs, and mix again until smooth. Increase the mixing speed to ensure that there are no lumps, and add the other 2 eggs. Keep mixing on medium speed until smooth. The mixture can also be combined in a food processor. Pour into the mold and place on a cookie sheet.

5 Bake in a preheated 325-degree oven for 1 hour. Turn the oven off and allow the cake to continue cooking in the remaining heat in the oven for 1 hour longer. The cake should be lightly browned on top. Let cool for a couple of hours before unmolding.

6 For the sauce: Strain the 2 c. apricot preserves and add the 2 Tb. cognac to the strained preserves. If need be, to make it of spreading consistency, add 1 to 2 Tb. water, depending on the viscosity of the preserves. Add the 1 c. each red currants and blueberries, and mix.

Pour some of the sauce mixture on top of the cake, just enough to coat the top.

7 At serving time, cut the cake into small wedges and serve with extra sauce and berries.

SUMMER CORNET SUSIE

This fruit-filled horn of plenty is made with a dough that doesn't have egg whites and, consequently, tends to stay crisper than standard cookie shells made with egg whites. Yet, if the dough is cooked and shaped into cornets, cookies (see Double-Decker Ambrosia, page 309), or cups (see Vanilla Ice Cream in Netty Cups with Spicy Cherries in Wine, page 280) a few days ahead of serving, be sure to seal the cookies in a plastic container so they don't get soggy.

The cornets can be brushed on the inside with chocolate, as done here, with melted jam, or they can be left plain. This summer fruit dessert can be transformed into a winter or fall dessert by using different seasonal fruits to fill the cornets. Pears, apples, bananas, oranges, pineapple, or other fruit can be used plain, as in this recipe, or rolled into jam and lemon juice and served with or without the whipped cream.

Yield: 12 cornets

CORNET DOUGH
¾ c. blanched almonds
2 Tb. flour
⅔ stick butter (about 2½ oz.)
1 Tb. milk
¾ c. granulated sugar

CORNET FILLING
4 oz. bittersweet or semi-sweet chocolate (see page 132), melted, or ¼ c. berry or fruit jam (optional)
1 c. heavy cream
2 Tb. granulated sugar
Confectioners' sugar for dusting (optional)

GARNISH
Mint leaves

SUMMER FRUITS ASSORTMENT
About 1 c. mixed fruits per cornet: wineberries, cherries, red currants, raspberries, loganberries, strawberries, and blueberries (see step 6)

1 Grind the ¾ c. almonds in the food processor with the 2 Tb. flour until very fine. (The flour will absorb any oil released by the almonds and will produce a finer mixture.) Add the ⅔ stick butter, cut into pieces, the 1 Tb. milk, and the ¾ c. granulated sugar. Process for 8 to 10 seconds, just long enough for the mixture to form into a ball.

Line a cookie sheet with a piece of parchment paper oiled very lightly on both sides and pressed flat on the cookie sheet. Cut the paper into fourths.

For the large cornets, place a good tablespoon of the dough on each of the four pieces of paper. Wet your fingers or a spoon and press the dough into disks about 2½ in. across, making them as round as possible.

2 Place in a preheated 350-degree oven and bake for approximately 12 minutes. The dough should spread and be nicely browned all around. Lift up each piece of paper, turn it over, and peel the paper from the cornet. Reserve the paper (it does not have to be oiled again) for the next cookies. →

3 The top of the cookie (side exposed during baking) will be the outside of the cornet, since it looks a little nicer than the underside. The cookies should be allowed to sit for 1 to 2 minutes after they are removed from the oven before rolling them up. (If rolled immediately, they will break apart.) If cooled too much, however, they will become brittle and can't be rolled. If this happens, return them to the oven and reheat them slightly until they become soft and pliable enough to roll. Roll each large cookie around a metal cornet or simply roll them free-form into a cornet shape without the metal insert, although the shape may not be as even as with the mold. As soon as the cornet is rolled, place a small ball of crushed aluminum foil inside to prevent the cornet from collapsing while it dries.

5 When the cornets are completely cold, brush inside with the 4 oz. melted chocolate or ¼ c. jam, or leave them plain.

8 For a different look, dust the surface of the fruit, cookie, and rim of the plate with confectioners' sugar just before serving.

6 Whip the 1 c. cream with the 2 Tb. granulated sugar until stiff. Place in a pastry bag with a star tip and partially fill the cornets with cream. Note the mixed fruits from left, foreground, and continuing counterclockwise: wineberries, cherries, red currants, raspberries, loganberries, strawberries, and blueberries.

4 To make single-portion cuplike receptacles that can accommodate whipped cream or ice cream as well as fruit, press the hot cookies (top side out) around half-cup molds (little Pyrex cups are ideal), pushing gently all around so they conform to the shape of the molds. Allow to harden before removing.

7 Arrange the cornets on individual serving plates. Add a little more cream to each cornet so it appears to be flowing out of the opening, and position a few decorative dots of cream around the plate. Then make an arrangement on the plate of all the summer fruit. Stick a few leaves of mint into the cream dots for color and serve immediately.

DOUBLE-DECKER AMBROSIA

This recipe is similar to Summer Cornet Susie, page 307, but uses only blackberries and raspberries. In addition to the whipped cream and the fruit, a sweet raspberry sauce is served with it and, because of that, there is less sugar in the whipped cream than there is in the recipe for Summer Cornet Susie. This beautiful presentation is easy to prepare but should be assembled at the last minute. The round cookies are made with the cornet dough, and if done ahead, they should be stored in an airtight container so they don't get soggy.

Yield: 8 servings (16 cookies)

1 cornet dough recipe (see Summer Cornet Susie, page 307)
2 c. raspberry sauce (see Raspberry Sherbet, page 282)
1 c. heavy cream
1 Tb. confectioners' sugar
About 1½ c. cleaned and hulled blackberries or loganberries
About 1½ c. cleaned and hulled raspberries
A few mint leaves for decoration
Confectioners' sugar for dusting

1 **To make the cookies:** Using 2 tsp. of the batter for each cookie, roll pieces of the batter into uniformly round balls, then press them down onto parchment paper. The rounder the ball, the rounder the cookie will be. If the cookies are not exactly round when they emerge from the oven, round them off with a knife or scissors while they are still hot.

2 Place about 2 to 3 Tb. of the raspberry sauce on each of eight dessert plates. Whip the cup of cream with the 1 Tb. confectioners' sugar until stiff, and spoon it into a pastry bag fitted with a star tip. Place a dot of the whipped cream in the center of the sauce on each plate and press a cookie into it. This will make the cookie sit above the sauce and hold it securely on the plate without sliding. Place 5 dots of whipped cream around the outside edge of each cookie.

3 Pipe whipped cream into the center and arrange the large blackberries and raspberries attractively around the periphery of the cookies on the plates. The dessert can be served this way, if desired.

For our double-decker presentation (above left), place a round cookie on top and press it lightly into the whipped cream to hold it in place. Pipe a dot of whipped cream on top in the center and decorate with a raspberry and a few mint leaves embedded in the whipped cream. Dust lightly with confectioners' sugar and serve right away.

1 **For the rich bread dough:** Combine the 1 envelope dry yeast with ¼ c. warm water and 1 tsp. sugar in the bowl of an electric mixer. Let proof for 5 minutes. Add the 1½ c. flour, 2 eggs, 2 Tb. butter, and ¼ tsp. salt, and beat with the flat beater for about 15 seconds on speed 1 (slow – see page 118, step 3), enough only to mix the dough slightly. Increase the speed to 4 (medium to fast), and mix for about 3 minutes. Cover the bowl with plastic wrap and let rise for 1 hour. With wet hands so it doesn't stick, spread dough on a jelly roll pan into a rectangle approximately 12 in. by 10 in. and ¼ in. thick. Let rise for about 30 minutes at room temperature and then place in a preheated 375-degree oven for about 20 minutes, until nicely browned. (This should be done ahead.)

PEAR BROWN BETTY WITH PEAR SAUCE

This dessert can be assembled and cooked a couple of hours before serving. It should be served lukewarm and the sauce should be cold.

The rich bread can be used fresh by itself, but for the recipe here it should be made ahead because it is best used slightly stale. It can be prepared several days ahead and kept in a plastic bag so it doesn't dry out too much. Leftover brioche, croissants, or pound cake can be substituted for the rich bread.

The pear mixture contains not only puréed pears but pieces of pear as well. Although the brown betty is cooked in individual molds in the recipe below, it can also be cooked in a large gratin dish, then scooped up onto dessert plates and served with the sauce.

The pear sauce can be served with crêpes or other desserts, and the pear brown betty can be served plain or with whipped cream instead of the pear sauce.

Yield: 12 servings

RICH BREAD DOUGH

1 envelope active dry yeast (¼ oz.)
¼ c. warm water
1 tsp. sugar
1½ c. flour
2 eggs
2 Tb. butter
¼ tsp. salt

PEAR MIXTURE

About 3 lb. ripe pears (9 large Bartlett, Anjou, or Comice)
¾ c. sugar
⅓ c. orange juice
1½ Tb. cinnamon
1½ sticks butter, melted (¾ c.)
½ c. raisins

PEAR SAUCE

1 lb. ripe pears (about 3)
¼ c. sugar
3 Tb. lemon juice
1½ sticks butter (6 oz.)
1 Tb. pear brandy

GARNISH

Lemon peel

2 **Make the pear mixture:** Cut the cool bread into 1- to 2-in. pieces (about 5 to 6 c. total). Wash the 3 lb. of pears, split them in half, and remove the cores. Reserve two of the pears and cut the remainder into 1-in. pieces.

3 Cut the two reserved pears into chunks and place them in the bowl of a food processor with the ¾ c. sugar and ⅓ c. orange juice. Process until smooth and well puréed. Combine with the bread and the diced pear, 1½ Tb. cinnamon, 1½ sticks melted butter, and ½ c. raisins. Press into buttered ¾-c. baba molds or a larger mold.

5 While the brown betty is cooking, **make the sauce:** Peel, core, and quarter the 1 lb. pears and put them in the bowl of a food processor with the ¼ c. sugar and 3 Tb. lemon juice, and process until smoothly puréed. Add the 1½ sticks butter and process; the mixture will look separated. Transfer to a saucepan and cook over medium heat, stirring with a whisk, until it comes to a strong boil, at which point the sauce will become smooth again.

4 Place on a cookie sheet and bake in a preheated 400-degree oven for 45 minutes for the baba molds and 1 hour for the larger mold. The mixture will rise in the oven; press down lightly to make level with the top of the molds. Cool slightly and unmold.

6 Cool the pear sauce and add the 1 Tb. pear brandy. Pour a few spoonfuls of the sauce on individual plates and center a lukewarm, unmolded pear brown betty on top. Garnish with lemon peel and serve immediately with extra sauce on the side.

CREPE FRANGIPANE WITH TANGERINE SAUCE

In making this dish, you will encounter several basic recipes: making crêpes, making frangipane pastry cream filling, and making tangerine sauce. Each of these recipes can be used in other combinations.

The crêpes can be used not only for dessert but also as a savory dish when filled with creamed chicken or fish, for example. In the recipe here, the crêpes can be made ahead because they are stuffed and served with a sauce. When served plain or with jam for breakfast, they should be made at the last moment.

For this dessert, the crêpes are served lukewarm and the sauce cool.

Yield: 20–24 crêpes (12 filled crêpes)

CREPES

1 c. flour
1 tsp. sugar
3 eggs
½ c. milk
⅓ c. water
2 Tb. butter, melted
1 Tb. rum

FRANGIPANE CREAM

¾ c. slivered almonds (reserving ¼ c. for garnish)
1 c. milk
2 egg yolks
¼ c. sugar

1½ Tb. cornstarch
½ stick butter (2 oz.)
1 Tb. dark rum

TANGERINE SAUCE

1 egg
2 egg yolks
⅓ c. sugar
½ c. tangerine juice
1 Tb. lemon juice
2 tsp. cornstarch
⅔ c. water
1 c. heavy cream
1 Tb. mandarin orange brandy
2 tsp. grated tangerine rind

GARNISHES

¼ c. browned slivered almonds (from Frangipane Cream)
Tangerine peel

1 **For the crêpes:** To make a smooth batter, put the 1 c. flour, 1 tsp. sugar, and 3 eggs with ¼ c. of the milk in a bowl, and mix with a whisk. You will notice that the batter is still thick and lumpy.

2 Keep working the batter without adding more liquid. Because the mixture is thick, the threads of the whisk will break down any lumps in the flour and make the batter smooth. When smooth, mix in thoroughly the remaining ¼ c. milk and ⅓ c. water, then add the 2 oz. melted butter and 1 Tb. rum and whisk until smooth. The batter should have the consistency of heavy cream; if it is too thick, add up to 1 Tb. more water. It does not have to rest.

3 **To make the crêpes:** Heat a 6-in. crêpe pan, preferably nonstick. When hot, spoon about 1 Tb. of the batter into the near side of the inclined pan. Shake the pan so the batter runs down the bottom of the pan and spreads over most of its entire surface.

4 The thinness of the crêpe is determined by the speed with which the batter is spread. As the batter touches the hot pan surface, it solidifies. If it is not spread quickly, it will solidify thickly, so it is imperative that the batter be moved quickly. It is better to have too little than too much batter in the pan. If there are holes in the crêpe, they can be filled in with a little more batter. Add a few drops of batter to fill any holes in the crêpe.

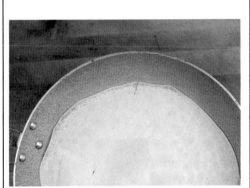

5 The edge of the crêpe is very thin and full of tiny holes. It is called a crêpe *dentelle,* which means "lace" in French. If the batter was liquid enough and it was spread quickly, the edge of the crêpe will look lacy.

6 Cook the first side of the crêpe for approximately 30 seconds. Then, flip it over. An alternative method of turning the crêpe is to use a fork. Lift up the cooked crêpe along the edge with the fork, then grab the crêpe between your thumb and finger, and turn it over.

7 Cook the crêpe for approximately 15 seconds on the other side. Then remove the crêpe to a plate so the side browned first is underneath. When the crêpe is stuffed and rolled, you want to have this side show because it looks best.

8 Note that the crêpe is very thin but elastic so it can hold a stuffing inside. If the crêpe were rich in cream or egg yolk, it might be thin but it would have a tendency to break. Stack the crêpes up on a plate, cover with plastic wrap, and set aside until the dessert is assembled. They will stay very moist and pliable and will separate easily when needed.

9 Spread the ¾ c. of almonds on a cookie tray and place in a preheated 400-degree oven for 6 to 8 minutes, until nicely browned. When cool, place ½ c. of the almonds in the bowl of a food processor and process until powdered. (Reserve the remaining almonds for use as a decoration.)

To make the frangipane cream: Bring the 1 c. milk to a boil in a small saucepan. Meanwhile, beat the 2 egg yolks with the ¼ c. sugar and the 1½ Tb. cornstarch. Pour the boiling milk on top of the egg yolk mixture, put it back in the saucepan, and bring to a boil to thicken. Mix with a whisk as it cooks to keep it from scorching in the corners of the pan. The cream should be smooth and thick.

10 Transfer the sauce to a bowl, let it cool to lukewarm, then mix in the powdered almonds, ½ stick butter, and 1 Tb. rum.
→

11 Spread 1 Tb. of the frangipane cream on each crêpe.

12 Roll each filled crêpe to make a little cylinder. Trim both ends with scissors to make a clean edge.

13 **To make the tangerine sauce:** In a saucepan, combine the egg, 2 egg yolks, ⅓ c. sugar, ½ c. tangerine juice, 1 Tb. lemon juice, 2 tsp. cornstarch, and ⅔ c. water, whisking to make the mixture smooth. Bring to a boil over high heat and strain immediately through a very fine strainer into a bowl. Add the 1 c. cold cream, 1 Tb. mandarin orange brandy, and 2 tsp. tangerine rind, and mix to blend.

14 To serve, arrange the lukewarm crêpes (they can be reheated in the oven) on a platter. Coat with the sauce and spoon additional sauce around them. Sprinkle the reserved almond slivers on top and decorate with a piece of tangerine peel. Serve immediately.

PRALINE-CHOCOLATE PARADIS

This very rich chocolate and praline dessert is sometimes served in small demitasse cups, decorated with chocolate leaves and raspberries. It can also be unmolded and placed in a chocolate wrapper made of bittersweet chocolate or a mixture of bittersweet and white chocolate. Both versions are shown here. About ⅓ to ½ c. of the mixture per serving is adequate since the dessert is so rich.

The chocolate leaves used to garnish the little demitasse cups can be made with dark or white chocolate. They are useful in many ways for decorating and as confections, and are easy to make: Leaves from a tree or a bush are gathered, washed, and dried, and then the undersides (where the veins are most visible) are coated with melted chocolate. Be careful not to use any poisonous leaves such as rhubarb or cherry. The chocolate leaves can be prepared ahead. The natural leaf is removed and discarded when the chocolate has set, and the chocolate leaves are kept refrigerated or frozen until needed.

Yield: 12–16 servings (16 demitasse cups, about ⅓ to ½ c. capacity each, or 1 large mold)

PRALINE
½ c. granulated sugar
¾ c. whole, unpeeled almonds

CHOCOLATE CREAM
10 oz. bittersweet or semi-sweet chocolate (see page 132)
2 c. cream
3 Tb. dark rum

CHOCOLATE LEAVES AND WRAPPERS
½ lb. bittersweet or semi-sweet chocolate and/or 2 oz. white chocolate

GARNISHES
1 Tb. confectioners' sugar
1 c. cream
A few fresh raspberries

1 Make the praline: Place the ½ c. sugar in a saucepan over medium heat and cook, stirring occasionally, until it caramelizes. You will notice that the outside edges of the sugar mixture will become liquid first. Stir that liquid into the dry sugar, let it continue to melt, then stir. It is likely that lumps of crystallized sugar will form. However, when the sugar reaches approximately 318 to 320 degrees and starts changing color and turning into caramel, the lumps will melt and the mixture will become smooth. Cooking dry sugar produces a very hard, brittle caramel, which is what you want for this recipe.

2 Add the ¾ c. almonds to the caramel, and continue cooking and stirring over medium heat for about 1 minute to brown and cook the almonds into the caramel.

3 Pour the almond praline onto an oiled metal tray, spread it out, and let it cool at room temperature or in the refrigerator for at least 15 to 20 minutes.

4 When the praline is well-set, break it up into pieces and put them in a mortar.

5 Using the pestle or a food processor (although the praline may damage the cutting edge of the blade), crush the praline into little lumps, the largest of which are not more than ¼ in. in size. You should have approximately 1½ c. At this point, the praline can be kept in a jar, refrigerated, for use as is to flavor sauces or powdered for serving with ice cream, pastry cream, etc.

6 To make the chocolate cream: Put the 10 oz. of bittersweet chocolate with 1 c. of the cream in a saucepan. Cook over medium heat, stirring occasionally with a whisk so it doesn't stick, until the chocolate melts.

7 When the chocolate-cream mixture is smooth, stir in the 3 Tb. rum and 1 c. of the praline mixture, reserving ½ c. of praline for decoration. Whip the remaining cup of cream until stiff.

8 When the chocolate-cream mixture has cooled to no more than tepid in temperature, combine it with the whipped cream.

9 Oil the demitasse cups (⅓ to ½ c. capacity) very lightly if they are to be unmolded. Fill them with the chocolate cream and set aside. When the top has set, cover with plastic wrap (so they don't pick up other tastes) and refrigerate. (They can be stored for several days in this manner.)

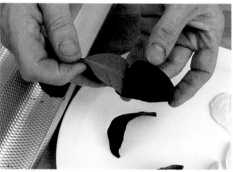

10 To make the chocolate leaves: Melt either the ½ lb. of dark chocolate or the 2 oz. of white chocolate in a double boiler. Using a spoon or brush, coat the underside of the thoroughly dried leaves with dark or white chocolate. Place in a French bread pan or ring mold that has a concave shape so the leaves can assume a curled shape.

11 Allow to cool, refrigerated, for at least 15 to 20 minutes; peel the natural leaves from the chocolate leaves, working quickly because the chocolate tends to soften in your hands. The chocolate leaves can be placed in a plastic container and kept, covered, in the refrigerator or freezer.

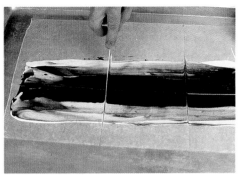

12 To give another look to the dessert, wrap it in chocolate strips. (For this you will need both the ½ lb. dark chocolate and the 2 oz. of white chocolate, melted.)

To make the chocolate wrappers: Pour a stream of the melted chocolate onto a piece of wax or parchment paper.

13 Spread the chocolate with a metal spatula to create a long, thin strip about 4 in. wide by 18 to 20 in. long.

14 Pour a thin strip of white chocolate on either side of the dark chocolate and spread with the spatula to mix it with the dark chocolate, creating a marblelike design.

15 After the chocolate has cooled for about 10 minutes (it is still slightly soft), cut the strip of paper lengthwise down the center and crosswise into thirds so each rectangle created is approximately 6 to 7 in. long by about 1½ to 2 in. wide. Refrigerate the paper-lined chocolate strips.

Run a knife around the praline demitasse desserts, shake slightly to loosen them (or, if necessary, wrap them with a towel that has been dipped in hot water and wrung out), and unmold them onto individual serving plates. Smooth, if desired, with a knife. Remove the chocolate strips from the refrigerator and leave them at room temperature for a few minutes to soften the chocolate.

16 When the chocolate is somewhat pliable, wrap the strips (paper-side out) around the praline so the white chocolate border is at the top and peel off the paper.

17 **For the garnish:** Whip the cup of cream lightly with the confectioners' sugar; it should still be soft and pourable. Arrange some of the cream around the desserts and decorate with crushed praline. Serve immediately.

18 For another presentation, serve directly in the little demitasse cups, decorated with chocolate leaves and raspberries. Serve the cream, sprinkled with the praline, on the side.

1 For the gourmand: In a mixing bowl, whip the 1 c. cream until lightly firm (do not over-beat). Meanwhile, place the 6 oz. chocolate with the ⅓ c. milk in a saucepan, and place over medium heat until the chocolate has melted and the mixture is warm and smooth. Add the 2 egg yolks to the chocolate with the 2 tsp. rum and mix. The chocolate will thicken slightly. In another bowl, beat the egg white until firm, then add the 2 Tb. granulated sugar and keep beating until firm and smooth.

CHOCOLATE GOURMAND

Chocolate gourmand is a rich chocolate mousse served home-style by scooping out portions of the dessert directly from the bowl at the table. It can be served with an array of different cookies, from Lime Tuile (page 326) to Chocolate Oatmeal Cookies (page 293), or with Home Cake (page 291) or Cinnamon Lemon Cake (page 286).

The chocolate mixture can be prepared several days ahead and kept refrigerated. However, it is important to cover the mousse snugly with plastic wrap after it has set, as the chocolate will have a tendency to absorb other tastes in the refrigerator.

Serve with a large spoon, scooping up little "egg shape" portions of the mousse for each serving.

Yield: 8 servings

CHOCOLATE GOURMAND

1 c. heavy cream
6 oz. bittersweet or semi-sweet chocolate (see page 132)
⅓ c. milk
2 egg yolks
2 tsp. dark rum
1 egg white
2 Tb. granulated sugar

TOPPING

½ c. heavy cream
2 tsp. confectioners' sugar

GARNISH

Candied violets

2 Pour the chocolate mixture into the beaten egg white and stir with a whisk just enough to incorporate. Add the whipped cream and fold in gently just until mixed.

3 Pour the mixture into an attractive serving bowl and refrigerate for approximately 1 hour. When the top starts to harden, cover with plastic wrap so the chocolate doesn't pick up tastes in the refrigerator. It should set for at least 4 to 5 hours or overnight, until firm.

4 **For the topping:** At serving time, combine the ½ c. cream with the 2 tsp. confectioners' sugar, and whip until the cream is firm. Spoon into a pastry bag fitted with a fluted tip and pipe rosettes of cream on top of the chocolate gourmand.

5 Decorate the top of the whipped cream mounds with small pieces of candied violets and serve plain or with a cookie or a slice of pound cake.

CHOCOLATE GOBLETS WITH ESPRESSO ICE CREAM OR COINTREAU STRAWBERRIES

These chocolate goblets are showy as well as delicious. They are beautiful chocolate receptacles, made by molding melted chocolate around inflated balloons. They can be filled, as done here, either with espresso ice cream or with a mixture of strawberries and Cointreau. Other filling variations include whipped cream, fruit salad, custard, or other kinds of ice cream served alone or with a sauce.

The chocolate accumulates in the bottom of the shells and forms a stable base as the shells harden on a tray lined with wax or parchment paper. These chocolate receptacles weigh no more than 1 oz. each when cold, and can be kept in a container in the refrigerator or even frozen. Even though all the 6 shells weigh only about 6 oz., it takes twice that amount of chocolate to make the goblets. The extra chocolate can be refrigerated and used again later.

The marbling effect in the chocolate can be made with white chocolate either on the surface of the chocolate goblets (as shown in step 6) or the white chocolate can be piped directly onto the balloons before they are dipped in the chocolate so the inside of the goblet has a marblelike effect. The balloons

used in this recipe are blown up to a circumference of 4 to 4¼ in. so the goblets are not too large, but a larger balloon can be used to create a single large receptacle to serve 6 to 8 people.

Be certain that the chocolate is only tepid or at room temperature when you make the goblets so the balloons don't burst in the process and splatter chocolate all over the kitchen. If the chocolate is too thick, add 1 to 2 tsp. of corn or cottonseed oil to liquefy it.

The coffee extract is made with a combination of boiling milk and finely ground French roast coffee. This makes a very rich coffee ice cream that can be served as a separate dessert by itself. Likewise, the strawberries combined with strawberry jam and Cointreau can be served alone or with whipped cream or Home Cake (page 291).

Yield: 6 servings

ESPRESSO ICE CREAM

1¼ c. milk
⅓ c. finely ground French roast coffee
2 c. heavy cream
5 egg yolks
½ c. sugar

CHOCOLATE GOBLETS FOR 6

About 12 oz. bittersweet or semi-sweet
   chocolate (see page 132)
2 oz. white chocolate
6 balloons

COINTREAU STRAWBERRIES

2 c. strawberries
¼ c. strawberry jam
1 Tb. Cointreau

GARNISH

6 chocolate-covered coffee beans
   (see introduction to Mocha Success
   Cake, page 255)

1 **For the espresso ice cream:** Bring the 1¼ c. of milk to a strong boil and add the ⅓ c. coffee; stir, cover, and let steep off the heat for about 5 minutes. Strain through paper towels. You should have about 1 c. of coffee extract.

Mix the extract with 1 c. of the cream in a saucepan and bring to a boil. Meanwhile, mix the 5 egg yolks and ½ c. sugar together with a whisk until thick (about 15 to 20 seconds), and add the boiling coffee-cream. Return the mixture to the saucepan and cook, stirring, until it reaches about 180 degrees, at which point the lecithin in the egg yolks will thicken the mixture. Be careful not to over-cook as it will tend to curdle if the temperature goes much beyond 180 to 190 degrees. Meanwhile, pour the remaining cup of cream into a clean bowl and strain the hot mixture directly into it through a very fine strainer. This will lower the temperature of the coffee-cream mixture and stop any further cooking. Cool and when at room temperature pour it into an ice cream maker and freeze according to the manufacturer's instructions.

2 Transfer the ice cream to a bowl, pack it firmly, cover with plastic wrap, and place in the freezer until serving time.

3 **To make the chocolate goblets:** Melt the 12 oz. bittersweet and 2 oz. white chocolates separately in double boilers, making certain that no water gets into the chocolate as this will thicken it and make it lose its shine. If the chocolate is too thick, add a little corn or cottonseed oil. Cool the chocolates to tepid (about 100 degrees). Blow up the balloons until they are 4 to 4¼ in. wide, then close them at the neck with plastic-coated wire twisters. Dip each balloon directly into the melted bittersweet chocolate, inclining it slightly to form a roundish shape on one side.

4 Twist the balloon and dip it in the chocolate again to create another large roundish shape around the base, lift it out and dip it again – 3 or 4 times in all – then place on a parchment-lined tray. Some of the chocolate will run down the balloon and accumulate at the base to form a thicker and more stable pedestal. Refrigerate until set or, if you want to add a white chocolate design, proceed with the instructions below.

5 For a different look, pour about 2 Tb. of the melted white chocolate into a paper cornet (see "Swimming Swans," page 234, steps 2–6), fold the cornet, and cut the tip off.

6 Pipe lines of white chocolate around the still-soft chocolate on the dipped balloon. The white chocolate will run slightly into the dark chocolate and create a marbled effect.

7 Or if you prefer to have the inside of the goblet marked with the white chocolate, pipe lines directly on the outside of a balloon.

8 Then dip the base of the balloon into the bittersweet chocolate, as described in step 3. Place on a tray and refrigerate until hard.

9 After the chocolate has set hard, open the balloon and release the air inside slowly. Although the sides of the balloon will separate easily from the chocolate around it, the goblet base may adhere more stubbornly to the balloon.

10 Pry up the balloon at the base with your fingers. If it takes too long, and the chocolate begins to soften, return to the freezer or refrigerator to harden slightly before finishing the removal of the deflated balloons.

11 The goblets, some smooth inside and some with white chocolate marbling, are ready to be filled. At this point, they can be stored in a container in the refrigerator or carefully wrapped in plastic wrap and frozen.

12 At serving time, **prepare the Cointreau strawberries:** Clean and quarter the 2 c. strawberries and toss them gently with the ¼ c. strawberry jam and 1 Tb. Cointreau. Spoon into the chocolate goblets.

13 For a serving variation, put a scoop of the espresso ice cream in each chocolate goblet, top with a chocolate-covered coffee bean, and serve immediately.

NOUGATINE SHELL WITH CHOCOLATE GOURMAND OR CHANTILLY

A nougatine is made from caramelized sugar and sliced almonds and can be either used as a garnish on cakes (cut into different shapes – from triangles to strips) or pressed into molds, as done below, to create small receptacles to hold different types of fillings. The nougatine can also be crushed into pieces and added to ice cream or pulverized and kept in a jar in the refrigerator to use, when wanted, in ice cream or custard cream as well as pastry cream. This recipe uses other recipes from this book, from the Home Cake (page 291) to the Chocolate Gourmand (page 318), for fillings.

Nougatine is hard to cut, particularly when it is too thick. To make it thinner (the thinner the better), cut out rough round or rectangular shapes to fit the molds you have selected, and then place them back in the oven to soften the nougatine until it is pliable enough to be pressed thinner.

Nougatine is better prepared on a dry day; it is difficult to keep it in areas that have a lot of humidity and moisture. Store in a cookie jar or plastic container with a tight-fitting lid so it doesn't get soggy and sticky.

Be extra careful when doing the caramel not to burn yourself. Pour it out onto an oiled marble surface or metal tray; don't use wood – it will stick. Be sure to lightly oil the dough scraper as well as your metal rolling pin (I have used a piece of cast-iron tube about 1¾ in. in diameter, which can be obtained from a local hardware or plumbing supply store) to keep the pieces of nougatine from sticking. (The metal rolling pin is also excellent for rolling out dough, since it is heavy, smooth, and stays cool.)

The caramel is made from dry sugar, although it can also be made from sugar and water. Dry caramel, however, produces a more brittle, harder nougatine that is less prone to stick.

Yield: 8 servings

NOUGATINE SHELL
1 lb. granulated sugar (about 2 c.)
2 c. sliced almonds (about 6 oz.)

CHANTILLY FILLING
1 c. heavy cream
1 Tb. confectioners' sugar

Cointreau, Grand Marnier, and/or rum (½ tsp. per portion to soak the cake)
3 to 4 sliced strawberries for garnish

OTHER OPTIONAL GARNISHES
Home Cake (see Poached Pears in Citrus Juice Lauren, page 291)
Chocolate Gourmand (see page 318)
Candied violets

1 Put the 1 lb. sugar in a saucepan and cook over medium to high heat, stirring with a wooden spatula occasionally (every 5 to 10 seconds). As some of the sugar around the outside edges of the pan starts to melt, stir it back into the dry sugar.

2 After 4 to 5 minutes, the sugar will begin to get liquid. Keep stirring. Lumps of crystallized sugar will be mixed with the melted sugar. Eventually, the lumps will melt as the temperature of the sugar goes higher.

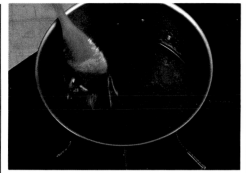

3 After about 7 to 8 minutes, the sugar will liquefy further and turn a caramel color, although there will still be some lumps in it. Lower the heat and continue cooking and stirring until the lumps have completely melted. The caramel will be slightly cloudy and a rich brown color. The total cooking time will be approximately 10 minutes, although it could take longer, depending on the size, the type of metal, and the shape of your pan, as well as the intensity of the heat.

4 Add the 2 c. almonds and stir gently to incorporate into the melted sugar. Keep cooking for 1 to 2 minutes, until the mixture liquefies again and becomes smooth.

5 Oil a marble slab or metal tray lightly with a tasteless oil (such as cottonseed or corn oil) and pour the nougatine onto it, using a wooden spoon to help scrape it out of the pan.

6 Lightly oil a dough scraper and spread the nougatine, being careful the hot mixture doesn't touch your fingers.

7 Using an oiled metal rolling pin, press down and roll out the nougatine further to make it smooth. It won't expand too much at this point but should form an irregular circle with a diameter of about 12 to 14 in. If you feel the nougatine is thin enough – no more than ¼ in. thick – and soft enough to handle at this point, begin cutting it into shapes using a big, sharp knife or cookie cutter.

8 If the nougatine is too hard to cut at this point, lift it up off the slab or tray, place it on a cookie sheet, and put it in a preheated 200- to 250-degree oven, checking it every 5 to 6 minutes, until it has softened again.

9 Remove the nougatine from the oven and roll it out again directly on the cookie sheet into a thinner layer. It should not be more than ¼ in. thick.

10 Press cookie cutters firmly into the soft nougatine. You may have to hammer the top of the cutters down with your metal pin to cut through the nougatine.

11 Using a large, heavy knife, cut out rectangles from the nougatine and place them directly on top of molds of about the same size. They should be a little too small to fit the molds at this point. Return the nougatine cutouts in their molds to the oven to soften further. Push the nougatine trimmings together roughly and return them to the oven to soften. When soft enough, roll them out again into a smooth, single piece. →

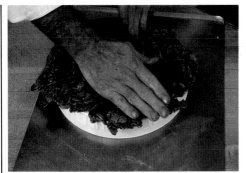

12 For a larger version of the nougatine receptacle, press a large piece of softened nougatine all around a lightly oiled inverted pie plate. It will conform to the plate to form a large receptacle. Trim the edges with scissors.

13 When the nougatine in the small molds begins to soften, remove the molds from the oven and, holding them with a towel, press the nougatine with the back of an oiled spoon to thin and extend it further up the sides of the molds. If the edges of the nougatine are jagged at this point, trim them with scissors to make them even. (The trimmings can be pulverized and stored, refrigerated, in a jar for use as a flavoring in ice cream, pastry cream, etc.) Set the molds aside.

14 After 10 to 15 minutes, the nougatine will have hardened in the molds. Using the point of a knife, pry the shells out of the molds. They should release easily.

15 To make a variety of desserts: Cut the home cake into ½-in. slices and then into round or rectangular shapes to fit the molds. Place the pieces in the appropriate molds and sprinkle with either rum (if you are using the chocolate gourmand filling), or Cointreau or Grand Marnier (if using the Chantilly filling).

16 **For the chantilly filling:** Whip the 1 c. cream with the 1 Tb. confectioners' sugar until stiff. Spoon into a pastry bag fitted with a fluted tip and pipe a mound of cream on top of the Cointreau or Grand Marnier–soaked cake in the molds. Decorate the top with sliced strawberries or other fruit.

17 Using an ice cream scoop, place a scoop of the chocolate gourmand on top of the rum-soaked cake.

18 Decorate the chocolate filling with a little rosette of whipped cream and a piece of candied violet and serve immediately. (These desserts should not be assembled more than 30 minutes before serving as the liqueur-soaked cake and fillings will make the nougatine shell sticky if filled too far ahead.)

CARAMEL BASE

⅓ c. sugar
2 Tb. water

CUSTARD

1½ c. milk
⅓ c. sugar
5 eggs
2 Tb. rum
1 c. heavy cream
½ c. coffee extract (see Mocha Success
   Cake, page 256, step 1)

LIME TUILE COOKIES

¾ stick butter
¾ c. sugar
½ tsp. vanilla
1 tsp. lime rind
2 egg whites
¼ to ⅓ c. flour
½ c. sliced almonds

CARAMEL CAGE

½ c. sugar
3 Tb. water

GARNISH

Fresh flowers

COFFEE-RUM CARAMEL CUSTARD WITH LIME TUILE COOKIES

Caramel custard is a classic French dessert — fundamental simple cooking of the home cook as well as the sophisticated cooking of three-star restaurants. This recipe is flavored with rum and coffee and served with a lime tuile cookie, although it could be served plain or with other cookies. The caramel cage, which decorates the top of the custard, brings it to another level of sophistication but is not necessary for a simple home dinner.

The custard must be cooked in a pan of lukewarm tap water, which should not reach the boil as the custard cooks. There should be enough water surrounding the custard to extend three-fourths of the way up the outside of the molds. If the water boils, the custard will cook too fast and the albumen (the egg whites) will develop and expand, forming little air bubbles around the edges of the custard.

The custard can be cooked up to 2 or 3 days ahead and kept, covered, in the refrigerator. In fact, the custard must be made at least 5 or 6 hours beforehand if it is to unmold properly. To test the custard for doneness, plunge a knife blade into it. The custard is ready when the blade comes out clean, not wet. But be careful when testing that you don't push the knife completely through to the base of the mold or the custard may split when you unmold it. The custard can be flavored with vanilla only or with coffee, rum, almond, chocolate, or any other flavoring of your choice.

The lime tuile cookies done in this recipe are very large and one batch yields about 10 to 12 cookies. They can be made smaller. The French word <u>tuile</u> means "tile," and these cookies are meant to resemble the red, curly roof tiles in the south of France. This classic curved shape is achieved by placing the hot cookies in a French bread pan or laying them on top of a rolling pin so they become rounded. If the cookies are made ahead, they should be stored in an airtight container so they don't pick up moisture and soften.

Yield: 8–10 servings

1 To make the caramel base: Combine the ⅓ c. sugar and 2 Tb. water in a saucepan. Stir just enough to moisten the sugar and boil over medium to high heat until the mixture turns a deep, rich caramel color. <u>Pour it into the bottom of a 6-c. soufflé mold</u> and allow to harden while preparing the custard. →

2 **To make the custard:** Put the 1½ c. milk and ⅓ c. sugar in a saucepan, and bring to a boil. Meanwhile, beat the 5 eggs in a bowl and combine with the 2 Tb. rum, 1 c. cream, and ½ c. coffee extract. When the milk is boiling, pour it directly into the egg mixture and mix well with a whisk.

3 Place the caramel-lined mold into another pan so it can be cooked in a water bath, and strain the custard mixture through a fine strainer on top of the hardened caramel. Pour tepid water around the mold; it should extend about three-fourths of the way up the outside of the mold. Place in a preheated 350-degree oven for 1 hour. It is important that the water not boil while the custard is cooking or it will get spongy around the edges. Should the water begin to boil, ladle some of it out and replace with a few ice cubes.

4 Cool the custard for 4 to 5 hours or overnight and cover it with plastic wrap. Do not unmold until serving time. To unmold, run a knife around the edge of the custard to loosen it all around, making sure that the flat side of the knife is flush against the sides of the mold and does not cut into the custard.

5 Place a serving platter or a glass dish with a pedestal base upside down on top of the custard.

6 Invert and remove the mold.

7 **To make the cookies:** Place the ¾ stick of butter and ¾ c. of sugar in the bowl of a food processor, and process for about 10 seconds. Add the ½ tsp. vanilla and 1 tsp. lime rind with the 2 egg whites and process for another 10 seconds. Then add the ¼ to ⅓ c. flour and process just enough to incorporate it. Remove from the bowl of the food processor to another bowl and stir in the ½ c. sliced almonds.

Butter and flour a large cookie sheet. Spoon approximately 2 Tb. of the cookie batter onto the cookie sheet for each giant tuile cookie (about 4 to a sheet) and spread each to a diameter of about 5 to 6 in. The batter should be thin enough so that the baking sheet is visible through it in spots.

8 Place in a preheated 400-degree oven for 10 minutes. The cookies should have spread a little more and be uniformly browned. Run a knife under the cookies while still hot (work quickly; they must be removed right away) and place them in a French bread mold or over a rolling pin to give them a curved shape. Be sure that the top of the cookie is the side that is visible when the cookie is served. If the cookies are not served as soon as they have set, put them in an airtight container so they don't soften.

9 To make a caramel cage: In a saucepan, mix the ½ c. sugar and 3 Tb. water just enough to moisten the sugar. Place on the stove and cook over medium to high heat approximately 10 to 12 minutes, until the mixture turns a nice caramel color. Set the caramel aside for 1 to 2 minutes to thicken a little before making the cage. If the caramel continues cooking off the heat and getting darker in color, put the pan of caramel into a bowl of cold water to cool it faster and thicken the caramel. Lightly oil (using tasteless oil) the outside of a 9-in. cake pan, the same shape but larger than the mold used to cook the custard. Drizzle the caramel in strips around the mold and then across the top and down the sides of the inverted pan, going from one side to the other to make a structure and base for the cage so it doesn't collapse (see "Swimming Swans," page 236, steps 18–21). The large, thick strips of caramel going from one side to the other will support the structure, and the thinner connecting threads can then be drizzled on. After 10 to 15 minutes the caramel cage will be set. Remove it by easing it off a little near the base on the sides; it should slide up the sides of the pan easily.

10 Place the cage on top of the unmolded custard and decorate with different colored fresh flowers, which can be inserted in the "iron grid" of the caramel.

Serve a spoonful of the custard with some of the natural caramel sauce and a cookie.

CREME BRULEE WITH VERBENA

Crème brûlée, a British dessert, is a rich custard and, for this reason, I cook it in small molds, approximately ⅓ c. each. Sometimes the dessert is made even richer by using only heavy cream, but I find that it is rich enough with milk and cream in equal proportions, as I have done here. Because crème brûlée is made mostly with egg yolks, it cannot be unmolded since there is not enough albumen (egg whites) to hold the cream (as done for Coffee-Rum Caramel Custard, page 325).

It is important that the crème brûlée be poached slowly in a water bath in the oven. Use lukewarm water from the tap. The water should not come to a boil as the custard cooks. If the crème brûlée is cooked too fast, the albumen will develop and start expanding and little holes will form all around the sides of the custard, making it look like a sponge when it should be very smooth and silky in texture.

I flavored the crème brûlée with verbena, which is one of my favorite herb teas, but it can be flavored with vanilla, rum, chocolate, or almond, according to your preferences. The lemon rind accents the taste of the verbena. Light brown sugar is used for the topping; dark brown would be too strong in taste and too dark in color.

The custard can be made 2 or 3 days ahead and kept covered in the refrigerator, but the brown sugar topping should not be broiled more than 4 or 5 hours before serving. If done sooner, the sugar shell will melt and turn liquid on top of the custard.

Yield: 8 servings

CREME MIXTURE

1 c. milk
½ c. loose verbena leaves (or 2 verbena teabags)
2 tsp. grated lemon rind
4 egg yolks + 1 whole egg
3 Tb. granulated sugar
1 c. cream

TOPPING

5 Tb. light brown sugar (about 2 tsp. per serving)

1 **For the crème:** Put the 1 c. milk, ½ c. loose verbena leaves or 2 teabags, and 2 tsp. lemon rind in a saucepan, and bring to a boil. As soon as it boils, cover, remove from the heat, and let steep for 5 minutes.

2 Beat the 4 egg yolks and 1 whole egg with the 3 Tb. granulated sugar and add 1 c. cream. Combine the steeped verbena mixture with the egg yolk mixture, stirring well to mix thoroughly.

3 Strain the crème mixture through a fine strainer.

4 Arrange 8 small molds (the ones used here have a capacity of about ½ c.) in a roasting pan and fill with the crème mixture. Add enough tepid tap water to the pan to come three-fourths of the way up the outsides of the molds. Bake the molds in a preheated 350-degree oven for approximately 25 to 30 minutes, until set. The water around the molds should not boil. Should the water begin to boil, ladle some of it out and replace with a few ice cubes.

5 Remove from the oven and let cool. When cool, cover.

For the topping: At serving time or not more than 1 to 1½ hours beforehand, spread 2 tsp. of light brown sugar over the top of each crème.

6 Place the molds under the broiler and broil (watching them closely) until the sugar bubbles and turns uniformly brown, approximately 3 minutes. Let cool for at least 10 minutes, until the sugar surface hardens, and serve.

To eat, crack the sugar shell with the back of a spoon and eat with a nice pound cake as an accompaniment.

ABOUT MENUS

A few years after we got married, Gloria and I started renovating an old farmhouse in upstate New York, and we got in the habit of writing down our menus when we had friends for dinner or for any special occasion. Our guests would always sign the menus, which served as mementos of the good times we had had together. We now have three large books full of these menus. To me they represent precious "rememberings of things past." In addition to their nostalgic value, they serve as a helpful guide in how to put together a menu, so I have illustrated some of the ones we enjoyed during the four years that it took to write The Art of Cooking and am including them here.

These illustrated menus were created with recipes from both volumes of The Art of Cooking and are only a small sample of all the possible combinations that can be made with all the dishes. In the first volume, the main courses of fish, poultry, and meat are presented with their own vegetables and garnishes. A salad and simple dessert added to these plats complets would constitute a full menu. The plat complet is the anchor or centerpiece of the meal, the pièce de résistance, and appetizers, salad, and dessert are chosen in conjunction with that central dish. If you prefer simpler, light meals – particularly at lunchtime – simply select a fish or poultry dish from Volume I and serve it with the accompaniments I have given and some fruit or a sorbet for dessert.

In the making of a menu, dishes are chosen according to the importance of the event, the time allotted to the meal, economic considerations, the tastes of the guests, and, more than anything else, common sense. A meal that starts with oysters in puff pastry should not finish with a raspberry puff pastry tart, a white sauce should

not follow another white sauce, and a pasta should not be served with rice or another doughy preparation.

Traditionally, a menu progresses from heavy to lighter dishes in contrast to the wine, which should start with the lightest and move up to the heaviest. When unsure, follow the recommendations of the experts. However, nothing is written in stone and, after you have learned that the acidity of a certain chardonnay complements the richness of salmon, if you still prefer red wine with your salmon, follow your own taste. By the same token, if I chose to serve a menu with two starches or two foods that have a similar texture, I would do it not out of inexperience but by choice.

Today's life-styles, which determine the length of meals as well as dietary considerations, are important factors in planning a menu. As much or more than the dishes themselves, the way a menu is put together and the setting of the meal reflect the personality and taste of the cook.

I have tried in the menus I've selected here to reflect seasonal changes and what is available at certain times of the year. Note that often the difference between a lunch and a dinner is simply that the menu is extended with salad followed by cheeses or served with cheeses (for more information about serving cheese, see the following page). Whether or not to make separate courses of the salad and the cheeses is entirely up to the host and hostess. Remember, however, that some of the greatest

wines complement cheeses well but may conflict with a salad, especially when it is seasoned with an acidic, vinegary dressing.

Just as the addition of salad and cheeses will extend your menu greatly, so will the addition of wine. For lunch we usually serve one wine, as opposed to two for dinner, a white and a red.

There are other adjuncts to a menu that will make it more sophisticated: hors d'oeuvres with aperitifs before dinner and, following the meal, brandy and petits fours or chocolate. So far as I am concerned, champagne is always welcome with a meal, preferably as an aperitif, although I enjoy it as well throughout the whole meal.

The two special dinner parties are composed of at least five courses, with a pause in the center when a granité, a palate cleanser, is served between the fish and the main course. I have included a couple of exotic ingredients here because these are special occasions, but if you cannot get caviar, you can always substitute smoked salmon or a pâté, and the fresh white truffles could be omitted from the salad.

The buffet is a relic of the old French service called the "service of confusion." As many as 500 dishes would be brought to the table in three courses, or mets – the number being a sign of the generosity of the host as well as the dexterity of the cook. It is still the custom today for a hostess to make many of her favorite recipes and display them on a buffet for a large group.

Since a buffet features approximately three times as many dishes as a regular menu, portions are cut down accordingly. A recipe serving 10 would be one of the dishes in a buffet for 30 people. The same idea applies in the fashionable tasting menus when the chef serves tiny portions of many dishes to show the extent of his repertoire.

Picnics are a favorite in our family. Different from barbecues, where the food is grilled outside, our picnic is composed of precooked cold or lukewarm dishes arranged in baskets with an emphasis on salads and pâtés, which "travel" well.

Brunch, a totally American meal, partakes of breakfast and lunch in a relaxing

weekend meal. Egg dishes, smoked fish, sausages, and poached fruits are emphasized, as well as good bread. Fruit juices and coffee and tea are de rigueur, and champagne lends elegance and gaiety.

Finally, there is the "linner," my family's contraction of lunch and dinner, a favorite meal on fall and winter Sundays. It doesn't start before 3:00 p.m. and is a relaxing, informal, low-key meal that usually goes on until 5:00 p.m. Soups, stews, or casserole dishes are often our choice for "linner," and Gloria's Bloody Marys are always served.

Remember that the best way to enjoy meals is with family or friends and that, as the French saying goes, "On ne mange bien que chez soi!" (The best place to eat is at home).

CHEESE

A tray of cheeses is usually *the* dessert at our house, and many friends who love food would concur. For Talleyrand, cheese was the greatest of desserts and Brillat-Savarin wrote: "A meal without cheese is like a beautiful woman with only one eye." In the same vein, Colette said that if she had a son, she would advise him "to beware of girls who don't like wine, truffles, cheeses or music . . ."

In shopping for good cheese it is often difficult to recognize the overripe from the underripe. The best way to buy cheese is to go to a reputable cheese store and ask for recommendations, sampling, if permitted, before you buy. Be aware that certain cheeses, especially fresh farm varieties, will not survive as long as a Brie, for example. And the Brie, in turn, will not survive as long as a dry, hard cheese such as Parmesan or Chester.

If there are no cheese stores in your area, buy your cheeses in a supermarket where there is a high turnover. The most important asset for judging quality is your nose; cheese should smell fresh and sweet with no alkaline odor. Even spicy, tangy cheeses should have a frank odor rather than smelling acidic or alkaline. Beware of bulging specimens, which indicate a second fermentation, and dry, discolored wrappers that stick to the cheese. A cheese should look pleasant and be plump, with a natural color.

The soft cheeses — Brie or Camembert — should be soft and springy to the touch, indicating that they are almost ripe. Look for the name of cheeses: If you buy a Parmesan cheese, look for a Reggiano, if you buy a Brie, look for Meaux, and if you buy a Stilton, look for the word Stilton printed on top.

Be sure to wrap cheeses individually and keep them refrigerated. Although they should be taken out of the refrigerator far enough ahead of serving so that they are almost at room temperature rather than ice cold, they should not be left out for so many hours that they become lukewarm, soft, and runny.

I usually serve the same wine with cheese that I had with the main course, but a spicy, tangy cheese (such as a dry goat cheese) may demand a special, full-bodied red wine.

Serve cheeses on a tray, perhaps wooden, or in a shallow wicker basket-tray with fresh leaves underneath. I serve, at most, three or four cheeses: a soft cheese (Brie, Camembert, a rich Boursault, or, for a stronger variety, a Liverot or a Pont Lévêque), a semisoft cheese (Beaumont, Reblochon, or Saint Nectaire), and a Bleu (the Bleu I like best is an imported Gorgonzola, but I also enjoy a real Stilton or a French Bleu de Gex). When I serve a fourth cheese, I choose a dry, hard variety (Parmesan or Crottin de Chavignol, which is a tiny, hard goat cheese).

At a formal dinner, the cheese is usually served between the salad and dessert courses. When it takes the place of dessert for an everyday dinner, I sometimes serve it together with the salad, especially if the salad has a mild dressing and contains garlic.

March 23

MOLLET EGGS WITH STEWED ASPARAGUS
volume 1, page 36

GRILLED SQUID WITH LEMON SAUCE AND BROCCOLI RAPE
volume 1, page 70

CHOCOLATE-ORANGE TART MARTINE
volume 2, page 188

Mondavi Fumé Blanc '84

SPRING DINNER

Dinner May 16

Wild dandelion Salad Lyonnaise

Grilled Leg of Lamb Robert

Puree of Spinach with Croutons and Eggs

Sakonnet Vidal 83

Cheeses

Chateau Gloria 75

Galette de Pérouges

Jacques 87

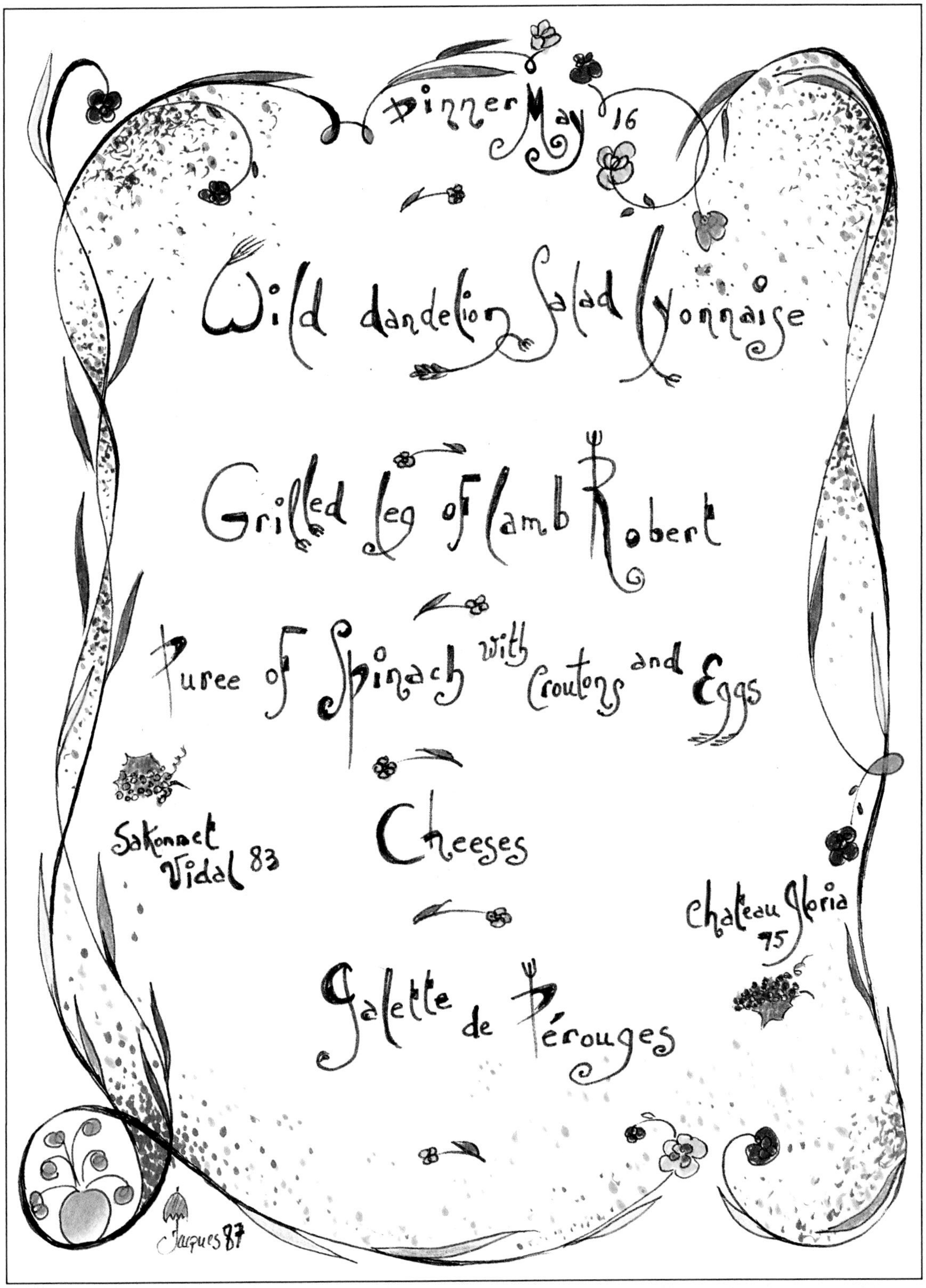

June 26

**GRILLED LAMB KIDNEYS WITH
STUFFED MUSHROOMS**
volume 1, page 301

LONG ISLAND BOUILLABAISSE
volume 1, page 151

STEW OF RED SUMMER FRUITS
volume 2, page 298

Cendré de Novembre Vin Gris '80

SUMMER DINNER

August 20

PIKE QUENELLES AND CHICKEN LIVER TIMBALE MERRET
volume 1, page 102

ESCALOPES OF VEAL COLETTE POTATOES PARISIENNE AND SWISS CHARD
volume 1, page 270

SALAD D'ÉTÉ
made with summer salad greens tossed with Mustard Vinaigrette
volume 2, page 90
or Walnut Dressing
volume 2, page 89

CHEESES

POACHED WHITE PEACHES WITH ALMOND LEAVES
volume 2, page 292

Rully '80
Rutherford Hill Merlot '81

December 13

Trimbach Sylvaner '79

Lunch Menu Dec 13

Black bean Soup Augier
bacon Corn bread

Chicken Jean-Claude with Waffle potatoes

Caramelized Apple loaf

Trimbach Sylvaner 79

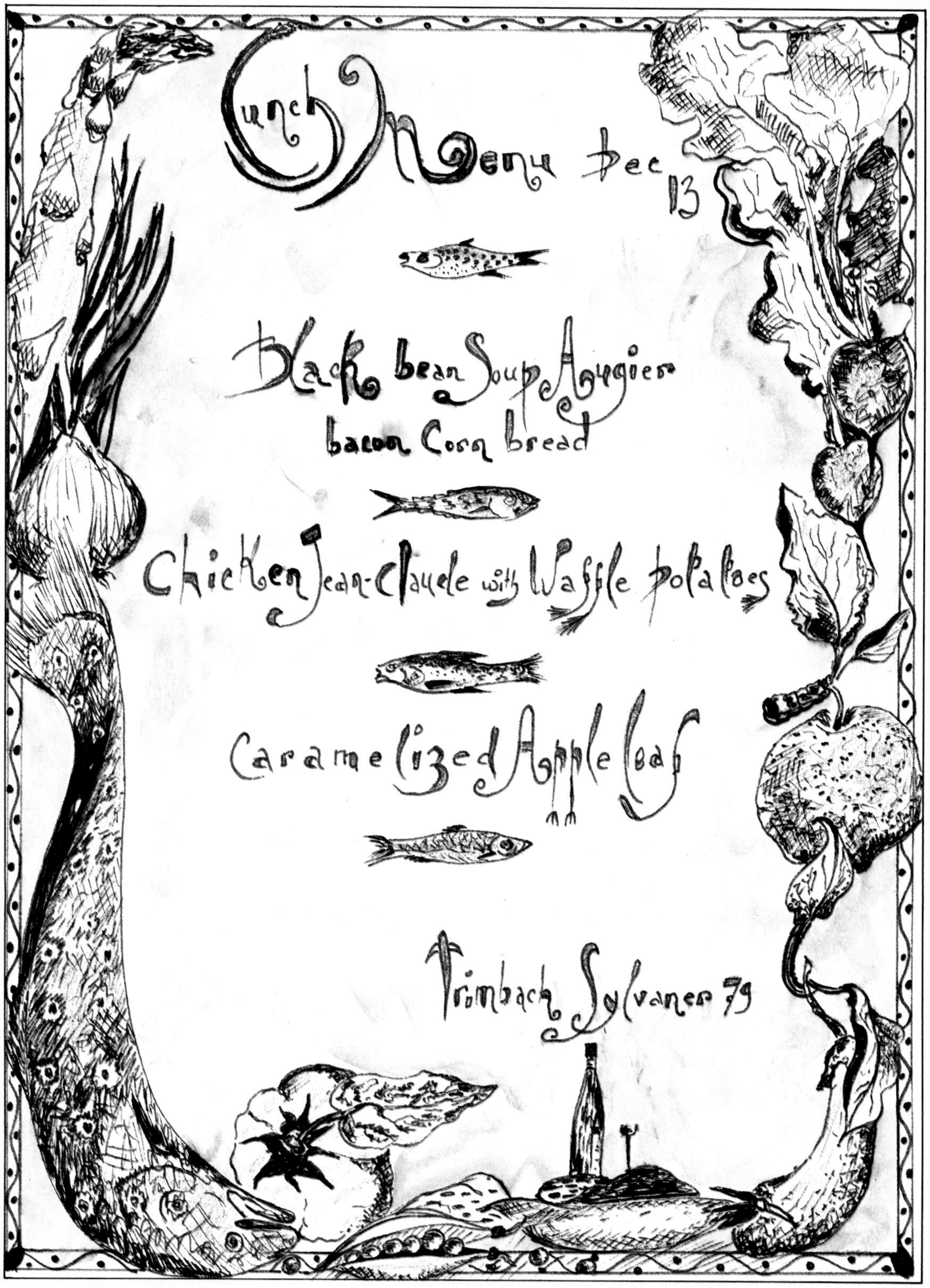

AUTUMN DINNER

September 18

FARMER'S-STYLE SOUP
volume 1, page 16

**STUFFED VEAL KIDNEY
BICHON WITH
POTATO AND TRUFFLE CAKE**
volume 1, page 305

WINTER SALAD
made with winter salad greens
tossed with Mustard Vinaigrette
volume 2, page 90
or Walnut Dressing
volume 2, page 89

CHEESES

CHOCOLATE CLOUD CAKE
volume 2, page 221

Pernand Vergelesses '80
Clos du Val Zinfandel '73

December 15

**PISTACHIO SAUSAGE IN
BRIOCHE WITH MUSHROOM
SAUCE**
volume 1, page 326

**ROAST MONKFISH IN
RATATOUILLE**
volume 1, page 114

CARAMEL SNOW EGGS
volume 2, page 247

Concannon Petite Sirah '82

WINTER DINNER

February 22

SHRIMP "BUNNIES" CREOLE
volume 1, page 80

CASSOULET PIERRE LARRE
volume 1, page 183

SALAD
made with winter salad greens
tossed with Mustard Vinaigrette
volume 2, page 90
or Walnut Dressing
volume 2, page 89

CHEESES

**POACHED PEARS IN CITRUS
JUICE LAUREN**
volume 2, page 290

Orvieto '76
Morgon '84

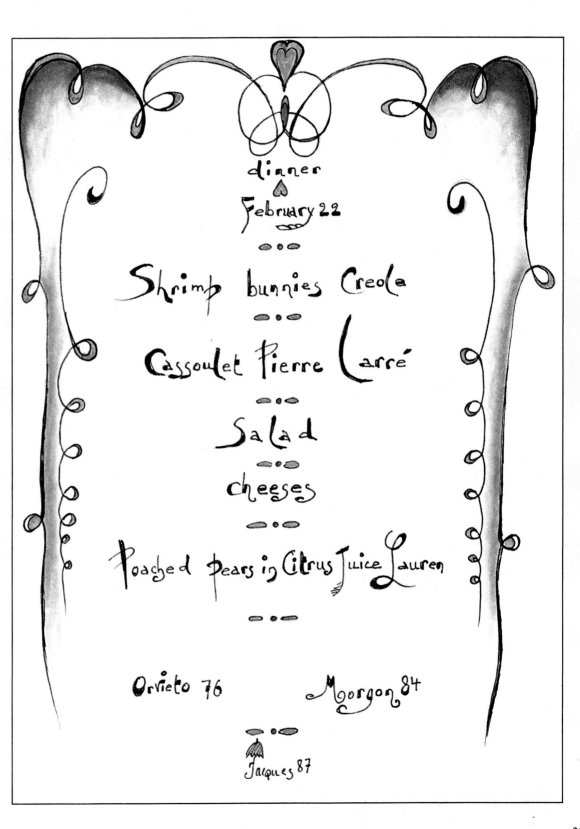

dinner

February 22

Shrimp bunnies Creole

Cassoulet Pierre Larré

Salad

cheeses

Poached Pears in Citrus Juice Lauren

Orvieto 76   Morgon 84

Jacques 87

December 18

**OYSTER AND CORN CHOWDER
WITH SMALL CORN BREAD**
volume 1, page 13

**FRESH FOIE GRAS WITH
COGNAC ASPIC**
volume 2, page 72
Chateau Yquem '70

**QUENELLES DORIA WITH
DUXELLES SAUCE**
volume 1, page 105
Chalone Chardonnay '80

GRAPEFRUIT GRANITE
volume 2, page 284

**ROAST WOODCOCK
WITH SOUFFLED POTATOES
SAVOY CABBAGE**
volume 1, page 193

BLACK TRUFFLE SALAD
volume 2, page 100

**CHEESES WITH WHOLE WHEAT
BREAD**
Aloxe Corton '70

**RASPBERRY SHERBET WITH
BLACKBERRY SAUCE**
volume 2, page 282

Coffee Express
Malvasia Cossart Madeira 1910

**CANDIED LIME AND
GRAPEFRUIT PEEL**
volume 2, page 201

**CHOCOLATE TRUFFETTES
(COFFEE-RUM)**
volume 2, page 202

**BRANDIED CHERRIES OR
CHERRIES IN MOUNTAIN BREW**
volume 2, page 111

Dinner December 18

Menu

Oyster and Corn Chowder + Small corn bread

Fresh foie gras with Cognac aspic

Quenelles Doria with duxelles sauce

Grapefruit Granité

Chateau Yquem 70

Chalone Chardonnay 80

Roast Woodcock with Souffle Potatoes
Savoy cabbage

Aloxe Corton 70

Black truffle Salad

Malvasia Cossart
Madeira 1910

Cheeses with Wholewheat bread

Raspberry Sherbet with blackberry sauce

coffee express

Candied Lime and Grapefruit peels

chocolate truffettes

Brandied cherries

Jacques 87

SPECIAL DINNER PARTY 2

June 19

CAVIAR WITH BLINIS
volume 2, page 106
Frozen Vodka

CONSOMME PRINTANIER WITH CHICKEN QUENELLES
volume 1, page 19

SALMON FILLETS IN BASIL SAUCE
volume 1, page 128
Meursault '76

WINE PLUM SHERBET
volume 2, page 285

BRAISED DUCK WITH GLAZED SHALLOTS AND HONEY SWEET POTATOES
volume 1, page 179
Cabernet Sauvignon Martha Vineyard Heitz '70

APRICOT AND PISTACHIO SOUFFLE
volume 2, page 266
Port Boa Vista '72

Coffee
Old Armagnac

DULCET CHOCOLATE SQUARES
volume 2, page 200

SUGARED PUFF PASTE STICKS
volume 2, page 197

MeNu

June 19
dinner

Frozen Vodka

Caviar beluga with blinis

Consommé Printanier
chicken Quenelles

Salmon Steaks in basil Sauce

Moeursault 76

Wine plum Sherbet

Braised duck with Glazed shallots
Honey Sweet potatoes

Cabernet Sauvignon
Martha Vineyard
Heitz 70

Apricot and pistacchio Soufflé

Coffee
Old armagnac

Port Boa Vista 72

Dulcet chocolate Squares
Sugared Puff Sticks

Jacques 87

Handwritten menu:

· Buffet · December 5 ·

Spicy Rum Cocktail

Carpaccio of white truffles

Salmon gravlax Evelyn

Homemade Sparkling cider

Smoked eel paté with eggplant marmelade

Cold Billi·bi

Chicken galantine with prunes

Sausage and potato Salad Jean-Victor

Grilled Shoulder of veal with herbed butter

Sanford Fumé blanc 82

Ham Georgia

Fromage blanc Victor with roasted garlic

Black raspberry Jam·Dartois

Givry red 80

chocolate whiskey prune cake

Gigondas 84

Vanilla ice-cream in netty cups with Spicy cherry in wine

Epi and crown bread with wholewheat dough

cheese bread

Jacques 87

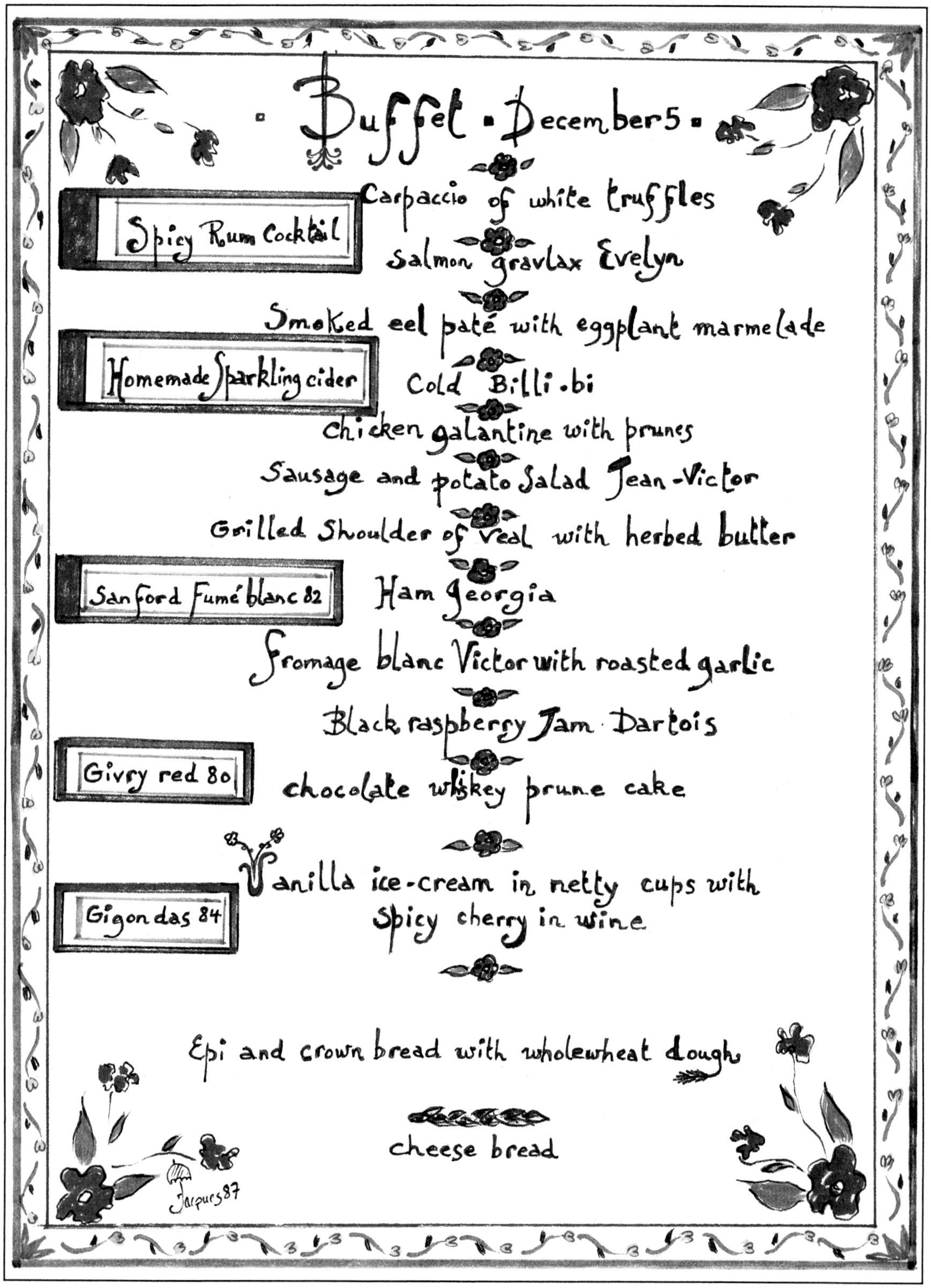

PIQUENIQUE
(EVERYTHING PRECOOKED)

LINNER

INDEX

A NOTE ABOUT THE AUTHOR

Jacques Pepin was born in Bourg-en-Bresse, near Lyon, and began cooking at the age of thirteen, when he apprenticed in his parents' Lyon restaurant. He studied in Paris at the Meurice restaurant and then at the famed Plaza-Athénée, where he trained under Lucien Diat. From 1956 to 1958 he was the personal chef to three French heads of state: Gaillard, Pfimlin, and de Gaulle.

In 1959 Jacques Pepin came to the United States, where he studied at Columbia University and earned a B.A. and an M.A. in eighteenth-century French literature. He appears frequently as a guest speaker on radio and television food programs and has written about food and cooking for *The New York Times, Bon Appétit, Food & Wine, House Beautiful,* and *Travel & Leisure.* From 1985 to 1987 *Gourmet* magazine featured excerpts from the two volumes of *The Art of Cooking.* Jacques Pepin spends about thirty weeks of the year traveling throughout the country to give cooking demonstrations. He lives in Madison, Connecticut, with his wife and their daughter, Claudine.

A NOTE ON THE TYPE

The text and display types were chosen for their appropriateness, clarity, beauty, contrast to each other, and association with France. They also represent the best in type design of two vastly different eras and are part of a long tradition and history.

The text was set in a digitized version of Garamond, which is based on letter forms originally created by the Frenchman Claude Garamond (c. 1480–1561). He was a pupil of Geoffroy Tory and may have patterned his letter forms on Venetian models.

The display type was set in a digitized version of Frutiger, which was designed by the Swiss Adrian Frutiger in Paris in 1976. It is based on the signage type he created in 1970 for the Roissy-Charles de Gaulle Airport and was originally produced in the United States by Mergenthaler-Linotype and in Frankfurt by Stempel. Frutiger also designed Univers and Serifa type faces.

Composition by Graphic Composition, Inc., Athens, Georgia
Separations by Color Response, Inc., Charlotte, North Carolina
Printing and binding by Arcata Graphics, Kingsport, Tennessee

Photography by Tom Hopkins

Design by Stephanie Guiomar Tevonian, Works design group